# Queen Anne
## Community on the Hill

**Dr. Kay F. Reinartz,** Historian/Project Director for *Queen Anne, Community on the Hill,* has extensive experience researching, writing and lecturing in the field of American cultural and social history. *Passport to Ballard,* 1988, won the Governor's Centennial Community Heritage Award. In 1989 Dr. Reinartz received the Association of King County Historical Organization's Individual Award for heritage leadership and the Ballard Chamber of Commerce Community Heritage award. *Tukwila, Community at the Crossroads* was published in 1991. In 1992 Dr. Reinartz received national recognition for her history work in King County from the American Association for State and Local History. Dr. Reinartz has lectured at universities in the United States and abroad. She has a Ph.D. in American Studies from the University of New Mexico, an M.A. in American History from the University of Minnesota, and a Master's in Urban and Regional Planning, with a specialty in Historic Preservation, from Texas A&M University. A native of Minnesota, she has made Seattle her home since 1965.

**Isabel Egglin** is a documentary photographer, a consultant for photo research and teacher on Queen Anne Hill. Her contemporary photography appears throughout the book. Her pictures are used to illustrate multicultural textbooks, journals and exhibits. She was the 1988 winner of a *Modern Maturity* magazine photography award.

**Laura Lewis** designed the book's pages. She is a graphic designer with her own firm, and her clients include corporations and public agencies. Design products include marketing materials, manuals and posters, as well as books. Other titles of local historical interest that she has designed include Emmett Watson's *Once Upon a Time in Seattle* and *My Life in Print, Tukwila—Community at the Crossroads*, and *The Friend of the Family—100 Years with Washington Mutual.*

**Jackie Brooks** illustrated the cover. She is a watercolorist and teacher, and a 26-year resident of Queen Anne. Her works have been accepted into more than 20 national and international juried exhibitions, winning numerous awards. Her paintings are included in many private and corporate art collections.

**Nan Davenport** designed the cover. A graphic designer, she is Publications Editor for the State of Oregon Department of Economic Development. She won a national award for her design, research, editing and production of the 1991 Oregon Directory of Wood Products Manufacturers.

Published by:
**The Queen Anne Historical Society**
P.O. Box 9180
Seattle, WA 98109

Printed in the United States of America by Valco Graphics, Inc., Seattle, WA.

# Queen Anne
## Community on the Hill

Queen Anne Historical Society
Publisher

Kay Frances Reinartz, Ph.D.
Historian

Isabel Egglin
Contemporary Photographer
and Photo Researcher

*1993*

*Partially funded by a grant from the*
*City of Seattle Department of Neighborhoods*

ISBN 0-9638991-0-4 (cloth); ISBN 0-9638991-1-2 (paper)
Library of Congress number 93-085195



## Staff

Historian/Author/
Project Director/Editor .......... Kay F. Reinartz, Ph.D.
Assistant Editor .......... Verna Ness, Ph.D.
Administrative Assistants .......... Leona Hilton, Anne Howe Johnson
Word Processor/Technical Assistant .......... Tracy Warner
Photographer .......... Isabel Egglin
Production Director .......... Mel Carlson
Book Design/Page Layout .......... Laura Lewis
Cover Painting .......... Jackie Brooks
Cover Design .......... Nan Davenport
Charts .......... Theano Petersen
Proofreader .......... Andrea Dupras
Indexer .......... Elspeth Pope

The book manuscript was reviewed by the members of the Queen Anne Community Editorial Advisory Committee.

## Community Editorial Advisory Committee

Lana Christman
Isabel Egglin
John Hennes
Del Loder
Loretta Morgan
Marion Parker
Val Reel
Robert Welden

## Finance Committee

Roger Billings
Fran Calhoun
Rick Dagg
Lisa Dankers
Bob Frazier
Dave Harvey
Mickey Canan Howard
Phil Howard
Tom Kildall
Eda Mendiola
Robin Milligan
Ron Metcalf

## Distinguished Queen Anne Citizens Committee

George Benson
Beth Brook
Bob Frazier
Emery Gustafson
Del Loder
Loretta Morgan
Florence Nelson
Marion Parker
Patricia Sobeck

## Leaders

Cathy Petito Boyce .......... Oral History Coordinator
Beth Brook .......... Distinguished Q.A. Citizens Coordinator
Mel Carlson .......... Production Coordinator
Lana Christman .......... Volunteer Coordinator
John Hennes .......... Technical Support
Phil Howard .......... Executive Coordinator
Mickey Canan Howard .......... Finance Coordinator
Hildy Ko .......... Acknowledgements
Mary Kridle .......... Oral History Transcription
Loretta Morgan .......... *Queen Anne News* Index Coordinator
Marion Parker .......... Home Base
Val Reel .......... Census Research Coordinator
June Sheppard .......... Acknowledgements
Barbara Wakefield .......... Business History Research Coordinator
Kay Yamamoto .......... School Research Coordinator

## Community Volunteer Support

Great efforts require special people. Everyone who worked on this book falls into that category. Hundreds have contributed bits and pieces of information, but due to space limitations are not listed here. If we have not mentioned your name please accept our apologies as well as our thanks for your assistance. The greatness is still yours to share.

## Lovers of History

Volunteers who made major commitments of time and talent to the community history book who are not listed elsewhere:

Robert O. Bishop, Sr.
Don Codling
Margaret DeLacy
Richard Frith
Laela Gray
Alan Gulick
Howard Hansen
Millie Hokanson
George Knutsen
Suzanne Lavik
Carl Nordstrom
Miriam Marston Owen
Patricia Paquette
Sylvia Peckham
Mona Secord
Kim Turner
Mary Wallon
Peggy Whippo

## General Volunteers

Molly Aasten
Jane Abrams
Corrinne Anderson
Dorthea Barnes
Ezra Basom
Betty Bebee
Nadine Belcher
Marie Bell
Bill Blair
Sue Bottemiller
Derek B. Booth, Ph.D.
Delora Bowie
Tim Canan
Jackie Cedarholm
David & Lila Chapman
Allen B. Codling
Georgia F. Cummings Codling
Sharon Davis
Mary Ann Egnell
Inga Ewbank
Alice Fairweather
Charles Farrell
Sally Flood
Jim Ford
Gary Gaffner
Alice Gates
Mary Haberman
Susan Hackney
William G. Hamilton
Richard Hamm
Barbara Hazen
Dan Healy
Scott Hennes
Anne Hoen
Mildred Hoffman
B.J. Hoover
Walter Hudi
Lauri & Kerttu Kivimaki
Margaret Lahde
Greg Lange
Anne Louie Locke
Michelle Lucien
Susan & Jim Mattison
Ellen McKoy
Arlene McDonough
Mike Mitchell
Dean Morgan
Peri Muhinch
John Nagy
Jim Nelson
Alice Osborne
Warren Parker
Charles Payton
Florence Pung
Dorothy Raymond
Joan Santucci
Carol Sauer
Ann Scdoris
Amy Seif
Henry Shaw
John Sheridan
David Spengler
Ann Stedronsky
Cindy Steingel
Chet Sundt
Helen Tapp
Pat Tewkesbury
George Thelen
Nile Thompson, Ph.D.
Ken Tollefson, Ph.D.
Sue K. Tripp
Sharon Tsutsui
Bonnie Vaughn
Kiyoo Yamamoto
Evelyn Youngren
Eric Waggoner
Robin Warner

## Special Thanks

Special thanks to Seattle Pacific University for co-sponsoring the community history book and providing the Research Center at 3215 3rd Ave. W. Generous assistance was given by Ivanelle Kirkpatrick, Public Relations; Gary Fick, Director and Anne Hill, Librarian, Weter Library; Ann King, SPU Archives; John Glancy, Publications Department; Bud Bylsma, Northwest Leadership Foundation for generously sharing the Research Center.

Special thanks to Miriam Walsh Lisco, Walsh & Assoc. for donating original poster design artwork; A & A Printing and Art Matni for poster printing; Alpha Graphics for leaflet printing; Salladay's Pharmacy, Queen Anne Pharmacy and Lisa Dankers Real Estate Group, copy service; Quorum Realty, fax and promotional support; and *Queen Anne News* and Pacific Media for publicity and printing.

Special thanks for research assistance to Scott Kline, Archivist, City of Seattle Archives; Ernie Dornfeld, Archivist, King County Archives; Carla Rickerson, Richard Engeman, Sandra Kroupa, Gary Menges, Special Collections and Preservation Division of University of Washington Libraries; Carol Winn, Manuscript Division, University of Washington Libraries; and Eleanor Toews, Archivist, Seattle School District Archives.

Special thanks to Rick Caldwell, Librarian, Carolyn Marr, Assistant Librarian, Howard Giske, Photo Curator, Museum of History and Industry. Also to Dr. Gary Zimmerman, the Pioneer Association of Washington; to Don Paulson, Old Seattle Paperworks; and to Paul Dorpat, Tartu Publications.

# TABLE OF CONTENTS

## PRELUDE


1 The Geology of Queen Anne Hill *by Bill Laprade* ..... 1
2 Off the Beaten Track: Native Americans and the Queen Anne District ..... 7
*by Erin Younger & Edward Liebow, Ph.D.*


## PART I — 1851 THROUGH 1929

*by Kay F. Reinartz, Ph.D.*


3 Oregon Trail Migrants to Puget Sound Country ..... 12
4 The Community of Pioneers North of Seattle—1853–1860 ..... 21
5 Building Homesteads and Families—The 1860s ..... 33
6 Pioneer Childhood on Queen Anne Hill ..... 44
7 Wilderness Lost—The 1870s ..... 53
8 Subdividing Eden—The 1880s ..... 61
9 Queen Anne Town—The 1890s ..... 73
10 Citizens Build a Good Community—1900–1929 ..... 85
11 Community Life in the Early Twentieth Century ..... 96


## PART II — COMMUNITY VOICES TELL THE TWENTIETH CENTURY STORY


12 Depression and War—The 1930s–40s *by Ron Palmer, Ph.D.* ..... 107
13 In Our Time—1950–1993 ..... 115
*by John P. Hennes, Editor, Lana Christman, Linda Humphrey McCallum, Marion Parker, Betty Renkor, Lt. Richard Schneider*
14 A Century of Schools on the Hill ..... 125
*by Dorothy McBride, David McNichols, Lit. D., Marion Parker, Kim Turner, Elizabeth Whitmire, Kay Yamamoto*
15 Going to Church *by Alison Nesmith* ..... 139
16 The Healthful Hilltop Air *by Marina King* ..... 149
17 Business Around the Hill *by Marina Gordon* ..... 158
18 Apartments and Development on the Hill *by Kim Myran & Scott Jennings* ..... 167
19 Community Life—Organizations and Newspapers *by Betty Renkor & Todd Davidson* ..... 178
20 Staying on Queen Anne Forever *by Del Loder* ..... 186

References ..... 191
Appendix A—Distinguished Queen Anne Citizens ..... 200
Appendix B—Business District Maps from 1915–1935 ..... 203
Appendix C—Street Name Changes ..... 207
Donors and Sponsors ..... 209
Index ..... 218


### ILLUSTRATORS:


Vonnie Anderson Burns ..... 12, 56
Tony Cresci ..... 10, 128
Mike Dowd ..... 139
Jennifer Egglin ..... 44, 47, 49, 58
Marina Megale ..... vii
Darcanne Preble ..... 17
Jim Stevenson ..... 89, 170, 171, 185
Dan Tuttle ..... 186
James Welby ..... 148

# Preface

Queen Anne, in the view of most Seattle residents today, is indeed the community on the hill. But Queen Anne is more than that. The Uptown area on lower Queen Anne, the western shoreline of Lake Union, today's Ship Canal and the tide flats of Smith Cove have all been part of the Queen Anne story since the beginning.

The history of Queen Anne is the story of a special place that was known and revered by Native Americans long before the European-American settlers. It is the story of a band of pioneers who built a sense of community through hardship and mutual assistance in the early years. This book chronicles how the modern community has taken shape and the influence that hill residents have had on the process in the nineteenth and twentieth centuries.

Queen Anne residents have always balanced the needs of their community with those of the larger city of Seattle. In return, Queen Anne's citizens have often actively demanded that aspects of Seattle's growth be controlled to preserve the family-oriented community we have known since our earliest days.

The writing of this history of Queen Anne had its origins in early 1989, the year of Washington State's Centennial, when Emery Gustafson began encouraging such a grass roots effort through his column "The Passing Scene" in the *Queen Anne News*. The Queen Anne Historical Society accepted the challenge and organized a History Book Committee to guide the effort towards such a community history book.

The effort to gather and organize material brought the realization that professional help was needed. Under the sponsorship of the Historical Society, the Book Committee selected Dr. Kay F. Reinartz, consulting historian and author of other King County community award-winning history books, to direct the project. A community Editorial Advisory Committee was formed to work with the historian in shaping the book and a Finance Committee was organized to raise the necessary funds. The History Book Committee obtained a grant from the City of Seattle Department of Neighborhoods to assist with research and writing.

Over one hundred community volunteers came forward to actively participate under the leadership and guidance of "Dr. Kay." Seattle Pacific University donated space for a History Book Research Center. Thousands of hours were donated by volunteers who researched land records, federal censuses, old newspapers and photo archives. An oral history team was trained and undertook in-depth interviews with community elders, recording their memories for this book to draw on in telling the story of their decades. The process of researching and writing the community's history as a group effort was a long journey. Any errors or omissions are unintentional and we apologize for these.

Dr. Reinartz assumed responsibility for the early history of Queen Anne and community writers took on the history since the 1930s, as well as special topics. Individual businesses and organizations were solicited for historical details and those submitted are chronicled here.

In addition to the material in this book, enough information was gathered to fill several additional books. These materials, in the form of a permanent historical archive, constitute our legacy to future researchers.

Tomorrow's Queen Anne will be built on yesterday and today. Those of us who have been actively involved with the project have gained an appreciation for the vision and spirit of those who made Queen Anne what it is. We who have shared in the researching of the history book will never again walk these streets without some story coming to mind about that particular place. You can share in that historical presence through these pages and through preserving a piece of your own history and depositing it in the community history archive for some future book committee to discover.

We congratulate Dr. Kay Reinartz, other writers, and the many, many volunteers and contributors who made this possible. Those now here and those yet to come will treasure the result of these efforts.

The Queen Anne Historical Society

# INTRODUCTION

Queen Anne Hill rises 456 feet above Elliott Bay at high tide. From the top of the hill are unparalleled views. The hill has been the home of American settlers since 1853 and was a hunting ground of the Native Americans long before that date. This book, the first to tell the story of the community on the hill, focuses on the period following American settlement.

The boundaries of the modern community have been defined in this book by Denny Way on the south, the Lake Washington Ship Canal and Salmon Bay on the north, Fifteenth Avenue W. on the west and the shore of Lake Union and Westlake Avenue N. on the east.

The history of the Queen Anne community is naturally interwoven with the history of the founding and development of Seattle. While the emphasis throughout this history is on activities that took place in the community, participation in Seattle's history is discussed whenever appropriate. Indeed, a number of the early residents of the hill actively participated in Seattle politics and economy and helped shape Seattle as well as Queen Anne.

The reader will note that the chapters discussing the nineteenth century focus on the Lake Union vicinity, specifically the lower south slope and the outlet of Lake Union. These two geographical areas were the locus of early development activity since they were connected to the Seattle community by water and rail transportation. The upper reaches of the hill were not seriously developed until the early twentieth century. Brief mention is made of the development of adjoining communities, such as Ross and Fremont, when their histories are intertwined with that of Queen Anne.

This history of the Queen Anne community is told by many voices. Voices speak to us from the nineteenth century telling us of the experiences, concerns and interests of the early residents of the hill. Emily Inez Denny, Abbie Denny Lindsley, Dr. Henry Smith, and Charlie Kinnear lend us insight into their times. The twentieth-century history is related by contemporary voices, all of whom are community residents. These writers each undertook researching the history and photographs for the subject area for which he or she was responsible. Thus, each chapter is the personal expression of that individual writer's interests and talent.

Those who have worked on the community history book have been a part of a pioneer effort. As the leader of this history project which combined professional historical methodology with grassroots community participation, I have served in many capacities, including historian, project director, teacher-trainer, author and editor.

*Tower Place Stairway*
*by Marina Megale*

Throughout the project my work has been complex and demanding. However, the burden has been lightened by the consistent assistance of special community volunteers who receive my heartfelt thanks, as does Tracy Warner, my technical assistant and word processing expert. Thanks also to the Community Editorial Advisory Committee for long hours of manuscript reading, intelligent comments and useful suggestions. Their total commitment to a high quality history book never flagged. We are all indebted to their excellent work. My husband and good friend Richard Frith has been tireless in his support throughout the project and receives my greatest thanks for all that he has done to make the project a success.

The storytellers are ready. Step back in time and walk now, in your mind, with the chroniclers and hear their voices.

Kay F. Reinartz, Historian
July 1993

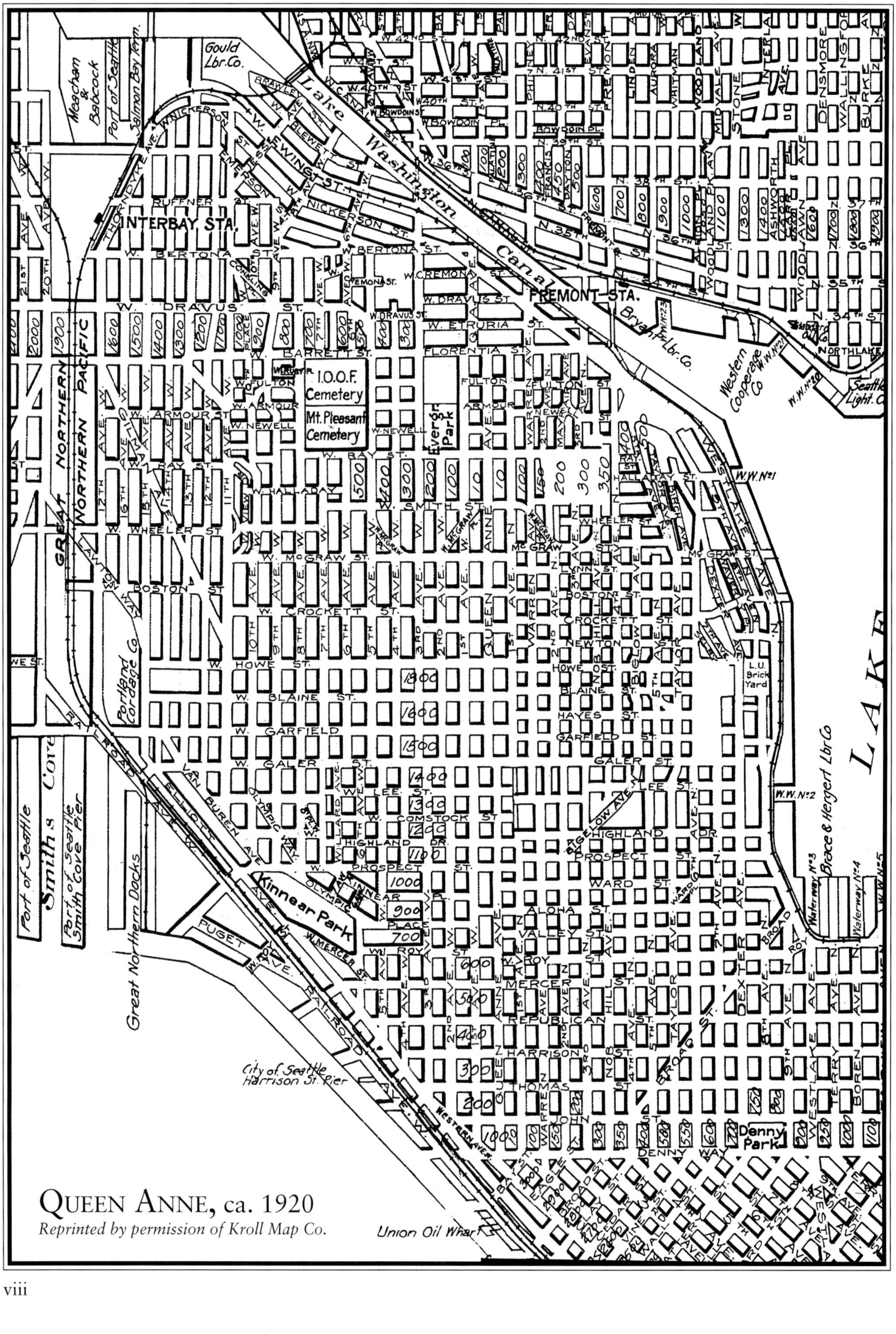


# QUEEN ANNE, ca. 1920

*Reprinted by permission of Kroll Map Co.*

Chapter One

# The Geology of Queen Anne Hill

by
Bill Laprade

The Puget Sound basin lies between the Cascade Range on the east and the Olympic Mountains on the west, and is open to the Pacific Ocean through the Strait of Juan de Fuca. Bedrock ranging from 10 to 50 million years old is exposed at the ground surface around the margins of the basin and occasionally south of Alki Point and Boeing Field in Seattle. Geologists estimate that the bedrock lies more than 1,500 to 2,400 feet beneath Queen Anne Hill, buried by glacial and non-glacial sediments in the past two to three million years.

The great ice ages commenced over three million years ago. Geologic evidence indicates that at least four and perhaps as many as six glaciations have occurred since the beginning of the Pleistocene Epoch. In the Puget Sound basin, ice originating in the coastal and inland mountains of British Columbia coalesced and progressed south, stopping approximately 50 miles south of Seattle. Since the retreat of the last glacial ice from the Seattle area about 13,500 years ago, the land has been modified by rising sea levels, erosion and landslides. The waters of Puget Sound reached their present level about 5,000 years ago.

Egg-shaped Queen Anne Hill is one of the original seven hills of Seattle. The others were Capitol, First, Beacon, Magnolia, West Seattle and Denny. The latter hill was removed in the Denny Regrade project. Queen Anne Hill lies between three bodies of water—Puget Sound, Lake Union, and the Lake Washington Ship Canal—and the central business district of Seattle. The deep depressions of Elliott Bay, Lake Union and Lake Washington are filled with water and the uplands are mostly covered with human development. Some of the water-filled basins, such as Lake Washington, Portage Bay, Lake Union and Salmon Bay, have been connected by excavated canals, and drainage has been redirected to serve human purposes.

## Vashon Stade Ice Covers the Hill

The geologic materials exposed on and around the margins of Queen Anne Hill were deposited during the Vashon stade of the Fraser glaciation, the last incursion of continental ice into the central Puget Sound area. A stade is a substage of a glacial period. Of the three stades in the Fraser glaciation, only the Vashon deposited sediment in the greater Seattle area. At its height, Vashon stade ice advanced past Olympia and covered Queen Anne Hill with more than 3,000 feet of ice.

Glacial remains of the Vashon stade on Queen Anne Hill are represented by four recognizable types: Lawton Clay, Esperance Sand, Vashon till and Vashon recessional deposits. Lawton Clay is the oldest deposit and the others are progressively more recent. All of these soils were deposited between 17,500 and 13,500 years ago. Only the recessional deposits were not overridden by glacial ice. A subsurface profile (see p. 2) through the hill from north to south shows the relationship of the units to each other. The interior of the hill is undoubtedly composed of Olympia non-glacial deposits from the interglacial period immediately before the Vashon stade and of sediments from older glaciations. These deposits and sediments, however, are not exposed at the ground surface or in shallow drill holes.

## Clay, Sand and Till

The oldest unit, Lawton Clay, is present below elevation 200 feet on the east, north and west peripheries of the hill. On the south slope, this material is covered with Vashon till. Lawton Clay can also be seen in building excavations on the north side of the hill and on the steep excavation slopes along Westlake Avenue. It represents the deposition of sediments in a lake that formed as the glacial ice advanced south and blocked the northern part of Puget Sound, eliminating the salt-water connection through the Strait of Juan de Fuca. The clay consists of laminated to massive gray silt and clay with scattered thin layers of fine sand. At Fort Lawton (Discovery Park), from which it takes its name and where it can be seen along the south beach, it is 82 feet thick; on Queen Anne Hill, it ranges from 125 to 175 feet thick, as measured above sea level.

Overlying the Lawton Clay is the most extensively exposed geologic unit on the hill, the Esperance Sand. It is found on the steep slopes and on much of the top of the hill. This deposit of sand, or mixture of sand and gravel, was laid down by streams issuing from the front of the advancing Vashon-Age ice sheet and for this reason is commonly termed advance outwash. It is currently thought that the entire width of central Puget Sound basin was filled to elevation 400 to 500 feet with this deposit before the ice overrode the area. On Queen Anne Hill, Esperance Sand is about 150 to 200 feet thick. It is found in the excavated slope to the northeast of the corner of Queen Anne Avenue North and Garfield Street, and it was well exposed during the excavation for the Queen Anne Pool at 1st Avenue West and West Howe Street. Perhaps the best exposure of this deposit is along the top of the south bluff at Discovery Park. The contact of the sand with the underlying Lawton Clay is commonly gradual and contains alternating layers of clay, silt, and sand.

As indicated on the subsurface profile, Vashon till overlies the advance outwash. Vashon till, composed of clay, silt, sand, gravel, cobbles and sporadic boulders, is commonly termed "hardpan" because of its very dense and compact nature. This deposit is the debris that was carried along the base of the glacial ice. It is not always present, but where it is, it ranges from a few feet to more than thirty feet thick. It is limited in exposure on the top of the hill, but it can be seen in building excavations in the lower south side of Queen Anne. One good viewing site is a parking lot excavation slope to the northeast of the intersection of Second Avenue W. and John Street, and it is also visible near the top of an old borrow pit just west of Twelfth Avenue W. and W. Howe Street.

The youngest geologic unit on Queen Anne Hill associated with glaciation is Vashon recessional outwash. It was probably laid down as streams flowed through the low area between Queen Anne Hill and Fremont when the glacial ice melted. Found along the south side of the Lake Washington Ship Canal, this outwash deposit consists mainly of medium dense, silty

## Geologic Profile of Queen Anne Hill

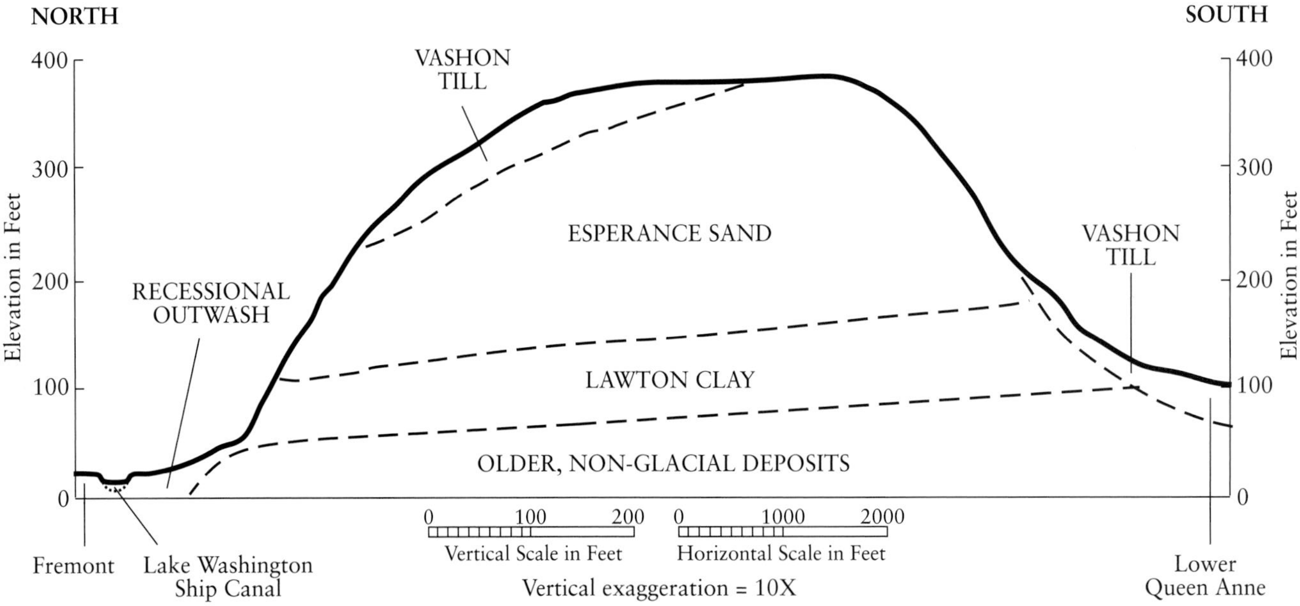


*Courtesy H. H. Waldron*

sand, with minor amounts of gravel. It is also deeply buried below fill in the Interbay lowland as that area served as an outwash channel during the recession of the glacial ice. Recessional outwash sand is also commonly found on the uplands in isolated pockets not more than a few feet thick, overlying till.

## Holocene Events

Following the recession and wasting of glacial ice in central Puget Sound about 13,500 years ago, geologic processes began that continue to this day: erosion and gully formation, lowland filling, hillside soil weathering, and landsliding. The rate at which these processes initially occurred is unknown, but it is likely that all of them were more rapid on the denuded, recently deglaciated slopes. For the past several thousand years, the rate of erosion, sedimentation and landsliding has probably been somewhat constant. During the same time period, sea level rose gradually about 300 feet to its present level.

When European-American settlers arrived in Seattle in the mid 1800s, Queen Anne's sister hill, Magnolia, was virtually cut off from the mainland by the nearly-connecting tide flats of Salmon Bay to the north and Smith Cove to the south. The tide flats were covered with soft mud and sand, and peat deposits dotted the surface. The edges of Interbay were mantled with landslide deposits that came from the hillsides to the east and west.

Minor gullies have developed on the post-glacial landscape throughout Queen Anne Hill, but only one has developed into a deep ravine. The half-mile long ravine on the northeast side of Queen Anne Hill has its mouth near the toe of the north slope and currently extends to Lynn Street on the south, following the right-of-way of Third Avenue North. A 1910 Seattle Engineering Department topographic map shows that this gully once extended much farther south, to the vicinity of Newton Street, but it was subsequently filled in. Prior to the placement of the fill over which the present roadway is built, a 300-foot long bridge spanned the creek along Boston Street over a 55-foot deep ravine.

Three geologic factors appear to be responsible for the formation of this gully: (1) erosion by the ubiquitous springs in the vicinity of North Queen Anne Drive, (2) the impervious till cap on the upland to the south of the gully, which promoted surface runoff of precipitation, and (3) the highly erosive Esperance Sand in the area between the springs and the drainage basin to the south. Two high structures, the McGraw Street Bridge and North Queen Anne Drive Bridge, were built across this ravine by the Seattle Engineering Department in 1936, with General Construction as the contractor.

Sediment, mainly silt and fine sand, carried off the hill by streams and landslides settled in the lowland areas, most notably Interbay, the ship canal area and Lake Union. The edges of those areas were built up and the deeper portions were made shallower by the accumulation of these fine soil particles over many thousands of years.

The slopes around the edges of Queen Anne Hill are very steep in many places. The soil on these slopes is loosened by gravity, root action, freeze-thaw cycles and chemical changes. Throughout the Puget Sound area, this loosened soil rind, termed colluvium, is commonly three to ten feet thick. Based on drill holes for residential developments, colluvium is as thick as 15 feet on the east slope, west of Aurora Avenue. The bowing and bending of the trees that grow on the hillside are a result of the downslope movement of the colluvial soil. This rind of colluvium is commonly involved in landslides, as it is loose and susceptible to the absorption of water in its inter-particles' void spaces.

Landslides were and continue to be an important geologic process in the sculpting of the hill's topography, especially on the east and west sides of the hill. Many of the landforms on these flanks of the hill still exhibit classic landslide topography, such as hummocky ground at the bottoms of steep slopes and steep-sided amphitheaters or bowls.

## The Springs

Springs are common to many of the landslide-prone areas on Queen Anne Hill and are located around all sides of the hill. They normally run throughout the year but are especially productive in the winter. On the east side of the hill, the spring line is between elevations 150 and 200 feet. On the north side, it is found between elevations 100 and 150 feet, and on the west side it is observed between elevations 125 and 200 feet. The most prolific springs on Queen Anne Hill existed on the south slope in the vicinity of Fourth Avenue North and Ward Street before they were incorporated into the city storm drainage system. Nearly all of the springs are found at the contact between the Lawton Clay and the overlying Esperance Sand. Precipitation infiltrates into the ground and travels vertically through the pervious sand until it encounters the top of the more impervious clay and silt of the Lawton Clay. The water then moves laterally until it emerges from the slope in springs. Many of the springs around the periphery of Queen Anne Hill were used for drinking water by early settlers.

Between 1882 and 1890, five spring-fed water supply systems known as Union, Maggs, Griffith, Kinnear and Peterson were installed on Queen Anne Hill. The Union Water System was one of the largest water supply systems in the city, yielding about 80,000 gallons per day. It was located at the large spring in the vicinity of Fourth Avenue North and Ward Street. The Maggs System, in the vicinity of Seventh Avenue North and Garfield Street, provided water to the southeast portion of the hill and portions of the Denny Regrade area as recently as 1950. Springs are still found scattered around the hill, but most have been captured by drainage trenches or tunnels and have been routed into the storm drainage system.

## Landslides

Landsliding is closely related to the presence of springs due to the internal pressures that build up in the ground when water is blocked or inhibited from escaping. The zone of particular hazard for landslides on Queen Anne Hill is defined by a band around the hill on the east, north and west sides. It is commonly referred to as "The Contact" because it is defined by the contact between the Lawton Clay and Esperance Sand. Larger slides appear to be related to a gradual increase in the water table over the winter months followed by an intense or prolonged period of rain. These slides are commonly slumps that form large amphitheaters. Such topography is common on the east side of Queen Anne Hill, uphill from Aurora Avenue and between Howe and Galer Streets, as well as along the west side of the hill, east of Elliott Avenue West and Fifteenth Avenue West, and between West Howe and West Comstock streets.

The West Galer Street landslides that occurred in 1909, 1916, and from 1951 to 1954 are examples of a slump. Much of the material that slid off the bluff just south of the ramp to the Magnolia Bridge came to rest behind a restaurant at West Garfield Street and Fifteenth Avenue West and was hauled away by Seattle Engineering Department crews during the 1950s episode. Horizontally drilled drains to relieve potentially destabilizing pressure deep in the ground were installed in 1988 during construction of residential units adjacent to the slide area.

On December 11, 1983, a large mass of saturated earth flowed down the east side of Queen Anne Hill, crossed Aurora Avenue and stopped on Dexter Avenue. Although this mudflow occurred along "The Contact," and natural spring seepage was a contributing factor, buried drain lines and fill placed on the hillside over the top of the spring water sources were also causes.

*Aurora slide of December 11, 1983, looking westward from Aurora Avenue. Large mudflows originated from a combination of old fill on a steep hillside, the ubiquitous natural springs in this location, and old drain lines probably related to water supply. Courtesy Bill Laprade.*

## The Denny Regrade

One of the most remarkable civil works projects in the Pacific Northwest was the removal of Denny Hill, just south of Queen Anne Hill, between 1903 and 1928. This area is now called the Denny Regrade. In a

*Denny Regrade No. 1 in 1910. Pinnacles of land remained where hold-out owners refused to sell. Those owners later were required to excavate at their own expense. Excavation after 1906 was made by hydraulic sluicing. Courtesy University of Washington, Asahel Curtis Collection.*

scheme envisioned and championed by R.H. Thomson, the Seattle City Engineer in the early 1900s, several parts of the city were regraded to open it up and improve the transportation network.

The regrading of Denny Hill was the first of these projects undertaken by the city and was accomplished in two phases. The first regrade, on what is now the western half of the area, was performed between 1903 and 1911 and used hydraulic sluicing methods to wash the soil into Elliott Bay. In 1928 the eastern half of the area was levelled using electrically-powered shovels and a complex series of conveyors. These two regrades accounted for the removal of six million cubic yards of soil from an area of 62 city blocks.

## LANDSCAPE CHANGES ON QUEEN ANNE HILL AND SURROUNDINGS

Lake Union was formerly connected to Salmon Bay by a small creek that was enlarged to a narrow canal for log transit. As part of an ambitious scheme to change the drainage of Lake Washington, between 1911 and 1916 the Sammamish River, the Cedar River, Lake Washington, Union Bay and Lake Union were directed through the newly-engineered Lake Washington Ship Canal. The Fremont Cut was part of this project. The excavation was made into Holocene-age alluvium and colluvium, essentially soft mud. Harder Vashon till and Lawton Clay were encountered in the bottom of much of the excavation. The excavation of mud, sand and soft clay was accomplished mostly by hydraulic sluicing and steam shovel. Much of the material was pumped onto adjacent low-lying ground. Concrete walls along the sides of the canal, extending several feet below water level for wave protection, are supported on piles.

The earliest transformation of Interbay was performed around 1910. This involved dredging a channel to lower the water table, thereby drying other areas for athletic fields. A limited amount of filling was also done at that time. Filling, chiefly as an open-air landfill

*Fremont Cut portion of the Lake Washington Ship Canal, looking northwest in 1912. Excavation was accomplished by a combination of sluicing and steam shovels. Note pipes used to carry excavated soil to disposal sites on the south side of the canal. Courtesy U.S. Army Corps of Engineers Collection.*

dump, continued intermittently from 1911 to 1968. The thickness of fill appears to have been about forty feet. The surface of the fill has reportedly settled a great deal and the presence of methane and other gases in the landfill has been well documented.

The construction of Aurora Avenue was completed along the alignment of Seventh Avenue North in 1932 as part of the Pacific Coast Highway chain. It significantly impacted the east side of Queen Anne Hill, cutting through the landslide zone there and triggering slope instability in several places. Landslides were curtailed after stabilizing measures were undertaken in 1933 by the Seattle Engineering Department. However, an occasional slide still occurs.

With regard to landscape changes, the two most geologically significant periods were probably the first few hundred years after the disappearance of the Vashon stade ice and the last one hundred years when European-American settlers moved in. Earlier modifications were large, with concomitant environmental consequences; smaller changes will be the watchword of the future. Limitations spelled out by Seattle's Sensitive Areas Ordinance and the State of Washington's Growth Management Act will enable us move into the twenty-first century in a sensible manner.

***Bill Laprade** has lived on Queen Anne Hill since 1974. His spouse, Mary Lou, teaches at John Hay School and two sons, Jed and Joseph, have been active in sports and community affairs on the hill. Bill coached soccer for 11 years in the Queen Anne Soccer Club. He is an Associate with Shannon & Wilson, Inc., a geotechnical engineering and environmental consulting firm, where he has practiced engineering geology for twenty years.*

Chapter Two

# Off the Beaten Track: Native Americans and the Queen Anne District

by
Erin Younger and
Edward Liebow, Ph.D.

In the late twentieth century there is evidence of neither native village sites in the vicinity of Queen Anne nor the large native population that once lived on Elliott Bay. However, a lengthy tradition of native settlement, predating those in almost every other corner of North America, has its roots on the shores of Puget Sound. A 1991 archaeological excavation at West Point below Magnolia Bluff has revealed artifacts 2,500 to 3,000 years old. Some contend that the area could have been inhabited 10,000 to 12,000 years ago. Because of the damp climate and acidic soils, few remains have been preserved or recovered and there is much to be learned.

When the first settlers arrived in 1851, there were several village sites clearly visible along the shores of Elliott Bay. These included the mouth of the Duwamish River southeast of Pioneer Square, the foot of what is now Bell Street, and Salmon Bay, in the vicinity of the Hiram Chittenden Locks.

From available information it appears that Queen Anne Hill was never a central location for Native American life or activities. It has, however, played a consistent role on the periphery. Its upper hillsides were used as hunting grounds and the meadows near its base were a traditional ceremonial and social gathering place for native people from around Puget Sound.

*Native American village at foot of Bell Street. Courtesy Queen Anne Historical Society.*

### Charlie and George Kinnear Jr. Visit a Native American Summer Camp on Elliott Bay, 1878

George and Angie Simmons Kinnear arrived in Seattle on September 28, 1878, with their two sons. The following day Charlie and George Jr. visited the local tribe's fishing and gathering camp on the beach. Charlie tells the story of the boys' adventure:

> *My little brother George, now deceased, and I ran down the hill, looked over the cliff and saw Indian wigwams about ten feet apart on the beach reaching from the foot of Marion to Columbia Street. In front of each was a little fire over which was four-foot square of slate; dangling from each were layers of salt-cured salmon eggs smoking for winter use. In front were many canoes drawn half out of the water, and in a constant stream fresh canoes came in bearing from three to nine bright, shining, silver salmon.*
>
> *Just beneath our station on the high bank were sixty-three long-haired, nude Indians (all their clothes in one pile) sitting in two lines facing each other, boards on their laps, stones in their hands beating the boards as they sang their wild chant. In the middle of each line was an Indian Chief with nothing on but a big red handkerchief around his neck. In one hand was a pair of small carved bones which—placed under the handkerchief—were changed from one hand to the other, the closed fists then swinging outward, again under the handkerchief, back and forth, and the opposing chief designated the hand supposed to be holding the bones. Both hands were then thrown upward, the bones going from the hand not guessed, and the score keeper deposited a stone indicating the loss. The bones then went to the opposite chief who made his trial. By and by all arose, the losing side sneaking along the beach to their wigwams, their squaws hurrying down launching canoes to go out onto the bay to catch more salmon to get more checkamen (money) to buy more mukamuk (food) and hyu ictus (many things), the stack of clothes divided into as many piles as there were victorious Indians.*

## Early Puget Sound Salish Culture

In the late eighteenth and early nineteenth centuries, the greater Puget Sound region was home to many different peoples whom anthropologists have come to call the Puget Sound Salish, referring to their related languages. Tribal names such as Duwamish, Suquamish and Snoqualmie are used to refer to larger groupings of different local bands. Aboriginally, the Puget Sound Salish identified themselves by family or household name and the village or location where they lived. For example, the Shilshole lived just inside of what is now Salmon Bay in a protected area called *hil-hole-ootseed*, in reference to the narrow entrance to the bay. Duwamish refers to the Native Americans living in the greater Seattle-King County area along the Duwamish River and its many tributaries.

As the various tribes lived intimately with the land, they named hundreds, if not thousands, of land forms and locations—beaches, trails, campgrounds, landmarks, and sites of mythological importance. In the Queen Anne area, Fourmile Rock, the large boulder at the foot of Magnolia Bluff, is said to be related to the mythic hero *Sta'kub*, who could take a gigantic dragnet made of cedar and hazel branches and throw it over the rock while standing on a distant beach.

## Spring and Summer Camps

As winter turned to spring, hunters began leaving the tribal villages to follow elk, deer and smaller game. When the salmon arrived in the bays and inlets around June to start their upstream journey, the winter villages broke up and temporary camps were established where the fish were most plentiful. Family groups continued to move through the season, following the ripening plants and berries, fishing, and gathering shellfish along the saltwater shores. As the fish were caught, women cleaned and cured them, drying them on racks or smoking them in small smokehouses.

The camps themselves consisted of simple, temporary structures of poles and mats that provided shelter from the elements and room for storage. The shores of Elliott Bay at night were dotted with fires of the many camps.

Summer was also a time for socializing and feasting. One of the most important social institutions was the potlatch, which was a great feast bringing together many people and requiring the preparation of great quantities of food. It also called for the accumulation and distribution of great quantities of gifts, including blankets, tools, cloth, pelts, carvings and jewelry. Gift recipients were expected to return the favor, thus establishing a complex system of social interaction and redistribution of food and wealth. Special events and rites of passage were occasions for potlatches, such as the conferring of a new name on a youth, the death of an elder, the return of the salmon to the rivers, or a successful hunt.

## Camping Grounds Around Queen Anne

When the settlers came to Queen Anne there were no permanent native villages on the hill, but seasonal camps abounded along its perimeter. The sandspit in the tidelands between Queen Anne and Magnolia, later Smith Cove, was a traditional Native American campground where various groups fished and gathered shellfish, which were smoked for winter consumption. Other seasonal food-gathering camps were located near the intersection of what is now West Thomas Street and Elliott West in Belltown, near First Avenue and Battery Street, and at West Point in Discovery Park.

The Native Americans often went to the hill to hunt. As recently as the 1980s, hunting artifacts have been unearthed in hill dweller's backyards. The intersections of Tenth and Eleventh avenues West and McGraw Street were also found to contain ancient shell middens—the equivalent of a prehistoric garbage dump—by geologist Harlan Bretz in 1913.

A very popular Native American camp was located on the shores of Lake Union in the vicinity of Westlake Avenue. A major focus of tribal activities during their stays at this camp was duck hunting. A favorite technique

*Potlatch Meadows, a traditional tribal gathering place, is now a part of Seattle Center. From the 1860s to the 1870s, it was the site of David and Louisa Boren Denny's homestead which they called "the house in the swale." Late in the nineteenth century the meadows were the site of a variety of activities including tent revival meetings and circuses. During the Spanish-American War, corrals were constructed at Potlatch Meadows to quarter army mules. Courtesy University of Washington.*

## The Powwow Tree

On the south side of Queen Anne Hill a cedar tree began to grow about the time of Marco Polo's first journey to China. Throughout the Crusades, the Black Death, and the discovery of North America, the tree continued to grow. Surviving the occasional forest fire that swept the region, the cedar became a true giant of the forest. It took ten men, standing with arms outstretched, to encircle it. Its noble head towered above all of its younger neighbors.

Native tribes recognized the significance of this ancient tree and revered it as sacred. They established the tradition of holding inter-tribal chiefs' councils beneath its graceful branches. Here disputes between the nearby Shilshole community on Salmon Bay and others were deliberated and problems of mutual concern were resolved. Native tribes called it the Powwow Tree.

Early explorers entering Puget Sound named the tree, which could be seen for miles from the water, the Landmark Cedar and used it as a navigation point, as did all ships entering Elliott Bay for nearly two centuries. It also became known to sailors as the Lookout Tree.

In 1891 the ancient landmark cedar was felled by Rudolf Ankeny to make way for a house being built for his daughter. This action was not taken without the Duwamish vigorously protesting the cutting of the sacred tree. Some members of the white community also supported the tribe's point of view. Before Ankeny destroyed the tree, the natives held a ceremony at the site and tribal tradition records that a curse was placed where the tree once stood. Located at 912 Second Avenue West, the Ankeny House is an example of late Queen Anne style architecture and a registered Historic Landmark.

*Illustration by Tony Cresci.*

was to paddle out on the lake with burning torches. On signal the hunters would startle the ducks by shouting, banging, and waving the flaming torches. The frightened ducks left the lake by flying low along a natural, open, marshy area leading to Puget Sound and directly into nets stretched across this "flyway" by the hunters. Entangled in the nets, the ducks were easily killed. According to anthropologist Thomas Talbot Waterman, "astonishing numbers" of ducks were caught this way, especially when the Duwamish were preparing for a potlatch.

## "Potlatch Meadows" at Seattle Center

The place that has become Seattle Center was a traditional gathering place of the Duwamish. Formed by a glacier, the flat meadow was kept clear of brush by periodic burnings by the natives. The Duwamish called the area *Baba'kwob* (prairies). Because tribal festivals were held there, the pioneers called the area Potlatch Meadows.

In 1966 local tribes held their first large scale powwow in a century on their traditional *Baba'kwob* grounds. The event was the War Dance, sponsored by the American Indian Women's Service League and the Seattle Indian Center. After performing the War Dance to large crowds at the Seattle Center Arena, the troupe of seven dancers went on to a three-month invitational tour of western Europe. The War Dance continued to be held at the Seattle Center annually for nearly a decade. The tradition was revived in 1986 with the United Indians of All Tribes Foundation's Powwow, observed annually during Seafair Indian Days. The powwow is now held at the Daybreak Star Indian Cultural Center at Magnolia's Discovery Park.

## Distinguished Native American Seattle Pacific University Graduates

Seattle Pacific University is proud of its Native American graduates, many of whom have distinguished themselves in a variety of fields. Among its illustrious graduates are Dr. William Demerts, who has served as a prominent federal Native American education official, Frank La Fontaine, a justice in the Colville Tribal Court, and Ronald Johnson, who served for years as President of the Indian Athletic Association. David Boxley, a Tsimshian artist, is locally and internationally renowned for his wood carving. Seattle Pacific University has instituted a minority student scholarship program that specifically includes Native Americans.

## Professors Support the Duwamish People

Seattle Pacific University's involvement with Native American affairs began in the 1970s when faculty and students assisted tribal groups in seeking sovereign status from the federal government. Ironically, the Duwamish, whose name appears first on the Point Elliott Treaty, were dropped as a federally-recognized Native American tribe in the early 1950s. No one knows precisely when or why this occurred, as there is no existing paperwork.

In 1976, the American Indian Policy Review Commission, a federal task force, recommended that a special procedure be established to consider requests of sovereign status from such tribal groups. The procedure for seeking federal acknowledgment is complicated and requires the applicant tribe to assemble detailed evidence of its community history. Several Seattle Pacific University faculty members have been very active in working with Puget Sound Indians in preparing this historical evidence: Kenneth Tollefson with the Duwamish and Snoqualmie, Michael Roe with the Cowlitz, Douglas Pennoyer with the Snoqualmie and Steilacoom, and Martin Abbott with the Snoqualmie.

## Daybreak Star Indian Cultural Center

Daybreak Star is located in Queen Anne's sister community, Magnolia. The center has been an enduring symbol of an urban tribal presence in Seattle since its founding in 1970. Native American culture is celebrated at the center in the form of ceremonies, festivals, dancing, singing and storytelling, and the public is often welcome to attend. In the 1980s a permanent exhibit on Native American culture and art was developed, which continues to expand.

The Daybreak Star Center was not established without a struggle. In the late 1960s, a group of Native American activists began meeting to discuss ways to persuade the city to allocate some of the newly-surplused federal lands at Fort Lawton to local tribes. The group eventually incorporated as the United Indians of All Tribes Foundation and developed a plan to use the land as a Native American cultural and educational center. Influenced by similar activism elsewhere in the country, including the militant advocacy of the American Indian Movement in Minneapolis and the Native American occupation of Alcatraz in 1969, members of the group occupied the site for three weeks. Negotiations with the City of Seattle and federal officials led to a lease on seventeen acres for ninety-nine years and financial assistance in developing the Daybreak Star Cultural Center. In 1993 the center is a dynamic place which both preserves the Salish peoples' culture and educates the public on the richness of their heritage.

***Edward Liebow*** *is a research scientist at the Battelle Memorial Institute and holds a Ph.D. in cultural anthropology. He is also an Affiliate Professor of Anthropology at the University of Washington and has published extensively on issues affecting contemporary Native Americans.*

***Erin Younger*** *is a Cultural Resources Specialist with the King County Historic Preservation Program. She has a master's degree in cultural anthropology and has published numerous articles on Native American art and a book on Hopi Indian photography.*

Chapter Three

# Oregon Trail Migrants to Puget Sound Country

by
Kay F. Reinartz, Ph.D.

*Why Did Americans Emigrate to the West? Some were prompted by mere love of change, many more by a spirit of enterprise and adventure; and a few, I believe, knew not exactly why they were thus upon the road. With these reasons was more or less mixed up a very important element—a desire to occupy the country as a basis of title in the dispute between the government of the United States and that of Great Britain.*

*Jesse Quinn Thornton*
*Oregon Trail Emigrant, 1846*

*Traveling along the banks of the Arkansas River the summer of 1852, the Ward pioneer party encountered an immense herd of buffalo—possibly a half-million animals—in Dillis Ward's estimation. Seeing that it was impossible to drive around the herd, the wagons drove into its midst, finding that the huge bison stepped back to allow them to pass through—like the waters of the Red Sea parting—according to one observer. The wagon train entered the herd at two p.m. and was clear of it after four and a half hours of steady travel. Original illustration by Vonnie Anderson Burns.*

As explorers and settlers found their way into Puget Sound they soon concluded that Elliott Bay offered the best harbor on the Sound. In 1851 two parties established settlements on Elliott Bay. In June, the Collins party arrived, composed of Luther and Diana Borst Collins and their children Lucinda and Stephen, Jacob and Samuel Maple, and Henry Van Asselt. This group selected land in the Duwamish River Valley, with the Collins' homestead located near what later became Boeing Field.

The following November, the second group, the Denny-Boren party, landed at Alki Point. This group of seven men, five women and twelve children included the first settlers destined to establish their homestead on Queen Anne Hill, Louisa Boren and David Denny.

Why did these Americans venture to the northwest wilderness of Puget Sound, which was not a part of the United States at this time? The answer is found in the history of the region and in almost two hundred years of its exploration.

## The International Struggle for the Northwest

The first known European to cross the 42nd parallel north (the present-day California-Oregon border) was the explorer Ferrero in 1543. Shortly thereafter Sir Francis Drake viewed the California coast and other explorers from Spain and England soon followed. The Spanish were the most active in exploring the northwest coastal waters and in 1775 Bruno de Heceta landed near the present Point Grenville. The year before, Juan Jose Perez Hernandez had observed Nootka Harbor on the west coast of Vancouver Island but did not go ashore. In the final decades of the eighteenth century, the Russians began establishing outposts along the Alaskan coast which were administered from New Archangel (Sitka). By 1800 the Russians were looking farther south, which concerned the Spanish.

In 1778 Capt. James Cook reached Nootka Harbor and, going ashore, claimed the area for England. George Vancouver sailed into Puget Sound in May 1792, naming many prominent natural features and also claiming that area for England.

The same year a momentous even occurred when the American, Robert Gray, discovered a very large river flowing into the Pacific. Convinced that he had found the long-sought "Great River of the West," he named the river Columbia for his ship the *Columbia Rediviva*. Gray's exploration of this and a subsequent trip in 1792 became a key factor in the American claim to the vast area that was called Oregon Country. The American claim was strengthened by President Thomas Jefferson's Lewis and Clark Expedition of 1804-06. The first permanent American settlement in the Northwest was Astoria, Oregon, a fur trading center established by John Jacob Astor in 1811.

Around 1838 the first American settlers arrived in the region later known as Washington. However, north of the Columbia River, the American influence was minimal. Under these circumstances the Hudson's Bay Company maintained unchallenged control over the Oregon Country wilderness, which extended from the 42nd parallel north to about the 54th parallel (present-day Prince Rupert, B.C.) into the early 1840s.

But between 1840 and 1860, the region destined to be known as the Pacific Northwest finally went to the Americans through their fulfilling three fundamental requisites for national title--discovery, exploration and occupation.

Increasing tension over occupation rights in the 1830s prompted the Americans to take dynamic action to solidify their interests and control over the area in 1843, the year the Oregon Trail opened. A provisional government was set up that was actually a republic within a republic, since the status of the region had not been determined at this time. In 1844 the newly-created territorial legislature met at Oregon City, drafted a code of laws, elected officers to govern and enacted a law defining boundaries. In 1846, after several years of negotiating, the 49th parallel north was agreed upon by the United States and England as the compromise boundary between parallels 42° and 54° 40'. Thus, control of the vast region below the 49th parallel passed from the Hudson's Bay Company to the Americans.

## Land Grants Entice Settlers

In the interest of hastening the settling process, thereby assuring possession of the northwest, the United States government passed a series of very generous land grant acts to attract settlers to this remote region. Most of the land in the Puget Sound area was acquired by the pioneers under one of three land acts: the Donation Land Grant Acts of 1850 and 1851, the Preemption Land Act of 1855, and the Homestead Act of 1862. Land was also obtained under the Timber Culture Act of 1873.

Historic records reveal many instances of settlers on Queen Anne saying they had "donation claims" when in fact their claims were preemption claims or obtained

## U.S. Government Land Grants in Washington Territory

| NAME OF ACT | PASSED-EXPIRED | ELIGIBILITY | AMT. OF LAND | COST OF LAND |
|---|---|---|---|---|
| Oregon Territory Donation Land Act | 1850-1850 | Single or married white males,married women and half-breed Indians over 18, settled in Oregon Terr. by 12/1/1850, must be or intend to become citizens | Up to 640 acres for a married couple, 320 acres for singles | Free except $10 filing and other fees. 7 years to prove claim. Must live on and improve land for majority of year |
| | 1851-1855 | Same, settled by 12/1/1855 | 320 acres/ married, 160 acres/single | |
| Preemption Act | 1841; extended to Washington Territory 1852-1891 | Heads of families, including widows, or single men or women over 21, who did not already own at least 320 acres. Claim allowed in addition to claim under Oregon Donation Land Act | 160 acres. Before 1879, only 80 acres within rail-road right-of-way | $1.25/acre, $2.50/acre within 40 miles of railroad from 1870-89. Residency and improve-ment required. Must pay within 12-33 months (in practice, often longer) |
| Homestead Act | 1862-present (now restricted to Alaska and territories) | Heads of households, or single men or women over 21, who lived on and improved land continuously for 5 years | 160 acres | Free except $10 filing and other fees. 7 years to prove claim |
| Timber Culture Act | 1873-1890 | Any settler, had to plant and maintain trees on part of land for 10 (later 8) years | Up to 160 acres of treeless land | Free, no residency requirements; 13 years to prove claim |

under the Homestead Act. Donation claim law required only paying for registration fees. The land itself was free. In contrast, land acquired under the Preemption Land Act cost $1.25/acre. Early settlers who qualified for land under the Donation Act could acquire an additional 160 acres under preemption law and an additional 160 acres after 1862 under the Homestead Act.

It is noteworthy that the 1850 act was only the second time in American history that Congress had given away land to encourage settling in a region. There were 1,018 donation land grants made to individuals under the 1850 and 1855 laws, a total of 300,000 acres of the most accessible land in Washington Territory. The vast majority of these grants were made to settlers in the region bordering on Puget Sound, with only 13 donation land grants being made in eastern Washington.

The conditions and qualifications required to acquire land under the legislation controlled the settlers' way of life throughout the first two decades of settlement on Puget Sound. The law required that the claimant live on his or her land the majority of the year and make substantial improvements, i.e., clearing the natural vegetation and planting crops. This process, known as "proving up," lasted seven years, after which time clear title, i.e., patent, was granted. The typical pattern for married couples was that the woman lived year-round on the claim alone or with the children, while her husband worked out in the logging camps or sawmills to earn needed cash.

Often claim law deadlines were not strictly enforced because of the difficulties in reaching the filing office, which was initially in Salem. Later, filing was done at the King County Seat, Seattle.

## The Settling of the Puget Sound Country

The beauty and outstanding abundance of natural resources in the Puget Sound country began to be widely known during the 1849 California Gold Rush, but the difficulty of reaching Puget Sound and the shortage of suitable farm land held people back.

Overland travel was blocked by dense mountain vegetation which made journeys by wagon nearly impossible. Water travel was considerably easier, but had its own set of dangers and drawbacks. Regardless of the route a settler took, the journey to Puget Sound was more complicated and dangerous than to other western areas open to homesteading. Settlers began trickling in during the 1840s, but Puget Sound Country did not attract settlers in significantly large numbers until the 1880s, after more accessible western lands were taken up and the railroad provided a fast, safe means of transportation.

## Travel by Sea

Puget Sound settlers had two sea alternatives to the overland trail—around Cape Horn or through the Isthmus of Panama. The Horn route often took a year, while the Isthmus route took four to six weeks. Sea travel cost more and presented real and imagined dangers for non-seafaring people. In addition, they were limited in the tools and equipment they could bring by ship, which excluded draft animals and heavy wagons. On the Puget Sound frontier, farming equipment and farm animals were scarce and expensive.

## The Oregon Trail

The historic migration of people across the Great Plains and Rocky Mountains to the Northwest began with the first wagon train out in 1842. Each spring from this year forward until 1883, when the transcontinental railroad was completed to the Northwest, ever larger numbers of daring men, women and children set off for the west coast. In response to the Oregon Territory Donation Land Act of 1851, during 1852 the trickle of migrants swelled to a veritable river.

A good crossing started in the early spring, when the green prairie grass provided food for the animals. The goal was to arrive in the Northwest in late August or September, with enough time to get situated before winter. Those people who made their way to Elliott Bay typically traveled by wagon to the Columbia River, thence down the river on barges, or followed the Barlow Road alongside the river. At Portland they caught a steamer for Puget Sound. By the late 1850s a road, barely passable by heavy wagon and a strong team, had been cut through the forest from the Cowlitz River to Olympia via Chehalis, and settlers drove their teams to Puget Sound Country.

The 2,000 mile overland journey to the Northwest normally took from four to six months, with ten miles the average distance in a 12-hour day. Most families had a heavy wagon pulled by a team of horses or oxen, and many drove milk cows and additional draft animals alongside. To reduce the weight of the load and break the monotony of riding in the jostling wagon most of the adults and children in a wagon train walked much of each day.

Prominent among the dangers implicit in the journey were route hazards, the weather, hostile natives, and disease. Larger wagon trains were safer from attacks by native tribes, while smaller ones made better time and had less trouble feeding the stock with available vegetation. More people died from disease, particularly cholera, than from all the other hazards together. An additional health hazard for women was pregnancy. Approximately one-third of all the married women began the journey in various stages of pregnancy. Many gave birth along the trail.

## Queen Anne's First Settlers in the Pioneer Vanguard

The Oregon Territory Surveyor General's report for October 23, 1852, notes that in 1852, 777 married couples filed for 640 acre claims and 202 single men filed for 320 acre claims under the 1850 Donation Land Act. Under Section 4 of Oregon Territorial Law, 80 couples filed for 320 acre claims and 20 single men for 160 acre claims.

The census taken the summer of 1853, a few months after Washington Territory was established, found that there were 3,965 settlers in the new territory. The county census shows King County, with 170 people, was one of the most sparsely populated. Other county populations were Clark, 1,134; Island, 195; Jefferson, 189; Lewis, 616; Pacific, 152; Pierce, 513; and Thurston, 996.

Numbered among the vanguard of 1852 who were destined to become the first European-American residents of Queen Anne were: Louisa Boren and David Denny, later married; Thomas Mercer and daughters Mary Jane, Eliza, Susannah and Alice; Dr. Henry Smith, Abigail Teaff Smith, his mother, and Ellender Smith, sister; and John Ross and Mary McMillan, who would later marry.

Four other young people who crossed to Oregon Territory in the summer of 1853 would assume prominent nineteenth century roles in Queen Anne community life. These were Clarence Bagley; Hester Ward, who became Thomas Mercer's second wife; and Hester's brother Dillis B. Ward and Sarah Isabel Byles, who would later marry. Nine-year-old Sarah Byles was a member of the famous Longmire party that made the first crossing through Naches Pass, where the wagons had to be lowered with ropes down the cliffs.

## Accounts of the Overland Trail

Narratives of the experience of traveling to Puget Sound Country over the Oregon Trail have been left by four of the first-comers to Queen Anne—Clarence

Bagley, David and Louisa Boren Denny, and Dillis B. Ward. The motivations for undertaking the move to the Northwest, as well as the character of the people, their intelligence, spirit, courage and resourcefulness, are reflected in their accounts of the journey west. These early community residents are a part of that great American nineteenth century epic—the Westward Movement—and their stories are tales of pure adventure. They are an important part of the Queen Anne community's frontier heritage.

## The Denny-Boren Party, 1851

Louisa Boren and David Denny were members of the Denny-Boren wagon train, consisting of four wagons, seven men, four women and four children including two babies, six weeks and four months old. The wagon party members were all Denny-Boren kissin' kin, with the families being connected by several marriages. They lived in Cherry Grove, Illinois. John Denny was the wagon train captain. By the standards of the day, a wagon train of only four wagons was considered far too small for safety. Undoubtedly, the outstanding physical and emotional health, as well as the intelligence and frontier knowledge and skills that characterized the women and men of this pioneer party, were a major factor in the safe journey of this group.

The family had been much encouraged to "pull up stakes and head for Oregon Country" by the glowing accounts in letters written by old friends who had gone west and were already homesteading in the Willamette Valley. They were also influenced by Gen. John C. Fremont's travel accounts. Finally, John Denny and son Arthur both wished for a change from the rigorous Illinois climate which caused them frequent lapses into malarial fever, commonly called ague.

The months of preparations that preceded the journey to Oregon Country are described in the words of Louisa Boren's great niece Roberta Frye Watt, as told to her by her mother Catherine Denny:

> *Hams were cured; blankets were woven; warm comforters made; and the household linen replenished. The women sewed far into the night making stout garments for themselves and the children. Even the children's little fingers were kept busy carding wool and piecing quilts. The cobbler came and made shoes for the whole family. New harnesses were bought and the wagons were provided with strong, heavy springs.*
>
> *The old homes were sold. The household goods were scattered among friends and relatives, for only the things that were absolutely necessary and those that could be packed conveniently into the covered wagons were kept. Most of the provisions were crammed into sacks to save the weight of boxes. . . . It was a saying in those days that nothing must be taken that was not worth a dollar a pound.*

## Louisa Boren and David Denny's Twice-Told Tales

Years later, Louisa Boren and David Denny, sitting in their home near Lake Union, were to tell their children the story of the journey with its many adventures. One such story was of how David, driving his four-horse team in the teeth of a driving hail storm, almost lost control of the animals as they reared and plunged, attempting to escape from their unseen, icy attackers.

The mountains were a real wonder to the party. Inez Denny, daughter of David Denny and Louisa Boren Denny, tells us that her parents found that "as they approached the upheaval mountainous country, they had a lively interest, a keen delight in the novelty of their surroundings, and surprise at unexpected features were aroused in the minds of the travelers." Getting the wagons over these mountains required endless ingenuity and patience. Louisa told her children, "What grinding, heaving and bumping over huge boulders! What shouting and urging of animals, what weary hours of tortured endurance dragged along!"

Crossing great arid stretches required special preparations. They crossed the Green River desert in one night—30 miles of "push" traveling by dim starlight. Finally, they reached the other side. Smelling water, the horses dashed uncontrollably into the river, taking the wagons with them.

As the journey became routine and the party crossed the Great Plains, the early exuberance waned. Inez Denny recorded for her parents:

> *Summer came on apace and the landscape became brown and parched. . . . Long days of travel followed the monotonous expanse of prairie, each with scarcely varying incidents, toils and dangers. The stir of starting in the morning, the morning forward movement, the halt for the noonday meal, cooked over a fire of*

*Original illustration by Darcanne Preble.*

## Death Along the Trail

The Denny-Boren pioneer party members were frequently saddened along the Oregon Trail by the numerous lonely graves of pioneers who, like themselves, began with high hopes but stopped forever along the way. One day they came upon an isolated grave on the side of a mountain piled high with stones to protect it from the ravages of wolves. The party shared a feeling of deep solemnity and gathered around the grave, where they prayed for the departed and joined in singing an old song:

*I came to the place*
*Where the white pilgrim lay,*
*And pensively stood by his tomb,*
*When in a low whisper I heard something say,*
*'How sweetly I sleep here alone.'*

*buffalo chips, and the long weary afternoon of heat and dust whose passing brought the welcome night, marked the journey through the treeless region.*

The day after the Fourth of July, an old Shoshone visited the camp, hanging around all day. He was friendly and caused no trouble, leaving at nightfall. The next morning, as the women were preparing breakfast, a single young brave rode into camp with a string of ponies, which he explained he wanted to trade for Louisa Boren. He became very angry when his offer was rejected and Louisa, concerned that he might swoop down on her with his horse and carry her off, quickly got into the wagon. While David stood guard by the wagon the group quickly hitched the horses and got underway "at a good smart pace." The brave followed the wagon train for several miles before accepting his failure to secure the beautiful Louisa for his wife. A short time after this incident, the wagon train was joined by the John Low wagon train which added two wagons and eight more people to the Denny-Boren Party.

On August 11, 1851, the wagon train arrived at The Dalles, 1,765 miles and 80 days after they pulled out of

Cherry Grove. They had lost no animals or people; there were no serious injuries or fatal illnesses; they still had food, money, energy and enthusiasm. The group had averaged an amazing 18 miles a day—a record few parties could report.

The party traveled down the Columbia to Portland with the women and two men traveling by boat, while the rest of the men drove the wagons on the rough Barlow Road. Because of drunken boatmen one of the boats almost went over the falls. However, Louisa Boren detected the fact they had overshot the pull-out point and forced the drunkards to pull ashore, thereby saving the entire party. At Portland the party temporarily settled in, while David Denny, John Low and Lee Terry, who was traveling with Low, went ahead to Puget Sound to scout for a favorable place for their settlement.

## The Bethel Party, 1852

It was estimated that over 50,000 emigrants took the overland trail the summer of 1852. Among these was the Bethel party. Clarence Bagley observed that the party could well have been named the "Seattle Party," for more than half of the members eventually settled in Seattle, and many played key roles in the development of the city. Foremost among these were future Queen Anne residents Thomas Mercer and his daughters Mary Jane, Eliza, Susannah, and Alice; Dexter Horton, Eliza Shoudy Horton, and daughter Rebecca; William Shoudy; Rev. Daniel Bagley, Susannah Whipple Bagley, and son Clarence.

In 1850 Rev. Bagley had decided to answer the call of his church for volunteer missionaries for Oregon Territory and began recruiting people for his party from his congregation in Princeton, Illinois. Thomas Mercer was among the men in Bagley's congregation struck with "Oregon Fever."

Susie Mercer reported from family discussions in the winter of 1851 that her father was persuaded to go to Oregon Territory for three main reasons: to escape the fever and ague that plagued the Mississippi Valley; better economic opportunities; and the offer of free land in Oregon Territory. Moreover, Oregon Territory was widely promoted by the government because of the boundary dispute with England.

While the men were enthusiastic about going west, the women, including Nancy Brigham Mercer, Thomas Mercer's wife, were less eager. They were more objective than the men about the real hazards of the journey, as well as the hardships of living on the frontier. They realized that it would be considerably more difficult to feed, clothe, educate and keep their families healthy in far-flung Oregon, not to mention the strenuous six-month journey.

## Thomas Mercer, Party Leader

From the beginning Thomas Mercer made a great effort to put together a strong, well-planned, well-equipped, healthy wagon train. He carefully researched the requirements of the trip and concluded that the common key errors were failure to plan for a healthy balanced diet throughout the trip, lack of medical knowledge and supplies to treat illnesses that occurred, and overloading the wagons. With this in mind, in addition to the usual supplies, they packed quantities of dried fruit, a variety of legumes, and whole wheat and rye flour. Many wagon trains survived for months on red or white beans, salt pork and white flour bread.

On April 20, 1852, the final goodbyes were said and the Bethel party wagon train pulled out of Princeton. The party consisted of 14 prairie schooners, the Bagley's spring coach, 44 horses, 22 men, seven women, and eight children. All of the women were married but one. Almost all of the members of the Bethel party were related to other members of the group. Additional wagons would join the group along the route, eventually making a total of 38 wagons.

Thomas Mercer, 39, was elected wagon captain, which made him responsible for all the decisions made—starting and stopping times, guard duty schedules, and settling disputes, although there were very few among the well-acquainted and religious members of the Bethel party. Mercer's logs of the trip were found in his house on Queen Anne Hill by his daughter Susie years later.

## Cholera, Scourge of the Oregon Trail

Contamination of the water supply with human and animal waste by earlier wagon trains made cholera the scourge of the Oregon Trail in the 1850s. The worst year was 1852, and members of the Bethel party report that at times they drove for hundreds of miles between the unbroken rows of graves. Looking for a way to pass the time, Susie Mercer, ten, and Clarence Bagley, nine, decided they would count the graves, with each child keeping count of one side of the road. The total for the day was 120.

The Bethel party had no deaths from cholera or

other causes. Thomas Mercer and Daniel Bagley both had a good understanding of basic medicine and they had packed into the wagons large quantities of treatment ingredients. At the first suggestion of cholera, they administered an effective herbal treatment consisting of a compound of hot bitter bark and roots simmered in water, which was then drunk. If taken soon enough, it was very effective in curing the disease. Many members of the Bethel party came down with cholera, but prompt and frequent administration of this herbal medicine overcame the deadly disease.

The Bethel party, prompted by their strong belief in treating one's fellow man with love, administered their medicine to many sick migrants they met along the trail. A few paid them, but they expected no payment. For years afterwards, Mercer and Bagley were often approached by total strangers who thanked them for saving their lives, or that of a friend or relative, on the Oregon Trail.

The party included many children and school was carried on during the journey, with studies beginning after they crossed the North Platte River. The older children taught the younger from graded readers and arithmetic books, and the adults helped the young teachers with their own lessons and advised them in teaching the little ones. Years later Clarence Bagley recalled that he and the other children received a broad education in plant and animal life during the course of the long journey. In addition, they learned practical skills, as they were called upon to assist with work around camp.

## Tragedy at the Dalles

The wagon train reached Fort Dalles, regarded as the end of the overland trail, on September 3, 1852, less than five months after their departure. The Bethel party averaged 12 to 15 miles a day, in spite of the fact that they did not travel on Sunday. No one had been seriously ill or died and they had lost only a single animal.

Their good luck turned at The Dalles. The weather had turned cold and wet, and Nancy Brigham Mercer became seriously ill with pneumonia, being drenched by river spray during the ten-hour journey down the Columbia River. Alarmed at his wife's condition, Mercer sent the main party ahead while he, their daughters, and Eliza and Dexter Horton remained behind to nurse Nancy. Nancy had been a strong, healthy woman but the long arduous journey had weakened her constitution and she died on September 21. She was 34 years old.

Autumn was in the air, however, and there was little time for lingering. They buried Nancy on the bank of the Columbia River and joined the others in Salem. Leaving his daughters in Eliza Horton's care, Thomas Mercer almost immediately took a ship to Elliott Bay to look for a claim. There he met David Denny, who took him up to the area north of the Seattle settlement where Mercer found land to his liking on a beautiful small lake not far from Puget Sound. Having made friends with the settlers, with whom he quickly established good rapport, Mercer declared he would return in March to build a cabin and prepare a home for his children, and then sailed back to Portland.

## The Ward Party

In the summer of 1853 the Ward party made its way to Oregon from Batesville, Arkansas. Among the travelers were Hester Ward, 27, and her half-brother Dillis B. Ward, 15, who wrote an account of their journey 50 years later, published in 1911 as *Across the Plains in 1853*. In 1859 the pair would come to Seattle and Queen Anne Hill, where they would make their mark in community history.

The extended Ward family's decision to move to Oregon was strongly influenced by health problems and disagreements with their church. The Wards were adamantly opposed to slavery and very angry when the Methodist Protestant Church decided to split into two branches, with the southern supporting slave ownership. The Wards' feelings were not shared by their neighbors, since the family was living in a pro-slavery region. In addition, after the Wards had moved to Arkansas, scarcely a month passed when some member of the family was not sick with malarial fever.

About this time, the Wards read a glowing description published in their church newspaper of the many attractions the Willamette Valley held for homesteading. Dillis relates that in the summer of 1852 they held "a brief family council, in which father, mother and the older children were all heard." The mutual agreement was to move to Oregon Territory and in the following months of preparation "little was thought of or talked about except Oregon and how we were going to get there. In the innocence of our childhood, we [children] looked upon the whole affair as a great picnic excursion."

Like so many of the emigrant groups that took the Oregon Trail in those early years, the Ward party was composed of several extended families connected by friendship and family ties. The party consisted of 25 persons, seven of whom were the children of Jesse

Ward's three marriages and his third wife's children by her previous marriage. Half of the party was young children—13 in all—plus four women, eight men, and eight wagons. Early in the journey the party was joined by other emigrants, making up a final wagon train of 18 wagons, 22 men, and 35 women and children.

The Wards left Arkansas March 9, 1853, and reached Salem, Oregon Territory, September 30th. The seven months on the trail were marked by numerous adventures, including hair-raising close calls with hostile Native Americans. Through a combination of luck, quick thinking and courageous action by many party members, there was no violence and no lives lost. At the time of Hester Ward's death, on November 13, 1897, the *Post-Intelligencer* printed an extensive account of this remarkable woman's life. Included was her story of confrontations with local tribes while traveling on the Oregon Trail. The newspaper account is verified by Inez Denny's memories of Hester Ward Mercer.

Hester's younger half-brother Dillis wrote his version of the same stories in *Across the Plains in 1853.* It is interesting to note that Dillis' version omits the role that Hester and other unnamed women played in saving two young women from abduction by native men. His account credits only the men for the rescue.

Hester's version of the incident is given here. About eight miles east of the North Platte River the Ward wagon train encountered a hostile Arapaho war party returning to their camp. After harassing the wagon train, they were frightened off by the train's bugler blasting on his horn. The emigrant train's trouble with the Native Americans had only begun.

> *Down in the valley through which the pioneers were compelled to travel they saw many little tents. Other Indians were camped there. The old chief and his party accompanied the emigrants. Every Indian showed an ugly disposition. The emigrants were compelled to stop in the midst of the tents in the valley. The old chief explained through an interpreter that his people had just come back from a great battle. They were hungry, he said, and wanted food and the emigrants would have to give it to them, for were not these whites, he said, passing through the sacred land of the Indian?*
>
> *The Ward party was a small one, it could muster but 22 men. Each man was well armed, but the Indians were mixing up with them and it would have been impossible to get together for united action. It was necessary to submit to the wishes of the Indians. Bacon, sugar, flour and crackers were given up and the old chief divided them among his people.*
>
> *While this division was being made young braves were busying themselves by annoying the members of the party. Among the white people was a young woman who had charge of two horses attached to a light covered wagon. Several of the braves took a fancy to her. They gave the whites to understand that any woman who could drive horses was all right and must not go any farther. Mr. Ward and his men had a hard time keeping the Indians from stealing the girl. Once they crowded about her and for a time it was thought that she would be taken by force. Several of the women went to her rescue. [Hester] was in the rescue party. She [along with the other women] shoved the Indians right and left and in the end the girl was rescued and smuggled into a closed wagon, where she remained concealed for some hours.*
>
> *Another young woman in the party had beautiful auburn hair. An Indian warrior took a fancy to her, thought she was the finest woman he had even seen, and said that his people would compromise if she were given to him for a wife. Again there was trouble and the girl had to be hidden in a closed wagon.*

The Indians kept up their annoyance of the party for some time, but finally their hunger got the better of them and they sat down to eat the food which the Ward party had under compulsion given them.

The Indian chief consented that the white people should take their departure. They were quick to do so and were soon some distance from the Indian camp.

In addition to trouble with native men, the Ward party experienced other disasters, such as one evening when all of their animals stampeded without observable provocation. Left without any means of moving their wagons, the stranded party waited for almost a week while some of the men, traveling miles on foot, managed to round up enough of their horses and oxen to move on. Several wagons had to be abandoned because there were no animals to pull them.

The Ward Party arrived at their destination, Salem, on September 30, 1853. Hester and Dillis settled down on the Jesse Ward homestead with their extended family for the next six years. The two would come to Seattle in the summer of 1859 to blend their history with that of other Queen Anne Hill settlers.

Chapter Four

# The Community of Pioneers North of Seattle— 1853–1860

by
Kay F. Reinartz, Ph.D.

*The noble army of courageous, enduring, persistent, progressive pioneers who threaded their way across the western wilderness prove that an age of marvelous heroism is but recently past.*

*The knowledge, foresight, faith and force exhibited by many of these daring men and women proclaimed them endowed with the genius of conquerors.*

*Inez Denny,*
*Queen Anne Pioneer*
Blazing the Way, *1909*

*Queen Anne Hill looking west toward Smith Cove, Magnolia Bluff and the setting sun. Courtesy University of Washington Special Collections.*

## PIONEERS IN THE WILDERNESS NORTH OF SEATTLE

On January 1, 1852, the European-American population in the vicinity of Elliott Bay was 31: 11 men, six women and 14 children. The next year, 170 residents were counted in the newly-created King County, Oregon Territory. By 1854 there were four claims on the west side of Lake Duwamish (Lake Washington), four more along the south shore of Elliott Bay, and one in Rainier Valley. Settlements were also quickly forming in the Duwamish and White river valleys.

The area north of the Seattle settlement is officially designated in the government survey as Township No. 25, North Range, No. 3, East, Willamette Meridian, Territory of Washington and includes districts that later became known as Denny Hill (Denny Regrade), Queen Anne Hill, Lake Union, Smith Cove (Interbay), Magnolia, Ross, Fremont and Salmon Bay (Ballard). Between 1853 and 1859 approximately 15 land claims were filed, mostly by single men, for land in this area north of Seattle. Some of the claims were only partially within the Queen Anne community and in a couple cases the settler's homestead is located just outside of the boundaries. In spite of their isolation, the north district settlers became well-acquainted and functioned as a single informal community working together, visiting, and looking after each other when illness or other trouble befell a household. All of these settlers are included in the following discussion of the early years.

These adventurous pioneers shared cultural, political and religious values. They were mostly American-born, not immigrants, and came to the Northwest from the middle states, e.g., Illinois, Indiana, and Ohio. They were very experienced with the conditions of living in a primitive outpost, far from the securities and comforts of civilization. With a few exceptions, they grew up in frontier conditions.

Those whose political allegiance is known were Whigs, abolitionists and pro-Union in the Civil War. They were remarkable in that many were intellectuals, deeply religious in the Protestant faith, and teetotalers. Their strong support of temperance was not in total harmony with frontier life, where hard drinking was commonplace and used by men to relieve the stress of an unbalanced social life. Although most of these pioneers were bachelors, the male leaders among the north district settlers had families with them, which critically influenced their shaping the course of local history.

While not far apart in terms of miles, the density of the virgin forest made travel slow and difficult, which in turn isolated each homestead. The native people's trails crisscrossed the area, connecting Lake Union with the bay and cove. The trails also connected their semi-permanent camps on Lake Union at Smith Cove, and in the vicinity of Battery Street. Trails also linked the permanent Shilshole people's village on Shilshole Bay to the camps and waterways. These native trails around the perimeter of the hill, as well as game trails, were used by the early settlers for many years and in some cases later became the routes of paved roads.

### People Settling North of Seattle, 1853-1859*

Louisa Boren, David T. Denny – 1851
Dr. Henry Smith, Abigail Teaff Smith, Ellender Smith –1852
Ira Wilcox Utter – 1852
Osborn Hall – 1852
John Ross – 1852
Edmund Carr – 1852
Henry Pierce – 1852
Thomas Mercer, Mary Jane, Eliza, Susannah, Alice Mercer – 1852
Frances McNatt – 1853
Erasmus M. Smithers – 1853
William Strickler – 1853
John H. Nagle – 1854
Osmine Frost – 1854
David Stanley – 1854

**Dates are those recorded by the settlers as their arrival dates. Claims were normally selected almost immediately upon arrival, although land records often give a later date for official commencement of residency.*

## THE DENNY BROTHERS EXPLORE SMITH COVE

In December 1852 David and Arthur Denny and William Bell, all members of the Denny-Boren party, decided to explore the area north of Seattle in their search for pasture land. The area was only vaguely known to the Seattle pioneers through accounts by the natives. Skirting around the west side of the two hills directly north of Seattle (Denny and Queen Anne) the trio fought their way through incredibly dense vegetation. Bell, discouraged by the steady rain and slow progress, turned back around 2 p.m., but the brothers continued on until they reached tidewater, called Shilshole by the native people (now known as Salmon Bay).

The early darkness of December overtook them, making returning to the settlement impossible. They had not come prepared for camping and had neither food nor bedrolls, and their clothing and matches were soaked. However, as seasoned frontiersmen they found dry wood inside logs and under downed timber and soon had a warm fire, ignited with the flash of David's musket. Sheltered from the cold winter rain by the wide spreading branches of a giant cedar, they passed a safe night. In the morning they trekked back to Seattle, meeting up with Bell in the cove which would become known as Smith Cove. Bell had come looking for them with his pockets full of hardtack.

That winter the Denny brothers showed the cove to several newcomers to Elliott Bay, including Dr. Henry Smith and Henry Pierce, and later Ira Utter and Osborn Hall. All found the cove a favorable location, as the land was relatively flat and open, making only light clearing necessary, and had direct access to Puget Sound. The main disadvantage of the site from the perspective of the newcomers was its proximity to the Shilshole village located on Salmon Bay, in the vicinity of the present-day Ballard Locks.

## THE SWEETBRIER BRIDE

About six weeks after he spent a damp night under the great cedar on the north side of the hill, David Denny and Louisa Boren were married on January 23, 1853. In the early morning, the couple had gone to the beach to collect clams and oysters for their wedding dinner. Next they gathered evergreens from the forest and fashioned garlands with which they decorated the fireplace mantel, doorway, window sills and dining table of Arthur and Mary Boren Denny's cabin. The bride helped her sister Mary prepare the wedding dinner of clams, oysters, salmon, wild duck, potatoes, baked beans, stewed wild berries, biscuits and cake.

Shortly past midday, Louisa climbed the ladder to the cabin loft and put on a soft white mull dress she had made in Cherry Grove and pinned in her hair a bit of cedar greens and bright berries she had also gathered that morning. David donned his only jacket, pinned some cedar and berries to the lapel and joined Louisa in front of the fireplace. With 15 settlers, including seven children, and a handful of native people looking on, David "Doc" Maynard,

*David and Louisa Boren Denny with daughters Emily Inez and Madge Decatur, circa 1858. Many years of friendship in Cherry Grove, Illinois, blossomed into a deep love and commitment for Louisa Boren and David Denny. Once in the Northwest they married, established a home and family, and embarked on a lifelong love affair with the Puget Sound Country. They found the challenges of pioneer life, and living dependent upon nature and the environment, exhilarating. They commented frequently throughout their lives that they never wished to be living "back east" where they could enjoy the comforts and refinements of a settled civilization. Courtesy Queen Anne Historical Society.*

Justice of the Peace, performed the civil ceremony. Henry Yesler, King County Clerk, recorded the marriage, the second one in Seattle, on a slip of paper which was given to the couple.

After the ceremony and wedding dinner, the bride and groom walked down the bluff to their canoe, laden with their few wedding gifts, including a pair of chickens from Doc Maynard—a valuable gift, for it meant a supply of fresh eggs. Before dark they paddled about a mile and a half north and climbed up the steep, muddy hillside to the cabin on their 320-acre donation claim, which they dated January 24th, 1853. The claim ran from Lake Union to Elliott Bay, with its boundaries on the north and south being marked by today's Mercer Street and Denny Way.

*David Denny built his bride a one-room log cabin on the bluff overlooking Elliott Bay, near the foot of Denny Way. Built of nearby trees without a single nail, Denny had the help of two native men. David laughingly told Louisa that their home had been described in the seventeenth verse of the first chapter of the "Song of Solomon": "The beams of our house are of cedar and the rafters of fir." Around her cabin door, Louisa planted sweetbrier roses, hence she became known as the "Sweetbrier Bride." Louisa Boren's roses were still found growing wild at the foot of Denny Way in 1931, when they were rooted out in the process of erecting a commercial building on the site. Original drawing by Emily Inez Denny, first-born child of Louisa Boren and David Denny. Courtesy Museum of History and Industry.*

## Henry Smith, Abigail Teaff Smith and Ellender Smith

In the summer of 1853 the Smith family from Wooster, Pennsylvania, established their homestead in the cove that lay on the northwest side of the hill, and the cove became known as Smith Cove. The family was Dr. Henry Smith, 22, Abigail Teaff Smith, 61, his mother and a widow, and sister Ellender Smith, 16. The Smith family had traveled with a wagon train the summer of 1852 that was organized under the epic name "Far West Emigration Expedition," with Henry serving as assistant to the expedition's physician, a former teacher in medical school.

Leaving his mother and sister in Portland, a settlement of about 150 people, Dr. Smith decided to walk north to Puget Sound country, which had been highly recommended to the California-bound trio. In the second week of his walk, in an unremitting downpour, he met and befriended Henry K. Pierce. They completed the journey together, traveling by water from Olympia to Seattle. Meeting the Denny brothers, they were shown the cove area where Smith selected land because he was convinced it was the natural route for the future railroad to enter Seattle. In addition, he saw the potential for large commercial docks where the cove opened into Elliott Bay. Pierce chose land on the north side of Salmon Bay.

After spending the winter in Portland with his mother and sister, Smith returned to the cove early in the spring of 1853 and built a log cabin. Abigail and Ellender came by ship in early summer and planted potatoes and onions. Soon after arriving at the cove Abigail Teaff Smith selected land and filed her own claim immediately north of her son's.

## The Friends Explore the White River Valley

Full of curiosity about the area, the two young Henrys, Smith and Pierce, spent what free time they could manage exploring. In the autumn of 1853 they headed over to the White River. As they paddled downriver one day, another canoe overtook them and pulled alongside. This canoe held a white man of short stature who wore overalls tucked into his boots, a blue flannel shirt and a slouch hat covering a head of long black hair. His companions were Native American paddlers. Smith relates:

> *We fell into easy conversation on that ever new topic, the weather, the wildness of the country,*

*richness of river bottom soils, etc., etc., and I eventually asked if he was looking for a claim.*

*"No," he said, "I am not much of a farmer... I have my hands pretty full already and expect to have more irons in the fire soon; the country needs workers."*

So the two canoes passed the hours, traveling side by side with the men conversing until they reached Seattle. Smith invited the stranger to visit him at his ranch in the cove and they parted ways.

A few days later Smith and his family, Henry Pierce, and every other man, woman and child around the Sound, crowded into Yesler's Mill to meet the newly-appointed territorial governor, Isaac Stephens. When the governor stood up, Smith and Pierce were astonished to see that it was none other than their fellow traveler of a few days earlier—still dressed the same as on that day. Smith immediately dubbed him "Puss'n Boots," a moniker applied to Napoleon, who also was short and wore his pants tucked into high boots. Many in the territory called Stephens "Hat and Boots," since that was often all one would see of him as he explored the region by native canoe. As he was paddled up and down the rivers of Washington, he would typically lie in the canoe studying a map spread across his chest and only his hat and boots visible. Governor Stephens was glad to see the two Henrys and made the promised visit to the cove a few days later.

The summer of 1854 was a busy one in Smith Cove. Lumber was hauled from Yesler's Mill to the cove by scow and ox team for a comfortable two-story frame house, which was built on Abigail's claim. (The exact location of this house is unknown.) Smith hired natives from the large camp located nearby to turn over the sod for an orchard. Then he, Abigail, and Ellender, along with native helpers, spent long days planting a large grafted apple orchard, the first of its type in King County. They began harvesting apples the third year.

## HENRY SMITH'S WALK IN THE WOODS

During the summer of 1854, Smith left his house one day determined to cut a trail to Seattle. At that time the only route to the settlement was via canoe. It was a bright sunny day, but within the hour clouds rolled in and he had to rely on his compass to determine the route. Smith noted at noon that the compass had reversed its poles and was elated, since he interpreted this to mean there were iron deposits nearby. He continued walking all afternoon—but without intersecting Seattle. Finally, at nightfall he spied a clearing and shake-built cabin. He immediately concluded that it was John Nagle's place east of Lake Union (Eastlake), and sat down on the rail fence to consider if he should spend the night with John or walk into the settlement. We have Smith's own words on what happened next:

*While sitting thus, I could not help contrasting his improvements with my own. The size of the clearing was the same, the house was a good deal like mine, the only seeming difference was that the front of his faced the west, whereas the front of mine faced the east. While puzzling over this strange coincidence, my own mother came out of the house to feed the poultry that had commenced going to roost, in a rookery for all the world like my own, only facing the wrong way. "In the name of all that's wonderful!" I thought, "What is she doing here? and how did she get here ahead of me?" Just then the world took a spin around, my ranch wheeled into line, and lo! I was sitting on my own fence, and had been looking at my own improvements without knowing them.*

## ELLENDER SMITH

Ellender Smith, 18 in 1854, is described by contemporary Cornelius Hanford as "a beautiful girl and lovely character." Needless to say, Ellender did not remain single for long. The energetic, enterprising businessman Charles Plummer was the lucky bachelor who married the rosy-cheeked Ellender Smith on New Year's Day, 1855. They were married in Plummer's newly-built mercantile, which was festively decorated with garlands of evergreen and holly. The sociable Plummer invited everyone in the community to enjoy a dinner and dance right there in the store. In the spring Plummer put his carpenters to work on a large home for his bride, which was the showplace of Seattle for years. Sadly, Ellender would die giving birth to twin boys in 1858.

## JOHN ROSS AND EDMUND CARR

In January 1853 two newcomers to Elliott Bay, John Ross and Edmund Carr, met and agreed to search for suitable land for their claims. A few days after New Year's Day they paddled a native canoe from the small freshwater lake (Lake Union) to Salmon Bay via a shallow, swampy channel which they portaged. The place where the waters of the lake flowed out to the sea they named the Outlet (vicinity of Fremont). Continuing west, Ross and Carr came to a shallow bay which they named Salmon Bay because the day they explored it the waters were teeming with salmon. The native people living on this bay called it Shilshole and themselves the Shilshole-ahmish (people of Shilshole). Ignoring the native's names, the settlers gave the name Shilshole Bay to the little bay north of Magnolia, by which name it is still known.

Attracted by the idea of convenient water transportation to Puget Sound, John Ross selected a 148-acre tract of land on the north side of Queen Anne Hill and built his cabin at the Outlet. Edmund Carr selected land about a mile farther west, on the south side of Salmon Bay, next to Dr. Henry Smith's. In the twentieth century Ross's homestead is the site of the Seattle Pacific University campus and Carr's land is occupied by Fisherman's Terminal.

## The Thomas Mercer Family

Back in Illinois in the winter of 1851, when Thomas Mercer was dreaming of Oregon Country, he envisioned his wilderness home being on a lovely lake. The fulfillment of his dream was Lake Union, which he described as "hidden away in the tremendous forest," and "a mirror-like lake surrounded by deep, dark evergreens of the primitive forest." Deer trails led from the forest to the water's edge and flocks of duck and geese made the lake their home. A Native American trail skirted the shore of the lake to the Outlet that led to Salmon Bay. Mercer called Queen Anne Hill "Eden," for he felt he had reached the Promised Land.

Thomas Mercer's claim lay directly north of David and Louisa Denny's claim, with today's Mercer Street marking the shared boundary. The eastern boundary of Mercer's claim was the meandering shoreline of Lake Union, the western boundary was about Queen Anne Avenue, and the northern boundary became Highland Drive.

Mercer furnished his rustic home with simple handmade furniture, three large double beds, a table and chairs. Some shelves and clothing pegs along the walls completed the rooms. A treasured piece of furniture in the Mercer home was a little blue rocker in which Nancy Brigham Mercer had rocked her babes back in Illinois.

After completing the two-story log cabin in the summer of 1853, he returned to Salem where his daughters were waiting, and brought them back together with his team and wagon. They traveled overland to Olympia, where everything was loaded onto the steamer for Seattle.

As the boat pulled up at Yesler's Wharf that sunny September day, all eyes were on Thomas Mercer's team of big horses, Tib and Charley, the first horses in the Seattle settlement. In the following days a steady stream of Duwamish people passed by Mercer's place to examine the team. With their first glimpse of the wagon they pronounced it to be a "*Boston kayim*," (foreigner's canoe). When they heard the creaking of the wagon as it was being pulled, they called it a "*chik, chik,*" a musically alliterative ex-

*The opening of Yesler's Mill in 1853 created a market for logs and those trees closest to the water were cut first. This rare photo, dated 1853, identifies the location as Queen Anne Hill. The logging operation is that of Hillory Butler and George Frye. Undoubtedly the logging camp is in the Smith Cove area. Courtesy Museum of History and Industry.*

*Initially, Thomas Mercer built a log cabin on this Lake Union claim in 1853. The next summer he built this farmhouse located near the intersection of Roy Street and Taylor Avenue N., for his four daughters Mary Jane, Eliza, Susannah, and Alice with lumber from Yesler's Mill. The Mercer homestead was the last standing pioneer house on Queen Anne in 1908. However, it was razed in the 1910s to make way for a building that was never erected and the site has been vacant ever since. In the 1990s the site of Thomas Mercer's homestead was being used as a parking lot. Courtesy Queen Anne Historical Society.*

pression which the girls took an immediate liking to, declaring it matched the creaking sound the wagon made as it bumped over logs, stumps and rocks.

Tib was coal black and Charley snow white. Mercer liked to joke that he had the "most perfectly matched team in town." This was indeed true, because it was the only team for several years. Tib was an exceptionally fine horse. On the overland journey, Native Americans they encountered had recognized this and had attempted to buy her several times. Charley died within a few years, but Tib lived many more long years and was well-known and loved by the Seattle pioneers. When his old friend and helper died, Mercer buried her in the orchard on the homestead and today her remains lie below the modern streets of brick and concrete in the vicinity of Taylor Avenue and Roy Street.

While Mercer's team attracted the interest of the natives, the pioneer women's hearts went out to Mercer's motherless daughters, and the girls were offered homes in other cabins. However, Thomas and his eldest daughter, Mary Jane, 14, were determined to keep the family together. Between the two of them they divided the most difficult homemaking tasks and the younger girls helped with the simpler chores. Susie Mercer recalled later, "we helped our father with just about everything." Mercer often told his daughters, "Now girls, whatever's worth doing is worth doing well." Susie liked to tell that "if we didn't do a job properly, such as sweeping, he'd sweep and show us how."

Fifty years later, Susie Mercer remembered her father's care of herself and three sisters in the 1850s, particularly "his patience, his sweetness, his kindness, [and] his constant thoughtfulness in raising the four motherless little girls." Susie relates how in the first cold winters, after they moved onto the homestead when they lacked adequate bed covers, to keep his two littlest children warm at night he slept crosswise in the bed with his arm around each child curled up in the corners. Susie Mercer commented on those days: "Looking back, I can't see where we had many hardships. Life was simple, but we had plenty to eat—lots of wild berries and salmon and trout."

The Mercer family soon had neighbors. David and Louisa Denny's second home on Queen Anne Hill, their "house in the swale" (vicinity of the Seattle Opera House), was about four city blocks away. However, the vegetation was so dense that it took David and Tom two months of hard labor with an axe, mattock and cross-cut saw to just make a narrow trail between their two places the winter of 1854-55. It took several decades of logging and clearing before they could clearly see each other's homes, although they could see the light from the cabin windows at night, which was a comforting sight. Inez Denny reports that "for many years we looked across the valley to see the smoke from the fire on the Mercer hearthstone winding skyward, for they were our only neighbors. . . . We were not so lonely as we might have been with no human habitation in our view. Then we knew we could always claim the cheerful greetings and friendly visits."

## Neighbors Around the Hill

Many who arrived in 1854-55 shared Dr. Henry Smith's vision that the valley between the two hills (Queen Anne and Magnolia) would become a center of the area. Indeed, many newcomers were convinced that "the city" for the region would grow in the Smith Cove area rather than the Seattle settlement. The cove was deemed a more favorable town site for commercial enterprises since the ground was level. Around the fireplace settlers talked of how the sloping hillsides to the east and west of the cove would be the perfect location for the city's residential district.

Among those filing claims for land around the cove between 1853-55 were Erasmus Smithers, Edmund Carr, Francis McNatt, Osmine Frost, and David Stanley, all single men. On the south end of Lake Union another bachelor, John Nagle, 24, a German immigrant, filed claim on a homestead. William Strickler, from Page County, Virginia, age 26, settled across the Outlet from John Ross. A man of good education and means, he quickly bought four lots of Carson Boren's land for $1000 in 1854. Just across the shallow tidewater of Salmon Bay Ira Utter, 24, and Osborn Hall, 22, two college men from upstate New York, had claims close to Henry Pierce.

Soon after Mercer arrived with his team, the bachelors homesteading on the north and west sides of the hill turned out to help widen and smooth the trail through the woods leading north from Seattle to the Mercer homestead at the foot of Eden Hill. Rough as it was, it was the first road built in the Seattle area. It ran from Yesler Way to the corner of Roy Street and Taylor Avenue.

## Two Old Men Join the Pioneer Community: Osmine Frost and David Stanley

Osmine Frost, already 45 years old when he arrived in King County in the summer of 1854, was old by frontier standards. Frost was born in 1809 and had grown up on the Kentucky frontier. He, like so many others, was directed to Doc Maynard when he arrived in Seattle, and Maynard suggested that Frost look at the district north of Seattle for a land claim. Frost soon selected a 160-acre section directly west of Henry and Abigail Smith's and Erasmus Smithers' claims in the cove. Little is known of Frost's background. Frost's closest neighbor to the west, David Stanley, came in the late fall of 1854.

At age 64, David Stanley was by far the oldest settler in the area north of Seattle, when the age of the average settler was about 24. Stanley was born in 1790 in Missouri and had considerable experience living in wilderness conditions. He befriended Henry, Abigail and Ellender Smith the day he appeared in the district. Dr. Smith tells the story:

> *David Stanley, an old man in his seventies, [Smith's guess] came to the cove one evening in the fall of 1854, looking for a claim. He came from Missouri, was low in stature and thin to flesh and his voice too, was thin from age. His beard was long and gray, and he wore a blanket overcoat that trailed to the ground. His wife, he said, who was much younger than himself, had deserted him for a younger, handsome man, and, feeling lonesome, he had concluded to spend the remainder of his life by the sea shore, where he could listen during the long nights to the waves beating against the rocks and the monotonous music, he thought, would lull his mind and keep him from thinking.*
>
> *The next morning was a rainy one, but the old man was anxious to get a claim before they were all taken, and he started off immediately after breakfast. It rained steadily and hard all day, and much of the time it fairly poured. All through this drenching storm he waded among beds of drooping ferns and brakes, and just at dusk returned, tired out and wet as a musk rat.*
>
> *"Rather a bad time for looking up claims, uncle," I said.*
>
> *"Yes," he said, "it has been mighty damp day all day."*
>
> *But the poor old soul had found a claim that suited him at the mouth of Salmon Bay. . . . There on the beach he built a little log hut and lived for nearly twenty years listening through the long nights to the music of the waves and the shrill cries of the sea-mews. What a weird story his thoughts would have made!*

Smith reports that over the years Stanley was robbed by the natives a number of times—they would enter his cabin when he was gone and take what they wanted.

## THE BACHELORS WORK TOGETHER

Needing cash for proving up their claims, in the summer of 1854 neighbors John Ross, William Strickler, Edmund Carr and Francis McNatt set up a logging camp near Olympia. At the end of the season they lashed their logs together with ropes and light boom chains, and floated them north toward Yesler's Mill. Alas, they hit rough seas and the raft broke up, leaving the logs floating off in every direction. As the logs disappeared over the choppy waves, the partners helplessly watched the entire summer's income vanish.

In spite of this loss, the following spring the four men launched another enterprise. Anticipating the logging of the dense virgin forest that covered the hills around Lake Union, they built a sawmill near Ross's claim at the Outlet and added a dam to hold back the logs and a footbridge.

Eager to bring work to their mill, the group asked the King County Commissioners, the official governing body for the region (Seattle was not incorporated until 1869) to improve the roads in the north district. They wanted the road to Mercer's homestead widened and leveled and a new road opened to their sawmill. The County Commissioners agreed to this and Carson Boren, Edmund Carr and John Nagle were appointed to view the route. The road was barely begun when the Indian War erupted and the brave little mill went up in smoke on January 26, 1856.

## PROVING UP THE CLAIM

The pioneers reaching the territory early received gratis land grants. However, the bargain did not come free of labor. In the first decade or more, most of the settlers proving up their land claims did little more than clear land and see that they had enough to eat. There was little cash to buy anything, hence literally everything was made at home.

With almost every square rod of land densely covered with luxuriant native vegetation, the process of converting the wilderness to farms was Herculean in scope and went on for decades. It was not uncommon for a settler to work steadily for more than 20 years to convert a 160-acre claim into a farm with at least 20 percent left unchanged, because the land was too marshy, hilly, or was left as a wood lot.

Clearing the claim naturally went faster with more workers. Family members were the main labor supply for most settlers. When a hired man was available for clearing land it was expensive; the going rate throughout the 1850s ranged from $40 to $60 a month or $2.50 to $3 a day. Many men hired labor out to earn needed cash.

Native American men were often hired to help with the logging and clearing at a rate of $1 a day. While some settlers complained about their work, the Dennys found the natives to be good workers. Inez Denny reports that "far from lazy, many of them were hard workers and would dig and delve day after day to remove immense stumps of cedar and fir left after cutting the great trees."

The settlers in the north district often worked together, rotating from claim to claim. Inez Denny tells that the main help for men with families were their wives and children. The most common task assigned to children was piling brush and keeping the fires going. They often made a game out of the chore. Inez writes "many a merry party turned out at night to 'chunk up' the blazing heaps; after nightfall, their fire-lit figures flitting hither and yon against the purple darkness, suggested well-intentioned witches."

## LAND RICH AND CASH POOR

In addition to hiring out clearing land, there were several other sources of cash. Yesler's sawmill, opened in 1853, paid mill hands $30 to $50 a month and more, dependent upon skill level and technical difficulty of the job performed. Farm hands were paid $30 to $40 a month, with room and board provided. Artisans and tradesmen, such as carpenters, mechanics, painters, coopers and tailors, made $3 to $4 a day.

The timber from one's claim could be a source of cash, depending upon the lumber market. During the San Francisco building boom, before the Indian War in 1856, sawed fir lumber sold for $25/1000 lineal feet (l.f.); cedar lumber $30/1000 l.f.; cedar shingles at $5/1,000; pilings, 3 cents/ft.; and squared lumber 16 cents/ft. By 1857 the California market was flat. Pilings for building docks and wharves, mostly around the Puget Sound, were the cash wood product in highest demand, and the settlers set aside all trees appropriate for this use as they cleared and burned the trees growing on their land. It was not until the late 1880s that the lumber industry boomed on Puget Sound.

## CIVIC AND PUBLIC SERVICE

King County was created in 1853 when it was still a part of Oregon Territory. It was up to the settlers scattered around King County to fill the civic offices required by the new status. Seattle was quickly designated the county seat, which placed pressure on those living in and near it to assume responsibility for these offices. A token payment accompanied a few of the offices, but most were strictly volunteer.

The group of settlers north of Seattle, as a whole, were well-educated and moved by a strong sense of community service. Thus, they accepted the duties of various civic offices more frequently than most. Dr. Henry Smith was appointed School Superintendent and Constable in 1853, and in 1854 Thomas Mercer was elected King County Commissioner, the highest office. William Strickler served as Probate Judge and was elected to the Territorial Council, the legislature in Olympia. King County records for the 1850s and 1860s show the north district settlers sitting in almost every petit and grand jury, as well as serving as county treasurer, auditor, tax collector, coroner, school superintendent, road viewer, and election judge. In a given year one individual often served in several capacities.

## THE NATIVE UPRISING

After several years of growing tension, open conflict developed between the Elliott Bay settlers and the Native Americans during the winter of 1855-56. All of the settlers living in the outlying areas moved into Fort Decatur, a crude blockhouse built in the vicinity of First Avenue and Cherry Street of logs David Denny had cut that previous summer on Queen Anne Hill. With over 70 people living in Fort Decatur that winter, conditions were very crowded. The Denny's second daughter, Madge Decatur, was born in the fort in March 1856.

By August 1856, all hostilities had ended and the native uprising was officially over. However, the next decade would prove a hard one for the settlers. Looking back 82 years later, Susie Mercer observed, "I am convinced that it was the faith and courage of the founders that made Seattle a great city. They [the pioneers] loved the city all the more because of the work and hardships they underwent."

Some of the settlers filed reports of their losses at the hands of the natives to the government in hope that they would be compensated—which they never were. The claims, however, provide some insight into the property and chattel of these community pioneers: David Denny, claim $97, canoe and stock; Dr. Henry Smith, claim $1728, loss of frame house and stock; John Ross, claim $1306, log cabin and stock; Ira Utter, claim $637.25, log cabin, canoe, furniture, and crop; Erasmus Smithers, claim $1306, dwelling and stock; Edmund Carr, claim $480, log cabin; David Stanley, claim $173.50, loss of crops.

*Thomas Mercer was immediately identified as a leader and was appointed or elected to numerous offices in the 1850s. Beginning in 1855 he served as Probate Judge for many years, which caused him to be called Judge Mercer the rest of his life. Mercer's Quaker roots had a profound influence on his life philosophy. He was described by his contemporaries as "quiet and peaceful," and "guided by a high sense of honor, such as gains the respect of mankind." Thomas Mercer died on May 25, 1898, at age 85, and is buried in Lakeview Cemetery. Courtesy of Museum of History and Industry.*

Genuinely interested in homesteading, the pioneers of the district north of Seattle were less discouraged than many who had hoped to "get rich quick" through business ventures or the rapid increase in the value of land they obtained through land grants. These men left, along with many others who feared future uprisings by the native people.

Those who stayed harbored unspoken anxiety over the prospect of other Native American attacks for years. Louisa Boren Denny told her children "for years afterwards it was easy to imagine Indians everywhere." Throughout the 1850s Thomas Mercer never went into the woods to cut trees or clear land alone, his daughters reported; one of the girls always accompanied him. While Mercer worked, her duty was to stand guard with her rifle at the ready in case hostile natives appeared.

## Respect for the Local Tribes is Returned with Respect

In the Battle of Seattle on January 26, 1856, the natives set fire to almost all of the outlying homestead cabins. When Tom Mercer, David and Louisa Denny, and Dr. Henry and Abigail T. Smith returned to their homesteads in the spring, they were astonished to find their dwellings intact, although many of their belongings had been taken.

Mercer's frame house of 1854 was not burned. After the war the local natives were asked why they had not burned Mercer's place. One replied, "Oh, [we thought] Old Mercer might want it again." The natives explained that Mercer was '*klosh tum tum*,' kind, friendly, literally a good heart, and '*he wawa-ed sahale tyee*,' prayed to the Heavenly Chief or Great Spirit. They had come to know and respect Thomas Mercer, whose wife had died and who was caring for his children alone. Mercer had always dealt with the them honestly and fairly, and had learned to speak their language. His gentleness, integrity and kindness had made a deep impression on them.

While his house was intact, the milk cow that Mercer had just bought was gone. The Mercer girls mourned the loss of their cow, which was a pet, as one of the major tragedies of the battle of Seattle.

Louisa and David Denny's house in the swale was also spared the torch. Dr. Henry Smith and Abigail Smith's frame house was burned to the ground, but the original log cabin and log cabin infirmary were left unharmed. Like Mercer, the Dennys and Smiths had learned the local native language and took a deep interest in tribal culture and way of life, for which they demonstrated great respect on many occasions. The natives noted this and in return respected Denny and Smith and their *klootchman* (women) as *tillicums* (friends).

### Naming the Lakes

By the summer of 1854 Thomas Mercer and his daughters felt settled on Eden Hill. Their new house was almost completed and they invited the entire Seattle settlement to come out to the lake for a Fourth of July picnic.

After the picnic Mercer called a community meeting to discuss names for the nearby lakes. *Hyas chuck* (big water) was christened Lake Washington, for George Washington, and *tenas chuck* (little water) was named Union Lake, although in practice it soon became Lake Union. Mercer selected the name Union, predicting that someday a canal system would be dug connecting the lakes with Puget Sound. Before the meeting broke up the group decided that the large beautiful island located in Lake Washington should be named Mercer Island, for pioneer leader Thomas Mercer.

## Marriages and New Beginnings

The winter the settlers spent living in the crowded quarters of Fort Decatur had its bright side, for it provided an opportunity for courting. In spring of 1856 Edmund Carr and Olivia Holgate, who had become acquainted teaching Sunday school at the Methodist Episcopal Church, announced their intention to marry. The Seattle settlement had shrunk from 250 to about 70 people, and those who remained were serious and resolute. However, they were also young and optimistic, and the very idea of a wedding and the belief in the future that it represents appealed enormously to everyone.

The community went all out in putting on a grand wedding celebration for the young couple, complete with a feast and wedding cake. Cornelius Hanford, Olivia's brother-in-law, comments on the wedding preparations:

> *The market was nearly destitute of delicacies usually supplied for such an affair, but it is wonderful how pioneer women, with scant provisions, can delight the appetites of the hungry when they try; they did try and made the feast a great success.*

In November 1857 Eramus Smithers, 27, of Smith Cove married the land-wealthy 28-year-old widow Diana Gilmore Tobin. After living a short time on Smither's claim in the cove they moved onto Diana's land, and in the coming decades they founded the city of Renton, which lies on her donation claim of 1853. Smithers held on to his 160 acres in Smith Cove to the end of the nineteenth century when his heirs sold the land.

## John Ross and Mary McMillan

Unable to work on his claim because he was harassed by the local natives, John Ross decided in the fall of 1858 to go to Portland and then on to Salem.

At Salem he met and married Mary Jane McMillan, age 15, the daughter of Rev. David McMillan, a well-known clergyman from Illinois. Mary McMillan was born in 1843 in Springfield, Illinois. In 1853, at age ten, Mary's family had come to Oregon Territory. John Ross was 32 at the time of their marriage.

The couple returned to Seattle, bringing with them from the Willamette Valley a quantity of fruit tree cuttings. They settled into a house in Seattle in January 1859, and John hiked out to his claim, packing the cuttings and a spade on his back. However, he reports in his land grant records that once again the natives drove him off, as they had in 1857 and 1858. John regularly "commuted" from Seattle to his claim on foot and by canoe for years to fulfill the proving up requirements.

Eventually Ross planted over 500 fruit trees and invested $3,000 in improvements. During these years Ross expanded his land holdings, filing for additional land on the north side of Salmon Bay under preemption law. In addition, he received a parcel of state school land on Denny Hill in 1860, as payment for carpentry on the Territorial University building.

## The Determined Few

The historic records for the settlers making their living north of Seattle in the late 1850s and 1860s are sketchy. However, it is known that after the native uprising they were reluctant to live isolated on their claims and many moved into the Seattle settlement, going out to their claims for day work. David and Louisa Denny moved into a three-room cottage in Seattle, which remained their principal residence until 1860. Between 1860-1870 the Dennys lived part of the year in the Seattle cottage and the other part in their house in the swale on Queen Anne Hill. The Thomas Mercer family moved permanently back onto their claim around 1860.

### Food and Supplies—1857 Prices

| | |
|---|---|
| Fresh Pork, per lb. | .20 |
| Bacon/ham, per lb. | .25 to .30 |
| Flour, per 100 lb. barrel | $10 to 60.00 |
| Potatoes, per bushel | $2.50 to 3.00 |
| Butter, per lb. | $1. to 1.50 |
| Milk, per gallon | .75 to $1.00 |
| Onions, per bushel | $4.00 |
| Eggs, per dozen | $1.00 |
| Beets, per bushel | $3.50 |
| Beans, per lb. | .09 to .12 |
| Sugar, per lb. | .12–1/2 |
| Candy, per lb. | $1.00 |
| Coffee, per lb. | .18 |
| Tea, per lb. | .75 and $1.00 |
| Tobacco, per lb. | .40 to .75 |
| Molasses, per gallon | .50 and .75 |
| Syrup, per gallon | .75 and $1.00 |
| Lamp oil, per gallon | $1.75 to 2.00 |
| Salmon, per lb. | .10 |
| Whiskey, per gallon | $1.00 to 2.00 |
| Oats, bushel | .70 to .80 |
| Nails, 100 lb. keg | $7.50 to 10.00 |
| Sawed lumber, fir per M | $20.00 |
| Shingles, per M | $4.25 to 5.00 |
| Piles, per foot | .05 to .08 |
| Square timber, per foot | .12 to .15 |

Chapter Five

# Building Homesteads and Families—The 1860s

by
Kay F. Reinartz, Ph.D.

*[We] were obliged to do whatever [we] could to obtain a livelihood; [we] were neither ashamed nor afraid of honest work and enjoyed the reward of a good conscience and vigorous health. Life held many pleasures and much freedom from modern frets besides. . . . We were happy then, in our log cabin homes.*

*Louisa Boren Denny,*
*circa 1876*

*Construction of the Military Road began at the time of the Native American hostilities, 1855-56, but the northern section was not completed until the middle 1860s. This section of the road went north from Yesler's Mill on Front Street (1st Ave.) circling Denny Hill (Denny Regrade) on the east side, and passing by the burial ground that became Denny Park. The road then continued along the east side of Queen Anne Hill. This section of Military Road was renamed Dexter Avenue for the pioneer friend of the Thomas Mercer family, Dexter Horton. Courtesy Washington State Historical Society, Asahel Curtis Collection.*

On November 9, 1860, Territorial Governor Henry M. McGill proclaimed November 29th "as the day of Thanksgiving and praise to Almighty God." In the district north of Seattle, neighbors congregated at Dr. Smith's, whose house was the largest, and as the rain fell outside they sat down to their first Thanksgiving Day celebration. There was much to be thankful for. Most of the pioneers had been on the hill or around the cove for at least five years and some nearly ten. No one had died in the conflict with the Native Americans. Houses, barns and fences had been rebuilt. The crops, gardens, herds and orchards were growing, there had been marriages and children had been born. Everyone was healthy and they were prospering. In spite of the hardships, they still believed in the future of the Northwest and most particularly Seattle.

## A Quiet Northwest Frontier Settlement

After the native uprising the rapid growth that had characterized Seattle from 1853 ended, and for several years no one started new business enterprises. Dillis Ward reports that when he arrived in Seattle in August 1859 there were no real streets, just a rough road that followed the shoreline with trails leading away from the water's edge up to the homesteads and businesses. There were no more than six houses in the settlement proper north of Mill Street (Yesler Way), with David and Louisa Denny's little cottage being the northernmost house.

Along Commercial Street, between Mill and Jackson streets, stood four dry goods and general merchandise stores. The post office operated out of Plummer's Mercantile. In addition, there were two restaurants, three saloons, two small lodging houses, a tin shop and a stove shop. Nearby was a blacksmith shop and tannery, as well as the Methodist Episcopal Church and the school house.

Although three wharves had been built, only Yesler's was maintained and it received nearly all of the business from ships picking up logs and pilings and dropping off supplies and merchandise. Yesler's sawmill, the only industry, provided five full-time jobs. A good deal of the money in circulation in Seattle was brought in by the loggers and lumbermen from the thriving milling centers of Port Orchard, Port Madison and other places along the west side of Puget Sound.

Elliott Bay was no longer regularly visited by coastal sailing ships looking for lumber cargoes and the flow of settlers slowed to a trickle. Gold reversed this trend. From 1855 to 1865 the discovery of gold in various locations throughout the Northwest created a series of little "gold rushes." Men weary of the monotonous round of cutting, clearing and burning slash dropped everything to join the excitement at Colville, Rock Creek, Stehekin, Lillooet, Wenatchee, Florence, Boise, and the Fraser and Thompson rivers, where streams yielded enough placer gold to bring in thousands of prospectors overnight.

It was the big Fraser River Gold Rush of 1858 that

### By the Dreaming Shores
### Lake Union in 1864

by Emily Inez Denny

On a pleasant day of early spring in 1864, a pioneer was driving his team of grays with a stout farmer's wagon on a road through the great forest of Western Washington Territory. . . . The little party was on its way to an inland body of water some distance from their small village at tidewater. . . . they walked along a narrow trail through dense woods to the shore. Here they looked out over the placid water to see a primeval forest on every hand, and absolute wilderness. From afar came the cry of a loon and an otter slipped into the water nearby and swam noiselessly away.

Here, indeed, were the Dreaming Shores. The past eons had woven a marvelous dress, like a rich mantle it hung from the shoulders of the hills and trailed its fringes in the waters. There was not a mark of fire or axe, no human habitations, no improvements whatsoever. . . . They saw on this fair day that all the trees and shrubs by a forward spring were in full array of fresh foliage and maple, dogwood, syringa, service berry, vine of honeysuckle crowded thickly among the great mass of dark green evergreen forest of fir, spruce, hemlock and cedar.

Thick forest they saw on all the Dreaming Shores and the surrounding hills. No taint of smoke or dust was in the air. No clamorous sound broke harshly on the ear. Only the gay voice of the little children, the thrushes singing in their shadowy retreats, low-lapping of little waves, soft sighing of a breeze in the tree tops.

brought energy and activity back to Seattle. The population grew, but it was lopsided with young single men. The 1860 census reports a population of 275 for King County and 160 for Seattle. Clarence Bagley records that in 1861 the community had 110 men, 25 women and 25 children. There was a total of 23 families, including several headed by a single man or woman. There were only two marriageable age women in the community—Kate Denny, Arthur and Mary Denny's daughter, and Susie Mercer.

## Isolated in Puget Sound Country

Isolation was the greatest tension source for everyone living around Puget Sound. The telegraph line from Portland had been completed in 1855 but was destroyed by the natives that winter. The telegraph connection to Portland, thence San Francisco and the rest of the country, was not re-established until 1866.

The handful of settlers remaining in 1856 attempted several plans to end their isolation, including cutting a road through Snoqualmie Pass and trying to organize a railroad company. Their plans were getting support from the federal government until the national disruption of the Civil War diverted all federal funds, without which such ambitious projects could not be accomplished. David Denny, John Ross, Thomas Mercer and Dr. Henry Smith were at the center of all these schemes.

## A Dearth of Roads

All roads around Seattle led to Yesler's Mill. After the native uprising, the local roads leading back through the hills and to the lakes were neglected and

*Lake Union was a pristine wilderness lake when the settlers came to the area in 1853. Thomas Mercer named it Union Lake in the belief that someday the lake would serve as a link uniting Lake Washington with the salty waters of Puget Sound. Courtesy University of Washington Special Collections.*

quickly became nigh impassable. Thomas Mercer and David Denny diligently maintained the road out to their homesteads, as well as the lane that connected Mercer's with John Nagle's place (Eastlake area). A trail led out from Mercer's homestead to his daughter Eliza and Walter Graham's place on Lake Washington. Inez Denny describes the Eden Hill road as "being most notable for ups and downs, stumps in the middle and numerous muddy places, but useful nevertheless."

## Marriages for the Mercer Family

Thomas Mercer's two older daughters had married in 1857. Mary Jane, at age 18, married Henry G. Parsons and moved to Olympia. Eliza Ann, at age 15, married Walter Graham and they homesteaded on Lake Washington.

While on a trip to Salem to purchase livestock in the summer of 1859, Thomas Mercer met Hester L. Ward, 28, and after a whirlwind courtship the couple married and returned to Seattle, bringing Hetty's younger half-brother Dillis B. Ward with them. After living a year in Seattle, Hetty and Tom moved permanently back onto Mercer's homestead on the hill.

## Natural Wonders

Natural wonders of the Northwest amazed and frightened the settlers in the 1860s. On April 2, 1859, they experienced their first serious earthquake. Inez Denny describes her family's experience:

> *Not a breath of wind was stirring, the stars were shining and reflected in the depths of the water, no storm was there, but the people saw the tree tops waving, like plumes of warriors swiftly riding and heard a sound like a cannonading, as thousands of trees fell crashing to the earth. The house . . . rocked like a boat, [and they] held to the door frames and looked out—soon it passed by—and it really was quite an earthquake!*

It is recorded that the earthquake lasted 90 seconds and seemed to move from the north to the south. While no damage was done, it had a sobering effect on the pioneers, few of whom had come from areas that had seismic activity on the scale of the Northwest.

Also troublesome to many of the settlers who had come from the New England or Midwest states was the Puget Sound weather. The mildness everyone seemed to agree was most desirable, but the periods of continuous rain were wearying to say the least, particularly in the dark winter months.

*"A Visit from Our Tillicum" by Inez Denny depicts the Denny family's house in the swale, later the site of the Seattle Opera House. Inez shows the sisters visiting with Indian friends through the open half-door locally called a "Seattle door." Courtesy Museum of History and Industry.*

The weather was normally gentle, lacking extremes. However, there were dramatic departures from this pleasant norm. The winter of 1861 was one to remember. What began in early December as a mild winter changed radically just before the Christmas holidays when snow began falling and continued falling for a week. When it stopped snowing the mercury dropped to four below zero, where it stayed for days. Tom Mercer and Louisa and David Denny lost fruit trees, but Dr. Smith's sheltered orchard in the cove was undamaged. Many homesteaders around King County lost livestock. There was snow on the ground until April and the pioneers always called this season the Big Winter.

## Lake Union: Community Ice Skating Pond

The winter of 1861 Lake Union was frozen solid one-half foot for four months. The little lake tucked away in the deep woods suddenly became a community social meeting place as settlers originating from New England and other cold parts of the country turned out in full force to ice skate. Some people miraculously produced ice skates from the bottom of trunks. Others

### The Mercer Family

Hester Loretta Ward was a very unusual woman, who was known for her ability to learn and adapt quickly, good judgment, and an all-prevailing courage and calmness in a crisis. Possessing enormous reserves of energy and stamina, she always did more work than most and yet had energy left for fun.

Born in 1826 on the Kentucky frontier, she became a highly skilled frontier woman at a young age. She lost her mother when she was an infant and at age 13, upon the death of her stepmother, she assumed the role of "woman of the family" by caring for four younger children born of her father Jesse Ward's various marriages. This role included caring for newborn infant Dillis Ward, Hester's half-brother.

In spite of the exceptionally heavy adult responsibilities placed on her as a young girl, she completed grammar school. Hester Ward was also a textile artist. She learned to weave while still a girl and often processed raw cotton or wool into fine threads and yarns, which she then wove into fabric. Over the years she originated many complex patterns which were expressed in useful textiles, particularly coverlets, tablecloths and clothing.

Inez Denny, who as a child often visited her and became her friend in adulthood, observes regarding Hester's character: "A more generous, frank and warmhearted nature was hard to find, the demands made upon it were many and such as to exhaust a shallow one." Hester Ward died in 1903 and is buried in Lakeview Cemetery by the side of Thomas Mercer.

On May 23, 1861, Susannah, age 18, married David Graham, the younger brother of her sister Eliza Anne's husband, Walter Graham. The wedding was held at the Mercer homestead with Rev. Daniel Bagley officiating. Susie was dressed in a simple dress of white lawn made by a local seamstress, while David wore his old black suit, long in the bottom of his emigrant trunk.

That evening Susie and David were shivareed by a group of men who out went to the Mercer's, where the newlyweds were staying. The gang stood around the outside of the house and pounded on tin cans, washtubs and anything else they found lying around to make a racket. They also sang nonsense songs to the newlyweds and then called for whiskey. Graham, like Thomas Mercer, was a temperance man but he finally went out and told the crowd to go down to the saloon to get what they wanted to drink. When he went down to the village the next morning, he found the men were still celebrating at the saloon. He ended their party by paying the bill.

After the marriage David Graham returned to surveying work, which took him out of the village most of the time. Susie lived with Rev. and Mrs. Bagley and attended the nearby Territorial University.

David Graham's pioneer dream included farming in the Duwamish Valley and he and Susie moved to a homestead in what became the Duwamish-Allentown district of Tukwila. Homesteading so far from Seattle was not totally to the sociable Susie Mercer's liking. She often went into Seattle to visit her family and friends via a native "canoe taxi" which she would catch by going down to the riverbank and calling, "*Mi-Ka Ticky Klat-a-wa Kopa Seattle*," (I need a ride to Seattle). Any native who wanted the job would answer her call and come by with his canoe and a clean cattail mat for her to sit on. For 50 cents, he would paddle her to the cove where she would walk around the hill to the homestead. It took almost an entire day to get to Eden Hill from the Duwamish homestead.

In 1862, Eliza Ann died, leaving William, four, and George, two, to be raised by Walter Graham. Grief-stricken, Thomas Mercer's heart went out to his son-in-law, who like himself had to face the task of raising his children alone.

In 1862, Tom's brother Asa Shinn Mercer came to live with the family. Twenty-two-year-old Asa would gain much notice in a handful of years in Seattle for his promotion schemes, including easing the shortage of marriageable women by arranging for two small parties of New England school teachers to come to Seattle to seek their fortunes. Asa Mercer married one of the teachers himself and they left the region a few years later.

*The Puget Sound climate in the nineteenth century was colder than in the twentieth century and during some winters there were heavy snowfalls and months of freezing temperatures. The winter of 1861 was the first such winter experienced by the Elliott Bay settlers. This photograph was taken in January of 1876. Courtesy Museum of History and Industry.*

ingeniously invented ice skates from things they had around their place.

The Seattle village dwellers made the two-mile trek to the lake walking up Front Street, around the east side of Denny Hill and along the Military Road, scrambling over deep frozen ruts, logs and skids until they veered off Military Road onto a path leading to the lakeshore. One person estimated that over half the population of the Seattle area joined in on the skating fun that winter.

## Storms and Drought

In the mid-1860s the area was hit by a cyclone. Inez Denny describes the storm as the Dennys experienced it in their house on the swale:

> *It began in the evening with a sky of livid hues, puffs of wind increasing every hour until one hurtling stream tore at the forest as with giant hands, uprooting great trees, twisting others off as though wisps of straw, lifting sheets of spray from the frothing waves; . . . Large stones were taken up from the high bank on the bay and piled on the roofs along with limbs broken from tough fir trees. Thousands of giant trees fell crashing and groaning to the ground, like a continuous cannonade; the noise was terrific and we feared for our lives.*
>
> *[Down along the beach] the Indian camps caught fire and long streams of flame flowed horizontally into the thick darkness beyond.*
>
> *The [family] prepared to leave [the house] and go to the big barn, substantially built of heavy timbers and standing on a more protected place.*
>
> *[They] put out all the fires in the house and [Louisa] wrapped the children well and all sat in one room—with the lanterns lit, waiting for a lull. [About midnight they] knelt and commended [themselves] to Him who rules the storm.*
>
> *Fortunately, [about 1 o'clock] the wind died down more quickly than it came and much relieved the people retired to rest. When morning broke some trees near the home were missed, the roads were blocked for many miles....*

The spring of 1866 was a particularly wet one. Early in June the rains abruptly stopped and the pioneers sweltered under temperatures reaching 114° F in the shade. In December 1867 the worst flood on record covered the region and many settlers in low-lying areas, including those living the cove, were forced out of their homes. Homesteads up on the hill suffered no losses. The next year the weather reversed and little rain fell.

## A SEASON OF FOREST FIRES

In 1868 the Puget Sound area experienced its most severe drought since the beginning of the settlement. From June 1 to October 29 no rain fell. A hot dry wind shriveled the crops in the fields and in July, forest fires began breaking out. By September fires were roaring throughout the Northwest from 600 miles north of the United States-British Columbia border, through Washington and Oregon territories, and into California. The drifting smoke was reported 1,000 miles west on the Pacific Ocean. The air was so filled with the acrid smoke of resinous woods as to be almost intolerable. There was no way to stop the fires and vast areas of forest were burned totally clear. The onset of the autumn rains finally brought the destruction to a halt.

During this season of forest fires, the south slope of Eden Hill burned. Inez Denny recounts how she and her sisters ran down the road to their farm with "the tall firs and cedars flaming far above their heads."

## THE BAGLEY FAMILY

In the autumn of 1861 Rev. Daniel Bagley moved his family from Salem, Oregon, to Seattle so that his son Clarence might attend the new Washington Territorial University, which had opened in 1860. They traveled over the newly-completed section of Military Road running from Seattle to Portland. Their arrival in late October brought everyone out into the dusty streets to see the first carriage to come into Seattle from "the outside" on its own wheels. Rev. Bagley agreed to teach the fall term at the university, with Clarence assisting him. When his father was away Clarence took over and taught all of the classes, which were grades 1-12. Eighteen-year-old Clarence Bagley was the envy of every young man in the area for he had a horse and buggy at his disposal for courting the young women. The drives were short since there were only two roads—the north route to Tom Mercer's place, and the south route over the ridge of Beacon Hill down to Lake Washington.

Rev. Bagley was disappointed with the university as a place for Clarence to complete his higher education. The Bagley family went back East in 1862 and Clarence entered Allegheny College, Meadville, Pennsylvania, Dr. Smith's alma mater. Before he left Puget Sound, Clarence Bagley had renewed his friendship with the Mercers and over the next four years, which included several trips back to Seattle, he courted Alice Mercer.

### The Primeval Forest Burns

by Dr. Henry A. Smith

As soon as the fire worked its way to the massive windrows of dry brush, piled in making roads in every direction, a circular wall of solid flame rose half way to the tops of the tall trees. Soon the rising of the heated air caused strong currents of cooler air to set in from every side. The air currents soon increased to cyclones. Then began a race of the towering, billowy, surging walls of fire for the center.

Driven furiously on by these ever-increasing, eddying, and fiercely contending tornadoes, the flames lolled and rolled and swayed and leaped, rising higher and higher, until one vast, circular tidal wave of liquid fire rolled in and met at the center with the whirl and roar of pandemoniac thunder and shot up in a spiral and rapidly revolving red-hot cone, a thousand feet in mid-air, out whose flaring and crater-like apex poured dense volumes of tarry smoke, spreading out on every side, like unfolding curtains of night, till the sun was darkened and the moon turned to blood and the stars seemed literally raining from heaven, as glowing firebrands that had been carried up by the fierce tornado of swirling flame and carried to immense distances by upper air currents, fell back in showers to the ground.

The vast tract, but a few moments before as quiet as a sleeping infant in its cradle, was now one vast arena of seething, roaring, raging flame. The long, lithe limbs of the tall cedars were tossing wildly about, while the strong limbs of the sturdier firs and hemlocks were freely gyrating like the sinewy arms of mighty giant athletes engaged in mortal combat. Ever and anon their lower, pitch-dripping branches would ignite from the fervent heat below, when the flames would rush to the very tops with the roar of contending thunders and shoot upward in bright silvery volumes from five to seven hundred feet, or double the height of the trees themselves.

Hundreds of these fire-volumes flaring and flaming in quick succession and sometimes many of them simultaneously, in conjunction with the weird eclipse-like darkness that veiled the heavens, rended the scene one of awful grandeur never to be forgotten.

## Alice Mercer and Clarence Bagley

Clarence Bagley and Alice Mercer planned to be married on Christmas Eve, 1865. Clarence completed his bachelor's degree at Allegheny College in early December and left immediately for Puget Sound, traveling via steamer and the Isthmus of Panama route. The timing was tight, but all was going well and Clarence was confident he would make Seattle with more than a week to spare—until the San Francisco steamer he was traveling on was delayed outside the Straits of Juan de Fuca by heavy seas.

For days Clarence walked the deck and prayed mightily. Finally the weather improved and the steamer passed through the treacherous waters of the Straits and made for Seattle. When they finally dropped anchor in Elliott Bay, late in the afternoon of December 24th Clarence saw that the storm that had delayed him so long had dumped quantities of wet snow on shore. But never mind, he would not miss his own wedding.

Around 6 o'clock that evening Thomas Mercer helped his 17-year-old, golden-haired Alice into the family lumber wagon, and Tib and Charley conveyed the family to the Methodist Church. Clarence recalls that he met Alice outside of the church and "she and I trudged through two feet of snow that led around the stumps standing in Second Avenue to the little building that was already filled by friends, young and old." The marriage of these two pioneers, who had come over the Oregon Trail as children with the Bethel Party, was the first formal church wedding in Seattle.

## COMMUNITY GATHERINGS

The pioneer historian Cornelius Hanford comments on the Seattle settlement in the 1860s:

*Life in the village was serious and strenuous. The friendship of neighbors was the principal source of good cheer, dispelling gloom. Neighbors visited each other, and those occasions were holidays for the visitors and the visited. Evening prayer meetings, spelling schools, and singing schools were means of assembling the community, and occasionally, questions of public concern were debated at meetings of the library association, which existed without a library.*

As the community grew there were regular church socials. Chicken dinners, oyster suppers and strawberry festivals were the most popular entertainments. George Frye organized a brass band in 1861 by persuading a dozen young men to buy and master the instruments. The Seattle Brass Band turned out for every community event and infused the occasion with musical delight.

## HYAS SUNDAY—THE FOURTH OF JULY

Without a doubt the Fourth of July celebration was the grandest event of the year for the pioneers. Beginning in 1852, the day was observed with speeches, picnicking, and dancing on a wooden platform built just for the occasion. The Native Americans, who attended this settlers' party, called the event *Hyas* Sunday, as they did all of the settlers' social gatherings.

The Fourth of July that the Denny girls remembered the best was held in the Methodist Protestant Church around 1864. The Denny family was a little late in arriving and the orator had already launched into his speech. Their commotion at the door of the church turned every head, and they beheld Inez, Madge and Abbie marching down the aisle, each respectively dressed in red, white and blue and proudly holding high a banner with mottos written with large letters cut out of the newspaper: "Freedom for All," "Slavery for None" and "United we stand, divided we fall." Each motto was encircled with a bountiful wreath of fresh red, white and blue flowers. The girls were wildly applauded by the audience, composed chiefly of young bachelors, who were by far the majority of the population.

## CHRISTMAS PARTIES

Beginning in the 1860s there was a regular Christmas party held in Yesler's Hall, attended by everyone in the community. At one end of the hall was a curtain that was dramatically drawn aside at the critical moment to reveal a tall Douglas fir glowing from the light of hundreds of homemade tallow candles. The graceful branches were festooned with strings of popcorn and local cranberries. Henry Yesler wore a Santa suit that his wife Sarah had made for him and handed out wonderful trinkets, many of which were not to be found in the Seattle mercantiles, but had been ordered from Victoria.

*The Smith family house on their "ranch" in the cove. With Mary Phelan Smith's death in 1880, Dr. Smith added on to the house to accommodate the family's frequent long-term visitors and his growing children. The house stood empty and deteriorating at 2827 Fifteenth Avenue W. into the 1930s, when it was demolished. Courtesy Museum of History and Industry.*

Louisa Boren Denny was asked on the fiftieth anniversary of the Denny-Boren party's arrival at Alki Point how the pioneers kept Christmas in the early years. Louisa, 76, responded with her characteristic energetic good humor:

*If you get up as good a Christmas dinner now as we could fifty years ago, I should like to help eat it. Here is one the Indians would call hyas closh muck-a-muck:*

   *Olympia Oysters, panned*
   *Clam Soup*
   *Fried Smelts*
   *Grouse Pie*
   *Roast Wild Goose – Giblet Sauce*
   *Roast Haunch of Venison – Native*
     *Cranberry Sauce*
   *Browned Potatoes – Creamed Carrots –*
     *Baked Squash*
   *Cole Slaw – French Dressing*
   *Huckleberry Pie – Cranberry Tarts –*
     *Clotted Cream*
   *High Buttermilk Biscuits – Fresh Churned*
     *Butter*
   *Coffee – Milk – Tea*

## THE TEMPERANCE LODGE IS FOUNDED

In the 1860s two important lodges were formed, St. John's Lodge of Free and Accepted Masons and the Order of Good Templars. The former did not involve north district settlers to any extent, but the latter was their organization. In the fall of 1865 Rev. A.C. McDougall came up to the frontier settlement from California and delivered a series of lectures on temperance at Headquarters Hall, the old Snoqualmie Hall on the second floor of Plummer's Mercantile.

McDougall's visit inspired many to increase their commitment to temperance, David and Louisa Denny among them. Around the Denny's kitchen table the Independent Order of Good Templars, Seattle Lodge No. 6, was formed. The settlers in the district north of Seattle were at the hub of the organization, with 20 percent of the charter members being from that area. Officers were elected, including David Denny, Lodge Chaplain; William Hammond, Secretary; John Shoudy, Financial Secretary; Louisa Boren Denny, Treasurer; John H. Nagle, Marshall; Gertrude Boren, Inside Guard and Inez Denny, Outside Guard. The group met regularly to discuss temperance goals and ways it could advance them in Seattle. Thirty years later this nucleus of temperance movement advocates would be at the center of a highly visible Prohibition political party championing the Queen Anne community's needs at City Hall.

## COUGARS, ELK AND BEARS

By the late 1860s there was still only a handful of settlers in the north district and game still roamed the area, although in ever smaller numbers. In 1854 David Denny had killed a nine-foot cougar, however, few wild cats of this size were seen by the pioneers.

*As the wilderness forest was slowly cut down the homesteaders were able to plant crops and create pastures for their livestock. This was called "stump farming" since the stumps of the giant virgin growth remained for decades. Courtesy University of Washington Special Collections.*

However, cougar were still common through the 1860s. Around 1867 David killed one on the north side of the hill near John Ross's homestead. The half-grown cat had been dining on one of Dr. Smith's sheep. David reported that it was the color of a deer. In September 1869 David Denny killed a 650 pound elk in the woods northwest of Green Lake.

John Wetmore, who was homesteading along Lake Washington, was having trouble with cougar attacking his herd of sheep. He heard that the Denny's little dog Watch was a good hunter and came over to borrow the small fierce dog. Watch successfully treed the cougar and remained below the tree all night. However, the cat finally escaped only to be later captured with a trap.

## The End of the Hermits

In 1887 Dr. Henry Smith wrote a series of articles called "Reminiscences" for the *Seattle Star*. In the November installment he commented on his hermit neighbors Ira Utter, David Stanley and Osmine Frost. He observed that all three of these men suffered from mental disorders, resulting from too much social isolation in Smith's opinion. Throughout the 1860s Ira Utter, who lived north of Smith Cove on Salmon Bay, diligently improved his land and bought additional nearby parcels. By 1869 he had become the largest landowner in the district north of Seattle, owning more land then even David and Louisa Denny. His holdings included 850 acres located on Queen Anne Hill, Denny Hill, the cove and Salmon Bay.

Utter never married and as the years went by he rarely went to Seattle and his neighbors saw less and less of him. Of the neighbors, John Ross knew him best, but no one seemed to really know him. Dr. Henry Smith says of his neighbor across Salmon Bay:

> *Ira W. Utter, the Salmon Bay hermit . . . was an educated man and more than ordinarily intelligent, but for twenty years he was the only white man on the north side of Salmon Bay, and solitude finally soured his mind so that he became suspicious and censorious and finally reason deserted its throne, and he ended his days, I believe, in an eastern asylum.*

On November 28, 1870, the *Weekly Intelligencer* announced the somber news that Ira Utter, age 46, "had been taken into custody on account of insanity, and his neighbor John Ross was appointed by the court as his guardian." On the same date it is noted that Utter had walked away from the county jail, where he was being cared for until his family arrived from the east coast. On January 9, 1871, his brothers George and Francis Utter arrived from Bridgeport, New York and after assisting Ira in putting his affairs in order, took him back home with them. He died in 1876 at age 51 in an asylum for the mentally ill.

The fate of Osmine Frost was not unlike that of Ira Utter. Frost lived alone proving up his claim for 32 years. His mental health deteriorated and he was sent by his neighbors to a mental institution in Portland. After eight years he was released and, returning to Elliott Bay, hired a boatman to paddle him around the Magnolia shoreline as he searched for his land papers. Before leaving for Portland he had buried under a large tree an iron box containing all of his documents, including his donation claim patent. Leaping suddenly from the boat into the water, which was icy cold and chest-deep on the old man, Frost scrambled ashore and ran into the woods. Although the tree was gone he proclaimed he had found the spot, and after ten minutes of digging, the box of papers was in his lap. Frost was jubilant. He lived on in the cove for a few more years, but the hard life and solitude seemed to have a deteriorating effect on his mental health. Dr. Smith observes the following about his hermit neighbor:

> *Solitude soured him also [comparing him to Ira Utter], and to such an extent that in order to seclude himself as much as possible from all mankind and to shield himself from assassination at the hand of the Rev. Daniel Bagley, H.L. Yesler, A.A. Denny and D.T. Denny, and other old timers equally harmless, he dug a cave in the hillside, where he passed most of his time, until his brother-in-law came last spring [1887] from the east, at the earnest solicitation of Mr. Bowman, and induced the old man to return with him. Verily it is not good for man to live alone.*

David Stanley does not appear to have been insane so much as highly eccentric. He often appeared at his neighbors' doorsteps, sometimes because his cabin had been stripped bare by the natives. Each time this happened over the years his neighbors, the Dennys, Mercers, Rosses, and Petersons, furnished the old man with food, bedding, and sympathy. Thus, did he live year after year in his shanty on the beach at the mouth of Salmon Bay until old age compelled him to accept the hospitality of friends. It appears that he died while living in the home of an unnamed neighbor in the north district.

Thus, young and old, the little band of stalwarts in the wilderness lived out the days of their years far from the comforts and cares of "civilization," their attention focused close to home on the needs of the season and their neighbors around the hill.

Chapter Six

# Pioneer Childhood on Queen Anne Hill

by
Kay F. Reinartz, Ph.D.

*The very thought of [pioneer child life] makes the blood tingle and the heart leap. No element was wanting for romance or adventure. Indians, bears, panthers, far journeys, in canoes or on horseback, fording rivers, camping and tramping, all in a virgin wilderness so full of grandeur and loveliness that even very little children were impressed by the appearance thereof.*

*The strangeness and newness of it all was hardly understood by the native white children as they had no means of comparing this region and mode of life with other countries and customs.*

*Inez Denny*
Blazing the Way, *1909*

*Denny children in the forest. Original illustration by Jennifer Egglin.*

All too often frontier history tells the story of adult pioneers' dreams, work, successes and failures, but the experiences of children are unknown. By rare good fortune written records have been left by the Denny and Mercer children themselves of their pioneer life on Queen Anne Hill in the 1860s and 1870s. Fortunately, Inez and Abbie Denny had both a gift for words and the discipline to write of the pioneer childhood they and their siblings enjoyed on the hill. In addition, Susie Mercer has left a modest collection of anecdotes published in the local newspapers.

## THE PIONEER CHILDREN

Half of the 24-member Denny-Boren pioneer party that landed at Alki Point on November 13, 1851, were children under ten years of age. None of these children lived on Queen Anne Hill, however.

The first children on the hill were the four daughters of Thomas Mercer, Mary Jane, 13, Eliza Ann, 11, Susannah, nine, and Alice, three, who came to live on the south slope with their widowed father in the summer of 1853. In 1854 David and Louisa Denny brought their nine-month-old baby Emily Inez to their cabin in the swale. Thomas Mercer's daughters loved to hike through the woods to Louisa's cabin to see the baby and visit. Inez Denny and Alice Mercer were four years apart in age and eventually became good friends.

Following the Native American uprising both families moved into Seattle. The Mercers moved back to the hill around 1861 and the Dennys spent their summers on the homestead and their winters in Seattle. When the Denny family moved to a new farmhouse on Lake Union in 1870, there were seven children ranging in age from 16 to one year: Inez, Madge Decatur, Abigail Lenora, John B., Anna Louisa, David Thomas Jr. (Davie), and Victor Winfield Scott. A twin son had been born with David, but died at birth. Cousin Billie Boren, who was Inez's age, was also a part of the family. More children came to the hill in the mid-1870s when the 11 Ross children and the seven daughters and one son of Dr. Henry Smith and Mary Phelan Smith joined the community.

Speaking for the pioneer children Inez says that, as children growing up on the hill, "we were seldom panic-stricken; born amid dangers, there seemed nothing novel about them and we took our environment as a matter of course. We were taught to be courageous but not foolhardy, which may account for our not getting oftener in trouble."

## THE NATIVE AMERICANS AND THE PIONEER CHILDREN

The Native Americans of Puget Sound country have always been a people with a great love of children. Inez Denny comments about the Indians, "How they admired the native white children! Without ceremony they claimed blood brotherhood, saying to the children, 'You were born in our *illahee* (country) and are our *tillicum* (friend). You eat the same food, will grow up here and belong to us.'" Often in the 1860s, the Denny children were lulled to sleep at night in their Seattle cottage by the *tamanuse* singing of the natives camped on the nearby beach (vicinity Battery St.)

The native children were usually amiable and friendly toward the

*Left: Emily Inez Denny, the Denny's first child, was an artist and writer who painted many scenes of the pioneer life she experienced. She published the narrative of her parents' pioneer experiences, as well as her own, in* Blazing the Way, *published in 1909. Her descriptive writing and character sketches provide priceless insights into the early community on Queen Anne Hill. Right: Abigail L. Denny was the third child of David and Louisa Boren Denny. Abbie wrote spirited accounts of the Denny children's life on Queen Anne Hill in the 1870s. Courtesy Museum of History and Industry.*

pioneer children. Inez recalls as a girl meeting little native girls singing and walking hand-in-hand along the beach or a woods trail. She asked them, "*Ka mika klatawa*?" ("Where are you going?") And they replied, "*O, kopa yawa*" ("O, over yonder"), nodding toward the trail stretching along before them.

Because of their parents' apprehension following the Native American uprising, the Denny children were only occasionally allowed to play with the native children and visit their beach camps. The children found the camps fascinating places of strong odors from salmon drying on poles over small fires and strings of clams hanging inside the mat houses.

Inez recalls only a single incident when the Denny children were treated rudely by an native child. She and Madge were visiting the camp at Smith Cove when a hostile little boy hurled a rock at Madge, hitting her in the head. To Inez he appeared filled with hatred and bitterness, and she wondered what had happened to make him so. She learned later that he was not of the Puget Sound people, but Snohomish, a group that harbored a deep hatred of the settlers because of bad experiences.

## No Fear of the Native People

Inez tells us that the Denny children

> *had no real fear of the Indians and never but once were we frightened by them. The first time was when we met ten big braves, wrapped in their blankets with one arm free, brandishing long knives and keeping time to a weird chant as they traveled at a dog trot along the road. They were mamooking black tamanuse (driving away evil spirits).*

The pioneer children were taught by their native playmates that the northern tribes, especially the Stickeens, should be feared for they were fierce head-takers. The Puget Sound natives greatly feared these people themselves. Indeed, Inez declares that the children feared the drunken white man much more than the sober Native American.

The Denny children learned that the greatest fear of their native friends was the frightful *statalth* or "stick siwash," which haunted the dark forest. These were ghosts of a race of people long dead who had been of gigantic stature. The ghosts were likewise very tall, dreadful and intent on chasing anyone they met in the woods on moonless nights. Inez reports one black moonless night a large brawny brave dashed into the Denny's farmyard running as fast as his legs would carry him. He was carrying a blazing pitchwood torch over his head as he kept looking back over his shoulder for the *statalth*.

When Susie Mercer first met native children she was astonished that she could not understand them when they spoke and vice versa. She and her sisters immediately decided to learn the local tribal language and to teach their native playmates English. Susie reports that "the Indians were slow to learn, and as a result all of us talked Chinook, even among ourselves." Inez and Madge Denny also decided to teach a native playmate to read English and every day they sat down with her for an hour with their graded reader and dictionary. The girl, who was very pretty "with long wavy black hair and bright color in her cheeks," had a lively curiosity and a zest for learning English.

## Cubs, Fawns, Crows and Beaver

The Denny children's native friends brought them pets, including bear cubs, mink, a raccoon and numerous wild birds. Once the children adopted several grouse chicks and raised them with the barnyard chickens until the day they flew off. A special pet bird was a crow named "Jim," who liked to help the children pick currants. As they worked their way through the thickets he would hover close by, opening his mouth to receive currants from the children. The greedy crow would eat berries so fast they would roll out of his mouth.

One pet they all adored was an orphan fawn which soon became their close companion, following them everywhere—into the house or out in the woods, wherever they went to work or play. A memory Inez treasured of Madge, her dear sister and good friend, was Madge as a girl "with her arms entwined about the slender neck of [the] pet fawn, her eyes shining with love and laughter, her burnished hair shimmering like a halo in the sunlight as she pattered here and there with her graceful playfellow." When they were busy berry-picking, which occupied them most of the time, the children had to keep a sharp eye on their buckets or the fawn would make lunch of hours' worth of work. The berries were preserved as part of the family's food supply.

One day a native friend walked into the Denny's farmyard with a beaver cub in a covered basket. The children kept the beaver as it grew, fascinated by the

Madge with her pet fawn. Original drawing by Jennifer Egglin.

replacement of its soft baby fur with strong stiff fur that shed water and protected the animal. The beaver was as tame as a kitten and would eagerly eat raspberry shoots and other fresh greens from the children's hands. Whenever there was a tub of water around the beaver climbed in and happily slapped the water with its broad tail, spraying a sheet of water in a ten-foot arc.

Louisa Denny, who generally approved of her children knowing and befriending the array of woods animals, finally objected to the full-grown beaver, which regularly flooded the house by diving into any tub of water placed on the kitchen floor. The pet went to the Territorial University students' dormitory, where it soon died. The children were told that the beaver died because the students "bathed it to death," but more likely it was fed the wrong food.

One day the Denny children reversed the situation with their native friends and gave a Duwamish woman a kitten for a pet. The woman had come to their house to trade clams for potatoes and was very pleased to receive the kitten, which she called *pish-pish* (cat) as she wrapped it in her shawl. The next day she reappeared at the Dennys' door, displaying her hands and arms which were covered with scratches made by the *mesachie pish-pish* (bad cat). Louisa soothed her ire by giving her some oven baked *supalel* (bread), which was highly-valued as a luxury by the natives, who rarely had yeast bread.

When one of the children's pets died, they invariably held a funeral with pomp and ceremony as they buried it in the orchard or flower garden. One time when a pet bird had died Madge, aged six, arranged a litter upon which the tiny corpse was placed, draped with white muslin and decorated with flowers. Two children carried the litter as Madge followed, singing seriously:

*We're traveling to the grave*
*To lay this body down*
*And the last word I heard him speak*
*Was about Jerusalem.*

## The Dennys' Dogs

The Denny family was very fond of dogs. David had brought his large black Newfoundland, Towser, out west with him and the dog was David's constant companion while hunting in the 1850s. Watch was a longtime family pet, although there is no record of the dog's origins. Jack, a yellow hound, was also a family pet and David's hunting companion in the 1860s.

Watch often accompanied the children on their adventures exploring the hill and cove, and at least once saved their lives. On a sunny April day, five of the children finished their work early and decided to take a walk west through the forest, toward Smith Cove and Elliott Bay. As as they walked along the beach at the cove, they went beyond the three big stones, the marker agreed upon with their parents as the farthermost distance they should go along the beach.

Admonishing Abbie, John and Davie to "stay together," Inez and Madge climbed up the steep hillside to gather some creamy white honeysuckle. They had just broken off some blossoms when they saw Watch become very excited about something that appeared to be in an immense hollow log. Every bristle on the bulldog's body stood straight up. He quivered with terror and animal rage, and was slowly, very slowly, backing toward the girls. Without any discussion, the girls took to their heels and scrambled and fell down the yellow bank to where the others were waiting. The troop stampeded down the beach and then up the trail to home, about a mile and half.

A few days later the Dennys were invited by their native neighbors to come to their camp in the cove to see the carcass of a cougar which measured about nine feet. With wondering eyes the children circled the huge beast, marveling at its great length, huge paws and hard white teeth protruding over shrunken lips. They were sure that this was the creature that had alarmed Watch a few days earlier.

### The Shore

by Madge Decatur Denny

*I saw the long line of the vacant shore*
*The sea-weed and the shells upon the sand*
*And the brown rocks left bare on every hand*
*As if the ebbing tide would flow no more.*
*Then heard I more distinctly than before,*
*The ocean breathe and its great breast expand,*
*And hurrying came on the defenseless land,*
*The insurgent waters with tumultuous roar;*
*All thought and feeling and desire, I said*
*Love, laughter, and the exultant joy of song*
*Have ebbed from me forever! Suddenly o'er me*
*They swept again from their deep ocean bed,*
*And in a tumult of delight and strong*
*As youth, and beautiful as youth, upbore me.*

## The Beach

On Saturdays in the 1860s and 1870s, when the children's lessons and work around the farm were well done, Louisa rewarded them by permitting them to spend the afternoon on the beach. Abbie tells us that "the beach was clean and beautiful . . . and we found treasures of little pink shells, agates, pebbles and many other things. The banks in the spring were all abloom with syringa, red flowers, coral, honeysuckle and spirea." When it was warm enough to swim the children went skinny-dipping. When a visitor to the farm once reported that he had seen them skinny-dipping the day before, they objected, saying that he had seen native children.

## Christmas

Christmas was observed each year beginning at the Alki settlement in 1851, when the children's gifts were trinkets Louisa had had the foresight to tuck into her emigrant trunk. In 1859 George Frye and Charlie Plummer decided there should be a Santa Claus for the children and dressed up as natives, wrapping themselves in blankets and carrying their trinkets in a sack. The children were ecstatic, no matter that Santa was "double" and appeared as a Native American.

Christmas trees were not a custom in the United States at the beginning of the nineteenth century. The custom was introduced in England by Queen Victoria's German husband, Albert, and thence it came to America. Around 1860 Louisa and David Denny had the first Christmas tree in Seattle. David cut a small Douglas fir and Louisa hung bright red Lady apples, sticks of candy, and little gifts on the branches.

After the Territorial University's 1860 opening, a Christmas tree was put up on a platform and Susie and Alice Mercer joined in the decorating party. They also made great ropes of spicy cedar with which they crisscrossed the central hall. Boughs of Douglas fir were ornamented with large glass balls. A program was put on for the community with the young children, including Inez and Madge Denny and Alice Mercer, singing Christmas carols and hymns.

## Children's Work

In the frontier home there was always an abundance of chores and tasks, and every pair of hands was needed. Children learned while still very young that they were expected to be industrious and useful to their parents. In fact, there were many jobs that could be done by even a five- or six-year-old child around the homestead. One such daily job was bringing the cows home from where they freely grazed among the stumps and natural clearings, where they found lush grass. This task often took real fortitude, for it meant going along trails "through the dark, thick forest in the deepening twilight that was impenetrable blackness in the wall of somber evergreens on either hand," in Inez's words.

Older brothers and sisters were responsible for watching out for the little ones. The garden always needed weeding and many hands were required for gathering the quantities of vegetables. The woodbox must be kept full, and water hauled to the house from the creek, lake or well. Children helped with all aspects of food preparation, including cooking, baking and the serving of meals.

*The girls' "skirt dance" and boys' kites. Original drawing by Jennifer Egglin.*

In the early pioneering days there was not the rigid differentiation between the roles of women and men, or of boys and girls. Inez Denny tells us that "the majority of the pioneer boys were expected to not be particular as to whether they did men's work or women's work." Cousin Billie Boren was "a notable example of versatility, lending a hand with helpless babies, cooking or washing, the most patient and faithful of nurses, lifting many a burden for the tired house-mother."

The children helped preserve the garden produce, such as stringing apples for drying. Another chore was selling surplus vegetables and flowers door-to-door. Susie and Alice Mercer also made the rounds of the village selling vegetables, milk and eggs from their farm.

On washing day children were pressed into service performing numerous tasks: tending the fire under the big kettle in the yard, rubbing soft homemade soap into the soiled places on the clothing and linens, and wringing out the washed clothes. The children then spread the clothes on bushes and branches to dry. Later they used clotheslines.

## THE WILDERNESS PLAYGROUND

The pioneer children had few toys and their playground was the green, tree-covered hillsides and brown beaches. For fun they dared each other to climb up the steepest, slipperiest banks above Smith Cove or to walk or run down the 50- and 60-foot logs that lay at odd angles across deep ravines or on steep inclines. Inez reports that the children went on with their usual outdoor games the year around, unless it rained unusually hard. They loved being outside and were restive if kept in the house for very long.

The children were not restrained in their athletic adventures for fear of damaging their clothes. The girls' dresses and boys' shirts were of cotton calico which cost only five cents a yard at Dexter Horton's store. Warmer dresses and trousers were made of linsey-woolsey, a home-woven blend of linen and wool fibers, and handknit wool sweaters, mittens and scarves kept off the damp chill from the bay in the winter time. The girls participated in making their own clothes, knitting and stitching the garments. Everything was carefully washed

### Cousin Billie Catches the Steamer

One summer around 1862 when cousin Billie was visiting, there was a lot of weeding to be done, which Louisa assigned to the children. The lad decided that he had had enough of weeding and walked down to Yesler's Wharf and caught the *Eliza Anderson* bound for Olympia and home. Since the *Eliza Anderson* made one run a week around the Sound, it was a week before the Denny family were assured that cousin Billie had arrived safely home in Olympia. Carson reported that when questioned about his unannounced leave-taking, the boy replied, "There was too much chickweed at Uncle David's, so I came home."

and mended over and over before it was handed down to the next child, or to a neighbor.

When the Chinook wind came singing across Puget Sound in January or February, the boys sent their homemade kites up, up into the sky at the top of Queen Anne Hill. On such windy days the girls would loosen their long hair, which was normally braided or held back in a net, and perform what they called a "skirt dance" by holding the hems of their skirts over their heads and running down the hill squealing with delight as their skirts ballooned out behind them like sails.

The cattle were another source of adventure. When David's range stock came around the homestead, which it did quite often, the children would run for a rope or rawhide lariat and lasso the calves. One day Inez and Madge enjoyed a wild adventure. Mounting a two-year-old heifer when it was lying down, they were startled when it leapt to its feet and, bellowing hideously, ran for dear life with the two girls clinging to its back. In seconds the entire herd began stampeding toward Lake Union—cows leaping over logs and calves bawling—with the girls astride the heifer in the middle of a cloud of dust, shrieking with delight and fright. They eventually flew off, landing in a soft sandy spot in the road.

When the Ross or Smith children came over to the Denny farm they loved to play on the teeter-totter. The Denny teeter-totter had the longest, strongest Douglas fir board that could be found laid across a large log. A huge stone was placed in the middle to hold down the board, which was then crowded with large and small children at either end until there was hardly any board showing. They then see-sawed the board up and down, with their eyes glued on the huge stone, prepared to leap aside if it started rolling.

Canoeing along the shores of Elliott Bay and later, when they were older, north and south along the sound, was a major recreation of the children, who all quickly learned to handle a native canoe. Most often the pioneer women and children used the style of canoe designed for the native women, a stable, lightweight canoe that was easily navigable, in contrast to the larger, heavier, fishing and war canoes used by the men.

At a young age all boys and any interested girls were taught to shoot well. David and Louisa's sons, as well as Madge and their nephew Billie, became good shots with both the shotgun and rifle at a young age and killed numerous bear, deer, grouse, pheasants, ducks, wild pigeons and other game for the family table. Thomas Mercer taught all of his daughters how to handle firearms. More than one girl brought down bear, as well as birds, elk, moose and deer.

## Toys

Toys were simple and homemade. The few toys a family had were shared by everyone. Dolls made of calico or corncobs were common, as were calico dogs, cats, rabbits, mice and horses. Children traded with the native children for their toys, including child-size bows and arrows. The bows were stained with berry juice and the arrows tipped with red, with duck feathers forming the vanes that kept the arrow flying straight.

Children often made their own toys, such as kites constructed of slivers of light wood and paper. Baseballs were made by winding a piece of rubber with yarn, then twine, and covering it with leather cut from the tops of old worn-out boots.

In the evenings children often played Authors, Hearts or other card games. Lucky children received in the mail *Youth's Companion* or *St. Nicholas*, popular young people's magazines from "back east." Each issue had crossword puzzles and pencil games, and was a treasure-trove of ideas for things for young people to make and do.

## Church on Sunday

The families living on the hill in the 1850s and 1860s shared a strong religious faith and many attended

## Madge Decatur Denny: Queen Anne's First Mountaineer

*Born March 16, 1856, Fort Decatur*
*Died January 17, 1889, Queen Anne Hill*

All of the pioneer children were adventurous, and some of them became mountain climbers. Named for the fort where she was born during the Native American uprising, Madge Decatur seemed to have been endowed with a fearless nature and an insatiable appetite for adventure. Her mother often noted that Madge approached everything in life with a calm, quiet courage. Madge was a strong natural athlete whose physical stamina and beauty impressed the community. By the time she was 14 she was a crack shot and could shoot off the head of a grouse at long range.

Inez says of Madge:

> *Courage, steadfastness and intrepidity were marked traits of her character. The surpassing loveliness and grandeur of the "world in the open air" appealed to her . . . even in extreme youth.*
>
> *Her nerves were of steel; she seldom exhibited a shadow of fear and seemed of a spirit to undertake any daring feat. To dare the darkness, climb declivities, explore recesses, seemed pleasure to her courageous nature. At Snoqualmie Falls, in the Archipelago de Haro, in the Jupiter Hills and Mount Olympus of the Olympic Range, she climbed up and down the steep gorges with the agility of the chamois or our own mountain goat. The forest, the mountain, the seashore yielded their charm, to her, each gave their messages.*

Endowed with great beauty and a keen mind, Madge was also well known for her cheerful temperament and keen sense of humor. She enjoyed keeping everyone laughing. She died at age 32 from an undiagnosed illness. *Courtesy Museum of History and Industry.*

church on Sunday. The boys' Sunday best consisted of "Buster Brown" style linen blouses, long trousers and cloth caps with wide visors.

The girls wore ankle-length full skirts held out by hoops and long, wide, stiffly-starched and beruffled pantlets. Abbie recalls these "as the bane of our lives, for we had to walk so carefully along the side of the road that their immaculate whiteness should not be marred by the dust. How we envied the little care-free 'Injuns' that we passed on our way to Sunday school. They did not have to hitch up their hoops in the back when they sat down or else have them fly up and hit them on the nose."

Abbie Denny has left a delightful sketch of her sisters' and brothers' experiences at church. Reaching the church each Sunday, they climbed what seemed like very high steps to small people, tip-toed in, and sat down on long painted benches in a "sniggering row to say their catechisms." When the teacher told the children how sin came about by Adam and Eve eating apples, the Denny girls agreed among themselves that "if the apples had been as green as the ones [they] had tried from the 'sweet June' tree, Adam would have let Eve eat them all."

The Sunday school teacher asked the children to prepare verses to recite, promising that the one learning the most by heart would receive a prize. One Sunday Anna Louisa, about six, put up her hand, indicating that she had a verse. Receiving a nod, she stood up, and facing the group blurted out at breakneck speed, so no one could stop her:

> *Matthew, Mark, Luke and John,*
> *Saddle a cat and I'll get on.*

After a stunned silence the entire Sunday school class erupted into a hysterical laughter, including the teacher.

When Sunday school was over, the children, like their parents, stood around on the church steps talking over the news, such as ". . . the folks up river, including the little Terry girls, were all flooded out by the early summer freshets . . . and had all come to Seattle in canoes." When they ran out of things to talk about they would wonder about "which Indian had fired the gun that had left bullet holes in the church window frames."

## Parties with the Neighbors

The main recreation enjoyed in the evening was getting together with the neighbors for taffy pulling, playing word games, or theatricals on the order of charades.

The older children enjoyed spelling bees, since being able to speak well and spell correctly was much esteemed at this time. "Spell downs," in which good spellers engaged in friendly competition, were popular. These were usually held at the schoolhouse and were well-attended. Singing was a favorite pastime of children as well as of adults. Singing schools were organized throughout the year, meeting in the evening, and it was a real step toward being "grown up" to be allowed to attend, usually at age 14 or 15. Many a courtship began at singing school.

Reflecting back on their pioneer childhood in 1906, Abbie Denny-Lindsley observes:

> *To some of our middle-aged citizens who were once the barefooted boys and girls who played in the roads that are now First and Second avenues, the past seems like a beautiful dream wherein people of another era dwelt: the red man with his picturesque garb of blanket and beads; the pioneer in his buckskin hunting blouse; the sailors from white-winged ships of foreign lands, and the jolly jack tars from the old man-of-war.*

Chapter Seven

# Wilderness Lost— The 1870s

by
Kay F. Reinartz, Ph.D.

The 1870s proved to be a watershed in the history of Seattle and its environs, marking the transition from wilderness to urban development. The troubled years following the Native American uprising had faded and, with the restoration of national peace after the Civil War, more people decided to take a chance on the Puget Sound country. Thus, toward the end of the decade noticeably more newcomers arrived in Seattle looking for a chance for a new start—and land. During this period all activities and development were confined to the lower south-sloping hill and the southern end of Lake Union.

Inez Denny provides a picture of the environment of the south slope of the hill in 1871, when her family moved into their house at Republican Street between Eighth and Ninth avenues N.:

> *The claim reached from Lake Union to Elliott Bay, about a mile and a half; a portion of it was*

*Among the settlers in the 1870s who found their way to Eden Hill was the Wilcox family, who built their home on the east side of the hill overlooking the Lake Union wilderness. Wilcox enclosed his house yard with a sturdy fence to keep the children from wandering into the woods and to keep the deer out of the garden. Courtesy Ruth Wilcox and Willa Fassett.*

*rich meadow land covered with luxuriant grass and bordered with flowering shrubs, the fringe on the hem of the mighty evergreen forest covering the remainder.*

*Hundreds of birds of many kinds built their nests here, and daily throughout the summer chanted their hymns of praise. Robins and wrens, song-sparrows and snow birds, thrushes and larks vied with each other in joyful song. The western meadow larks wandered into this great valley, adding their rich flute-like voices to the feathered chorus. Woodpeckers, yellow hammers and sapsuckers beat their brave tattoo on the dead tree trunks and owls uttered their cries from the thick branches at night.*

*Riding to church one Sunday morning we beheld seven little owls sitting in a row on a dead limb of a tall fir tree, about fourteen feet from the ground. Winking and blinking they sat, silently staring as we passed by. [We also saw] rare birds peculiar to the western coast, the rufous-backed hummingbird, like a living coal of fire, and the bush titmouse which builds a curious hanging nest, also visited this natural park.*

## LIVING OFF THE LAND

In the 1860s and 1870s the settlers lived out their years in predictable cycles marked by clearing land, planting, cultivating, harvesting and preserving food. Most settlers drew on the abundance of nature and literally "lived off the land" for 30 years. Homesteads were expanded with barns and outbuildings constructed to shelter growing herds of cattle and farm equipment. The men were able to obtain more help with the clearing and farming from growing sons and newcomers.

The pioneer women found help with the household work by hiring Native American women. Roberta Frye Watt, the Eden Hill Dennys' cousin, reports that it was a slow process to train a native woman how to do housekeeping chores "correctly." Often they would wash the worn clothing with such great vigor that they rubbed holes in the cloth. If not watched closely they would lay the wet clothes on the ground to dry, often soiling them in the process. Louisa Boren Denny reports, regarding the natives who she hired, "after they had learned how, [they] could wash the clothes as white as any of the modern steam laundries, and with less wear." When it came to floor washing, however, native women confined their efforts to the middle of the floor and no amount of instruction could get them to wash in the corners.

*A pioneer woman airs her bedding in the spring sunshine. Part of a woman's work was making numerous featherbeds and quilts for her family. Many women used quilting as an opportunity to express their artistic talent in original designs. Courtesy University of Washington Special Collections.*

## "CHINA BOYS"

The arrival of Chinese men in the region proved to be a boon for the pioneer household, for they relieved both the women and men of many of their more tiresome chores. Brought to the United States as contract labor to build the railroads, by the 1870s Chinese men in the Puget Sound region formed a substantial source of domestic labor, which would later lead to trouble for them in the 1880s.

The Chinese were quick to learn the techniques of American-style housekeeping and, once trained, rarely deviated.

Moreover, they were generally very dependable and good-natured. Called "China boys" by the settlers, they were appreciated by many. They freed the women from the most onerous of the household chores, such as the bimonthly mountains of laundry, washing up from cooking, and weeding the large garden, while the men were relieved of chopping and carrying wood and building fires. Frequently a family's China boy liked to take full charge of the house, including caring for the children. Often a warm relationship was established between the family and its Chinese help, who would often come back to visit a family after moving on to another job.

## HOME MEDICINE

David Denny commented in an interview in the 1890s that his family enjoyed splendid health and in 24 years they consulted a physician only four times. These years included Louisa delivering children seven times, including twin boys.

The settlers in general were very healthy and there were infrequent injuries in the forest and around the homestead. Some men, like Thomas Mercer, were skilled in home medicine. Healing the sick was usually considered a part of women's work, however. It seemed that whenever the women got together they always spent some time discussing treatments for health problems, since most felt they could never know enough. For their remedies pioneer women drew on foodstuffs and spices, as well as herbs and plant materials.

BUSINESS DIRECTORY.

**THE GREAT**

**MEDICAL DISCOVERY!**

**Of Washington Territory.**

MERCER'S PANACEA!

**Prepared by Dr. Thomas Mercer, of Seattle, W. T.**

This preparation is carefully prepared by Dr. Mercer, who gives his personal attention thereto.

After years of experience he presents this compound, Tonic and Cathartic, to the public, as better calculated to assist nature in overcoming disease than anything yet offered by the faculty, in all cases of general derangement of the system.

It promotes digestion and stimulates different organs into healthy action.

**As an Appetizer it Has no Equal.**

It is particularly beneficial in eradicating from the system the Effects of Syphilis.

As a Cathartic it is unsurpassed, being unaccompanied with griping and pain.

Dr. Mercer has also a preparation which he calls

THE LADIES BALM,

Being expressly designed for female derangements. He has also prepared a

PULMONARY SYRUP,

Which is unsurpassed for Coughs, Colds and all derangements of the lungs.

**All the Above Medicines are Purely Vegetable.**

M. A. KELLY, Agent at Seattle; PATERSON & MANN, at Olympia.

**Patronize Home Skill.**

Dr. Mercer refers to the citizens of Seattle and Puget Sound generally, who have used his medicines. THOMAS MERCER.

*Courtesy University of Washington Special Collections.*

## THE WILDERNESS LAKE IS TRANSFORMED

Between 1870 and 1890 Lake Union was destined to be transformed from a beautiful wilderness lake to a busy industrial area. In 1872 the Seattle Coal and Transportation Company started the first commercial activity on the lake. Coal was barged from the Renton mines up Lake Washington to Union Bay on the *Addie*. After portage to Lake Union it was reloaded on the *Linna C. Gray*, a side-wheeled barge with narrow-gauge rail tracks bolted to the deck. The *Linna C. Gray* docked near the intersection of Valley Street and Westlake Avenue, and when the coal cars rolled off the barge a locomotive hauled them over a wooden trestle up Westlake Avenue to Pike Street, and then on to the bunkers at the foot of Pike (Pike Place). There the coal was loaded by hand into the holds of ships that took it to San Francisco and the East Coast markets. Seattle Coal and Transportation shut down its Lake Union operation in 1877 when the Seattle and Walla Walla Railroad completed its road to Renton.

In the 1870s people moving to the outskirts of Seattle were looking for small farm acreages. Lake Union attracted many and by the mid-1870s homes began to dot the shores, with cultivated orchards and orderly gardens replacing the tangle of vine maple, salal, Oregon grape and ferns.

The winter of 1875 was a hard one and the ice skates were brought out again. Every evening bonfires blazed on the shores of Lake Union and skaters cut the ice in swoops and curves within the arc of light cast by the fire. Young lovers found it convenient to drift off for

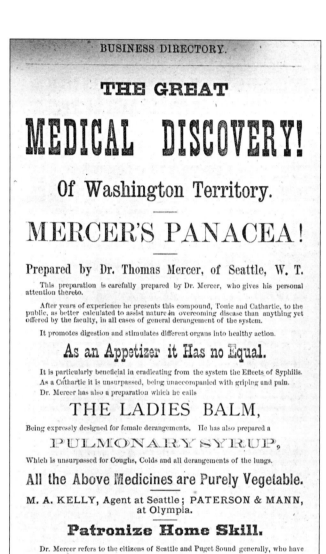

## A Pioneer Woman's Garden

Keeping a garden was very important in maintaining a healthy diet for the pioneers. Vegetable gardens nurtured their bodies and flower gardens nurtured their souls by providing beauty and memories of old homes left behind.

Louisa Boren led the way in developing beautiful flower gardens in the settlement on Elliott Bay. Many of the cabin door gardens in Seattle and on Queen Anne Hill in the 1860s and 1870s were propagated from seeds and cuttings from Louisa's garden.

Louisa built her flower garden from native plants she gathered in the wild as well as in the time-honored gardeners' way of exchanging seeds and plants with friends. In addition to Sweetbrier roses there were pink Mission roses, brought to Fort Steilacoom by the mission fathers in the 1840s, which her brother Carson brought to her from Olympia. From the woods came blue and yellow violets, and the fragrant lady's slipper, the favorite flower of the pioneer children. The arching stalks of the native false Solomon's seal with its white star flowers leaned over delicate lavender Oregon iris, red columbine and bleeding hearts.

In the spring the garden was a burst of color, with the fragrant purple lilacs and white spirea in the background, fronted by white trillium, erythroniums and purple lupine. The intense scarlet of the red currant exploded here and there in the garden, while the soft pink of the native rhododendron marked the corners of the cottage. The native trumpet honey-suckle covered the garden gate.

White stones from the beach were carefully placed to form neat borders around the colorful beds. With the help of an old Native American woman, Louisa carried from a distance rich soil black with humus. Lime was obtained by crushing the oyster shells that lay on the beach in profusion.

When the Denny family moved to their farm on Lake Union around 1870, Louisa cultivated an even larger flower garden where "old and new garden favorites ran riot." This garden was resplendent with Japanese and ascension lilies and velvety pansies, and fragrant with roses of all varieties. Louisa obtained from mail order catalogues fancy tulips, English violets and other exotic plants. Her scientific interest in plants was well developed and she often experimented with her plants, cross-breeding them and grafting freely. Inez reports that wherever her mother cultivated a garden it elicited much enthusiastic praise.

When the Civic Auditorium, which was built on the site of the Dennys' house in the swale, was dedicated, an elderly Clarence Bagley placed in the cornerstone a little sprig of Sweetbrier rose in memory of the gardener, Louisa Boren Denny.

*Louisa Boren Denny, 1828-1916. Pioneer, community leader, midwife, natural medicine practitioner, horticulturist, seamstress. Louisa Boren Park, Capitol Hill, is dedicated to this Queen Anne pioneer woman. Original painting by E. F. Hines. Courtesy Museum of History and Industry.*

*Original illustration of Louisa Boren Denny's 1860s garden by Vonnie Anderson Burns.*

a few minutes into the darkness down by the lake. The cold soon drove them back to the warmth of the fire where noses, hands and toes could be warmed up, and a cup of hot coffee was available from the big smoke blackened pot nestled in the glowing coals. Occasionally, a skater broke through the ice, but no one drowned.

## Schooling for Infants and Teachers

When it was time for the Denny children to begin school, the family was living in Seattle in the winter and on the homestead in the swale during the growing season. Louisa, who was a certified teacher in Illinois, taught her children and the younger Mercer daughters at home when they were living on their claims. During the rest of the year the children attended the Seattle village school.

The Mercers and Dennys attended the Territorial University when it opened in 1860, where the older girls were in the secondary class and Inez and Madge Denny attended the very large "infant" classes. Each pupil had a small slate on which lessons were written, as paper was in short supply on the frontier and expensive. The girls cleaned their slates with a sponge attached to the slate by a string and water kept in a little bottle in their pockets. The boys, on the other hand, often did not bother with the sponge and water, but would spit on the slate or lick it off and dry it with a sleeve. A favorite prank of the boys was to get up on the roof of the university and walk around the edge of the building to "show off."

In the winter the classroom was a potpourri of odors from the home remedies for colds and coughs. Red flannel bands saturated with turpentine or kerosene were wrapped around the necks of many pupils. Others sported neat little bags of "assafidity" or camphor around their necks. Some had been sent to school with small cotton bags of powdered sulfur in their pockets and instructions to "rub it on their hands anytime they touched anything" to ward off skin infections. The scent of onions wafted over all. Onions were a basic ingredient in most cough treatments.

The university also offered secondary schooling and teacher's training. In the winter of 1861 Dillis Ward studied for his teacher's certificate and became one of the first to graduate from Washington Territorial University as a certified teacher. Tom Mercer's daughters and the Denny children all completed secondary school at the university.

## The Ross School

It was a long way from the Ross farm to Seattle and in 1878 Mary Ross decided to open a school for the younger children in her home. A second-floor bedroom was converted into a schoolroom, and John built plank desks and benches from cedar growing on the farm. Lima Penfield was hired as teacher for $20 a month, plus room and board with the Rosses.

The neighbors sent their children over to Mary Ross's home school and soon a larger place was needed. With the help of neighbors, John built a small two-room schoolhouse on the Ross homestead which served until 1903, when a larger building was erected on the north side of today's ship canal.

The older Ross children, like other young people on the north side of the hill pursuing a secondary education, made a two-hour journey over water and land to reach the Central School on Marion Street. Arising around 5 o'clock in the morning, the girls would help their mother in preparing breakfast and school lunches while one of the boys milked the family cow. Their five-mile route to school was as follows: a walk to the shore of Lake Union where they would take their canoe and paddle to the south end of the lake; from there they walked up the narrow-gauge railroad track to Pike Street and then over to Marion Street.

*Some of the ingredients used in old home remedies. Original drawing by Jennifer Egglin.*

The Ross children, like all of the children in the nineteenth century, did a great deal of walking. For example, a really wonderful outing was to go over to play with the Smith girls at the cove. From the Outlet the Ross children would follow a trail through the woods to the cove and then walk along the beach when the tide was out to the Smiths' house—a trip of three to four miles, each way.

## Seattle Gets a Fine Teacher

In May 1877 Dillis and Sarah "Belle" Byles Ward returned to Seattle after seven years at the Skokomish Indian Reservation School. Their family of five was increased by the birth of Mabel in June. After a business venture fell through, Dillis began teaching grammar school the fall term at the rate of $65 a month. For the next ten years, he divided his time between teaching, business ventures, and community service. In the 1880s he would become a prominent Queen Anne leader and land developer.

Dillis Ward was an excellent teacher. A Works Progress Administration writer's project, which during the Depression collected the memoirs of northwest pioneers, recorded the following commentary on Ward by an anonymous former student:

> *D. B. Ward was accredited with being the best disciplinarian of any grade school teacher in the territory. While the discipline he maintained was well nigh perfect, yet I never saw him display any temper. He was always genial, often giving happy exclamations, his facial expression inviting and pleasing—yet his power of control over pupils was something extraordinary, and for years the annual presentation of the banner for highest degree of order and discipline maintained in school was presented to him.*

## The Donation Claims are Subdivided

In the 1870s Puget Sound was discovered by those seeking homes in the far west. In 1867 Seattle had 400 residents; in 1874 there were 1800. The population doubled or tripled almost yearly from 1870 forward. Finally, after more than two decades of patient waiting by the early settlers, it happened—with the demand for building lots in the vicinity of Seattle, land value began to increase.

The entire district north of Seattle to Salmon Bay (Ballard) became officially known as North Seattle in this period of development. Subdividing activity on the hill began slowly with nine plats filed between 1869 and 1881. Most of the areas platted were on the south slope or top of the hill.

The first plat on record for North Seattle was D.T. Denny's North Seattle Addition (Mercer St. to Denny Way, Warren Ave. to Elliott Bay), filed by David Denny and his father John on July 13, 1869. The next year, James Law platted Law's Second Addition in the first of a number of "wildcat subdivisions," so-called because they were situated far from current development, "out where the wild cats live!" Law's land was situated on

### The Ross Family

In the spring of 1873, the Ross family moved from Seattle to their homestead on the north side of the hill. That summer the family members lived in Ira Utter's old dirt-floored cabin while John was completing their own two-room cabin on the south side of the Outlet, in the vicinity of Third Avenue W. and W. Dravus. He soon built this five-bedroom house for his large family which eventually numbered 11 children. Mary Jane McMillan Ross founded the first school on Queen Anne Hill in this home near the Outlet in 1878, where her 11 children were educated together with neighbor's children. This house was destroyed in 1915 during the construction of the Lake Washington Ship Canal. John Ross died May 3, 1886 at age 59 and is buried on his donation claim in the historic Odd Fellows Lodge section of Mount Pleasant Cemetery. *Courtesy Metro Seattle Environmental Laboratory.*

*In the nineteenth century Lake Union frequently froze solid for months, much to the delight of the settlers. Courtesy University of Washington Special Collections.*

the top of the hill (Galer to Howe; 3rd W. to 9th W.). Law had acquired the land under preemption in the 1860s for $1.25 an acre and sold 32 lots for an average price of $10 a lot.

Conservative Thomas Mercer was closely watching the Seattle scene. In August 1870 Mercer made his move. He filed his first plat, named Eden Addition (Mercer to Aloha; 6th N. to Lake Union), and offered lots bordering on the southwest end of Lake Union for suburban homes. In January 1871, Mercer filed Eden Second Addition (Aloha to Highland Dr.; 6th N to Lake Union). The summer of 1871 witnessed brisk land sales in the immediate Seattle area and between 20 and 40 real estate transactions were filed each week for lots selling from $50 to $500.

## The 1870s Land Boom

In 1872, 431 real estate sales were recorded for Seattle and environs. The long-awaited real estate boom was on. That year saw phenomenal growth in Seattle, with 74 buildings constructed: 39 houses, one church, one ice skating rink, and the remainder for business enterprises. Clarence Bagley observes that "the buildings, with a few exceptions, were better and more substantial than ever before, and the downtown district was being extended and the residence districts began to climb the hills."

In November 1872, David Denny subdivided 500 acres of unimproved land on the shores of Lake Union, calling the plat Denny's First Addition. Denny promoted his subdivision by placing an elaborate advertisement in the newspaper describing the land and its advantages. Prices ranged from $30 to $100 with the usual terms of the day—about ten percent down and monthly payments of $5. In June of 1875 he platted Denny's Second Addition and offered house lots for $50 to $100 each and land at $50 to $100 per acre, in five- or ten-acre parcels. In July, hoping to stimulate building in his subdivision, Denny offered a free second lot to all purchasers who would promptly build a house on their first.

Denny would soon regret having subdivided such

### A Washington Territory Civil War Hero Moves to the Hill

In 1873 David and Susie Mercer Graham moved back to Queen Anne Hill and built a home on Thomas Mercer's donation claim at 320 Ward Street. Capt. Joseph Dickerson, who had been living with them on their farm, also made the move. A bachelor, Dickerson was an integral part of Susie and David's family for 40 years.

Capt. Dickerson, as he was known, was honored in Washington Territory as a hero. He served in the Civil War as the color bearer for the Washington and Alaska Division of the Grand Army of the Republic, the northern forces. He was one of two soldiers from the Northwest honored with a gold medal for bravery in the field of battle. President Abraham Lincoln presented Dickerson with the medal and raised him to the rank of captain for refusing to surrender the Union flag, although surrounded and under heavy fire, at the Battle of Antietam. Dickerson died at 320 Ward Street in 1916.

## The Denny Cabin

David T. Denny began dealing in real estate in the 1870s. In 1889 his son-in-law Edward Lindsley, Abbie Denny's husband, built David Denny a real estate office at Temperance Avenue (Queen Anne Ave.) and Republican Street. The log cabin remained on its original site for 77 years, during which time it saw use as a church, school, tavern and home.

In 1988, the old cabin occupied a lot whose owner announced his intention of demolishing the building and converting the land to parking. The Queen Anne Historical Society was unsuccessful in its attempts to acquire and preserve the building. The building was eventually bought by commercial interests in Federal Way which planned to use it as the centerpiece of an "Old West" theme shopping mall. The plan was abandoned, however, and the cabin sat deteriorating for ten more years. In 1992 the Federal Way Historical Society gained ownership of the cabin, relocated it, and began restoration work. The cabin remains in Federal Way at the time of this writing. *Courtesy University of Washington Special Collections.*

large tracts at this early date, for he was now taxed at a per lot rate rather than at the farmland or unimproved vacant land rate. As the land sold very slowly until the late 1880s, these taxes were a heavy burden and helped contribute to Denny's financial collapse in the 1890s.

From 1876 to 1877, Belltown was the fastest growing area of Seattle as well as its most favored residential neighborhood. Named for William and Sarah Bell's donation claim, it soon had the feel of a village with shops and its own school, which had been built for $2,700. Directly north of Belltown, only small areas of Denny and Eden hills had been logged, and they remained covered with forest.

The great windstorm of 1875 marked a turning point for the north district. In March of 1875 a hurricane ripped through Puget Sound. The *Post-Intelligencer* reports that "it blew down thousands of trees, a number of houses, barns and small sheds were lashed to foam." Clarence Bagley comments that "when the storm was over, the whole country had undergone a change. The timber was cleared so we could see the territorial university from the landing at Lake Union. Fifty-six trees blew across the railroad track, from the lake to Fourth Avenue, nearly three quarters of a mile. It took 14 men working steadily from daybreak to 2 p.m. to clear the track."

During the winter of 1878-79 a large number of houses were built along the rail line of the Seattle Coal and Transportation Company to Lake Union. This was considered a superior building site.

## The Kinnears Come to the Hill

George Kinnear, 42, working as county clerk of Woodford County, Illinois, had been following the development of the Northwest for several years. In 1874 he visited Puget Sound and after looking around he purchased property on the south side of Eden Hill. In 1878 he and his wife Angie Simmons, 34, sold all of their Illinois land and moved to Seattle with their sons Charles nine, and George six.

A few days after they landed, Kinnear and Charlie set off on foot to look at their land. A short distance from where the Kinnear Mansion was to be built (Queen Anne Avenue between Roy and Aloha), the pair met Dr. Henry Smith driving his wagon into town. Smith cordially introduced himself and regaled them with his favorite story about the day in 1853 he spent walking in a circle trying to find Seattle. Smith later described Kinnear as "honest, energetic, kindhearted, clearheaded and generous."

Kinnear lost no time in establishing himself at the hub of land development activity in the Seattle area. He was a long, lean man who could walk through the woods all day without tiring. With a keen eye he noted where the slopes were and calculated which would be the most favorable districts for residential suburbs for the growing town. In 1884 he subdivided his land as Kinnear's Addition, built a road and launched a new era which would transform the wilderness of North Seattle forever into a residential district of Seattle.

Chapter Eight

# Subdividing Eden— The 1880s

by
Kay F. Reinartz, Ph.D.

In 1883 the land contiguous to and directly north of Seattle, now bounded by Howell and McGraw streets, Sixteenth Avenue W. and Lake Union, was annexed by a citizens' petition containing a minimum of 20 percent of the electorate who had voted in the last election. Thus did the majority of the area of Queen Anne come under the jurisdiction of Seattle. The balance of the community's geographic area was annexed to Seattle in 1890.

At the time of annexation, the district north of Seattle to Salmon Bay was commonly referred to as North Seattle. Throughout the 1880s the Queen Anne Hill district was known by various names, including Galer Hill, Queen Anne Hill, and occasionally Queen Anne Town. The name Galer derived from Jacob Gaylor,

*Looking south from midway up Queen Anne Hill, circa 1889. The Seattle boom that began in the 1870s quickly transformed the city into a busy urban center with the north district being developed to the foot of Queen Anne Hill. Developers began moving up the hills as the demand for residential suburbs increased. In the center of this photograph is the Denny mansion on Temperance Street (Queen Anne Avenue.) The topography of the south slope is characterized by steep grades alternating with somewhat level benches. Being the most desirable building sites, the benches were developed while the steep areas were left. Courtesy Washington State Historical Society.*

## The Queen Anne Style

The community name Queen Anne is the result of the historical coinciding of the ornate Queen Anne style of architecture with the North Seattle building boom. The ornate Queen Anne style, introduced from England to the east coast in the 1870s, reached Seattle in the 1880s at the peak of land development on the south and west sides of the hill by home seekers prosperous enough to afford "a little style" in their new home.

In his *Documented History of the Origin of Washington Geographic Names,* Edmond Meany confirms that the Queen Anne community name did, indeed, arise from the architectural style. Meany observes, "about 1880, such citizens as C.B. Bagley, F.H. Osgood, A.B. Stewart and others, built homes in the then-prevailing Queen Anne style of architecture. Rev. Daniel Bagley jokingly asked folks if they were not 'going out to Queen Anne Town?' The name persisted to the wonderment of new-comers."

*Three variations on the Queen Anne style found on Olympic Place at Second Avenue W. The house to the far right is the Ankeny House, where the Duwamish people's powwow tree was located until cut in 1891. Courtesy Queen Anne Historical Society.*

who built an imposing home on the southern crest of the hill in 1884 fronting on what became Gaylor (Galer) Street. The scant references to Galer Hill in the historic record suggests that this name was short-lived.

The name Queen Anne Town begins to appear around 1885, mainly in real estate promotion literature. Belltown had been the residential suburb of choice in the mid 1870's. Ten years later it was Queen Anne Town. Realtors sensed the name—a combination of aristocratic elegance and romance—would have a potent appeal in a still rough, unfinished city. In 1889 a typical land promotion bill declares:

> *Queen Anne Second Addition! The last opportunity to get in on the ground floor in Queen Anne Town! A sightly location! A view of the salt water from every lot! First 60 lots $300 each. Remember that the lots are 30 x 120 in size; that the alleys are 16 feet and the avenues are 74 feet wide.*
>
> *For the benefit of non-residents (as all Seattle's citizens are aware of the fact), we might mention that this addition is the cheapest property on the market; that the most aristocratic resident portion of the city is in North Seattle, and that this addition is within easy walking distance of the present terminal of the electric and cable roads.*

The name Queen Anne Town appears in a few official City of Seattle documents in the 1890s. After 1900 "town" disappears with the district being known simply as Queen Anne Hill.

On March 15, 1885, the Dennys, Thomas Mercer, George Kinnear and Walter Graham petitioned the city for: "a good passable wagon road [to] be opened connecting Temperance [Queen Anne Ave.] to Farm [Aurora] Street. This street is to be named Mercer Street." April 20, 1885, the city announced: "request granted." And so Mercer Street came to be.

## Seattle Booms

By 1880 the growth that had begun in the 1870s was like a locomotive with a full head of steam and a clear track. In a decade Seattle changed from a small lumbering center to a dynamic city many called the "Young Chicago." In 1883 the railroad was completed to Seattle from Tacoma, providing a direct link with eastern markets and, most importantly, a quick and easy way for people to move to King County, Washington Territory. And move they did. People were proud of what they called "the Seattle Spirit" which was carried out to the newly-developing suburban areas including Queen Anne Town.

## NORTH SEATTLE BOOMS

In the ten years, 1880 to 1890, more than 50 plats were filed with King County for subdivisions north of Denny Way. About 65 percent of the land that comprises Queen Anne was subdivided in this decade. Careful study of the plats reveals that other than a handful of subdivisions filed by David and Louisa Denny, Thomas Mercer and Dr. Henry Smith, the subdividing of the hill and cove area was done by land developers new to the Northwest. Indeed, many had come specifically looking for investment opportunities. Where the donation claim settlers led, many quickly followed. Development was initially along the west shore of Lake Union and the lower south slope of the hill, where transportation was accessible.

Thomas Mercer completed subdividing his donation claim 30 years after he arrived on the hill, with the filing of Mercer's Addition on February 2, 1882, and Mercer's Second Addition, April 14, 1883. Mercer's lots averaged $300 for a 30 x 120 foot lot.

With his new-found wealth Mercer built a comfortable home on Lombard (6th Ave. W.) between Ward and Prospect streets for Hetty and himself. Tom, 70, and Hetty, 55, continued as they had always been, modest and unpretentious. They had no interest in becoming a part of the fashionably self-conscious Queen Anne "society" represented by the Kinnears, Bagleys, Clises, Wards, Wheelers, and Churchills.

Throughout the 1860s David and Louisa Boren Denny had steadily bought land adjacent to Lake Union. By 1880 they were the largest landholders in the Lake Union district, holding over 1,000 acres, 320 of which was their original donation claim. They subdivided their great land holdings in 11 plats between 1869 and 1889. The final plat, Denny's Home Addition, was for their grand Queen Anne style home, Decatur Terrace. David Denny began his real estate sales activity in partnership with his father John, and when John died, David and his son John B. worked together.

## DENNY & HOYT—LAKE UNION LAND FOR SALE

In 1880-81 the land on the west side of Lake Union, including the Outlet, was logged off. In 1886 David Denny formed a real estate partnership with Judge John P. Hoyt, Supreme Court Justice of the Territorial Court, who presided over the 1889 Washington State Constitutional Convention. Denny & Hoyt Addition, platted March 1, 1888, was a huge subdivision bounded by Florentia Street to Woodland Park and Third Avenue W. to N. Thirty-ninth. Laying out five-acre parcels, they

*Queen Anne as seen from approximately Seventh and Spring streets, circa 1883. Note the single winding wagon road leading to the hill. As Seattle boomed in the 1880s the south side of Queen Anne Hill was subdivided. The north sides of the hill remained wooded into the 1920s. Courtesy Museum of History and Industry.*

Already flour, lumber, paper, furniture, boots and shoes, boats and car works fill the atmosphere, as the mystic problem of a great future comes

Floating on the Crown of Success.

TO CONCLUDE.

It is necessary to have people to do this; great works are only accomplished by the toils and labors of man. To accommodate them,

We will SELL HOMES SITES of this very property at $100 per lot cash.

Or, $100 per lot; $25 cash, balance monthly payments.

Or, We Will Give You a Lot, if you will build a snug home

TO COST $500.

Or, if you wish, we will arrange to build one for you at a slight additional cost.

We are, fortunately, yours,

WARD & GRIFFITH,

AGENTS FOR THE ADDITION,

OCCIDENTAL BLOCK

*1880s real estate advertisement; contemporary recreation by Theano Petersen.*

used their influence to bring the railroad through the Outlet. Denny & Hoyt's subdivision stimulated the rapid development of the northeast side of Queen Anne Hill and the formation of the Ross and Fremont districts.

## L.H. Griffith & D.B. Ward, Land Brokers

In the spring of 1886, land developer Lyman H. Griffith arrived in Seattle and soon formed a partnership with Dillis B. Ward, under the firm name of Ward & Griffith. This was a most fortuitous move for Ward, since Griffith was a highly competent investor with a real knack for picking good investments and making them work—and pay off handsomely. Later Ward worked with Griffith in the Griffith Co., a separate corporation. Ward's fortunes steadily rose after the partnership was formed. From the beginning Griffith, who came to town with ample capital, operated on an expansive scale.

In 1888 a syndicate of investors from Fremont, Nebraska, bought most of the Denny & Hoyt Addition. The Griffith and Co. land office in Fremont, named for the old home in Nebraska, advertised and sold lots for anywhere from $75 to $500.

Griffith understood the best way to attract buyers was to develop amenities. Thus, to create jobs and start an industrial core, in the summer of 1888 he and Dr. E.C. Kilbourne built the Fremont Mill at the Outlet. They dredged the natural drainage path from Lake Union to Salmon Bay to allow the passage of log booms as well as lumber barges. Mills appeared along this canal, as it was called, nearly 30 years before the completion of the Lake Washington Ship Canal. A wagon bridge was built in the vicinity of the Outlet connecting the north side of Queen Anne Hill to the budding Fremont townsite.

There was an immediate spurt of commercial construction around the Outlet and the Griffith Company provided a public water supply by tapping into a large spring on Nils Peterson's property on the north slope of Queen Anne Hill (vicinity Queen Anne Bowl).

## The Ross District Flourishes

The areas immediately adjacent to Fremont ben efited from Griffith's efforts to build up the district. Across from Fremont, a thriving community quickly formed around the Ross School on the old Ross Homestead (vicinity of 3rd Ave. W. and Nickerson St.) In 1888 the Ross Post Office was established in a corner of the general store, the Ross Marche, at Third Avenue W. and Nickerson. A flag station for the railroad was opened and the little village became known as Ross Station.

Up the hill from Ross Station was the large, prosperous Nils B. Peterson farm. In the 1870s Peterson purchased a large tract of John Ross's donation claim running from Mount Pleasant Cemetery east to First Avenue W. In addition to selling water to the Griffith Co., Peterson developed his own water system from the large spring.

## The Lake Union Road to Seattle

In 1890 Griffith, David Denny, Edward and Carrie Blewett, and a handful of other investors on the northwest end of Lake Union put their money together to finance the construction of the Lake Union Road, planned to include both a wagon road and rail tracks. The route followed the western shore of Lake Union

*The original Lake Union Road was built on trestle to avoid the marshy shoreline of Lake Union. Today Westlake Avenue follows this route. Courtesy University of Washington Special Collections.*

and connected the Ross District to Seattle.

In 1891 the entire area, which was still unincorporated King County, with the exception of Fremont, was annexed to the City of Seattle. The privately-funded Lake Union Road was only partially completed and 102 property owners and residents of the district promptly petitioned the city to complete the roadway. After considerable bickering, the city agreed—with the $6,000 lien lodged against the road by the construction company split between the citizens and the city. The road was built on a trestle above the marshy lake shore. Westlake Avenue N. now follows the old Lake Union road.

Beginning in the early spring of 1888, the steady rapping of hammers and purring of hand saws never stopped, as more than 100 houses were built on Queen Anne Hill between May and October. The vast majority of the houses were built between Mercer Street and Denny Way, with 90 percent being situated between Fourth Ave. N. and Westlake avenues. The most popular streets were Poplar (Taylor), Lombard (Sixth Ave. N.), Farm (Aurora), Dexter, Park (Eighth Ave. N.) and Rollin (Westlake). The streets surrounding the Denny Cemetery (Denny Park) began to be lined with houses. West Avenue

*South end of Lake Union circa 1888, with Western Mill and commuter steamer* Maude Foster. *Courtesy University of Washington Special Collections.*

## Commuter Ferry Service on Lake Union

A major drawback to buying land on the north and east sides of Queen Anne Hill in the late 1880s was the difficulty of getting to Seattle. The old Lake Union Road that roughly followed the west edge of the lake did not go through to the Outlet, but only served the southern end of the lake. The Griffith Co. overcame this problem by operating a little commuter steamer, the *Maude Foster*, on Lake Union which provided comfortable, convenient and efficient travel to Seattle.

Passengers were picked up at several docks around the lake and for a nickel homemakers, students and mill and construction workers were carried to a landing at the foot of Rollin Street (Westlake), near the Western Mill. The foot ferry was met by the Lake Union horse-drawn trolley, which carried the commuters to the heart of the town at Mill Street (Yesler Ave.). A special commutation fare of 15 cents included both the trolley and steamer.

Developers promoting their subdivisions around Lake Union gave star billing to the Lake Union Commuter Ferry. The completion of the Lake Union road and the Lake Union Electric Trolley Line in the early 1890s brought the Lake Union ferry service to an end.

### Wanted: A Good Framing Carpenter

By 1888 housing was very scarce in Seattle. It was often next to impossible for a family to rent a house. While waiting for their homes to be built, large families might live in one or two rooms in a boarding house, or in a tent pitched near the homesite. The ink was often barely dry on the land contract when work crews arrived with axes, saws and mattocks to clear away timber and to grub out the stumps. Next wagons drawn by two, four or six horses, for the sites high on the hill, pulled up with loads of lumber.

Only those building fine mansions called on the services of an architect. A good framing carpenter had basic house-building skills and for those who wanted "something special" in their cottage or bungalow, builder's pattern books and plans were available. J. Friedlander, an enterprising architect, regularly advertised to builders that they could purchase cottage plans from him for $15, while a two-story house plan cost $20. *Courtesy Museum of History and Industry.*

(Western) was rapidly transformed in the late 1880s by a neat row of houses scattered from Depot (Denny Way) to W. Harrison streets. On September 15, 1888, the *Post-Intelligencer* reported:

> *There is not a portion of the city undergoing more important changes than that section of North Seattle known as Denny Park Addition [Harrison, Denny Way, 9th N., 4th N.]. New houses are going up on every hand, streets being graded, lots cleared and sidewalks laid. At one point on Depot Street, which runs through the addition, a few blocks south of the Children's Home, several business houses are being started. In a whole block where a year ago there was nothing but brush and stumps now there are cozy homes. Not less than 100 new houses have been erected in that section during the past twelve months and fully twenty more are now in the course of construction.*

## BIGELOW THE BUILDER

Isaac N. Bigelow is an example of many of the land developers on Queen Anne Hill in the 1880s. He came to Seattle from Nova Scotia in 1875 and bought large tracts of land on the east side of the hill, which he subdivided.

In February 1882 and April 1883 Bigelow's First and Second additions were platted on the east crest of the hill (McGraw, Galer, First N., Nob Hill Ave.). In the next six years Bigelow transformed these additions into residential neighborhoods by building streets of houses, which he then sold. His house lots went for $75 and $80 and he enjoyed brisk business with more than 40 sales in 1888. His prices went up with the intensified demand for building sites brought by a great population increase. Bigelow built his own elegant home at 912 Queen Anne Avenue.

## PLANKED STREETS AND EIGHT-FOOT SIDEWALKS

As the number of houses dotting the slopes of the hill rapidly increased, so too did the need for roads. The construction of houses across the south slope of the hill made for heavy traffic through the stumps and slash on the unpaved dirt lanes, which were dust-bins when they were dry and muddy streams when it rained.

After North Seattle's annexation to the City of Seattle in 1882, property owners worked together to realize improvements in their rugged hill district. Between 1884 and 1898, approximately 40 petitions requested street grading, planking, paving, widening, extensions, improvements and sidewalks. Land developers often initiated these petitions.

Wood was plentiful and cheap at that time, and planks initially made a dry clean roadway, although they had their drawbacks. Street planks were good for about ten years, after which time they inevitably broke down from wood rotting and the planks separating. Accidents on plank streets were common and there were many serious injuries to horses and people when a wagon or buggy overturned, throwing out passengers and freight alike. In some cases injured parties sued the city for not maintaining the plank road.

As the plank streets got old they became spongy with water, as well as horse droppings, and gave off a "royal odor." In 1891 wooden planking was found to be a source of disease and infections, and Seattle shifted from planking to vitrified clay brick, which continued to be the main street surfacing until 1920. Bricks were considered the best wearing street surface but offered hazards, becoming dangerously slippery when wet and affording horses, and later cars, poor traction on inclined surfaces. The paving bricks for the North Seattle streets came from Port Townsend, Victoria and Japan. But mostly they came from the Denny Clay Co., operated by Arthur Denny and sons.

Legend asserts that Queen Anne Hill's steep streets were paved with cobblestones brought into Elliott Bay as ballast in foreign ships, but there is no verification of this story Some of the cobblestones, however, came from the San Juan Islands. In 1993 portions of some streets, such as the steepest grades of Fifth Avenue W., remain paved with the original cobblestones.

Careful tracking through the street improvement records shows that between 1884 and 1898 all of the north-south streets, from Denny Way to W. Highland Drive, were graded. All of the east-west streets from Fairview Avenue N. were also graded, with the exception of the those between Taylor and Warren avenues. Taylor Avenue was graded to Boston at the top of the hill and Garfield Street was mostly graded.

Grading simply meant a level roadbed—made of dirt. None of the Queen Anne streets enjoyed the benefit of paving in the nineteenth century except for a few sections that were paved with planking. The most noteworthy of these were Warren Avenue from Denny Way to W. Highland Drive, and Taylor Avenue from Denny Way to Ward Street. The record shows instances when property owners built roads and sidewalks at their own expense.

## BUSINESS AND MANUFACTURING ACTIVITY IN NORTH SEATTLE

Old Sanborn fire maps show a number of business enterprises in North Seattle in the 1890s. In 1893

*Cable powerhouse for the street trolley system, 1889 Depot Street. David Denny named the street marking the southern boundary of his donation claim Depot because he was convinced that the railroad would be laid along the route. The name was changed to Denny Way in 1895. Photo circa 1890. Courtesy University of Washington Special Collections.*

the Front Street Cable Railway Power House and Car Barn had been built on the southwest corner of Second Avenue and Eagle Street. Down on Lake Union, the Seattle Steam Laundry opened its doors in 1893. Just below Kinnear Park was the Johnson Mill, consisting of a working wharf and several buildings.

The Elliott Bay waterfront in the vicinity of Yesler's Mill was becoming crowded with mills by 1880 and enterprising millers looked for new locations. In the spring of 1882 two mills opened on Lake Union. By 1884 the Lake Union Mill was bought by a corporation in which David Denny and son John B. had controlling interest, and renamed the Western Mill. Using the latest sawmill equipment and techniques, the Western Mill had a diversified product line and a large capacity. Following practices of the day, all of the sawdust, shaving and refuse slabs, which ran into thousands of cords per year, were thrown into Lake Union. The *Post-Intelligencer* announced on August 3, 1890:

> *The greatest factor in the pollution of the waters of Lake Union is the Western Mill. All of the sawdust, shavings and thousands of cords of slabs are thrown into the lake there. . . . The most damage is done by the slabs as they have bark on them and make a strong tannic acid. This acid is a slow poison and makes the water absolutely black. A law passed in the last legislature forbidding the throwing of this refuse into lakes or streams where fish resort to spawn, the penalty being $100. Fish spawn in this lake to a large extent.*

After public outcry the mill stopped dumping its scrap wood into the lake and began burning it, thus filling the air with clouds of smoke and fine ash. John B. Denny designed an elevated carrier to haul the refuse from the mill to the burner which was located across Rollin Street (Westlake), against the east side of the hill. David Denny lost the Western Mill as part of his financial collapse in the Panic of 1893.

*The Kinnear mansion, 809 Queen Anne Avenue, established Queen Anne Hill's south slope as a fine residential neighborhood, and soon others built mansions nearby. Directly below the house was a swamp with pollywogs and waterbugs scooting between the tall grasses. In the mid-1880s Angie Kinnear frequently looked out of her south windows to see bears munching on the succulent roots of the skunk cabbages. Eventually the swamp was drained, filled in, and made into a street named for the Kinnears' son, Roy, born in 1881. Courtesy Old Seattle Paperworks.*

## The Avon Club and Ladies Musical Club

When Dr. Fredrick Churchill moved to Seattle in 1884, the city gained not only a good physician but an outstanding musician, Martha Blanke Churchill. The daughter of a Professor of Music at the Hamburg Conservatory of Music and a child prodigy, Martha Blanke had studied with several prominent German masters including Franz Liszt. She concertized both in Germany and the United States, coming to America at age 16. She married Churchill while living on the east coast.

Martha Churchill organized the Avon Club, which became one of the city's most active cultural organizations. Edmond Meany comments on the club of which he and fiancée Lizzie Ward were active members. "They were happy meetings, and our programs were always rich in enjoyment of music and literature. We were always treated to performances on the piano by Mrs. Churchill, who was one of the most brilliant pianists on the Pacific Coast." In 1891 Martha and a number of Avon Club members formed the Ladies Musical Club with Martha Churchill as its first musical director. Over a century old in 1993, the Ladies Musical Club continues to be a significant musical organization in Seattle.

## OTHERS JOIN THE KINNEARS ON THE HILL

Among the newcomers to Seattle in the spring of 1883 were John Ritchy and Rebecca Means Kinnear. George Kinnear's younger brother, John, 41, had been a prominent lawyer in Paxton, Illinois, and immediately plunged into politics, serving as the King Country representative in the Territorial Legislature in 1884. He played a role in framing the Washington State Constitution in 1888 and in 1889 ran a close race with Elisha P. Ferry for first governor of the new state. After losing this election, he served in the new Washington State Legislature as a senator in 1890 and 1891. Throughout his political career John Kinnear supported progressive legislation, including women's suffrage and workers' rights.

John and Becky Kinnear built their mansion close to brother George's place at 348 Olympic Place. The house was perhaps even more elaborate than George and Angie's, with fresco paintings on the ceilings of the public rooms and ornately hand carved woodwork throughout.

## THE WARD FAMILY'S HOMES AND LIFE ON THE HILL

According to his son-in-law Edmond Meany, Dillis B. Ward liked to say, regarding his land development which he pursued for 28 years, "I made and lost two fortunes." Ward subdivided much of the west side of Queen Anne Hill in the 1880s and 1890s while with L. Griffith. As Ward's ventures experienced ups and downs, the family's houses were "up and down." In 1880 he took an entire city block of land at Ward Street and Dexter Avenue and built the family a large house with a barn for a driving team and cow. By the late 1880s Dillis and Sarah had realized a good profit from

*The Ward family. The marriage of pioneer Sarah "Belle" Byles and Dillis B. Ward in 1863 was a long and happy one. The family home near the intersection of Ward Street and Dexter Avenue and later at 104 High Street (Aloha) was a community focal point. The Wards' children were as active as their parents and during the 1880s and 1890s temperance meetings, Bible study and musical evenings alternated with parties in the rose garden and big dinner parties alive with animated conversation. This massive oil portrait hangs in the Pioneer Museum, Pioneer Association of the State of Washington. In the center of the portrait are Sarah Isabella Byles Ward and Dillis B. Ward surrounded by their children left to right Lizzie, Clarence, Maud (back) and Kate. In front are left to right Agnes and Mabel. Photographed by John Hennes.*

the real estate boom and built a 14-room mansion on three and a half city lots on the corner of Kentucky and High streets (1st Ave. N. and Aloha St.).

Dillis B. Ward was one of those who lost in the Panic of 1893, and he and Sarah moved from their High Street mansion in 1895 to a place they rented at Fourth Avenue and Blanchard Street. A few years later, with an improvement in their fortunes, they built their last house at 1225 Sixth Avenue W. where they lived until Dillis' death in 1922 and Sarah's in 1928. They were married 60 years.

*The William Shoudy House, on the east side of Queen Anne Avenue between John and Thomas streets, was set like an elegant wedding cake in the forest. Every Fourth of July Shoudy took his daughters to the tower room where they climbed out onto the roof and nailed a row of American flags to the widow's walk railing. Shoudy was elected Mayor of Seattle in 1883 on the Populist ticket as a compromise candidate for a city torn with dissension after the crisis over the civil rights of the Chinese. Courtesy Queen Anne Historical Society.*

## Transportation Improves

In 1887 the Seattle Lake Shore and Eastern Railroad completed the heavy rail tracks running along the north shore of Lake Union. A cable streetcar line was laid out in 1888 which ran along Second Avenue and divided at Pike Street, with one line going out to Lake Union. The North Seattle streetcar rattled through Belltown and up the slope to Queen Anne Town. An extra horse was kept stabled at Second Avenue and Battery Street to be hooked up to the streetcar to help it climb the hills.

In 1888 a streetcar franchise was granted David Denny, Judge Thomas Burke, John Leary and others for the West Seattle, Lake Union and Park Transit Co. The company had an ambitious plan to build a street railway that would run from West Seattle to Lake Union. Around 1889 a wooden trestle was erected along the southwest side of the lake upon which Rollin Street (Westlake Ave.) and the streetcar tracks were built side by side.

## Voting Rights for Washington Women, 1883-1888

Since the late 1840s American women had been struggling to achieve full legal rights including the right to vote in all elections. Many in the North Seattle district were ardent feminists and strongly pro-women's rights. Among these were all of the Dennys including son John, who married his Oregon Law School classmate Carrie V. Palmer, who passed the bar shortly before dying of tuberculosis in 1891. Louisa, Madge and Inez Denny were very outspoken on women's issues and were leaders in organizing support for suffrage for Washington women.

Others who went on public record in support of women's suffrage included John and Rebecca Kinnear, George and Angie Kinnear, Dr. Henry Smith, Clarence and Alice Mercer Bagley, Thomas and Hester Ward Mercer and their children, Dillis and Sarah Byles Ward, Edmond and Lizzie Ward Meany, and John and Mary McMillan Ross.

In 1883 the dominant issue in the Territorial Legislature was women's suffrage, which was passed as Council Bill No. 44 granting women voting rights in local and state elections. It was signed into law by Governor Eugene Semple. The women of Washington were granted voting rights in local and state elections. In acknowledgment of women's newly-won citizenship rights, a blue-ribbon group of pioneer women were appointed to the next King County Court Grand Jury, including Louisa Boren Denny of Queen Anne.

## The 1886 Battle for Civil Rights for the Chinese

Tension in the western territories over the presence of the Chinese came to a head in Seattle in the

### John McGraw

Born in Maine to a lumber man and an Irish immigrant, John McGraw left home at age 14 with little formal schooling, but with ambition and common sense. After arriving in Seattle, in a single year he worked in a hotel and as a policeman, Seattle Police Chief, Harbor Master, Fire Warden and King County Sheriff. He played a key leadership role in peacefully quelling the attempt to drive the Chinese out in 1886 and 1887, but in that year's election was voted out as sheriff.

He began studying law at night and was admitted to the bar. He served as King County Sheriff another term, as well as the president of the First National Bank. In 1892, with the backing of the Masonic orders around the state, he was elected governor on the Republican ticket. Seattle went wild with jubilation and there was a torch-light parade. The second governor of the new state was one of them!

However, the governorship was very difficult for McGraw, since the financial crisis of 1893-96 hit full force during his term. The state was in a crisis and his personal finances were devastated by the end of his term. He settled on Queen Anne Hill and eventually prospered through real estate dealings. McGraw Street is named for this prominent early civic leader and community resident.

winter of 1886. A combination of racism and fear of competition on the job market led to a violent confrontation in Seattle between those defending the Chinese civil rights and those determined to deport them, as was done in Tacoma.

In Seattle the forces supporting the civil rights of the Chinese under the United States Constitution won the day. A major role was played by George Kinnear, who was put in charge of the citizens' volunteer militia, the Home Guard, which he successfully trained to maintain civil order. As a whole, those living on Queen Anne Hill supported the rights of the Chinese, such as young John McGraw, who as King County Sheriff played a major role in quelling the violent mob that attempted to forcefully drive out the Chinese people in Seattle.

One night David and Louisa Denny, who supported the Chinese, had a visit from a gang of men with guns looking for trouble. The men tramped through the mud and encircled the house, demanding that Denny, "the friend of the Chinese," come out. The mob focused their verbal attacks on the Dennys' employing Chinese houseservants and renting an area known as China Gardens (vicinity of the Seattle Opera House) to the Chinese. The Dennys stood their ground and the mob dispersed.

## THE LOYAL LEAGUE

In 1886 the Loyal League was formed by citizens of Washington Territory who supported the civil rights of the Chinese. Many of the men and women living in North Seattle were founding members of the organization. Their names appear here in acknowledgment and respect for their courage in going against the current of the times. In some cases names which the reader might expect to find here, e.g., Thomas and Hester Ward Mercer, are missing because those individuals were out of the area during this historic period. (Source: Cornelius Hanford, *Seattle and Environs*, Seattle: Pioneer Historical Publishing Co., 1924, 122.)

Clarence Bagley
Alice Mercer Bagley
Isaac N. Bigelow
Edmund M. Carr
S. D. Crockett
David T. Denny
Louisa Boren Denny
E. Inez Denny
Madge D. Denny
John B. Denny
Loretta Denny
Walter Graham
Elizabeth Graham
George Kinnear
John R. Kinnear
John H. McGraw
Edmond S. Meany
A. L. Palmer
Carrie V. Palmer
Ann M. Pontius
David Ross
Dillis B. Ward
Sarah I. Ward
Sarah B. Ward

*In 1887 George and Angie Simmons Kinnear deeded to the city 14 acres of land on a high bluff offering a grand view of Elliott Bay and the open waters of Puget Sound. Situated on Olympic Place, the park was made into the showplace of the Seattle Parks Department at the turn of the century. Eventually a tree from every state in the Union was planted in the park, and it was often referred to as the "Park of State." Since the 1920s the plantings have been greatly simplified, with the elaborate Victorian gardens replaced with rolling lawns and a few native shrubs. The park has been the frequent site of gatherings and concerts for over a century, and a favorite place from which to watch the Fourth of July fireworks display over Elliott Bay in the 1980s and 1990s. Courtesy Old Seattle Paperworks.*

Chapter Nine

# Queen Anne Town— The 1890s

by
Kay F. Reinartz, Ph.D.

Between 1880 and 1890, Seattle's population grew from 3,533 to 42,837, a twelvefold increase. Queen Anne resident Thomas Prosch oversaw the 1890 census and reports that the rate of growth greatly intensified as the decade wore on. For example, the 15,727 people counted in 1889 were more than double the count taken 12 months earlier.

*Polk's Seattle City Directory* for 1890 lends insight into the people making their homes on Queen Anne Hill at that time, although it provides only a partial picture in emphasizing men's occupations and overrepresenting the middle and upper classes. Of those registered with Polk's, professionals, merchants and semi-professionals make up 38 percent. Artisans account for 25 percent, with the construction trades dominating, in the following order: carpenter, plasterer, painter and bricklayer. Service jobs are listed for nine percent, and unskilled labor for 22 percent.

*By 1896 all of the south slope had been cleared of forest and a half century would pass before large trees once again graced the hillsides. The streets lay like ribbons across the land in the new subdivisions. The unpaved streets became a quagmire in wet weather, and the wheel ruts were turned into gullies as the rain water coursed down the hill. Here the Front Street cable car carries its passengers up the hill via Queen Anne Avenue. Courtesy Museum of History and Industry.*

In 1890 compensation for work varied, as this sample shows: waiter, $30/month; housemaid, $10/month; laborer, $2/day; farm hand, $26 - $30/month; milker, $30/month; teamster, with wagon and team, $6.50/day; mill worker, $3.50/day, $30/month. Many laboring and service jobs included room and board. Most workers were not members of unions at this time; however, pay scale records for union workers were definitely higher.

*Hanson & Hourn cash grocery on the northwest corner of Taylor Avenue and Florence Street, 1890. Taylor Avenue was an important thoroughfare and the best route to the top of the hill at this time. Courtesy Museum of History and Industry.*

## A HOUSE ON THE HILL

The price of Queen Anne view property shot up during the 1890s and never came down. The views from Queen Anne Hill already had a hefty price tag in 1890. One realtor advertised a "Queen Anne Town Tip-Top View" corner lot with 125-foot frontage as "view perfect and can't be shut out," for $2,760. Some prime view locations were very high, but there was, in fact, quite a range. With the old growth trees cut and no commercial or apartment highrises, almost any location offered an unobstructed view in 1890. Many of the "view" properties of that era lost their views within a few years as trees grew and other houses were built.

The following is a sampling of 1890 prices: a view lot in Kinnear's Addition, 60 x 120 ft., $850; a double corner lot in Nob Hill Addition, $1,000; a choice lot on Roy Street, $1,600; a corner lot on Temperance Street, 100 x 100 ft., $4,000; two blocks in Mercer's Addition, view, $3,000; a lot in Bigelow's Addition, $300 - $500; corner lot Temperance and Banner (1st Ave. W), $6,000. Inside lots (non-view) were cheaper, e.g. Denny's Third Addition, $280 a lot, and Denny's Fourth Addition, $160.

Comparison of Queen Anne lot prices to those in nearby districts is useful. In 1890, a Capitol Hill double view corner lot near Madison and Sixth Avenues cost $10,000; a corner view lot at Madison and Ninth, 60 x 120 feet, cost $5,500. In contrast, over in Ballard and in Dr. Kilbourne's Green Lake Addition 25 x 50 foot

### The Sarah B. Yesler Women's Hotel

A constant problem for women arriving alone in Seattle was "Where to stay?" In September of 1892 this problem was somewhat alleviated by the opening of the Sarah B. Yesler Women's Hotel on Temperance and Depot streets (Queen Anne Ave. and Denny Way) in Queen Anne Town. The new hotel management announced in the *Post-Intelligencer* that "the hotel was designed to meet the needs of women and girls coming to the city on business or pleasure, and for the business women of our city, many of whom by honesty and fidelity have enabled to push their way along most of the lines of industry in which a success involves tact, rapid movement, and faithfulness to detail."

The Sarah B. Yesler Hotel offered spacious quarters with wide halls, a pleasant dining room with good food, neat and airy chambers, a sewing room with a modern sewing machine, and large parlors beautifully furnished with a piano, for visiting and recreation. The cost was $4 to $5 per week.

house lots went for $100 to $150. B.F. Day was asking $200 to $300 for lots in his large subdivision just north of Fremont.

Terms of purchase varied, but long-term mortgages were almost nonexistent. Usually the seller asked for one-third to one-half down, cash, and the balance due within one to five years. A typical modest transaction for a $800 lot would be $350 cash down, and the balance due within two years, in regular payments at 8 percent interest.

The year-end new construction report in Seattle for 1890 shows that 151 new homes were built in the Queen Anne district, mostly on the lower south slope. Twenty percent of these new homes cost under $500; 15 percent, $500 to $999; 38 percent, $1,000 to $1,999; 24 percent, $2,000 to $3,999, and three percent, $4,000 to $10,000.

A sense of the cost and values of the times is found in an advertisement which offers the following on Queen Anne Hill for $18,000:

> *A large, fine residence and two lots, terrace and otherwise neatly improved. House has 10 rooms, is heated throughout with steam. A conveniently arranged stable for horses and a cow. This property is probably the best situated for view of any in that select neighborhood. Easy terms of payment.*

*In 1898 Charles Wilke built a comfortable, modest 4-bedroom home for his family at 1920 Second Avenue N., which was out in the country at that time. Wilke was a framing carpenter and put a large sign on the roof of his barn "Chas. Wilke, Carpenter and Builder." As land values rose Wilke cut his orchard, to the south of his house, and built more houses which he sold. Wilke built a number of houses in the eastern and central neighborhoods of Queen Anne. Members of the original Wilke family lived in the home until 1969. The old farm house was designated a historic landmark on the Federal Register, the house was in good repair and still home to the family in the 1990s. Courtesy University of Washington.*

## Much of the Hill Still Wooded

While the south side of the hill buzzed with construction, elsewhere the hill was a quiet, rural place, although no longer wilderness. On the north side a rough trail led from the Lake Union Road to Mount Pleasant Cemetery at the top of the hill. Around the north and west sides of the hill, near the top where it was flatter, homes were clustered in clearings in the woods. Lacking roads, residents made their way on paths through the trees.

Homemakers on the west side of the hill ordered groceries and household supplies from a little store at the foot of the hill. Twice a month a horse drawn two-wheeled cart hauled the goods up to a central point near Eighth Avenue W. and W. McGraw Street and hilltop dwellers walked down with wheelbarrows and small wagons to haul their things home.

In 1892 C.G. Carlson established a dairy farm on the west side of the hill, at the 1900 block of Tenth Avenue W. Carlson let his cattle graze freely and they often made their way through the woods to W. Highland Drive, where they could be seen contentedly munching in the gardens and on the carefully-tended lawns surrounding spanking-new grand houses.

This was not a unique situation, for livestock roamed freely all over the hill. Once again the citizenry pelted City Hall with petitions. In 1894 the Herd Laws were passed as general animal control laws requiring that all domestic animals, including dogs, be confined. Loose animals were incarcerated in the city barn, where the owner could collect the missing animal only after paying the poundman a fine of $6 for every 24 hours in the pound, and $2 if the owner caught up with the poundman and the offending animal before they reached the city barn.

People living on the northeast side of the hill walked down to the thriving Ross Station district to buy their groceries and dry goods at the Ross Marche Mercantile

*Queen Anne Hill, First Avenue N. at Garfield Street, March 1891. Courtesy University of Washington Special Collections.*

or Robinson's Hardware. The streetcar barn was at Third Avenue W. and Nickerson and it was only a short walk to Fremont, where the Interurban streetcar could be caught to downtown or the city of Ballard.

The children living on the north side of the hill loved to play around the canal, where the mills and boats provided endless entertainment. In the summer of 1895 the Marston boys—Clarence, Martin, Archie, and Charlie—took an adventurous trip on the canal. They fixed up an abandoned rowboat they found in the mud along the canal, and one sunny day in August they floated out toward Shilshole Bay on the morning tide. These lads, who had recently moved from the drylands of central Washington, looked with wonder at the throbbing mills with their great log booms as they floated past. The screeching of saws was replaced by the screeching of seagulls as they drifted out the mouth of Salmon Bay into the Sound. Throwing their fishing lines over the side—right into a school of trout, they later related—the boys proudly brought home eight good-sized fish for supper. It took them three hard hours of paddling against the tide to get back to Ross Station.

*The Bolcom Canal Lumber Company, Twelfth Avenue W. and Nickerson Street in the Ross Station district. In the 1890s, decades before the Lake Washington Ship Canal (1917), the natural waterway that drained the fresh waters of Lake Union into the salt waters of Salmon Bay was dredged to make it a navigable by shallow draught vessels. This waterway was known as the canal and soon was dotted with lumber mills. In the period 1890 - 1905 the following mills were in operation on the canal between Ross and the Ballard Bridge: Canal Mill, on Blewett Street (off Nickerson east of the Ballard Bridge); Central Lumber, Bertona Street; Gould Lumber, Nickerson; Loeb Mill, Ewing Place and Third Avenue W. (north of Nickerson); and Phoenix Lumber & Fuel, Nickerson. Courtesy Washington State Historical Society Museum, Asahel Curtis Collection.*

## The Temperance Movement on Queen Anne Hill

The Good Templars Lodge No. 6, formed in 1866, had waxed and waned over the years, with its membership varying from 300 to just the Dennys and a few friends. The membership had averaged 75 until the late 1880s when the national Temperance Movement came to Seattle with the new arrivals from "back east" and membership swelled accordingly. One of these newcomer activists was George Cotterill, who was Good Templars of Washington Secretary in 1889.

Evidence abounds of the strong temperance feelings of a substantial portion of the Queen Anne Town population. For example, in 1892 residents on the north side of the hill banded together with others living in Ross, Fremont, Edgewater, Latona and Green Lake on a simple petition to the city stating:

> *We, the undersigned citizens, . . lovers of sobriety, and being opposed to the "Liquor Traffic," do hereby earnestly beg of your honorable body and pray that you do not [sic] grant an extension of the saloon limits to, or within our borders.*

The petition carries 120 signatures. The saloon limits were not extended and the City Council received the following expression of appreciation:

> *The Lake Union Women's Christian Temperance Union [W.C.T.U.] hereby tender you their most hearty congratulations and thanks for your prompt action upon the "closing ordinance" for saloons.*
>
> *We can assure you that you have the approbation and most hearty "God speed" from the truest and best of the citizens for any and every righteous ordinance passed by your honorable body.*
>
> *We feel your own consciousness of well doing must add to your satisfaction, this with the assurance that you're in the approval of the most honorable, the truest, and sturdiest of the people should give you courage to stand bravely for the most righteous laws.*
>
> *You have our most fervent "God Bless you."*

## THE TEMPERANCE MOVEMENT GOES POLITICAL

In the late 1880s North Seattle residents began pressuring Seattle City Hall for public works and utilities, the need for which intensified as the population grew at a furious rate. Granted, a few streets were graded and improved; however, the residents continued to be without satisfactory water and sewer systems or fire protection. Queen Anne Town's leaders moved the community's needs to the political arena in the fall of 1890.

Under the name Prohibition Party, with temperance as their political rallying point, a slate of candidates was drawn up together with a party platform which directly challenged City Hall. While temperance people from all over Seattle participated, Queen Anne residents were at the top with Dillis B. Ward running for mayor and David T. Denny for city treasurer. George Cotterill served as Prohibition Party Secretary at the party convention on September 10, 1890.

Addressing the convention, Ward pointed out that in the past he had not believed in bringing politics into city affairs, but, he emphasized, "there had been errors in city government and they had to blame it on the party in power." Pinpointing exactly what the issues were, Ward cited the lack of a good water and sewer systems for Seattle's residential suburbs, including Queen Anne.

The Prohibitionists did not win the election of 1890, but they demonstrated that they had considerable strength in the city. The groundwork for this political party was laid by the Queen Anne pioneers.

## Community Members Continue Working Together for Improvements

Not discouraged by losing the election of 1890, on July 19, 1891, Queen Anne Town residents held a large outdoor mass meeting to work out a strategy for bringing the needs of the Queen Anne community to the attention of the Seattle City Council. With Dillis Ward as chairman and George Kinnear, secretary, committees were formed to pursue the areas of water, sewage, fire protection and improvement of Kinnear Park. When the community group met the next Saturday evening, they adopted the following resolution:

> *The people of Queen Anne Town feel that they have been paying their proportion of the expenses of public improvements in other parts of the city long enough to entitle them to some recognition at the hands of the council of their own needs.*

The citizens' committees were very effective and the concerns of Queen Anne received the attention of City Hall. The improvement of Kinnear Park was the first accomplishment. In the coming years community meetings were held on an irregular basis—usually in response to a specific issue. The favorite winter meeting place was the old streetcar house of the North Seattle electric rail line.

As the 1894 election drew near, the Prohibition Party put together a slate of candidates, and a platform that was a mix of Prohibition values and demand for utilities for the residential districts. Once again Queen Anne leaders were at the forefront and, while the Prohibition Party did not win the election, it did influence the winning party and City Hall sufficiently to heed the requests of the suburban districts, which were registered mainly through citizens' petitions.

## Fire Protection Improves

Beginning in 1888, Queen Anne residents, who had no fire station in the district, continuously petitioned City Hall for more than two decades for fire protection improvements. The citizens' efforts were finally rewarded, and in July 1890 the city put Queen Anne on the list of districts slated to receive a chemical fire-fighting wagon and a fire station, which was built on the corner of Banner and Lee streets in 1892. Ironically, the community had a fire station, but still no fire protection since the city did not equip the station.

*Queen Anne's first firehouse was built in 1893 at the corner of Banner and W. Lee streets (103 W. Lee St.), later the site of St. Anne School. Courtesy Last Resort Fire Dept.*

The summer of 1893 the situation reached somewhat of a crisis. First four houses went up in flames on "Bigelow Row" in July. On August 29th the home of prominent citizen C.E. Bowman, at the corner of Benjamin (Lee) and Poplar (2nd Ave. N.) streets, burned at midday. The *Post-Intelligencer* reports:

> *The family was at lunch, when a neighbor rushed to the door and yelled that the house was on fire. . . . A telephone alarm was sent in, but by the time the chemical engine reached the top of the long, steep hill, the building was all ablaze and beyond all hope of saving the slightest remnant of it. A line of hose was run up from an engine stationed at the end of Front street cable line, but the house was in cinders before this feat was accomplished.*
>
> *The question of having fire protection for this portion of the city has been discussed for a long time past, but nothing has been done, and every building that takes fire up there is almost sure to be destroyed before the department can reach it. Citizens of that part of the city have become indignant at the long delay in giving them an engine, and will urge immediate action upon the council.*

The Bowman fire was followed with a huge outcry from Queen Anne Hill, and the Lee Street Fire Station was finally equipped with a horse-drawn hose wagon, carrying 1,000 to 2,000 feet of hose on a reel, which could fight fires with water drawn from hydrants. For fires high on the hill above Bradley Street (W. Highland Dr.) the station was given a chemical wagon that carried a self-contained, pressurized firefighting system.

## Water Service on Queen Anne Hill

The public record contains more than 35 citizens' petitions submitted by Queen Anne residents between 1889 and 1899 requesting the provision of municipal water and sewer service. In 1891 all of North Seattle became a part of the Seattle Municipal Water System. Up to that time about a half dozen private water companies provided the community's water service. The terms of the water franchises given to private companies by the city varied greatly, and none of the franchises gave exclusive rights to lay pipe in any street. Thus, residences on a given street often were serviced by different water companies whose pipes often lay parallel underground.

The private water companies seldom put in fire hydrants and tended to use substandard equipment that was prone to failure. For example, when both of the water companies servicing the south side of the hill had simultaneous equipment failures in November 1889 Queen Anne Hill residents experienced a "water famine." What was expected to be a few days' inconvenience dragged on for half a month without water. The hill had few wells but people managed to "get by" on water from the pure springs that flowed from the hill in a number of locations.

The largest private water company was the Union Water System, incorporated in February 1882 by David Denny, Edgar Bryan, Walter Graham, Samuel Milham, James McCombs and William Graham. Initially, the company's water source was a large spring located in the vicinity of Fourth Avenue N. and Ward Street, later the location of the Queen Anne Pumping Station. The 80,000 gallons a day that flowed from the springs were soon insufficient.

Looking for an alternate source of water that could

### Water Systems on Queen Anne (ca. 1880s–1914)

| SYSTEM NAME | SOURCE | AREA SERVED | DATES | SPECIAL FEATURES |
|---|---|---|---|---|
| Griffith System | North side of QA Hill near Florentia & Evanston Sts. (now 3rd N.) | Most of Fremont. | 1888-1897 | Discontinued after building of Lake Washington Ship Canal. |
| Kinnear System | Spring in Block 4, Comstock Addition. | 12 lots in George Kinnear's Addition north of QA Drive. | 1888-still operating 1914 | Pure water filled 4-inch pipe at spring head in all seasons. |
| Maggs System | Spring between 6th & 7th N., Garfield & Galer Sts. | East to Lake Union, west to 2nd W. & Roy St., Elliott Bay & Battery St. | Aug. 26, 1889 until ca. 1911 | Franchise granted by Ord. #1188. Grading of Dexter Ave. made system inoperative. |
| Northern Pacific & Great Northern System | | Interbay | Abandoned between 1900-13 | |
| Peterson System #1 | | SW slope of QA between W. Galer & W. Prospect | 1890, abandoned between 1900-13 | Feb. 24, 1890 Ord. #1300 granted franchise to Nils Peterson. |
| Peterson System #2 | Spring in ravine near 3rd W. & Raye St. | A few houses on the north slope of QA Hill. | 1900-still operating 1914 | On a different Mr. Peterson's (not Nils) private land. |
| Union Water System | Spring near 4th N. & Ward St. (80,000 gal./day). Then, 348-ft. well at top of QA Hill. Then, pump from Lake Union. | | Incorporated Feb. 27, 1882 | One of the largest of the old systems. Incorporators included D.T. Denny. Used wooden bored pipe. |

*Source: The Seattle Municipal Water Plant, John Lamb, 1914.*

### Early Seattle Water Rates (1881 and 1887 Ordinances)

**Ordinance No. 253**, passed Nov. 12, 1881. Enfranchised Spring Hill Water Company. Rates set by this ordinance (per month except where noted):

- Family: $1.50
- Lot 60x120 ft.: $2/year
- Boat: 50¢/1st 1,000 gal.; 40¢/subsequent 1,000 gals.
- Hotel: $5/100 rooms; $1.50/additional 50 rooms
- Livery stable: $3
- Saloon: $1.50
- Restaurant: $2.50
- Barber shop: $2.50 with bath; $1 without bath
- Store: $1.50
- Factory: 30¢/1st 1,000 gal.; 20¢/subsequent 1,000 gals.
- Laundry: $4 if 300 gal./day or less; same proportion if more
- All others: 50¢/1st 1,000 gal.; 35¢/subsequent 1,000 gals.

**Ordinance No. 883**, passed Dec. 3, 1887. Rates set by this ordinance (per month except where noted):

Single Family Dwellings, household purposes:

| Size | 1 story | 2 stories | 3 stories | 4 stories | 5 stories |
|---|---|---|---|---|---|
| 1,000 sq. ft. or less | $1.50 | $1.50 | $1.75 | $2.00 | $2.25 |
| 1,000 to 1,500 sq. ft. | $1.75 | $2.00 | $2.25 | $2.50 | $2.75 |
| 1,500 to 2,000 sq. ft. | $2.25 | $2.50 | $2.75 | $3.00 | $3.25 |

Business Establishments:

- 40¢/100 cu. ft. for bills over $10
- 25¢ for bills over $50
- 20¢ for bills over $100.

*Source: The Seattle Municipal Water Plant, John Lamb, 1914.*

make use of gravitational flow, the company began drilling at the top of the hill and built a large wooden water tank as a reservoir. At 348 feet water was reached but, lacking any artesian force, the well had to be abandoned. The company then decided to use Lake Union as its water supply and pumped lake water to the tank at the top of the hill, where it flowed through wood pipes to the company's customers.

Between 1891 and 1895 the City of Seattle bought the Union Water Co. and most of the other private Queen Anne water companies. The city took over the existing pipelines, which were hopelessly clogged by the middle 1890s since most had used half-inch pipe. Only a few homes were served by private water companies into the twentieth century.

The hill community's water problems did not disappear when it became part of the municipal system. Almost every summer people living at the top of the hill had to haul water to their homes from late summer until the autumn rains came. In 1894 the city built a 100,000-gallon water tank at the top of the hill as a reservoir for the dry season to alleviate this problem.

## A Desperate Need for a Public Sewer System

In the 1880s each house in Queen Anne Town had its own outhouse over an open cesspool. Gray water from household cleaning, bathing and dishwashing was thrown on the ground, usually very close to the house. Naturally these activities quickly resulted in a high level of soil pollution. The problem was augmented by the rainy climate.

The growing sense of desperation that residents felt with increased population pressure after 1888 is expressed in a June 1, 1891, petition for a sewer along Temperance Street from Bradley Street (W. Highland Dr.) to the bay: "Your petitioners . . . and all others on [Temperance Street] are entirely without sewage facilities, and fear that with the coming of warm weather a great deal of sickness will result unless the relief they pray for is granted."

In the 1870s a simple public sewer system was built in the central part of Seattle. Primitive flush toilets were installed and the sewage was carried via wooden box sewers and dumped raw into one of three natural waterways, Elliott Bay, Lake Union and Lake Washington. This meant that 65 percent of the city's sewage went, untreated, into freshwater lakes. Most of the Queen Anne community's sewage floated into Lake Union.

In December 1885, the City of Seattle passed an ordinance requiring all inhabited property be connected to existing sewer lines and the citizens' demands for a comprehensive public sewer system was legitimized. The city, however, had not anticipated the huge population influx that began in 1888 and it was caught unprepared. The key problem of how to dispose of the enormous volume of sewage became the chief issue in Seattle in 1890 and Queen Anne residents played leading roles in the ensuing battle.

After the Great Fire of 1889, Lake Union rapidly deteriorated into a cesspool. Observing this, David, Louisa and John B. Denny drew up a protest petition which was strongly supported by their neighbors in North Seattle, 78 of whom put down their signatures. The text of the petition reads:

> *We the undersigned residents of the Northern part of the City of Seattle, having learned of a project to use Lake Union as a cess pool, and having also learned of a remonstrance having been presented to your Hon. Body against the use of the same lake for such purposes, even temporarily, we wish to hereby add our protest in strong terms, against any such action of the city authorities.*

The city engineer and health officer agreed that turning the city's lakes into open cess pools would be disastrous and began looking for a solution. Benezette Williams, a consulting engineer hired to solve the problem, developed a plan that divided the city into three districts: Lake Union, Intermediate and Central. The Lake Union district included sewer service for Queen Anne, however, the plan anticipated the early addition of a separate Queen Anne district. The Lake Union district would have a collection point at the south end of the lake with the sewage transported the shortest distance to the Sound via a tunnel.

Under the plan each district would have a complete system including 50-60 miles of eight-inch and larger mains, tunnels and outlets leading to the Sound. Untreated sewage would be dumped into the deep waters of Puget Sound with limited drainage into Lake Washington. Storm water would drain into the lakes.

## THE COMMUNITY FIGHTS THE DESTRUCTION OF LAKE UNION BY SEWAGE POLLUTION

When the Williams plan was made public but not acted upon, alternate plans were brought forth, all of which dumped quantities of raw sewage into the lakes. A public discussion ensued with 81-year-old Thomas Mercer and 60-year-old David Denny in the forefront of action. On July 21, 1890, a petition prepared by Mercer and Denny was presented to the mayor and Seattle Common Council.

In forceful language, Judge Thomas Mercer challenged the city plan under consideration whereby all of the sewage beginning at Bismark Street (Terry Ave.) and along Rollins (Westlake) to Lake Union would be collected in wooden box sewers and discharged directly into the lake. Moreover, all of the sewage generated on the thickly-populated south slope of Queen Anne was to go into the lake.

The petition includes an ugly, but realistic picture of what the plan would do to Lake Union. It would be transformed into "a murky, bubbling cesspool of deadly poisonous waters, discharging noxious gases and emitting indescribably repulsive odors" and, they concluded, "this in what was touted to be one of the city's most desirable residential districts."

The second point of the petition focuses on the fact that Lake Union was the main water supply for over 500 families in Queen Anne, Ross and Fremont served by the Union Water Co. The pollution of the lake waters with sewage would leave North Seattle residents without water and the Union Water Co., of which David Denny was a principal, would sustain a major business loss.

## THE LAKE UNION SEWAGE TUNNEL

Under pressure from powerful North Seattle leaders supported by the residents, as well as advice from the city engineer, it was decided to proceed immediately with the Williams plan.

By fall all was ready and excavation of the tunnel began simultaneously at Lombard (6th Ave. N.) and Republican streets and at the tunnel's Elliott Bay opening, which was at the foot of Mercer Street. The Lake Union tunneling went slowly, but smoothly. In contrast, the excavating effort from Elliott Bay was a nightmare. Mixed in the sand and gravel, which were easy to tunnel through, was a potpourri of clay, cut by seams of water bearing sand, boulders, plastic clay, silt and quicksand that flowed like water. The tunnel was timbered as the workmen progressed, but the walls collapsed again and again and one worker was killed. Finally, when the crew hit a pot hole that turned out to be an underground lake situated under Lombard and Mercer, the city engineer admitted defeat.

*Construction of a public sewer system was a dominant issue in the early 1890s. Begun in 1890, the Lake Union sewer tunnel channeled North Seattle's raw sewage into Elliott Bay rather than Lake Union. The project ran out of money and it was 1894 before the tunnel was completed. Within the context of the period, the decision to avoid dumping raw sewage in Lake Union reflected sensitivity to environmental issues. This man is resting on a wooden storm sewer outfall pipe draining into Lake Union. Courtesy Seattle Engineering Dept.*

The tunnel route from the bay was altered so that the outfall was at Republican Street and the tunnel then angled to follow the center line of Depot Street. This made it possible to extend the outfall into deep water entirely within the limits of public streets. The grade required placed some sections of the tunnel 150 feet underground. Even after the regrade of Denny Hill parts of the tunnel were still 50 feet underground. The tunnel was lined with locally-made vitrified brick.

Paying for the Lake Union sewage tunnel left no funds for the sewer mains the residential neighborhoods desperately needed. An editorial appearing in the *Post-Intelligencer* on March 8, 1891, expresses the mood on Queen Anne at the time:

> *The necessity for a sewer system has been felt by Seattle for several years. . . . residents near Lake Union, in Queen Anne Town, and the vicinity of the gulches further east are crying for aid, and the only response they get is from the doctor and the undertaker. The blank spaces are filling up and the accumulation of refuse matter of all kinds is reaching a point of extreme danger.*

As the debate over the cost of the sewer system dragged on, the city's sanitation deteriorated. In 1892, three-quarters of the area within the city limits and half of the population were reported without sewer service. The threat of a cholera epidemic pushed the city to

*Built in 1892, Decatur Terrace, David and Louisa Boren Denny's mansion at 512 Temperance Street, was the epitome of the Queen Anne style. In 1891 David Denny put all of his and Louisa's assets behind the public street railway because he felt it was extremely important that the rapidly growing city have a good public transportation system. By 1894 everything they had, including Decatur Terrace, went into the hands of receivers and the Dennys moved out to their old hunting cabin at Licton Springs to live with daughter Inez. David T. Denny died on November 25, 1903, at age 71, and Louisa died August 18, 1916, at age 90. They were buried at Oak Park Cemetery, a burial ground they had established with a gift of land. Oak Park is now part of Washelli Cemetery on Aurora Avenue N. Courtesy Queen Anne Historical Society.*

action in 1894. To finance the utility the city adopted the system whereby the city pays for the mains and the property owners are assessed the cost of installing the lateral sewer lines servicing their property.

## Electric Lights and Telephone Service

Electric lighting was introduced to Seattle in 1885 by the Seattle Electric Light Co. In 1889 the Pacific Electrical Company was formed and in 1891 the two companies consolidated under the name the Union Electric Co., which served North Seattle and Queen Anne until 1899.

Clarence Bagley reported that he paid $7.50 a month in 1890 for one-third the candle-power service that he enjoyed in 1929 for a mere $3 a month. Most of the mansions built in Queen Anne in the 1890s had incandescent lights.

Street lighting in the residential districts was haphazard in the 1880s and 1890s, with electric incandescent fixtures slowly replacing gas lamps piecemeal. There were no uniform standards in the design and performance of street-lighting fixtures.

Queen Anne residents, displaying their characteristic initiative, peppered City Hall with petitions requesting street lighting, with a total of 11 petitions being tendered between 1889 and 1894. Residents complained in 1890 that there was not a single street light along Republican Street from Temperance Street (Queen Anne Ave.) to the waterfront. In 1894 irate citizens reported that there was still not a single street light north of Bradley Street (W. Highland Dr.) and demanded the situation be rectified. In their petitions Queen Anne residents generally asked for 30 candle-power incandescent and arc lights. These petitions were effective and Queen Anne was proud of being one of the best-lit districts at night by the late 1890s.

The Sunset Telephone Company opened its first office in Seattle in 1884. By 1890 the system served the entire city. Rates were set at $5 for a business and $3.25 for a private residence per month, by city ordinance in 1894. The system gradually expanded and in 1912 it absorbed the Independent Telephone Co., Sunset's only competition. By 1916 there was a Telephone Exchange Building on Garfield Street at Fourth Avenue W. on Queen Anne Hill, one of eight such buildings in the city.

*Farm Street was so named in the 1880s because it led from Seattle to a district of small farms overlooking Lake Union. The road's name was changed to Seventh Avenue N. around 1895. In a replatting of the Denny & Hoyt Addition in 1888, Dr. Kilbourne, a principal in the Griffith Co., named the northern section of Farm Street Aurora for his hometown of Aurora, Illinois. Eventually the entire roadway became known as Aurora Avenue. This photo shows old Farm Street about 1899. Courtesy Museum of History and Industry.*

## A Bicycle Built for Two

The arrival of the first pneumatic-tired safety bicycle in Seattle early in 1893 touched off a bicycling craze that lasted for a decade and had a noticeable impact on the city. Queen Anne Hill resident George Cotterill, a young engineer who was City Engineer Reginald Thompson's assistant, was at the center of the bicycling movement.

Cotterill and the

## George F. Cotterill

Cotterill played a leading role in many Seattle public works, including securing the Cedar River water supply system for Seattle, designing and building the initial municipal sewer system, platting the Seattle harbor, and designing and improving the streets and parks system.

Cotterill spent years in public office, serving as State Irrigation Commissioner 1903-05; State Senator, 1907-11; Mayor of Seattle, 1912-14; Chief Engineer, Washington State Department of Highways, 1916-19; Port of Seattle Commissioner, 1922-34. He began his political career as a Republican, was a Prohibitionist in the years 1890-96, and became a Democrat the rest of his life.

George F. Cotterill was platting the west slope of Queen Anne Hill in the 1890s for the city when he found the site for his home, which he built in 1910 at 2501 Westview Drive. The house is built in the early Northwest style and has a sweeping view of Puget Sound and the Olympic Range. The nine-room house is sheathed in rough sawn cedar. The home is protected from alteration by a Seattle Historic Landmark designation.

Cotterill was married to Cora R. Gormley of Seattle, with whom he raised two adopted children. Cora died in 1943, and George at age 92 in 1957.

Queen City Bicycling Club worked hard for street improvements by petitioning and lobbying. In 1896 the city's several bicycle clubs united to build bicycle paths. Queen Anne and Magnolia hills held much appeal for the bicyclists because of the grand views. One of the bicycle paths followed the route of Olympic Place to the Kinnear Park viewpoint. Another bicycle path was built around the east side of Queen Anne Hill beginning at Mercer Street and circling around to Fremont where it followed the canal, then turned south into Smith Cove and crossed over to Magnolia on the Grand Boulevard Bridge (W. Dravus St.). From there, another path followed the pioneer wagon road to Magnolia Bluff.

The bicycle path network was designed, financed, built and maintained by Queen City Good Roads Club, with the city providing additional financial support with funds collected for bicycle licenses. Queen Anne Hill became a focus of the club's work, partially because of the central role that George Cotterill played in the club leadership. Cotterill was the chairman of the Paths Committee. As a club volunteer he designed, surveyed, laid out, and supervised the construction of 25 miles of bicycle paths. These paths eventually became the basis of Seattle's boulevard system built later for automobiles. For example, Thorndyke Avenue and Magnolia Boulevard follow routes first laid down for bicyclists.

*Street construction and public utilities installation work around the turn of the century. Courtesy University of Washington Special Collections.*

Chapter Ten

# Citizens Build a Good Community—1900–1929

by
Kay F. Reinartz, Ph.D.

In the period following statehood, 1889, Washington experienced its own version of the great American westward movement. In three decades the number of people living in the state increased fifteen fold. In 1900 the state population was 518,013, and in 1910 it was 1,141,990. This 120 percent rate of increase was six times the national average.

Seattle was the fastest growing place in Washington. Its population increased from 42,837 in 1890 to 237,194 in 1910. Seattle's population in 1910 was about half of the population of the entire state only 20 years earlier. For the Puget Sound region the first decades of the twentieth century were a time of amazing economic, social and political transformation. Tens of thousands of foreign born immigrants poured into the state, along with people from the midwest, old south and Atlantic seaboard.

*Streetcar No. 312 traveling down Queen Anne Avenue at Prospect Street, circa 1905. This streetcar, which navigated the steepest street in Seattle, became popularly known as the Counterbalance. The hill continues to be called the Counterbalance more than half a century after the counterbalance streetcar went out of service. Courtesy Queen Anne Historical Society.*

Washington historian and regionalist Lancaster Pollard's population studies of this period reveal that by 1910 the ratio of newcomers to the established population was greater in Washington communities than anywhere else in the United States. Pollard's research also shows that in many communities the flood of newcomers submerged the previously established community culture. Ballard, Queen Anne's neighboring community to the north, was one such community. There the influx of Scandinavian immigrants who came in after 1900 essentially obliterated the established culture, which was basically east coast Yankee.

## IMMIGRANTS FIND HOMES ON THE HILL

Analysis of the population information from the 1900, 1910 and 1920 federal census shows that the Queen Anne community did not attract foreign-born immigrants at the same rate as Ballard and many other King County communities. The below discussion is based on numbers derived from a hand tabulation of census tracts for Ward Eight, which encompasses the Queen Anne district. The Interbay district is not included.

In 1900 Washington's population was 23 percent foreign-born while the population of Queen Anne was just 20 percent foreign born. Only fourteen percent of these immigrants originated from non-English-speaking countries. The flood of immigrants from abroad peaked around 1910 when the state census showed that 33 percent of Washington residents were foreign-born immigrants. At this date 25 percent of those living on Queen Anne were foreign-born. By 1920 immigrants accounted for only 25 percent of the state population and ten percent of Queen Anne's population. Only six percent of these were from non-English-speaking origins.

When compared to other King County communities, Queen Anne's immigrant population is remarkable for the high proportion of immigrants from English-speaking countries, specifically England and Canada. In both 1900 and 1920, 40 percent of all immigrants originated from these two countries and constitute the largest cultural group. In 1910, the peak of Scandinavian immigration to the Northwest, only 28 percent of the immigrants on Queen Anne claimed England or Canada as their homeland. Those with Scandinavian origins dominated in 1910 and were second to Anglo-Saxon in all of the census.

Living on the west side of the hill in the 1920s at Second W. and W. Howe St., Stuart Prestrud recalls his block had Jensens, Sandstroms, Olsens and Sundes. The vast majority of immigrants were young single people.

### English and Canadian Immigrants Come to Queen Anne Hill— The Criddle Family

Fredrick P. Criddle's family was among those from England and Canada which came to the community around the turn of the century. Fred's mother, Isabella Powell, came from New Brunswick, where her Tory ancestors had gone after the American Revolution. Fred's father, William J. Criddle, was born in Cornwall. Times were hard in England in the 1880s and Fredrick Criddle's grandfather, Fredrick J., who was a carpenter, decided to come to the states with his partner, also a carpenter.

Leaving their families in the Old Country, in June 1889 the pair was working in Connecticut. One evening, as they were reading the newspaper after dinner at their boarding house, William turned to his friend and said, "See that huge fire that they had in Seattle?" The other replied, "Yes, and there will be a building boom out there. Let's go out." The following Friday they drew their pay, packed up their tools and few belongings, and caught the train for Seattle. "Grandpa always told the children." Fred recalls, that "Denny Hill was still smoking when I got here!" In fact, there were no fire hydrants on Denny Hill in 1889 and the fire was left to burn itself out.

After two years of working and sharing a room in a boarding house, the two men had established themselves sufficiently to send for their wives and children, which included seven Criddles. After renting a little house on Valley Street, just off Taylor Avenue N., Criddle built his family a home near the intersection of Elliott Way and Mercer Place. Large old maple trees found at that place once surrounded the Criddle house.

## COMMUNITY RESIDENTS PREDOMINANTLY NEW ENGLANDERS AND MIDWESTERNERS

The census shows that not only were the majority of Queen Anne residents American-born, but they came from a handful of states. In 1900, 40 percent came

*Anne Craig displays her pet parrot and her garden at 200 Florentia Street in 1915. Annie and her husband Charles bought the lot and built their home around 1897, after having rented a house at 232 First Avenue for several years. Charles, who worked as a tallyman for the Stetson and Post Lumber Co., died in 1899. Left to support her family, Annie began taking in laundry. By 1909 she had formed the Flatow Laundry Co. with her neighbor Isador Flatow. Annie Craig was vice president and Flatow president of the Belltown-based enterprise. It is most likely that Craig managed the laundry while Flatow oversaw the pick-up and delivery end of the business. Courtesy Paul Dorpat.*

from five states, which were, in descending order of representation: New York, Illinois, Wisconsin, Ohio and Pennsylvania. In 1910, 46 percent of the community's adults originated from seven home states: Washington, Illinois, Minnesota, New York, Ohio, Iowa, Wisconsin and Nebraska. Reflecting the maturing of the children of the pioneers, those born in Washington were the largest group for the first time on record in 1910, when they comprised ten percent of the whole. Census patterns for places of origin changed very little from 1900 to 1920.

## THE QUEEN ANNE COMMUNITY, MYTH AND REALITY

From the 1890s Queen Anne Hill had a reputation of being a community of grand houses. In fact, elaborate mansions represented only a small part of the community's residences. For each mansion built there were hundreds of attractive middle-class houses, and modest, yet neat and charming, laborers' bungalows and cottages. The census for 1900, 1910 and 1920 verify that the Queen Anne community was composed, not of wealthy lumber and land barons, but "average" people, who had begun simply and through hard work, careful management and perseverance, prospered. They achieved a comfortable home and a good education for their children, in a safe and caring community which they helped build.

The census data for 1900, 1910 and 1920 reveals that through the period more Queen Anne residents worked as laborers than any other occupation, with one man out of every three being a laborer. Artisans rank second, with the building trades dominating, e.g. carpenter, plasterer, bricklayer and painter. Approximately one out of every five adults worked as an artisan, a percentage that remained constant for 30 years.

The only occupation to show substantial growth between 1900 and 1920 is business. Business occupations such as merchant, clerk, sales, bookkeeping and general office work, grew from 18 percent of the total to 31 percent—a 72 percent increase. This noteworthy change in the occupations of community residents is reflected in small drops in a variety of other occupations such as farming, services, artist and musician. By 1920 the number of government workers had almost doubled from 1900 but was still only five percent of the total.

The Queen Anne community has had a reputation in the twentieth century for being the home of a high proportion of professionals. From 1900 to 1920, professionals consistently accounted for only ten percent of the total occupations.

## A COMMUNITY OF YOUNG PEOPLE

In 1900 the population was young with two out of every five residents being under the age of 30. One out of every four residents was a young adult between

16 and 30 and only one resident in ten was more than 50 years old. The dominance of youth intensified in 1910 when three out of every five residents were less than 30 years of age.

In 1900 the typical household size was two to nine people, with the average being 4.4. Two out of three residents rented their home rather than owned it. Nine percent of the households were headed by a woman. One out of seven households took in boarders, who rented rooms and took their meals with the family. Six percent of the community residents reported that they were boarders. Families were large, typically with four or five children under age 16.

In 1910, at the height of the immigration period, households on Queen Anne were slightly smaller, and 14 percent were headed by women. There were fewer children under 16. They accounted for only 22 percent of the total population in 1910, as compared to 37 percent in 1900.

## A Home of One's Own

The preponderance of young married couples and unestablished newcomers is reflected in the fact that in 1910, 82 percent rented their homes, as compared to 62 percent in 1900. In addition, 28 percent of households took in boarders. It was not uncommon to have three, four or more children sleep in one room in order to be able to rent out extra bedrooms.

The 1920 census shows that the population had noticeably changed. It appears that the dramatic influx of young single people had leveled off and the population picture as a whole was similar to that in 1900, with two notable exceptions: a) home-ownership was at the highest level to date with half of the households now owning the house in which they lived; and b) people over 50 were becoming more a significant population factor, with 17.4 percent of the people belonging to this age group.

## A Trolley to the Hilltop

The flood of newcomers to Queen Anne naturally built their homes progressively higher up the hill. Because the top of the hill is relatively flat, construction leapt from the lower areas to the top around 1900, leaving a belt of more difficult construction sites to be developed later. This pattern, however, left the early homeowners at the top of the hill without transportation down to the city.

*Alfred Hoglund, who eventually made his home on a 5-acre tract on the north side of the hill, like many other immigrants from Scandinavia, found the Northwest much to his liking. He declared that in many ways "It was like the Old Country!" Young Hoglund was proud of his good team, which allowed him to earn a living as a teamster. Courtesy Maxine J. Schuetz.*

A citizens' committee formed in 1902 dedicated itself to bringing public transportation to the top of the hill. Members carefully analyzed the grades involved and concluded that the streetcar lines had to travel from Eighth and Westlake avenues north up the "easy grade" on the east side of the hill, to Fifth Avenue N. and Newton Street. An alternate route via Kinnear Park was also deemed feasible. A counterbalance system to get the streetcar up Queen Anne Avenue was also recommended in the plan which was presented to the Seattle City Council.

The logic of the plan, coupled with the eloquence of the spokesmen, resulted in the eventual building of both streetcar lines and the counterbalance. These trolley lines were extremely important at the time, for they established a thoroughfare from the business center of Seattle to the existing and potential homesites on the upper reaches of the hill, as well "to all the northern part of the city," as the citizens' resolution states.

## Queen Anne Boulevard

Enjoying success in their quest for thoroughfares, in 1906 the Queen Anne committee appeared before the Seattle Parks Board proposing the development of a scenic route at the top of the hill to be called Queen Anne Boulevard. At this time John Clise was a member of the Parks Board and received support for the idea from other Queen Anne residents on the board, J.M. Frink and George Cotterill. In addition, John McGraw appeared before the Parks Board and spoke on behalf of the proposed route.

The Seattle Parks Board opposed the idea of the boulevard, since it was not a part of the new Olmsted Plan for Seattle's boulevard and parkway system. The proposed route followed ordinary city streets, which did not meet the 150 foot minimum width called for by the Olmsted Plan to provide space for tree plantings and other amenities. The Parks Board finally agreed to the plan with the provision that the community pay some of the costs of development of the scenic route.

Constructed between 1911 and 1916, the boulevard was the only route by which commercial vehicles could reach certain sections of Queen Anne Hill. Queen Anne residents were happy with the boulevard for a time, but by the 1930s the complaints began pouring in and have not stopped since: "maturing trees are blocking the views; tree roots are buckling the sidewalks; and the sewer lines are clogged by roots." The Parks Dept. understood that many of the problems arose from the "cutting of corners" at the beginning and the failure to follow the standards established for boulevard throughout the city. For decades to come Queen Anne Boulevard would be a headache for the city parks and engineering departments.

## The West and North Slopes are Developed

The Panic of 1893 caused only a brief pause in the real estate market in Seattle's residential suburbs. Between 1899 and 1918, 25 subdivisions were platted for Queen Anne Hill.

While Queen Anne Hill's south slope was filling up, there were large undeveloped tracts on the north side of the hill facing Phinney Ridge and Salmon Bay. In 1926 Queen Anne Park was subdivided. Looking back to that era George Knutsen, whose family lived nearby, recalls, "The north side of Queen Anne Hill was interesting in those days. A lot of construction and activity of a growing district. It was a neighborhood of sawmill workers." The concrete streets of the Queen Anne Park subdivision had just been poured when the Great Depression hit. The developer went broke and the project was taken over by others.

*The scenic route called Queen Anne Boulevard winds around the crest of Queen Anne Hill nearly 3½ miles, providing grand views in all directions. Called a boulevard, the route follows various streets, including W. Highland Drive, Bigelow Avenue N. and W. Raye St. The route includes several retaining walls, the best known being the Wilcox Wall at Eighth Avenue W. and W. Highland Drive, built in 1909. Doris McClure Linkletter, whose family lived nearby on Eighth Avenue W. remembers going for walks as a child with her father up the long stairway to W. Highland Drive. She, like many youngsters before and since, marveled at the wall, which appeared to be constructed of wood, for the surface had wood grain and knot holes, yet was as hard as the concrete sidewalk. Illustration by Jim Stevenson. Courtesy Queen Anne Historical Society.*

*Looking northeast from corner of 10th and Lee Street May 1903. The west side of Queen Anne Hill continued to be rural with small farms, typically on five acres, connected by ungraded country lanes. Courtesy Olmsted Associates, Inc., Seattle Municipal Archives.*

Dozens of houses stood half-finished for years.

The new subdivisions on the north and west slopes were quickly dotted with new houses, which the proud owners all too frequently were forced to travel through mud or dust in season to reach. So aggravating were the dirt streets that the planking of Tenth Avenue W. and McGraw Street in 1902 triggered a mini building boom.

The conditions were similar on other parts of the hill which had been occupied longer, with the exception of the south slope. Thanks to persistent citizen action in the 1880s and 1890s, south slope dwellers enjoyed the amenities of graded and planked roads and sidewalks, as well as access to the municipal water and sewage systems.

## The Queen Anne Improvement Clubs

Continuing the tradition firmly established in the 1890s by Dillis B. Ward, George Kinnear, Judge Eben and others of organizing community pressure on Seattle City Hall for improvements desired by Queen Anne residents, the Queen Anne Improvement Club was formed around 1901 with the expressed mission of "bringing the needs of the Queen Anne Community before the Seattle City Council."

People living all over Queen Anne Hill developed a strong sense of neighborhood early on. Certainly the hilly topography coupled with the fact that everyone traveled by foot or by public transportation brought neighbors into frequent contact which encouraged the formation of friendships and mutual interests. Many of

### The Knutsen Dairy — Good Norwegian Quality

In 1902 Knute Knutsen and his wife Sigrid Rongve Knutsen immigrated from Voss, Norway to Washington, making their home in Georgetown. In the next ten years several children were born and the young couple worked hard and saved. In 1911 they moved to Queen Anne Hill, making their home at Fourth Avenue W. and Fulton Street. Knutsen rented a barn at Third Avenue W. and Armour Street and began dealing in cattle, for which there was quite a demand at that time when many people kept their own cow.

As the Herd Laws curtailed cattle grazing, the demand for milk increased and the Knutsens started a dairy. They bought the milk from farmers in the Duwamish and White river valleys, who sent the tall cans into Seattle fresh each morning on the Interurban electric train. The Knutsens picked up the milk at the Interurban Station on Spokane Street and delivered it to homes on the hill six days a week by horse-drawn wagon. The milk was kept cool with wet burlap jackets and ice placed around the cans. The Knutsens quickly established a reputation for pure, raw milk and cream of "good Norwegian quality," and always received top rating from the Seattle City Health Inspector.

Later the Knutsens kept their own dairy herd, grazing the cows in pasture close to the barns at Third Avenue W. For many years the dairy prospered on Queen Anne, with the only competition coming from Harry Gould's dairy located at Fourth Avenue W. and Raye Street. Gould, who had made a stake prospecting for gold in the Alaskan fields, called his business the Golden West Dairy. Later more competition came from Apex Dairy on Queen Anne Avenue and W. Dravus Street, and Vitamilk at the foot of the north slope of Queen Anne Hill.

Knute Knutsen and son William eventually moved the dairy to Bothell, were they served Seattle until 1990.

*At the beginning of the 1920s the northwest side of Queen Anne Hill, in the vicinity of Mount Pleasant Cemetery, called Queen Anne Park, was still woods and many north slope dwellers cut their Christmas trees there. Wolf Creek ravine is located on the right. The Mayfair Land Company's 30-acre subdivision, one of the last major land development ventures on the hill, was located in this area. The columes of smoke are from the sawmills along the canal. Courtesy Washington State Historical Society.*

the neighborhoods formed their own local improvement clubs. These neighborhood improvement clubs were often led by women who were more persistent in pursuing local improvements than the men, whose work and interests took them away from the home neighborhood.

The improvements that initially concerned the clubs were not glamorous. They began with the basics: graded and paved streets and sidewalks; fire protection; sufficient water mains to support fire fighting; street lights; and sewer mains. Normally the clubs worked for these improvements through the established systems of citizens' petitions and letters, and community delegations appearing at Seattle City Council meetings to speak on behalf of community interests.

One of the first accomplishments of the Queen Anne Community Club was the paving of eight blocks of dirt road on the north side of the hill around 1905.

As basic utilities and public works improvements were achieved, the improvement clubs shifted their focus to the development and maintenance of parks, playgrounds and tennis courts, as well as community celebrations and festivals. Often the improvement clubs undertook extensive fundraising to pay for special projects, such as additional books for the community library or play equipment for the children's playground. In the 1920s the improvement clubs folded or were absorbed into the Queen Anne Community Club.

*The flat top of the hill attracted people and by 1895 there were sufficient children for the Seattle School District to build West Queen Anne School on Fifth Avenue W. between Galer and Lee Streets. The native forest had been destroyed in the development process and the small trees seen here were planted by the homeowners who found their stark streets most disagreeable. Courtesy Washington State Historical Society.*

## Prosperity, Petitioning, Paving and Plumbing

The city engineer's records show few street and utilities improvements

*Street construction on Queen Anne Avenue, 1902. The street is being expanded to include travel lanes on both sides of the trolley tracks. Note the difference between the right lane, which is graded, and the left lane, which has had only minimal grading. Wooden sidewalks were typically eight feet wide. Courtesy Queen Anne Historical Society.*

for Queen Anne in the first years of the twentieth century. This situation changed because of two factors. First, the city-wide adoption of the Local Improvement District (LID) system for building utilities, which places the cost of improvements on the property owners. The second, and most critical factor, was leadership provided by the neighborhood improvement clubs.

In 1907 Queen Anne's neighborhoods began to hum with the work of street paving and the laying of sewer and water mains. A quick analysis of the record provides insight into geographic focus of the activities. The 19 separate improvements completed in 1907—street grading and paving, water mains and hydrants, and lateral sewer lines principally—concentrated on First through Fifth avenues north. In 1908 the focus shifted to Mercer and Westlake.

By 1909 the Queen Anne improvement program had worked up a real head of steam. More than 31 improvements were completed on several parts of the hill, especially in the Ross district and Rodgers Park area, as well as Galer, Republican and Fourth N. Between 1907 to 1914 the community received hundreds of miles of sewer lines, water mains and paved streets.

As the son of the Chief Inspector of the Seattle Water Dept., Charles H. Jenner, J. Kirkham Jenner had a keen interest in the municipal water system. He recalls that the water main running in front of their Nob Hill home in 1925 "was made of wood, coopered from staves like a barrel and bound by iron rings every several inches." Ten-year-old Kirk and the other neighborhood children loved to watch the Water Dept. crew repair leaks. The men would first dig up the street and find the leak, then, Kirk recalls, "they would sit around the excavation, carving little wedges of wood with their pocket knives" which they pounded into the leaking area. The wedges swelled with the moisture and made a permanent seal.

Street improvements varied with the terrain. Streets at the top of the hill were macadamized, while those around the edges of the hill, particularly on the west and north sides, were simply graded dirt. In some cases planking was placed over the dirt. Frequently, dirt streets had pedestrian plank walks across the street at the intersection to keep pedestrian's feet out of the mud. In 1914 the engineering department stopped using planking entirely in favor of macadam and concrete surfacing. On ordinary side streets sidewalks were usually two-plank wide paths running alongside the road. By the 1920s all sidewalks were made of concrete, as were curbs.

Between 1915 and 1930, a total of 143 separate projects brought good quality paved streets, water mains, sewers and sidewalks to most parts of the hill. By comparison, utilities construction work has continued on a greatly diminished schedule throughout the rest of the century.

Gradually electrical and telephone wires have been put underground with this improvement beginning on the south slope and working around to the north side.

In 1900 the Queen Anne post office was opened on Queen Anne Avenue between Republican and Harrison.

## Streetcar Barns, Substations, and Water Towers

From early in the twentieth century the City of Seattle maintained a number of public utilities in the Queen

## Observatory Park

The first Queen Anne standpipe under construction in 1901. The water tower was built at First Avenue N. and Lee Street. Located literally at the top of Queen Anne Hill, the 60-foot tank was encircled by a spiral stairway leading to the roof from which there was a grand view. In May 1902 the standpipe area was designated Observatory Park and the public was free to ascend the stair to enjoy the view. In 1904 a second tank was built.

From the days of the Mercers and Dennys, people living on Queen Anne Hill have noted that sound often carries very well up the hill, undoubtedly because of the presence of large surrounding bodies of water. In 1919 Florence Spaulding, a 20-year-old University of Washington student, wrote to a friend of watching and hearing the jubilant Armistice Day celebration, marking the end of World War I, from Observatory Park. She wrote "Because of the flu Mother wouldn't let me go to town, but we climbed the big water tower to see the fireworks, and we could actually hear the people downtown hollering." By the time Florence's son Carl Nordstrom was old enough to enjoy climbing to the top of the towers for the view, Observatory Park was closed (1934). *Courtesy Seattle Water Department.*

Anne community area including the Aloha Street Substation, the 365 Ward Street Pumping Station and the Animal Control Center on Elliott Avenue. Nearby in Interbay is the Salmon Bay Fishermen's Terminal, Port of Seattle. In 1917 there were streetcar barns at 309 W. Ewing and Nickerson at Third Avenue W. The Municipal Street Railway Maintenance Shop was at Aloha Street and Dexter Avenue. Puget Sound Traction Light and Power Station was at Fifth Avenue N. and Mercer.

*Because the south side of the hill had been developed early, by the 1920s tree lined avenues and mature shrubs gave a grace to the neighborhoods not available on the other sides of the hill. Courtesy Washington State Historical Society, Asahel Curtis Collection.*

## Fire Protection Improves

One of the Queen Anne Improvement Club's crowning achievements was the securing of adequate fire protection between 1900 and 1929. The steady laying down of water mains and installation of fire hydrants at frequent intervals, as well as the steady water pressure provided by the Queen Anne water tower, greatly aided effective firefighting. After 1910 noticeably fewer homes were reduced to cinders in minutes as owners stood helplessly watching.

In 1900 the community had a single fire station at First Avenue W. and Lee Street. Old Chemical Wagon No. 3 was replaced in 1902 with a combination hose and chemical wagon, which was a converted 1890 Holloway chemical wagon. A new fire station was built for this equipment directly south of the water towers on Lee Street.

In 1903 the new two-story Fifth Avenue W. Fire Station opened at 1520 Fifth W. Late that year the two-

*Engine House No. 8, 1417 Warren Avenue next to the Queen Anne standpipe, had sleeping quarters upstairs for the firemen and room for two gleaming fire wagons. Courtesy Last Resort Fire Department.*

bay station got a brand new shiny American Metropolitan 550 gallon-per-minute steam pumper and the unit's name was changed to Engine Company No. 8. This was a major improvement since the steam engine could pump water at greater pressure than that available at the hydrant.

In 1908 Queen Anne received two new fire stations. The Fourth Avenue N. Station, at Fourth Avenue N. and Thomas Street in lower east Queen Anne, was built to replace the firehouse that would be razed during the Denny Regrade. Temporarily closed from 1921 to 1924, this station served as the Fire Alarm Office from 1924 to 1960. It was razed in 1961 to build the Space Needle.

The Warren Avenue Fire Station was built in 1908 at 1417 Warren Avenue N. Engine Company 8 moved to this station and a few months later Ladder Company No. 6 moved into the Fifth Avenue W. Fire Station. Receiving the ladder company was a "feather in the Queen Anne Improvement Club's cap," since there were only three ladder companies in all of Seattle at that time. The ladder company engine was a Seagrave city service ladder truck with two 35-gallon soda-acid chemical tanks and hose reels. All of the ladders were ground ladders and the longest could be extended 45 feet. Late in 1909 the second bay in the Fifth Avenue W. Station was filled by Hose Company No. 24, which had been used at the Alaska Yukon Pacific Exposition that summer.

Within minutes of the fire alarm sounding, the fire station bays would burst open and the big horses dashed out, hooves pounding the cobblestones as they went flying down the street to the blaze. Spike and Frank provided the horse power at the Fifth Avenue W. station in the 1910s. The brown and black pair were well known to the neighborhood children, who loved to hang around the station petting the horses, feeding them sugar lumps and staring in awe at the big red engines, which the firemen were always polishing. Sometimes the firemen let the children sit in the driver's seat for just a moment, but only a moment. "We might be called to a fire any minute!" they were told.

Queen Anne had advanced from one to four fire stations in less than a decade. The next change was the replacement of horse-drawn equipment with motorized trucks. All of the firemen and the neighborhood were out on the street on November 14, 1914 to see the splendid new Gorham-Seagrave 800 pumper truck drive up to the Warren Avenue Fire Station. With built-in hose storage the need for a separate hose wagon was eliminated.

With the shift to motorized equipment everyone was concerned with the fate of Spike and Frank. Spike retired to a ranch in Bothell, where he was cared for by a fireman's father, and Frank, leaving his old partner-in-harness, retired to the grassy fields of the Sulphur Springs Point resort on Lake Sammamish. Reports were that whenever either horse heard an alarm his ears perked up and he expectantly ran to the barn—undoubtedly looking for his engine.

In 1924 the Lee Street station got a new Seagrave 800 with a 40-gallon soda-acid chemical tank. The Fifth Avenue W. station was sent a 1913 Seagrave city service ladder truck that had been used in downtown Seattle.

William C. Hunter, who grew up in the Ross district in the 1920s, tells us about the impression the motorized fire engine made upon the children in his neighborhood:

> *The main arterial thoroughfare from upper Queen Anne was Third Ave. West. Down this street came the fire engines from upper Queen Anne. For roughly eight blocks there were no major intersections, so the fire engines . . . roared along without slowing until they reached Dravus St. For nearly two blocks before the junction with traffic, Third West was flanked on the east side with high cement bulkheads, which bounced the sound of the approaching fire truck, amplified it, and gave loud warning to the entire neighborhood west of the bulkheads that a fire truck was coming!*

*We children stopped our play, and ran to get a glimpse of the great red truck. It was a sight and a sound to behold as the driver reduced his speed. That added to the terror and fascination of the scene. The big engine belched and backfired, and thundered on its way. The siren was one of the old fashioned ones which had to be hand cranked. The same man who cranked the siren pulled the cord on the bell, so as the big engine rolled by, it was roaring, thundering, wailing and clanging.*

*Some of the neighborhood children circulated the rumor—which I think they really believed—that it was those men on the red truck who started fires! They regarded the noisy fire truck as a sort of demonic invasion from Hell, to set fire to some home in our neighborhood. I am not sure that I ever believed what they told me, but I will admit that the rumor added just a tinge of fear to my fascination with fire trucks.*

## A Legacy of Parks Grace and Enrich the Community

Kinnear Park was given to the community by George and Angie Simmons Kinnear in 1889. It was only the first of many parks that have been given to the community by Queen Anne citizens. These include Franklin Playground and Kerry Park.

In the twentieth century, midway down the south slope of Queen Anne Hill an ample spring gushed forth. George Kinnear had piped this spring in the 1880s as the water supply for his home and gardens, as well as Delamar, his nearby guest house. In 1904, wishing to protect the spring and the storage tank beside it from private and street development, the Kinnears deeded the site to the City of Seattle "as a park forever," reserving the right to "maintain or rebuild any part of the system."

This was named **Franklin Playground** in 1909, in honor of Kinnear's friend Mayor John Franklin Miller; the same year the site was graded and turned into a park. The water tank was covered with land fill, with access retained through a manhole. A clay-surfaced tennis court, swings and teeter-totters were added and the playground landscaped.

The popularity of the tennis court brought forth a small petition from annoyed neighbors who did not enjoy the exuberant shouts of the players or the resounding whacks of well-placed rackets sending the ball. The Queen Anne Hill tennis fans successfully countered with a petition, thick with signature sheets, for the retention of the courts. The courts continued to be used for decades until weeds and rain won the battle for the clay surface.

At the top of the south slope of Queen Anne Hill, about 50 feet above Franklin Playground, there is a rather narrow bench of land along W. Highland Drive, between Second and Third avenues. It was too narrow to be suitable for a home site, and remained overgrown with grasses and wild flowers until the 1920s when it became Queen Anne's most popular viewpoint, **Kerry Park.**

In 1927 Albert S. Kerry Sr. and his wife deeded the land to the City of Seattle to be dedicated to "park purposes." The Kerrys' plaque, mounted on the park wall, expresses their desire "that all who stop here may enjoy this view." Delighted with the wonderful site, the Parks Department developed it as a viewpoint park with a low wall at the top of the slope, cinder walks and a drinking fountain which served as the park's modest centerpiece. The park was immediately popular and the heavy use of the drinking fountain became a first class nuisance to those living in the nearby homes. Every time the drinking fountain's handle was turned the neighbors' plumbing would bang loudly. Franklin Playground, located directly below the viewpoint, was administratively absorbed into Kerry Park.

High up on the southwest brow of the hill is **Phelps Park**, dedicated on July 7, 1904 in honor of Thomas Stowell Phelps, who, as lieutenant on the ship *Decatur*, aided in repelling the Native American attack in the Battle of Seattle in January 1856. Located on the southwest corner of W. Highland Drive and Seventh Avenue W. this site was selected to honor Phelps because, from the viewpoint, one would have been able to see the ship *Decatur* lying in the harbor. Years later this park would acquire two additional names: Marshall Viewpoint (1960) and Betty Bowen Viewpoint (1977).

Chapter Eleven

# Community Life in the Early Twentieth Century

by
Kay F. Reinartz, Ph.D.

*Queen Anne is more than a neighborhood—it is an atmosphere. . . . Everywhere on Queen Anne you are on a hill, you feel it when you can't see it . . . the local paper speaks of "the hill" and "hill people" and a "hill boy" or "hill girl"—everything but hill-billy.*

*Almira Baily*
Post-Intelligencer
*October 31, 1927*

Living on Queen Anne Hill in the early decades of the twentieth century was a time of close relationships with family and neighbors. Life for most people was centered around the home and local institutions,

*The automobile became available to many families by the 1920s and just going for a drive was found to be a wonderful way to spend a day. Here the Sandvigen family enjoy a summer outing in the family's flivver. From left to right: Emelia Black, unknown, Delma, hired girl, hired girl, Carrie Melby with veil (cousin), father holding Alex and mother holding Emma. Gilbert in front of car with Buster. The collie dog was named Rover. Courtesy Queen Anne Historical Society.*

including the school and church, and community organizations. A very large proportion of the families were young and there were many children. The majority of married women with young children devoted themselves to full-time work as homemakers, while their husbands typically traveled by streetcar to jobs in other neighborhoods or in downtown Seattle. Most unmarried women held jobs.

## GETTING AROUND: TROLLEYS, STREETCARS AND THE COUNTERBALANCE

From 1900 through the 1920s almost everyone walked or took the streetcar everywhere—to church, to work, to shopping, to school, to parties and funerals. Many traveled to their own weddings on the streetcar. Traveling by streetcar helped neighbors get acquainted and was the beginning of more than one friendship and courtship. The fare was a nickel in the 1910s and increased to three single-trip tokens for a quarter by the 1930s.

In the 1920s there were four streetcar lines on the hill. Both the north Queen Anne and east Queen Anne routes came up the hill via Taylor Avenue N. to Boston Street and Queen Anne Avenue, where they separated. The east Queen Anne route ran to Blaine Street where it turned left and terminated near the High School. The north Queen Anne car went across to McGraw Street and Seventh W., where there was a T-style turn-around.

The west Queen Anne line, popularly known as the Counterbalance route, came straight up Queen Anne Avenue. In 1905 this line replaced the old Front Street cable line that ran up the hill as far west as W. Highland Drive. The Counterbalance was a simple, efficient system for getting the trolley up the steep hill. At the foot of the hill the motorman or conductor got out and attached the car to a "shoe" which in turn was attached to a huge underground counterweight equal to the weight of the trolley car. When the car was at the bottom of the hill, the counterweight was at the top, and vice versa. When the car reached the top of the hill the counterweight was disconnected near Lee Street, a block and a half above W. Highland Drive. The west Queen Anne streetcar then proceeded on to Sixth Avenue W. where the route terminated at Sixth Avenue W. and McGraw Street.

The fourth streetcar line was the Kinnear line. It started up Queen Anne Avenue, turned west at Roy Street and ran past Kinnear Park to Tenth Avenue W., where it terminated at 10th W. and McGraw Street. People also walked down the hill to catch street cars.

### Tales of the Counterbalance

On several occasions the eight-ton counterbalance weight broke loose, creating a slight earthquake when it reached the bottom of the hill under the street.

Roy Kinnear, who grew up next to the Counterbalance, recalled that when the car was coming down the hill, the conductor would yell, "Look out for the curve!" Occasionally the force of the car going over the abrupt dip that characterizes the topography of the slope would throw someone right out of the car. One woman was killed this way in the 1910s.

The roar of the metal-on-metal wheels was deafening as the car careened across Aloha Street, but those living nearby became accustomed to the racket. Kinnear declared that if the Counterbalance stopped earlier than the usual midnight hour, his family would wake up because it was too quiet.

Fred Betts reports that as a lad he once sneaked into the Counterbalance tunnel and rode

the counterweight to the bottom of the hill and back again to the top—petrified with fear every inch of the way. In 1939 the counterbalance system was replaced by a trackless trolley system. *Courtesy Queen Anne Historical Society.*

The car out to Ballard was caught on Fifteenth Avenue W. in Interbay.

Before automobiles became common at the end of the 1920s, only a few of the more wealthy kept a horse and carriage. These were mostly on the south side of the hill. There were a few livery stables at the perimeter of the hill where a horse and buggy or wagon could be hired.

## Making a Home on Queen Anne Hill

Between 1900 and 1930 most married women devoted their time and talent to homemaking and caring for their families. However, there was a beginning trend for more married women, particularly college-educated, to be working outside of the home. Homemakers had a big job. They were expected to make a major contribution to the family economy by producing and processing raw materials rather than buying end products. Through their efforts they reduced the household costs of cooking, sewing and home management, and often greatly improved the standard of living afforded by their husband's earned income, which was often very modest.

Most purchases were made at neighborhood shops. Miriam Marston Owen recalls the little business centers around the hill from 1910 on had food shops and dry

*The red Wet Wash Laundry wagons were a familiar sight on Queen Anne Hill in the early years of the twentieth century. With their plant at 222 First Avenue N., the company used "New system 44 wet wash" which provided the cleanest, brightest laundry with only three days between pick up and delivery. Courtesy Queen Anne Historical Society.*

### The House that Davidson Built

The influx of people to Queen Anne Hill between 1900 and 1929 created a steady demand for houses that was recognized as a business opportunity by Fredrick J. Davidson, a skilled carpenter, who immigrated from Canada around 1903. Davidson soon established himself as a contractor and built over 150 houses between 1910 and the late 1920s.

Built mostly of brick, Davidson's houses were noted for their high-quality construction and modern features including built-in central heat (hot water radiators), good plumbing, and adequate electrical wiring—qualities that were missing in many houses constructed in that era. Davidson kept in his employ Sam Ernst, plumber, and John Beattie, electrician, both Queen Anne residents.

Davidson built custom houses as well as blocks of homes which he sold prior to construction. His final and major work was developing the entire block bounded by Bigelow Avenue N., Fifth Avenue N., and Boston Street and Lynn Street. The several dozen homes were all pre-sold. The average price of a Davison house in the 1920s was $12,500, house and lot.

Son Howard Davidson recalls that while he was growing up the family frequently moved from one house to another in his father's developments. For a time they lived at 2312 Bigelow N., as well as 2302 Fourth Avenue N. Davidson operated his business out of his home, with the records kept in a large roll-top desk in the dining room. Jane Skinner Davidson, a former school teacher, assisted her husband with telephone and paper work.

Many of Fredrick Davidson's quality houses continue to be home to community residents. Houses by this skilled builder may be seen at the corner of Second Avenue N. and W. Highland Drive, 370 Lynn Street, 1701 Nob Hill Avenue N., and 310 and 314 W. Prospect Street.

## Grocery Shopping in 1920

by Anne Howell Johnson

When we lived down on Olympic Way, Dukelow's Grocery was just next door and there was a vegetable man that came around with his horse-drawn wagon, but Grandma liked to go down to the Pike Place Market for the household's vegetables and meat. We took the streetcar, which stopped right in front of our house and dropped us off at First Avenue and Pike Street.

The Market was always exciting to me. As we made our way down the aisles, I nose-high to the counters, the Italians shouted the virtues of their produce, and the Japanese bowed and smiled. The odors of fresh fish and newly baked goods are unforgettable. If the doughnut machine was working at the bakery I was "parked" there to watch the dough being plopped into the hot fat to start its journey on the circuitous route to come out golden brown at the end. After a while of pressing my nose to the window, the baker would give me one. When Grandma collected me, we would go across the street to Mengadoht's Meat Market. Mr. Mengadoht was German, as was my grandmother. While they dealt and visited I received another handout, this time a chunk of baloney or a wiener. Then back on the street car we would go, Grandma loaded down with at least two shopping bags full of the week's victuals.

Later, when we moved to the vicinity of Sixth W.

and McGraw Street, I took over most of the family's grocery shopping. Those were the days when the customer went to the counter and the clerk picked out the items you requested. Cans or other merchandise stored overhead along the walls were retrieved by the clerk climbing up on a ladder or reaching up with a special tool designed to grasp the can. Peanut butter came in bulk and was scooped out into cardboard cartons with wire handles. Cheddar cheese came in big wheels coated with cheesecloth and paraffin, was cut into triangles and wrapped with white butcher paper. When you were a little kid, you were always the last to be waited on.

Alas, the days for the merchants to hand out free goodies are over. *Courtesy Queen Anne News.*

goods stores which offered fabrics by the yard and sewing notions, as well as inexpensive children's clothing, e.g., socks, underwear and play clothes.

Between 1900 and 1930 doorstep delivery was common. In addition to the regular rounds of the milk and ice wagon—the latter followed by youngsters begging for "a little piece of ice"—there were bakeries, dry goods stores, pharmacies, laundry and fuel enterprises delivering to the door. Normally, the homemaker had a standing weekly order, or called in a special order. No charge for delivery.

Jobs were often hard to find in the Seattle area between 1900 and 1920 because of the huge population influx. However many people, particularly immigrants, pursued activities common at that time in Europe—vending from door-to-door. Such "permanent" vendors included fish mongers and farmers from outlying areas as far away as Poulsbo, who served both new and established customers with standing weekly orders for their fresh green produce, eggs and butter. Other venders did not raise their products, but bought them at wholesale prices from a railroad "fresh produce car," which stood on a sidetrack alongside the ship canal between Ross Station and the Ballard Bridge.

Kirk Jenner remembers that a highlight of the week for the kids in his neighborhood was the regular visit by the garbage truck, pulled by four huge Percherons. About once a month another interesting entrepreneur, the junkman, made the rounds with his small wagon drawn by a single horse. The children marveled at how the junkman tethered his horse by placing a lead weight on the street which he attached to the end of the reins.

Coal and wood for heating and cooking were needed by every home in this era. Bob Bishop recalls working one summer for the Consolidated Fuel Co., whose office was beside the Uptown Theater. Bob says he and his brother "backpacked garbage cans of coal, cradled high between our shoulder blades, to flats and apartments."

## Community Organizations

In the 1920s clubs and community organizations flourished on Queen Anne Hill as people got together over mutual interests, hobbies or community concerns.

Many of the clubs formed during this period lasted only a few years and little more than their names are known 80 years later. These include the Townsend Club, for retired community members, the Queen Anne Knickers Club, the Queen Anne Men's Club and the Women's Single Tax Club. The Town Meeting Club provided a forum for debating issues of the era, such as the League of Nations as a peace keeping organization or the merits of the unicameral legislature.

Clubs focusing on history, world cultures, literature, music and the arts were very popular and included the Queen Anne Study Club, Orptic Club, Fortnightly Club, and the Aspasia Club. The Fortnightly Club, formed in 1894, is still active in the Queen Anne community a century later.

The Queen Anne Nomadic Circle was a popular intellectual club whose members wrote stories. Open to women and men alike, the club provided both an outlet and guidance to those interested in being writers. The club published, in the *Seattle Mail and Herald* on January 3, 1903, an installment of "Dr. Allen's Temptation," a novel the members had collectively written:

> *This story is a combined product of the 15 to 20 ladies and gentlemen who constitute the literary circle known by the name "The Queen Anne Nomadic Circle." For several years a part of the evening's program of this circle has been the reading of a chapter of an original story. During the year, from October 1 to June 1,*

### Helen Tillman Zednick—Queen Anne Community Leader, 1914-1930

> *The future history of America will be shaped in a large measure of the character of its homes. If we continue to be a home-loving people, we shall have the strength of character that comes only from a wholesome family life and our development will be sound and in the right direction.*
>
> *Helen Tillman Zednick, 1926*

Helen Tillman Zednick grew up in Seattle in the 1880s and graduated from the University of Washington in 1911 in journalism. She was a member of the first University of Washington women's rowing crew, which distinguished itself by becoming national champions.

Helen Tillman married Victor Zednick in 1914 and the couple settled on Queen Anne Hill. In the next two decades the Zednicks were prominent in both Queen Anne and the region for their leadership in public affairs. Victor's ambitions are well known, for they took him into politics first as a member of the State Legislature and eventually as Lt. Governor. Helen's work was more focused on Queen Anne and Seattle activities and community service.

Soon after settling on the hill she founded the Aspasia Club, geared toward the intellectual needs of women college graduates. Under Helen's leadership the Aspasia Club, West Queen Anne Parent-Teachers Association, as well as the Century Club, a city wide organization in which she served as leader, undertook many valuable community service projects in the 1910s and 1920s.

Helen Zednick's management abilities were soon recognized by Seattle's Mayor Bertha Landes, who appointed her to various municipal committees.

Helen Tillman Zednick's work supported her belief that good homes are the backbone of a good America. In 1924 Herbert Hoover, as Secretary of Commerce, appointed her Director of the Better Homes in America Committee for the Northwest. The Better Homes movement was a nation-wide federal program established to improve the standard of living in the American home. In her role guiding the federal project in Seattle, Zednick stressed the importance of aesthetics and beauty in the home environment to nurturing spiritual values and a peacefulness in family life.

*Courtesy Helen Zednick Mercier*

*each member contributes a chapter, and the story is then complete. For the Mail and general reading public, the resulting novel will be published in serial form, a chapter from each member of the circle each week.*

*The cold winters characterizing the nineteenth century became rare in the twentieth, and Queen Anne children rarely had a chance to built a snowman. Proudly posing with their snowman ca. 1921 are, back row: Marion Baker (Marion), second from right; Eleanor Delong, third from right; Mary Gove Wallon, fourth from right. Front row: Elizabeth Wallon (Brazean) second from left; Alice DeLong (Wolgemuth), fourth from left; and Lewis Arthur Wallon Jr. (Bud), extreme right holding snowball. Courtesy Mary Wallon.*

## Queen Anne Community Club

Undoubtedly, the Queen Anne Community Club, organized in 1922, was the most significant community organization of the decade. The club evolved from local improvement clubs and served as the community's voice at Seattle City Hall.

The club's initial project was the paving of the lower section of Taylor Avenue. Accomplishing this goal, the club brought about other community improvements such as street paving, lighting, drinking fountains and playfields. The club grew from 40 to 2,000 members in its first seven years.

The heavy debt caused by the building of a clubhouse in 1927 forced the club to spend most of its efforts in the early 1930s raising money to pay for the building located at the corner of Queen Anne Avenue and Garfield Street. This activity drove members away and the club never regained its popularity of the 1920s.

## Recreation

The main forms of recreation for most people continued to be that enjoyed in the nineteenth century, namely family gatherings, visiting with neighbors, and church and school centered activities. For many the work week was six 10-hour days, and Sunday was set aside for church, leisure and socializing. Fred Criddle recalls that in the late 1910s almost every Sunday after church his family walked from their home on Fourth Avenue W. and Smith Street to their grandparents'zx home on Bigelow Avenue N. and W. Garfield Street. Other Sundays the grandparents walked to their house. In the summer, they might all walk to Kinnear Park after dinner to hear the band concert and for the little children to play on the swings. Then there was the walk home, about ten miles total walking for the "day of rest."

## Children's Life in the 1920s

Most children were given little money because the average parent did not feel they needed any since their needs were looked after by their parents. However, enterprising children often found ways to earn a little of their own.

Many boys delivered newspapers in the 1920s. Ted Delius earned money with his magazine routes. He sold *The Saturday Evening Post, Liberty, and Ladies' Home Journal.* His business involved finding customers, delivering the magazines, collecting the money, and paying the magazine company. Ted sold monthlies for ten cents and weeklies for five cents. His commission was two cents per magazine. When business was good Ted would buy a Coke and Sunfreeze slice at the grocery store on Saturday.

*Queen Anne High School girls enjoyed playing tennis at the several tennis courts around the hill that were built between 1910 and 1930. Left to right: Mayme McDonald, Agnes McDonald, unknown, Ava Cocknane, Margaret McLane, unknown. Courtesy Margaret Pontius.*

At age 13, Kirk Jenner managed to land a good job with *The Seattle Times* as a combination copy and office boy. He worked Friday evenings five to nine, all day Saturday, and Sunday morning. He traveled by streetcar at first, but by the time he was 15 he was walking to and from work. Kirk recalls "I rather enjoyed the walk which was about five miles, but in reality there was no easy way to get there by streetcar."

With the $6 he made each weekend Kirk bought his mother her first washing machine. Still proud of his gift 50 years later, Jenner remembers, "It was a used Savage rotary type with a copper tub and cost $65. I paid for it on the 'easy payment plan' which took about a year. Mother really appreciated the washer and never again had to use the scrubbing board in the bathtub."

George Knutsen remembers that in the 1910s, after they had finished their supper time chores, he and other children in the neighborhood would walk over to the movie house and sit in the alley behind the building listening to the organ playing as it accompanied the silent picture show.

Kids living on the north side of the hill would save up a few pennies and then head down Third Avenue W. to the big store, the Ross Marche, across the street from Seattle Pacific College on Third Avenue W. Bill Hunter relates, "To us children, the exciting thing about the Ross Marche was its supply of penny candy, visible on shelves behind a big glass case. A penny was big money in those days, and it was an event to be relished to choose from a dozen possibilities your kind and flavor of candy."

## Playing on the North Side of the Hill

In the 1910s most children had few toys, but playing outside year around offered plenty of fun. Donna Everett Williams moved with her family into their new home at the corner of Fourth Avenue N. and McGraw Street around 1904 when there were only three houses in the immediate vicinity. The Everett children's favorite place to play was a "canyon" formed by the stream

*On Tuesday afternoons in the 1920s, Stu Prestrud recalls, the children living on the west side of the hill would run to the Eleventh Avenue W. overlook after school to watch the* H.F. Alexander *depart on its weekly voyage to California. On alternate Saturday mornings they again gathered at the overlook for the excitement of watching the green-hulled President liners back out of Pier 41, later Pier 91, to begin their voyage to the far-away Orient. Courtesy Museum of History and Industry.*

## The Circus

by Ted Delius

When the circus came to town from the early 1900s until 1927 its tents were raised on the vacant land south of Mercer Street from approximately Fourth Avenue N . to about the Nob Hill area.

Ringling Brothers and Barnum and Bailey paraded the circus animals up Warren Ave., much to the pleasure of pupils at Warren Avenue Elementary. Many boys from Warren Avenue School and Mercer School earned tickets of admission by doing such chores as carrying water for the elephants and spreading straw and sawdust on the grounds. There was a large performing tent and a sideshow tent where the kids were not allowed.

A favorite for some children was a sort of wild west show with Indians in full regalia, complete with feathered headdresses, riding ponies, shouting and shooting blanks. When the circus folded its tents and left town the grounds were searched for coins that, hopefully, had been dropped. One little girl was sure that one day she would find a diamond ring somewhere in the trampled straw. *Courtesy University of Washington, Hamilton collection.*

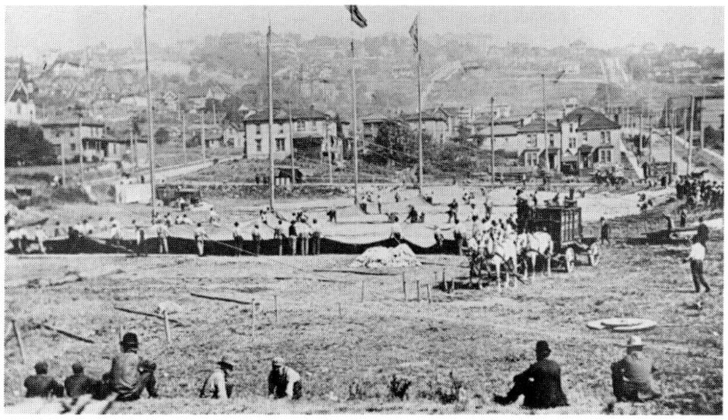

which was the outflow of Nils Peterson's big spring up the hill. It was a dark, mysterious place filled with huge ferns, skunk cabbage, cattails and tall grasses. It was cool in the summer and a grand place to hide. As a part of street construction in the 1910s the stream was diverted into a storm sewer and the children's canyon became Third Ave. W.

Bill Hunter recounts playing on the north side of the hill, near Evergreen Park (Rodgers Park) around 1918:

> *Above the bank was a wooded area, in which we climbed trees, built tree houses, and played "Pioneers and Indians." There was a thick patch of blackberry bushes up there, which bore berries prolifically. One day I got so absorbed in picking and eating berries, I found myself helplessly trapped by the sharp barbs of surrounding bushes. The more I struggled, the worse I was trapped. One of my playmates had to go home and bring my Dad up to rescue me. He brought up a butcher knife and ball bat, wore gloves, and by hacking and beating the bushes, he finally set me free.*

The play area enjoyed by the Everett and Hunter children was destined to become the first park on the north slope. In 1883 B. F. and Frances R. Day, north slope real estate developers, had given the city a five-acre parcel on the north side of the hill. After lying untouched for 30 years, in 1909 an adjoining 50-acre tract was purchased, and the park was named Evergreen Park for its beautiful grove of fir trees.

The park was improved in 1914 when the North Queen Anne Elementary School was built at the northern end of the park, which was at Second Avenue W. and Florentia Street. Much to the consternation of the neighbors, the improved park attracted the north slope youth. In May 1915, R.H. Lyon complained to the city:

> *In the two past months several evenings each week a gang of hoodlums have made this park a resort, some evenings for an hour or two only, and other evenings for a greater portion of the night, and have kept up a constant pounding, whistling and yelling, with the use of loud, vulgar, profane and obscene language. . . . This condition has become intolerable and a park that should add greatly to the desirability of the location for residence has been rapidly turned into a public nuisance and [is] being used for illegal and immoral purposes.*

In 1919 Evergreen Park was renamed Rodgers Park for David Rodgers, who is credited with having "done more than anyone else in placing the name of Seattle in the foremost rank of the shipbuilding industry."

## The North Slope Parent's Nightmare

In the 1920s a problem developed in the north slope neighborhood that was to remain "the issue" for years. The trouble centered on a gravel pit originally dug by Nils Peterson in the 1870s, when he excavated sand for construction projects. Located at Third Avenue W. and Florentia Street, just south of the North Queen Anne grade school, the gravel pit was a favorite place of the children. Bill Hunter remembers that

> *It was a marvelous sandpit! It was roughly 300 by 400 feet. The sand was an excellent quality that would have been suitable for an ocean beach, and it was great for tackle football [but] only fair for sand lot softball. Its greatest virtue was that on two sides, there were sheer banks, about 25 or 30 feet high. We kids dared to dig steps in the face of a bank, and then climb precariously to the top. If you fell, you lit in soft sand below. That was the 'Mount Everest' of our neighborhood.*

In the 1920s the Queen Anne Sand Co. began working the high grade deposit and soon created a very large, deep pit. The pit naturally filled with water running off the nearby slopes. The children loved to play around this "little lake." Occasionally a child went home dripping wet after slipping into the pit, and parents constantly warned their children "Stay away from the pit!" The problem of the gravel pit was to reach a crisis in the 1930s, when a neighborhood boy drowned.

## Diversions on the West and East Slopes

By 1910 the streets on the east side of the hill were constantly filled with playing children. Recognizing the need for a regular playground, the East Queen Anne Improvement Club laid their desire before the Seattle Parks Department, which quickly purchased a 1.4 acre parcel bounded by Howe and Newton Streets, Second Avenue N. and Warren Avenue. Eventually the park became known as the East Queen Anne Playground.

In 1914 a tennis court was built in the park. The next season a group of boys began showing up as early as 4:30 a.m. to enjoy tennis at dawn. For two hours or more they would play game after game of fast, hard-hitting tennis. Those sleeping in the nearby houses were awakened by the smart walloping of the ball. Neighbors complained to the Parks Dept. Superintendent, such as Jeannette Macdonald, who declared that "it is absolutely impossible to get any sleep after they start in."

*Dubbed "Little Howe" by the neighbors, the East Queen Anne Playground was originally divided into two levels divided by a retaining wall. The upper level was an open, grassy play area which eventually had playground equipment, while the lower level had a wading pool and shelter. Ruth Gove Herr happily recalls the playground from her childhood in the 1920s "the wading pool was always a great source of fun and games." Courtesy City of Seattle Archives.*

## The Best Hill in Town for Sledding

Early in the century there were many hard winters with sufficient snow to make for splendid sledding. The two favorite hills were Third Avenue W. and Queen Anne Avenue. The latter was like a roller-coaster ride with the sledder's stomach making "flip-flops" with each dip up and down—and then the final wild stretch, flashing across Mercer Street and finally slowing to a stop. It was a ride well remembered by the children when they were 80 years old.

Will Hunter lived on Fourth Avenue W., a street less busy than Third Avenue W. and, best of all, without significant intersections. Will and his sister and brother Helen and Phil would trudge six blocks up the hill and then jump on their sleds for the thrilling ride down. The hill got steeper the farther down they went and the only way to control the speed was dragging their feet in the snow. Often kind adults scattered an abundance of ashes on the road at the bottom of the hill near the college, which helped prevent crashing.

In the summer the kids would swim in the canal between Ross Station and the Ballard Bridge. Some also went swimming in Lake Union, although their parents frowned upon it because it was very polluted. Undoubtedly, the place where children growing up on the hill spent the longest hours year round was the Queen Anne Library.

## THE QUEEN ANNE LIBRARY

From the 1890s, when the women of the Women's Christian Temperance Union (W.C.T.U.) opened a reading room in North Seattle, many had longed for a library on the hill. In 1912 the community was selected by the Seattle Library Board as the site for a branch library. Funded by the City of Seattle, a Carnegie Corporation grant, and a $500 donation from Col. Alden Blethen, Queen Anne resident and owner of *The Seattle Times*, a building site was selected at Fourth Avenue W. and W. Garfield Street after much controversy and community bickering.

January 1, 1914, was a community Red Letter Day—the beautiful new library was opening. All day long Queen Anne residents crowded into the new library to inspect the handsome golden oak paneled rooms well appointed with reading tables and comfortable chairs. All eyes hungrily studied the titles on the long shelves—a total of 5,000 books. The anticipation of long happy hours "with a book" filled many with joy that day.

The new library was open daily under Head Librarian Frances L. Holmes. Helen Watson, the first Children's Librarian, pledged: "The work of the branch with the children of the Queen Anne community will always be of paramount importance." And the Queen Anne children soon found their way to the little library in droves. In 1914 a distraught parent wrote to Miss Watson:

*Dear Madam: Will you please stop John and Mary from getting any more books as we can't get anything out of them at all—they won't go to bed at night and won't get up in the morning and won't do anything but read when they do get up.*

*The Queen Anne Library, W. Garfield Street and Fourth Avenue W., was designed in the English Scholastic Gothic style by architects Somervell and Thomas. Upon completion, the local press called it "one of Seattle's most beautiful public buildings." Courtesy Seattle Public Library.*

The new library had a special children's story room which was crowded every Saturday morning from 1914 through the 1940s with children coming to hear stories and book talks. In the 1960s, the room was converted into the library office.

The library has served the community's children in a variety of ways over the decades, including library lessons given in the elementary, middle schools and junior high schools by librarians, library visits by school children, cooperative creation of young people's reading lists, preschool children's programs, puppet shows and films.

## The Library Helps the Community in Times of Need

During World War I the Queen Anne Library auditorium became a community focal point. It was there that many activities geared toward helping "win the war," took place, including meetings of the Home Guards, Council for Defense, Red Cross auxiliaries, Minute Men, and the Council for Patriotic Services, which sold war savings stamps. The women gathered here several nights a week to knit warm socks, mittens and vests, and prepare dressings to be shipped overseas.

The war over, the library staff wrote a weekly "Book Notes" column for the *Queen Anne News*, designed to increase the community's awareness of its library resources. During the Depression years the community turned to the library as never before and circulation increased to a record 197,222 books for the year 1932. The city's tightened budget had reduced the size of the staff which worked even harder to serve the many readers. To ensure the upkeep of the book collection, librarians made home visits after work to retrieve overdue library materials. At the end of the 1930s the auditorium was used for two years by the Works Progress Administration (WPA) statewide Library Services Project which left the library much improved with new lighting, bookcases and paint. From the beginning, the Queen Anne Library has been a major community resource.

In 1970 Florence Ekstrand, retired editor of the *Queen Anne News*, reflecting back on the 1920s, observed:

> *The 1920s were a pleasant interlude [during] which Queen Anne families saw no reason why they and their offspring would not go on forever picnicking and swimming along Lake Union's shores, or exchanging pleasantries with others who rode the East Queen Anne trolley home in the February dusk.*

Chapter Twelve

# Depression and War— The 1930s–40s

by
Ron Palmer, Ph.D.

By 1930, the population of Queen Anne was about 30,000. The scarring of the land that had occurred with the transformation of the area into an urban environment had disappeared as the trees planted along the residential streets began to tower over the homes. Some thought that the hill was becoming sociologically stratified with an upper class living in the south slope view homes, the workers lower down on the hill around Warren Avenue and the middle orders scattered in between and on the flatlands of the summit.

With the 1930s came the Great Depression. The Aurora Bridge, completed in February of 1932, soon claimed its first suicide victims. A shantytown or "Hooverville" emerged in the Interbay flats. At the same time foreclosure vacated many houses in the

*The George Washington Memorial Bridge under construction, 1931. The bridge linked Aurora Avenue with the north side of Lake Union and has been locally known as the Aurora Bridge since its opening. Courtesy Puget Sound Maritime Historical Society.*

district. Work slowed on Queen Anne Park, a projected exclusive residential area on the north slope of the hill. A bright note was the improvements that many of the Queen Anne parks received from the Works Progress Administration during the late 1930s. As a community Queen Anne's response to those hard times showed its resilience in economic initiatives, political activism, civic cooperation and community creativity.

*Dexter Avenue and Crockett Street, looking south, circa 1933. Dexter Avenue follows the course of the Military Road, which was built on a Native American travel route which skirted the hill. The levelness of the land and proximity to water transportation on Lake Union made Dexter Avenue a desirable building site in the 1890s. Courtesy University of Washington, Special Collections.*

## Economic Initiatives

"Getting by" became the primary objective in the 1930s. Lee Steen, a Queen Anne roofer, maintains that he kept busy even in "the darkest days of the depression," and that "the work [was] there and all you [had] to do is go after it and once you [got] it, expend every effort to give your customers the best possible work." Paul Mooney recalls, "I'll always be grateful to my boss who kept me on the payroll even though there was nothing to do."

The National Recovery Act (NRA) represented a major effort to defeat the Depression. State Senator George Lovejoy headed the drive for enrollment in the program on the hill and Charles Gerrish, a local merchant, claimed the distinction of being the first merchant to display the Blue Eagle. According to the *Queen Anne News*, Queen Anne went one-hundred percent for the NRA. By fixing a national minimum wage, determining maximum working hours, and establishing industrial codes, General Hugh Johnson, the NRA's chief, predicted that prices would rise, consumer power would increase, men would go back to work and the Depression would be licked by snowfall. Although the Supreme Court later declared the NRA unconstitutional, the spirit of cooperation continued in several local and enduring organizations.

## Political Activism

The hottest political issue centered on repeal of Prohibition. Silas Rich and the Women's Christian Temperance Union led the forces to maintain it, arguing that repeal would menace business interests, increase the number of injuries and deaths in factories and on highways, and siphon needed resources away from productive enterprises.

Victor Zednick, perennial Republican candidate for the legislature, Ben Paris, well-known sportsman and owner of several billiard parlors, and C. F. Miskey, president of the Democratic Club, led the movement on the hill for repeal. Zednick presented extensive reasons for repeal in a series of articles in the *Queen Anne News*. But the argument that Prohibition had taken away a prime source of money for the government and put it in the pockets of an undesirable class appeared to clinch the issue. Queen Anne voted three to one in favor of repeal, and every precinct selected Zednick and Paris as delegates to the "repeal convention" in 1933.

## Civic Cooperation

While partisan politics occupied a large share of Queen Anne's attention, economic deprivation elicited non-partisan charitable and philanthropic activity for Queen Anne citizens. They exceeded their goals in the yearly Community Fund drives. Reginald Parsons headed the planning group of the Community Fund, the ancestor of United Way. In the Red Cross drives, which began in 1932, Queen Anne led every residential district in both dollars contributed and memberships registered. Dr. Oscar Proctor and Judge Charles Moriarty headed the city-wide campaigns in 1934 and 1938, respectively. In addition, Queen Anne strongly supported Goodwill Industries, the Children's Orthopedic Hospital, Seattle Children's Home, and St. Vincent DePaul.

The 1930s proved difficult for the Queen Anne Community Club. It never decided whether it should focus on politics or entertainment. Even though entertainment would attract 300-350 attendees when James Bailey showed his travel movies or Mrs. Charles Moriarty played the violin, sustained cooperation proved elusive. Participation was characterized by intensity of support for a specific issue. In the 1930s, the principal community issues included: 1) a drive to save the Queen Anne Clubhouse, 2) efforts to obtain a field house for the district, 3) opposition to spot zoning, 4) a campaign to close the sandpit on the north side of the hill, and 5) measures to combat juvenile delinquency.

*The Works Progress Administration (WPA) improved Queen Anne's parks and built many sidewalks during the latter years of the Great Depression. The network of footpaths that honeycomb the hill include numerous stairways built by WPA labor. Photo by Isabel Egglin.*

Efforts aimed at saving the Queen Anne Clubhouse from foreclosure had failed, and with its loss attention focused on a plan for a city-managed field house on the site. The Queen Anne Community Club gathered petitions to the City Council carrying 2,500 signatures. Community leaders spoke on behalf of a field house, pointing out that community money already invested would cut the cost in half, but they did not get the field house.

Queen Anne citizens regrouped for a 1937 assault on the City Council. A new umbrella organization, the Queen Anne Council of Clubs (QACC), sought to mobilize community support. A mass rally of 1500 on the West Queen Anne Playfield whipped up support for the request as bands played, leaders spoke and everyone sang and danced. In the council chambers, future governor Arthur Langlie supported the presentation made by the QACC. The Queen Anne residents made their points: 1) over $40,000 had been included in the budget for Woodland Park ("The children of Queen Anne should have preference over goats, deer and snakes. While the snakes keep warm, our children are out in the streets seeking places to play!"); 2) Queen Anne had not received its fair share of park funds (although it had one-seventh of Seattle's population, it received only $82,000 of the $6 million Park Department expenditures between 1929 and 1937); and 3) failure to invest in youth resulted in rising juvenile delinquency.

The request failed again, but the campaign process had a healthy community impact. The street dance on the West Queen Anne Playfield proved a popular innovation, and repeated events drew thousands of participants. Editor of the *Queen Anne News* Clyde Dunn observed, "Queen Anne is at the threshold of a new era. Awakening to the fact that their community has been ignored and neglected. . . the citizens of this district are now aroused to the point of taking direct action."

A prime goal of the North Queen Anne-Nickerson Community Club was the creation of a park and playfield between Rodgers Park and the North Queen Anne School. Unfortunately, the property belonged to Queen

Anne Sand and Gravel and Washington Sand and Gravel. The QACC urged closure of the sandpit and, after several months of negotiation, the Board of Public Works ordered the companies to cease operations by the end of 1938. When Seattle Pacific College leased the Queen Anne Bowl area to the city in 1939, the whole tract was developed as a recreational area.

*Queen Anne Bowl showing a section of Third Avenue W. Encompassing the former site of a gravel pit that was the focus of community agitation throughout the 1930s as a community safety hazard, the area became a playing field in the 1940s, shared by Seattle Pacific University and the community. Note North Queen Anne Elementary School in the upper left side of the bowl. Courtesy City of Seattle Archives.*

The primary motivation for much community action was the welfare of children; the field house and parks were to serve the kids. The QACC determined the ideal ratio of park and play area at one acre for every 50 residents. Queen Anne fell far short of the ideal: only one acre for a thousand residents. The QACC sponsored forums, lectures, and articles on delinquency, parent-child relationships, and child development to improve the quality of life for the district.

The YMCA provided a key antidote. In October 1937 it acquired the old Congregational Church building at 1520 Queen Anne Avenue and established a clubhouse. The soul of the YMCA was popular secretary Harold Nickerson, a graduate of Coe School, Queen Anne High School and the University of Washington. As the *News* reported, "hardly a boy grows up in the district without feeling the imprint of the Y's body and character-building program." Camp Orkila in the San Juans highlighted the year's calendar and Hank Ketcham, who would later achieve national fame as the creator of the cartoon strip "Dennis the Menace," led the pack in registering for camp each year.

## COMMUNITY CATHARSIS

Activity provided an antidote to Depression anxiety. For many unemployed young men, Al's Hamburger Shop at Queen Anne Avenue and Galer Street provided a place to hang out and create their own ambience. Others spent their time playing softball and other sports on the graveled field at Second Avenue W.

Sports events attracted major interest in the 1930s. Queen Anne produced championship teams and outstanding athletes, many of whom later excelled in college and in the pros, such as Rainiers' baseball star Edo Vanni, and Johnny Cherberg, who quarterbacked the Grizzlies and Huskies, earned "Man of the Year" honors in 1938, coached at Queen Anne High School, and went on to later fame as University of Washington football coach and Lt. Governor of the State of Washington.

Social events provided by the Queen Anne Club, the Queen Anne Men's Club, or the Merchant's Club included dances, community picnics, "Queen Anne Days" at the Puyallup Fair, and caravans to baseball games. Area churches combined to sponsor two sunrise services on Easter Sunday, at Washelli Cemetery and Volunteer Park. The services drew 25,000 to 30,000 as a highlight of the religious calendar.

## Out of Isolation

For some Queen Anne residents, events in the international arena appeared as distant, surrealistic images. As Jim Kaldal recalls, "I was in high school when the war started. We weren't very worldly. The war wasn't real; it was so far away. As class president, I spoke at commencement in 1939 and said nothing about the war and how we'd probably be involved someday."

The German invasion of Holland and Belgium on May 10, 1940 produced a radical change. Gathering on street corners, in barbershops and living rooms, Queen Anne residents listened avidly for the latest news from the front. A variety of programs on Queen Anne focused attention on the troubled Eastern Hemisphere. For instance, Dean Vernon McKenzie, who had visited Europe annually and actually interviewed Hitler and Mussolini, talked to the Queen Anne Community Club about the Ethiopian situation.

The war prompted a change in the Community Fund drive. Re-labled the "Greater Defense Chest," the campaign became a battle for "humanity, democracy and the American way of living." Leola Bowen served as colonel for Queen Anne and Mrs. Robert Cowan headed the Youth Service Project. Enthusiasm and sacrifice resulted in outstanding success with $959,575 raised, and 11 Queen Anne women received merit awards for their leadership and work in this important project.

The Queen Anne Community Club promoted civil defense measures. Organized drills were held every Monday night at the Field Artillery Armory. Others became more directly involved. In 1939, Cal Butterworth, a leading mortician, organized an ambulance company as part of the 41st Infantry Division. Of the 50 members, half came from Queen Anne. For many, the dollar for attendance at biweekly meetings

### Mickey Mouse Club

by Marion Parker

Mickey Mouse Club—it was a steady source of entertainment on Saturday afternoons in the late '20s and early '30s when I attended. We would form a single line outside the Queen Anne Theater until the doors opened at 1 p.m. Admission was 10 cents. On stage, Seymour Kail, a popular Queen Anne High School upper classman, was emcee. He later won acclaim as a Marine Corps officer in World War II. He led us in the song, and in the proper cheers.

*Oh, I am called little Mickey Mouse,*
*Got a sweetie down in the chicken house,*
*Neither fat nor skinny*
*She's the horse's whinny,*
*She's my little Minnie Mouse. . . oh-o-o-*
*When it's feeding time for the animals*
*And they howl and growl like cannibals,*
*I just turn my heel,*
*To the henhouse steal,*
*And you hear me sing this song. . .*
*Oh the old tom cat with his meow, meow, meow [with feeling]*
*And the old hound dog with his bow-wow-wow [more feeling!]*
*With the cows and the chickens*
*They all sound like the DICKENS—*
*When I hear my little Minnie YOO-HOO [time to yell it out!]*

No, we weren't called Mousketeers—no costumes—just fun! Then on screen, a comedy and a serial—and a final "so long" until the next week!

*Queen Anne Theater, 1529 Queen Anne Avenue, formerly the Cheerio. Cinema in the 1930s and 40s meant double features and limited engagements on a three- to four-day rotation. For kids, the Mickey Mouse Club featured prizes, puzzles, and parades and attracted 600 members on Saturdays. Courtesy University of Washington Special Collections.*

*The Erik Hokanson family on their doorstep in the 1940s. From left to right: Erik, Bina, Patricia, Randolph, recently returned after musical study in Europe, Barbara, Dorothy. Courtesy Millie Hokanson.*

was a real incentive. There was not much equipment—the stories about wooden rifles are true.

## ON THE EVE OF WAR

In politics, the Republicans began to regain the influence they had enjoyed before the Depression. Representative George Kinnear served as the standard-bearer for the G.O.P. on Queen Anne from 1938 to 1942. Senator George Lovejoy headed the Democratic leadership on the hill. From the momentum of the Democratic landslide of 1932, Lovejoy still faced little opposition in 1940. Two-term representative Howard Payne, however, would feel the heat of the Republican resurgence.

Political excitement peaked with the mayoral contests of the 1940s. Earl Millikin carried Queen Anne colors into the fray. Following service in the artillery in World War I, Millikin returned to teach history and coach at Queen Anne High School from 1919 to 1930. After a stint as president of the Northwest Football League, he served as County Auditor from 1934 to 1940, winning the 1938 election by 73,000 votes.

Queen Anne received direct benefits from Millikin's election. On March 28, 1941, Millikin was inaugurated; on March 31, the resurfacing of McGraw Street began. In fact, Millikin undertook to fulfill the aspirations of Queen Anne residents with such enthusiasm that *Queen Anne News* editor Curtis Barnard felt obliged to defend him against charges of favoritism.

Two major issues attracted Queen Anne residents' attention during this period. The first was the transportation revolution, incorporated in the Beeler Plan of 1939 which replaced the trolleys with buses. The second controversy arose from a recommendation by Jesse Epstein to build a low-cost housing project in the Warren Avenue district. Fear of threats to economic and social values on the hill galvanized property owners. As Curtis Barnard explained:

> *We're not attempting to unfurl the banner of race prejudice—we're merely trying to point out the economic and social effects which we believe to be the logical consequence of such a proposition. We're not opposed to social reform, but we do not believe it should improve the status of the underprivileged by tearing down the values which hardworking men have created.*

Queen Anne residents and the Queen Anne Chamber of Commerce helped lead the fight to keep the Warren Avenue Project from materializing. Joined by the Municipal League, the Seattle Chamber of Commerce, the Master Builders Association and the Real Estate Board, they argued that the Warren Avenue proposal should wait until sufficient time had elapsed to demonstrate the worth of Yesler Terrace, a project conceived by Epstein which was in the vanguard of low-income housing in America.

## The Impact of Pearl Harbor on Queen Anne

On December 7, 1941, many Queen Anne residents sat in churches. As worship services concluded, ministers told parishioners that the Japanese had attacked Pearl Harbor. World War II had begun.

*Counterbalance conductor in front of streetcar shanty at the upper end of Queen Anne Avenue. On August 10, 1940, motorman W.W. Wiley took the last trolley on the Counterbalance route. The event became an occasion for a much-condemned riot in which Queen Anne boys smashed windows, ripped seats, and cut trolley rope. The result was over $200 in damage and two boys were thrown in jail. Courtesy Old Seattle Paperworks.*

Queen Anne citizens aided the war effort through civilian defense, the Red Cross, victory gardens and conservation, in addition to working in defense production. A call went out for 400 air raid volunteers. The tepid response prompted an open letter to the *News*: "What's the matter with you fellows on Queen Anne Hill? Are you waiting for the Japs [sic] to rap at your front door or put a bomb in your front room before you decide to help us out? Why not do it now before they arrive?"

Many Queen Anne residents refused to let air raid wardens inspect their homes to verify that they were prepared for an air attack. Meanwhile anti-aircraft guns were installed in the north section of Mount Pleasant Cemetery.

Over 75,000 Seattle homes had victory gardens and Queen Anne citizens received tips for better production through Leah Griffin's weekly columns in the *News*. Griffin also provided a rationale for raising food in the backyard: the need to feed England and the Allies, to save on transportation costs, to improve nutrition for inductees (a shocking number failed physical exams), and to express reverence for the land.

Queen Anne shared in the national experience of economic regulation and some residents still treasure their "War Ration Books." Directors of the Office of Price Administration appeared at forums in the community to explain price controls and gauge the neighborhood's response to the program.

The outbreak of war had a direct impact on the lives of Japanese-Americans living on Queen Anne. While few in number, the Japanese-Americans had made important contributions. For example, Yoshi Miyauchi was a track star and valedictorian of his 1935 Queen Anne High School class. As Teresa Machmeier, a teacher at West Queen Anne Grade School, remembers:

> *The day after Pearl Harbor was a somber Monday. . . The Japanese students were badly treated. It was terrible to see the other children put down the Japanese children merely because of their race. Actually, it had been a joy to have these Japanese students in class because they were excellent students. After Pearl Harbor, even the storybooks on Japan in the libraries were taken out and thrown away.*

The *Queen Anne News* voiced the opinion that since every other American contributed to national defense through "dollars and cents, personal sacrifice, civilian defense or actual bloodshed...the Japs [sic] should not hesitate to cooperate with the federal government by leaving all defense areas at once."

## POSTSCRIPT TO WAR

Everyone who lived through the war cherishes memories. For many, the return of prosperity meant steady work and a larger income in defense industries such as Boeing. Charles Gerrish kept up his grocery business during the war and remembers selling big orders to Russian boats—thousands of dollars worth of cigarettes, meat and produce. Doris Linkletter remembers riding the bus and walking a lot, instead of driving the family car. Peggy Parcel worked as a legal secretary and volunteered for the Red Cross. She recounts that one Queen Anne woman hid a Japanese lady in her home so she would not have to go to an internment camp. Stanley Gallup, who lived across the street from the Japanese consulate, vividly recalls the Sunday the National Guard came and watched while the diplomats burned papers in barrels throughout the day. "Then, they were gone."

High school principal Otto Luther would observe that "relative to graduates, Queen Anne is most proud that [out of] 2,500 men from Queen Anne in the service in World War II, one out of four of them were commissioned officers." Some became heroes. Perry Dahl, mobilized with the National Guard in 1940, entered the Marine Corps in 1942, became a P-38 pilot and shot down ten Japanese fighter planes. John McClintock, Jr. received the Bronze Star for valor in Italy; Robert Smith, the Silver Star in the Solomon Islands; Maynard Kelley, the Navy's Distinguished Flying Cross in Okinawa; and Bob Galer, a star basketball player and ace pilot in the Marines, the Congressional Medal of Honor for exploits at Guadalcanal. But as Jim Kaldal remarked, "Most of us did a job and we survived."

Queen Anne entered the television age with Don Nelson offering a weekly column introducing the new wonder and answering questions such as "Do I need the room darkened?" "Do I need a radio for sound?" " Do inside antennas work?" New construction accelerated, including the Wedgewood Building (1946), Bartell's ("The most modern drug store in Seattle," 1948), A&P Grocery (1949), Public School Administrative and Service Center (1949), Post Office Building (1949), United Sales Company (1949) and the Electrical Workers Building (1949). Perhaps the most noteworthy and long-awaited project of this period was the completion of the $431,000 Queen Anne Field House in 1949.

Republican dominance continued in the post-war years on the hill. Queen Anne lawmakers included State Senator Victor Zednick, Representatives George Kinnear and B. Roy Anderson, and County Commissioner Harold Sparkman. While Earl Millikin attempted a political comeback in the 1946 race for state senator, he suffered a convincing defeat at the hands of Zednick. Allan Pomeroy, an Assistant United States Attorney and Queen Anne class of '23, ran for mayor in 1948 as an outsider challenging William Devin and the downtown clique. But Devin mobilized the Queen Anne establishment, including Reginald Parsons, Charles Moriarty, Donald McFee, and the Republican legislators to turn back Pomeroy's effort. In 1948's presidential election, Queen Anne supported Thomas Dewey with 5,935 votes and 4,805 votes for Harry Truman. In the legislative contests, Kinnear and Anderson outpolled Democrats Edo Vanni and Lou Cohen by 2,000 votes.

Major issues which stirred Queen Anne during the late 1940s included the promotion of home playgrounds in 1946, a successful drive to halt construction of an airfield proposed for Interbay in 1947, a campaign to keep Boeing from relocating in 1949, and perennial initiatives to increase parking along Queen Anne Avenue, reduce the activity of juvenile "gangs" and their mischief, and to improve streets and parks.

At home, twelve radio stations and the Federal Old Line Insurance Company with offices in the former Queen Anne Community Club Building, promoted community sing-alongs with the distribution of thousands of songbooks. The community supported the Famine Emergency Drive for Europe and China, the March of Dimes, the Community Chest, the American Cancer Society, and World Relief. Queen Anne feted her city championship football teams in 1945 and 1948. And the decade ended with Jack Morris and Don Sprinkle preparing the first Queen City Bowl game, touted as "the most spectacular grid and half-time show ever attempted in Seattle."

***Ronald Palmer*** *Ph.D. was a resident of Queen Anne 1958-1991, former professor of History at Seattle Pacific University, and past President of the Queen Anne Historical Society.*

Chapter Thirteen

# In Our Time—1950–1993

by
John P. Hennes, Editor, Lana Christman,
Linda Humphrey McCallum,
Marion Parker, Betty Renkor,
and Lt. Richard Schneider

## The Way We Were

by John Hennes

The end of World War II found Queen Anne short of housing, overdue for improvements in its schools and parks, and sharing in the struggling post-war economy. One theme runs through the years from 1950 to today: Queen Anne's residents want a community good for families in which to live and grow. Forces that appear to threaten this are strongly and vocally resisted. Many Queen Anne families today have roots that go back several generations; most new residents have chosen Queen Anne because of its physical setting and its community values. The thread of preserving both the past and the family community runs through every

*Queen Anne's first entry in the Seafair Parade and Miss Seafair competition was Sally Dailey, Queen Anne High School, Class of 1953. The float, sponsored by the Queen Anne Commercial Club, took second place overall. Courtesy* Queen Anne News.

decade. The highlights of the era from 1950 to 1993, as seen from the contemporary perspective, are given below.

**1950** The Big Blizzard, January 13.
Queen Anne Field House opened.
**1951** Dennis the Menace created by Hank Ketcham.
**1956** Johnny Cherberg elected Washington State Lt. Governor.
Parsons Memorial Gardens dedicated.
**1958** Luther Field constructed.
**1960** Interbay dump and landfill in Smith Cove closed and nine-hole golf course developed.
Marshall Viewpoint donated to the city.
**1961** Large Safeway on top of Queen Anne Hill opened.
**1962** Century 21, the 1962 Seattle World's Fair opened. The fair grounds now form Seattle Center.
Columbus Day storm.
**1964** McClure Middle School opened.
**1965** April 29 earthquake, measuring intensity between 6.5 and 7 on the Richter scale.
**1967** The NBA professional basketball team, the Seattle Supersonics, opened season at the Coliseum.
**1968** Forward Thrust bond issue passed giving financial support to Queen Anne parks.
Small developments at Kerry Park, Coe School, and Soundview Terrace.
Love Israel, formerly Paul Erdman, established his "Church of the Armageddon" on Queen Anne.
**1970** The "Boeing Bust" of 1970-1971. Boeing Co. employment dropped from over 100,000 to 40,000.
Port of Seattle Grain Terminal opened.
"Bhy" Kracke Park opened.
**1971** Queen Anne Parks Committee acquired property for Mayfair Park.
**1974** Hansen Bakery Company building redeveloped into a shopping complex.
Queen Anne Community Pool opened.
**1978** King Tut exhibit showcased in Seattle Center.
Seattle School District moved from voluntary to mandatory bussing.
**1981** Queen Anne High School and West and North Queen Anne Elementary Schools closed.
Queen Anne High School students assigned to Franklin School in South Seattle.
Queen Anne Helpline formed to help the needy.
Queen Anne Thriftway remodeled.
**1983** Bagley Wright Theater opened.
**1984** Jesse Wineberry elected to State Legislature (Queen Anne High School, class of 1973).
**1989** Queen Anne Library reopened after extensive renovation.
Blackstock Lumber Co. fire.
**1990** The S & M Market closed its doors in May.
**1992** Demolition of the Hansen Baking Company.
Queen Anne a popular film location for Hollywood movie companies.
City-wide mandatory water rationing left Queen Anne's lawns brown.
**1993** The inaugural day windstorm on January 20, the biggest since the 1962 Columbus Day storm, blew through the northwest.
The City of Seattle proposed a new "Urban Village" including parts of Queen Anne in response to Washington State's 1990 Growth Management Act.

## New Parks Shaped Our Community

by John Hennes

On Queen Anne the issue of parks has always brought out the community in its attempts to balance development with preservation.

A field house had long been sought for Queen Anne. In 1936 the Queen Anne Community Clubhouse on Queen Anne Avenue was proposed by the Council of Queen Anne Clubs for conversion to a field house suitable for official park activities, but the proposal did not succeed.

The focus for a field house location moved to the West Queen Anne Playfield, commonly known as Howe Field, located between First and Second avenues W. and W. Blaine and Howe streets. The dirt field was used in the fall for Queen Anne High School football practice.

The West Queen Anne Playfield site gained support and plans to vacate the area north of W. Howe Street for a field house and community building were pursued. But a strong reaction from some Queen Anne residents to the incipient loss of houses led, in 1946, to a petition drive opposing extension of the field. A counter-statement from a wide variety of school and youth groups contained endorsements for the expansion.

Finally, in 1948, following much community input, the plans for a field house were authorized at the West Queen Anne Playfield. On April 28, 1950 the Queen Anne field house was opened. A dance for Queen Anne High School students followed that evening, kicking off years of youth activities.

Expansion of West Queen Anne Playfield to include the area between Second and Third avenues W. was financed by passage of the Forward Thrust bond issue in February 1968. In 1972 the Queen Anne Recreation Center, as the complex of field and field house was then called, was completed.

*In September 1977, as part of a "Saturday in the Park," program, an old-time band concert in Kinnear Park was sponsored by the Queen Anne Historical Society. Courtesy University of Washington Library, Special Collections.*

Funds for the Queen Anne Swimming Pool were also part of the Forward Thrust bond issue. A pool to serve the Queen Anne-Magnolia area had been a goal for decades, but all proposed locations met with controversy. The West Queen Anne/McClure Junior High site was the ultimate choice. Ten homes were razed along First Avenue W. between W. Howe and W. Crockett streets. In 1977, after a cost of $846 thousand plus the land purchases, the Queen Anne Pool was opened.

*Parsons Gardens, 650 West Highland Drive, was formerly the private garden of Reginald and Maude Parsons, whose home is on the left. It was given to the city in 1956 by their children and has since been used for weddings and small community gatherings, as well as for the solitary pleasures of garden lovers. Photo by Isabel Egglin.*

As far back as the Olmsted Report in 1904 there were proposals for waterfront parks along Elliott Bay. That report recommended acquiring land at the foot of Denny Way. It also suggested a Harbor View Park in the area bounded by First Avenue, John and Bay streets, and the water, including the high bluffs there and the railroad tracks, then on trestles. In 1968, **Myrtle Edwards Park** was developed from Bay Street N. to Pier 88, the old rock-fill pier at Smith Cove.

The Forward Thrust vote also included funds for two neighborhood mini-parks. **Mayfair Park**, at Second Avenue N. and Raye Street, fits into the side of a northeast Queen Anne Hill ravine. It occupies 16,448 square feet and contains a variety of small park environments.

**"Bhy" Kracke Park**, located at 5th Avenue North and Highland Drive, is named for Werner H. "Bhy" Kracke. Its unique design features a steep winding trail linking the lower level, containing a playground, to the middle and upper levels, which provide a wonderful view.

**Marshall Viewpoint,** the park across the street from Parsons Gardens overlooking the Sound, was a gift to the city in 1960 from George and Margaret Marshall. A section of the park had been named in honor of Admiral Thomas S. Phelps, who in 1855 was aboard the gunboat *Decatur* during the "Battle of Seattle." Several sections of sidewalk art by Northwest artists are a memorial to Betty Bowen, civic leader and preservationist.

**Kerry Park Outlook** on W. Highland Drive between Second and Third Avenues W., was enhanced in 1971 by a well-known sculpture, *Changing Form*, by local artist Doris Totten Chase.

*Counterbalance hill in our time. This February 1973 scene from Queen Anne Avenue and Mercer Street shows the electric trolley bus and wires that have been part of Queen Anne since the 1940s. Bayview Manor Retirement Center on the left is on the site of the landmark Kinnear Mansion destroyed in 1959, to the dismay of the community who loved the elegant Queen Anne style house with its beautiful gardens and fountains. Courtesy University of Washington Library Special Collections.*

## GREENBELTS AND LANDSLIDES

The idea of greenbelts was proposed in 1954 and incorporated into the City Council's 1957 Comprehensive Plan. A greenbelt was defined as "an area in public ownership or control left primarily in its natural state." The rationale included to provide buffer zones, to prevent development in areas unsuitable for buildings, to maintain belts of natural landscape for recreation, and to avoid continuous development.

The initial two proposed Queen Anne greenbelts were on the northeast and southwest hillsides. The two areas have been subject to extensive landslide damage over the years, caused by the collection of springs and underground waterflow that underlies much of Queen Anne. An updated Greenbelt Ordinance was passed by the City Council on May 1, 1983. Despite these ordinances, and without the funding to attain public ownership, development continues to some extent along the areas. Current construction technology has permitted limited building on steep sites formerly considered "unbuildable."

## OUR LIBRARY CONTINUES TO SERVE

by Marion Parker

As it did during World War I, library circulation decreased during World War II. Gasoline rationing, long work hours, and the opening of the Magnolia Branch Library in 1943 all contributed to the decline. Among the wartime patrons were service personnel stationed at the Coast Artillery Anti-Aircraft Battalion located on Mt. Pleasant Cemetery grounds.

The 1950s found much interest among borrowers in civil defense preparation. New local television publicity for the public libraries featured Laura Wang, Queen Anne children's librarian.

Larger book budgets in the 1960s supported new services for the increasing number of community college students. In the mid-1970s the microfilm catalog, with its microfiche supplement, was installed and eventually supplanted the card catalog.

The library established a Neighborhood Resource

Center in 1978, offering information on the community council activities as well as other city government policies. The north windows of the library were replaced in 1978 with a vivid art glass mural of five panels created by Richard Spaulding, who said, "It captures the flow of the architectural style of the Carnegie-designed 1914 building."

With a 1984 bond issue the Queen Anne Library was renovated, receiving new plumbing, heating and electrical systems, seismic protection, cabinet work, and a handicapped entrance on the west side of the building.

Computer terminals for the use of the staff and the public were installed in 1992. The library is in step with the future.

## FIRE STATIONS TODAY

by Lt. Richard Schneider

The end of World War II brought about in 1947 the shortening of the firefighters' long wartime work hours. This resulted in a reassignment of personnel and the subsequent closing of five stations, including numbers 4 and 24 on Queen Anne.

Station No. 24, at 1520 Fifth Avenue W., was closed in 1954. Fire Station No. 4, 223 Fourth Avenue N., had been used only as a fire alarm communications center from 1924 until it was razed in 1961 to make way for the Space Needle in 1962. Fire Station No. 20, Fourteenth W. and Gilman, originally the "Interbay" station, was replaced in 1949 by a new station constructed at 3205 Thirteenth Avenue W.

For years the northwest corner of Warren Avenue N. and Lee Street has been city property, housing tennis courts, the tank and tower of the Water Department, and Fire Station No. 8 at 1417 Warren Avenue N. By the 1960s the station had become old and a replacement was built at 110 Lee Street to house Engine No. 8 and Ladder No. 6. The old station was promptly razed and two new tennis courts replaced it.

## THE CIVIC CENTER

by John Hennes

The Seattle Center as it exists in 1993 had its start with the Civic Auditorium, Civic Ice Arena and Civic Field which were built in 1927, using a voter-approved bond issue to match a fund bequeathed to the city by businessman James Osborne when he died in 1881.

The Civic Field, originally carrying the name Auditorium Field, was inaugurated on September 28, 1928 with a football game between Queen Anne and Broadway high schools. The Seattle Indians, the city's first professional baseball team, were also a regular occupant of Civic Field.

In 1939 the Washington State Armory was constructed to house the National Guard. After World War II the Civic Field was sold to the Seattle School District

*This pre-World's Fair view of the Civic Auditorium, taken in 1959, is looking east across Third Avenue N. at Mercer Street. The Seattle Center Opera House was built within the shell of the cavernous 1927 auditorium. The World War I Doughboy statue is now located on the south side of the Opera House. Courtesy University of Washington Library Special Collections.*

for $1 and rebuilt and enlarged to 12,000 seats. It opened in the fall of 1948 as the High School Memorial Stadium. In 1950 a Memorial Shrine was built on the entry plaza to honor the young men and women who had attended Seattle public schools and died in World War II.

By the 1950s, there was a regular pattern of dances at the armory, concerts, roadshow musicals and graduations at the auditorium, and football games at Memorial Stadium.

## CENTURY 21, THE WORLD'S FAIR

by John Hennes and Linda Humphrey McCallum

Passage of a 1956 bond issue started the next phase of the Civic Center's development. By the following year plans were underway for a 74-acre home for an international exposition. The Civic Auditorium was transformed into the Opera House. The massive armory became an equally massive Food Circus. The graceful United States Science Pavilion and the intriguing Washington State Coliseum with its "bubbleator" elevator were built. The Gayway Amusement Area moved into the space east of the Food Circus. The Warren Avenue School playground became the site of the International Fountain.

The development of the World's Fair site required the removal of many blocks of houses and small apartments, Fire Station No. 4, the Warren Avenue School, and other small commercial buildings. Streets were closed, people displaced, new apartments speedily built for the Fair; the face and tenor of uptown Queen Anne was forever changed.

The architecture of the Seattle Center is the legacy of the Century 21 Exposition. The World's Fair got off to an excellent start when it was assumed *a priori* that architects would be involved. A Design Standards Advisory Board was appointed and well-known northwest architect Paul Thiry was named Chief Architect. Thiry designed the Coliseum as the Washington State "World of Tomorrow" exhibit.

Minoru Yamasaki boldly proposed building the new Opera House within the shell of the existing Civic Auditorium, a move that would give the city a building worth several million dollars more than the bond issue allotment of $3.5 million dollars.

Yamasaki's design for the United States Science Pavilion, done in association with Seattle architects Naramore, Bain, Brady and Johanson, was by far his greatest contribution to the Center. His interest in Gothic forms led to the five open-ribbed vaults which form the focus of what is now called the Pacific Science Center. Alistair Cooke of the *Manchester Guardian* and "Masterpiece Theater," in spite of his outspoken criticism of the Fair in general, was awed by the serene structure and noted, "It is as if Venice had just been built."

The most enduring symbol of the Century 21 architecture is the ever-dominant Space Needle. The revolving saucer atop a dramatic 600-foot pedestal was the brainchild of Eddie Carlson, Century 21's greatest promoter. Carlson, who made his name in the hotel business and ultimately became the president of United Air Lines, had been in Stuttgart, Germany on vacation when he was struck by the visual dominance and profitability of the television tower there. He consulted with Ewen Dingwall, Century 21 chairman, and architect John Graham, who proposed the idea of a spinning restaurant. Victor Steinbrueck, Professor at the Univer-

*The Century 21 Exposition, always referred to as the World's Fair by Seattleites, led to several permanent Seattle landmarks. The 608-foot Space Needle and the seven-acre Pacific Science Center, pictured here during construction in 1961, are known throughout the world. Courtesy Museum of History and Industry.*

sity of Washington School of Architecture, was called in and eventually designed the delicate tripod which supports a futuristic saucer and restaurant. A mid-level banquet facility, part of the original plan, was added in 1982 to celebrate the 20th anniversary of the Needle.

The International Fountain, a concrete and colored-glass tile musical extravaganza designed by Tokyo architects Hideki Shimizu and Kazuyuki Matsushita, was the winner of a $250,000 international competition. Its 117 water jets shoot streams 100 feet into the air to the accompaniment of music and light changes.

## The Seattle Center

by John Hennes

By the close of the six-month Seattle World's Fair in October 1962, ten million people from around the globe had visited the Queen Anne area. In 1963, the city regained control of the grounds and the Seattle Center Advisory Commission was formed.

Professional basketball arrived in Seattle as the NBA Seattle Supersonics opened the 1967-68 season at the Coliseum. The team, named after the supersonic airplane the Boeing Company was then developing, played its first 11 years at the Coliseum before moving to the Kingdome for the 1978-79 championship season. In 1985 the Sonics returned to the Coliseum, where the team remains today. Plans for a major rebuilding of the Coliseum—lowering the floor, adding seats and boxes, remodeling locker rooms and other major fixes—are scheduled to be finished in 1995.

From 1974 to 1976 Memorial Stadium hosted a professional team, the Seattle Sounders of the North American Soccer League.

In 1978 the King Tut Exhibit, on a world tour, was showcased in the Center's Flag Pavilion and was a prime ticket for thousands from the northwest. In 1982 the Seattle Repertory Theatre, matching a $4.8 million bond issue, completed construction of the Bagley Wright Theater, named for its first president, in the northwest corner of the Center. The Intiman Theatre company moved into the Repertory's former site near the Fitzgerald Fountain.

Each year the Center hosts three large festivals: the Folklife Festival on Memorial Day weekend, the Bite of Seattle in mid-July, and Bumbershoot on Labor Day weekend. Several hundred thousand people attend each of these events.

Currently, plans for major renovation of Center facilities are funded by a $25.8 million 1991 levy. The Seattle Symphony is separately engaged in its development of a state-of-the-art symphony hall on the north side of Mercer Street between Second and Third avenues N.

The growth of the Seattle Center parallels the changes in Queen Anne as a whole. Traffic and parking are constant issues in the 1990s. The "Mercer Street Mess" is a byword for the traffic problems connecting lower Queen Anne with the I-5 freeway. But the role of the Center as a home for the performing arts has led to growth of the Queen Anne area as a desirable location for theater groups and artists.

Traditions from the old days endure. High school football games are still played at "Civic Field," dances are still held at the armory, children still play at the Warren Avenue playground (the International Fountain area), and Potlatch Meadows continues to be a peaceful gathering place.

## The Love Family

by Lana Anderson Christman

In 1968, Love Israel, formerly Paul Erdman, came to Queen Anne Hill to establish his church. Earlier that year, he and Logic Israel, Brian Allen, had a vision of an alternative society in which members would love one another, work in harmony and share the common good. The society family took form as a new religious group, the Church of Armageddon, and offered an alternative lifestyle as the Love Israel Family.

The Family's structure was wholly authoritarian, with Love Israel at its head. Several Elders consulted and counseled Love Israel. Upon joining the Family, followers' first names were discarded for a new name chosen by Love Israel fitting the follower's demeanor, such as Serious, Strength or Meekness. Israel, "the chosen people of God," was used as the common surname.

By 1972, the Family had grown to 60 members and owned seven homes on the hill. At the heart of the commune-like Family's living space was a beautifully landscaped outdoor sanctuary between 8th and 9th avenues W. in the vicinity of Mt. Pleasant Cemetery.

As its numbers grew, the Family became more involved in the Queen Anne community. Toys and musical instruments were sold out of their woodworking shop and a natural food store was set up. An empty lot behind these businesses on W. McGraw Street was turned into a small park.

Serious and Logic Israel were elected to the Queen Anne Community Council. Serious was on the council's Land Use Review Committee and was described by a council member as "charming, even charismatic, and always in favor of preserving the livability of Queen Anne Hill." They were also hired by the city to maintain Parsons Gardens.

By 1982, there were approximately 300 members of the Love Family occupying 12 to 15 homes on the hill. A large house for Love Israel and his household was developed in the 500 block of W. Halladay Street.

The threshold into the world of the Love Israel Family was the "Open Door Inn" at 617 W. McGraw Street. A Family guest-house across the street sheltered people for longer stays. Overcrowded at times, travelers would pitch tents in the small park behind the Open Door Inn.

In late 1983, a dispute with a Family member regarding money irreparably damaged the church and its followers. About 30 of Love's remaining followers were forced out of their Queen Anne headquarters by a legal settlement.

Today the small but loyal band of 35 adults and 52 children, including Love Israel, live on a rustic ranch outside the town of Arlington in Snohomish County.

*The 600-foot high television broadcast towers on Queen Anne can be seen throughout greater Seattle. This 1993 photo, taken from Capitol Hill, shows, from left to right, KING, KOMO, and KIRO towers along with the former Queen Anne High School. Photo by Isabel Egglin.*

## Those TV Towers

by Betty Renkor

During the December holiday season, a visitor gazing toward Queen Anne might be entranced by the sparkling, colorful lights stretching hundreds of feet up into the night air as, for a few weeks, the KING Television broadcast tower becomes a cheerful beacon in the dark winter sky. Many Queen Anne residents live in the shadow of the KING tower or the two other huge steel towers, KOMO and KIRO, that dominate the residential neighborhood and which are not complementary to its character. The towers also raise concerns for some about stability during earthquakes and danger from radiation.

The history of the towers starts with an old grocery store on Galer Street at Third Avenue N. The store was the site of a 100-foot radar tower used by the military in World War II. In 1947, radio station KEVR bought the old store tower, hung radio broadcast equipment, and established the first FM radio station in Seattle. On Thanksgiving of the following year television station KRSC delivered the first television broadcast in the northwest from the same tower. It was Seattle's move into the future. With less than 1,000 television sets in the area, the inaugural November 25, 1948 broadcast of the cross-state high school football matchup between West Seattle and Wenatchee was seen by fewer people via the airwaves than by the 12,000 people who attended the game at the newly-reopened Memorial Stadium. In 1949, KING bought KRSC, the first sale of a TV station in the U.S.

Extensive testing prior to 1952 confirmed the 450-foot high Queen Anne location as the best in the immediate Seattle area for television broadcasting. A Federal Communications Commission (FCC) freeze on TV licenses kept Queen Anne free of other such towers until 1952 when the FCC freeze was lifted. KOMO television rushed to erect its own tower.

Two broadcast towers in the heart of a vital community were enough for many Queen Anne residents. Objections to an additional tower became focused in the Queen Anne Community Club's 1957 protest of KIRO Television's plans to build a new tower at 1520 Queen Anne Avenue. In spite of community protest the KIRO tower was built in 1958 at the site of the Queen Anne YMCA building, which was razed. The day the KIRO tower was completed, Superior Court Judge Henry Clay Agnew ruled the tower had been placed at the location illegally. Zoning laws had changed since the application was filed in 1951, but the judge allowed the tower to stay.

By the mid 1980s, the three towers ranged from 556 feet to 613 feet above ground level. The construction of substantially taller buildings downtown, most notably the Columbia Center, caused increasing interference with the signals. The three stations in 1986 proposed higher towers, to make them 1,349 feet above sea level. The Queen Anne Community Council denounced the tower expansion and some Queen Anne residents organized the Citizens Against Tower Expansion (CATE). "We do not believe 919-foot towers belong in our neighborhood," Linda Dagg, a member of CATE, said at a June 1992 rally opposing higher towers.

In 1992 the City Council passed an ordinance limiting tower height to 1,100 feet above sea level. If the new ordinance applies to the existing broadcast towers, they could be raised only about 100 feet, but the broadcasting companies believe they have vested rights to build towers to 1,349 feet above sea level. The issue is still open.

## Residential Architectural Trends on Queen Anne Hill Since 1950

by Linda Humphrey McCallum

The flourishing of traditional architecture on Queen Anne Hill at the turn of the century was followed by a predictible swing to modernism, starting in the 1950s. The ubiquitous brick rambler, loosely patterned after the "Prairie Houses" of Frank Lloyd Wright but without their grace or ornament, spread across the top of the hill, as gracious older homes and existing vacant lots made way for this efficient icon of 1950s popular culture.

From the 1960s' "New Frontier" modernism of the Seattle Center to the respectful and meticulous restorations conducted since the 1980s, late twentieth-century Queen Anne architecture has generally reflected the changing styles of modernism throughout the country. Good examples of most styles of the Modernist Movement were built on the hill.

In 1952 architect Robert Reichert threw the neighborhood of 2500 Third Avenue W. into a frenzy when he constructed what was to be the first contemporary house on Queen Anne Hill. Built to accomodate himself, his mother and a large pipe organ, the structure reflected the size and shape of the instrument. But that was not what alarmed the neighborhood. The stucco-faced structure was covered with black and white abstract graphics, complete with a wave pattern washing over the roof. The black fence surrounding the property was detailed with pivoting rings that spun with the wind currents. Concrete obelisks covered with hieroglyphics stood sentry in the garden. Today nothing remains of the original graphics or the stuccoed exterior. While Reichert may have shocked his neighbors, he was remembered in 1990 for his daring with an exhibition of his work at the Seattle Art Museum.

In the 1960s, a regional movement developed which became known as Northwest style or Northwest Timber style. One Seattle architect who was influenced by this movement, as well as by the Frank Lloyd Wright School, was Ralph Anderson. While many homes on Queen Anne Hill were designed by his firm, the earliest and most significant dwellings are the residence at 18 Highland Drive (1965) and Pifer House (1970) at 1317 Willard Avenue W. Both of these homes are characterized by exaggerated vertical volumes with wide overhangs to fend off Northwest rain. Large windows admit a maximum of light and simple, monochromatic colors define the exteriors.

In 1968 Seattle architect Gordon Walker stretched the concept of "contextual architecture" by designing a concrete-block house at 411 W. Comstock Street. It took its inspiration from the Bauhaus School, a German design movement of the twenties, which saw structures pared to their essential elements. The simple, unadorned Bauhaus style led architects of the mid-twentieth century to eschew ornament and rely on the natural material of a structure to give it elegance. Walker was fascinated with the use of concrete block for construction. His clients, the Raffs, wanted a house that would accomodate their Oriental rugs and a huge number of books. The house is very woody inside, with cedar trim and ceiling, oak floors and wood partition walls. Over the years the natural landscaping has softened the exterior lines of this very modern version of the traditional brownstone.

Bruce Goff's highly decorative approach can be seen at 173 Ward Street in the Taylor house, a project of many years and much love. The owner, Gene Taylor, had seen Goff's work in the midwest. Decorated with a mosaic of tiny gold and blue mirrored squares, the house is actually a remodel of a conventional lapped cedar siding structure. The Taylors converted the house over a 12-year period, doing most of the work themselves.

The 1980s and 1990s had their share of million-dollar-plus-homes testing the buildable limits of Queen Anne lots. Too many were built without architectural plans and little reverence for the character of the

*The Taylor home, 173 Ward Street, was designed by Bruce Goff. Photo by Isabel Egglin.*

surrounding homes. Many more Queen Anne residents caught the "restoration fever" that had begun in the 1980s. At the time of writing literally hundreds of houses on the hill are being painstakingly remodeled. With the resurgence of interest in the Arts and Crafts style, many Queen Anne bungalows with original box-beamed ceilings, built-in columns and turn-of-the-century light fixtures have became highly desirable. Some renovations, including additions, are so successful that it is hard to distinguish old from new. One highly accomplished renovation designed by Brandt Hollinger of Geise Associates is the 1914 Craftsman style home at 501 W. Comstock. The garage and sunroom on the Fifth Avenue W. side of the property are 1989 additions so perfectly replicating the original Oriental railings and brick parapets that most people cannot distinguish the remodel from the original.

The "classic box," a familiar housing style in the 1910s and 1920s, fell victim to aluminum and asbestos siding in the 1940s and 1950s. But even these homes have come back to life, some with more daring than others. The box at l953 Sixth Avenue W. was converted by architect Lane Williams in the mid-1980s to an intense blue stucco in the "Japonaise" fashion, reflecting both Modernist and Post-modernist influences.

The epitome of restoration is the magnificent gambrel-roofed Georgian colonial at 678 W. Prospect Street. Purchased by the Belanich family in 1991 and meticulously restored by Dean Polley and Mervin Wolf, this replica of a Brookline, Massachusetts historic home was built in 1905 by F.H. Osgood, the engineer who had been brought from Boston to build the Queen Anne Counterbalance.

While loving recreation of the past can be expensive, the idea of authentic renovation has spread over the hill as the working class bungalow takes on new life and the classic box once again displays its elegance. Although modern architecture has become a valued part of this eclectic neighborhood, the ongoing movement toward restoration is a statement of our appreciation for the history of Queen Anne Hill, its residents, and its architecture.

***Lana Anderson Christman** attended John Hay and McClure schools. As volunteer coordinator she was an effective leader in the Queen Anne community history book project. She makes her home with her husband Bryan and daughters Alexandria and Cassandra in West Seattle.*

***John Hennes** grew up on Magnolia, was a founder of the Queen Anne High School Alumni Assoc. and was editor of the association's newsletter, the KUAY, for nine years. He lives on the north slope of the the hill with his wife Margaret Ladhe.*

***Linda Humphrey McCallum,** a graduate of Queen Anne High School and Stanford University, is the Seattle City Editor for* Metropolitan Home *magazine. She has written about architecture of the Northwest for several local and national publications and is co-author of the book* American Design: The Northwest.

***Lt. Richard Schneider** is the historian for the Seattle Fire Department.*

Chapter Fourteen

# A Century of Schools on the Hill

by
Dorothy McBride,
Donald McNichols, Lit.D.,
Marion Parker, Kim Turner,
Elizabeth Whitmire, Kay Yamamoto

## Part I
## Public Elementary, Middle, and High Schools

by Dorothy McBride, Marion Parker,
Kim Turner, Elizabeth Whitmire, Kay Yamamoto

In the 1890s Seattle was a frontier seaport. By contrast, within the decade following the Alaska Gold Rush, Seattle was a fast-growing city, well known as a good place to settle down, raise children and live well. This change in image was tied in part to the foresight and intelligent planning by the city's educational community. As the city expanded northward, early settlers on Queen Anne Hill took a keen and active interest in the establishment of schools in their area.

*West Queen Anne School art class has a lesson in "the power of image selection," circa 1914. Courtesy Washington State Historical Society.*

## WEST QUEEN ANNE, 1889-1981

In 1889, the year of Washington's statehood, the first public school was built on Queen Anne Hill. An unpretentious "shack school," Queen Anne School, with grades one through three, was located on a clearing on a lot bounded by Gaylor (Galer) and Lee streets, and Anna and White streets (Fifth and Sixth Avenues W.) The older boys and girls continued to attend Denny School in Belltown until Mercer School opened in 1890.

In 1895 a six-room Romanesque-style brick building was constructed and by 1902 six more classrooms for the higher grades were added. As principal of Queen Anne School in 1901, Adelaide Pollock became the first woman principal of a Seattle public school. She served until 1918 when she resigned to serve overseas with the Red Cross.

To ease the overcrowding which Queen Anne School was experiencing, an annex was built at the present site of Frantz H. Coe School in 1905, and the East Queen Anne annex was constructed in 1905 at the first John Hay School site. About 1908 the name Queen Anne School was changed to West Queen Anne School to avoid confusion with other schools being developed on the hill. Even with the annexes, enrollment at West Queen Anne continued to increase so quickly that by 1914 stair landings were used as study halls. The final addition of an auditorium and ten rooms was added in 1916. The auditorium, soon used as a meeting room and a polling place, aided the school's recognition as a community asset.

West Queen Anne was to realize much change from the mid-1950s to the 1970s. To alleviate crowding, in 1954-55, seventh and eighth grade classes from Queen Anne elementary schools were moved to the new Junior High School opened in the Queen Anne High School building. When the Warren Avenue School was closed in 1959, West Queen Anne School was flooded by students from as far south as Stewart Street.

The decade of the 1960s was a period of stable enrollment. However, by 1970 enrollments began to decline rapidly, leaving empty classrooms. In 1977, in compliance with federal guidelines for desegregation, bussing became mandatory. This resulted in West Queen Anne becoming a K-3 school, with the fourth through sixth grades being bussed out of the area.

Culminating a long struggle on the part of the community to prevent West Queen Anne School's closure, in 1975 the building was entered on the National Register of Historic Places. In 1977 it was also declared a Seattle City Landmark. To celebrate this occasion and the building's 80th anniversary, the P.T.A. held an open house attended by over 700 people.

In 1981, despite opposition from the community, West Queen Anne was closed, as were North Queen Anne Elementary and Queen Anne High School. The closures were an economic necessity for the Seattle School District. In 1984 West Queen Anne was converted to 49 condominiums.

For nearly 90 years, the halls, classrooms and playgrounds of West Queen Anne Elementary School served the needs of the hilltop community, wearing their age proudly and gracefully.

*During the Great Depression, an elaborate banking procedure was installed in a West Queen Anne classroom converted to a unique "Banking Room" which was operated by seventh and eighth grade student tellers. This city-wide program, which continued until 1974, was sponsored by the Washington Mutual Savings Bank, and it taught children to save regularly. Courtesy Seattle Public School Archives.*

*Mercer School was named for Thomas D. Mercer, the Queen Anne pioneer whose four young daughters Mary Jane, Eliza, Suzie and Alice were the first school children on Queen Anne Hill. In the 1850s they attended Catherine Blaine's home school and then the Territorial University, which offered secondary education. Photo taken circa 1900. Courtesy Queen Anne Historical Society.*

## Mercer School, 1890-1931

In 1890 the Mercer School was built at Fourth Avenue N. and Valley Street on Mercer's donation claim. Almost immediately overcrowded, an addition and an annex were built in 1892. Considered Seattle's finest school in 1892, the Mercer School was a part of the Seattle exhibit at the International Columbian Exposition, Chicago, as an example of Seattle's modern education facilities.

Following the construction of Warren Avenue School in 1902, enrollment at Mercer declined. The building was closed as a regular school in 1931, but continued to be used as an adjustment school until 1940. It was next used as a training school for district custodians, until it was finally removed in 1948 to make way for the School District's new Administrative and Service Center.

### Learning to Keep a Store

In 1978, Follow Through, a continuation of preschool Head Start, was placed at West Queen Anne, sharing the building with the regular student body. In 1979, Follow Through students operated a classroom store, using Nelsen's Grocery as their wholesaler. With the cooperation of restaurateur Victor Rossellini, the class was able to use the store profits for the learning experience of dining in a fine restaurant.

## Interbay School, 1901-1930

The Salmon Bay School Annex was built in 1901 at 16th Avenue W. and Barrett Street. In 1902 the name was changed to Interbay Annex, and operated under the supervision of the Salmon Bay School (now Lawton School). In 1903 an eight-room permanent Interbay School building opened for classes, with Miss L. Maxine Kelly as principal, at a monthly salary of $105, and five teachers.

Miss Kelly, during her twenty-nine year tenure, reported on the delights of working with a student population which she titled "a melting pot of nationalities." Included were Russians, Latvians, Austrians, Germans, Lithuanians, Icelanders and Norwegians. There was even an ethnic mix among the teachers, some from the British Isles, Denmark, and "one Manx."

In 1916 a kindergarten was added, and in 1920 the enrollment peaked at 519 students. With the opening of the Magnolia School and St. Margaret Parochial School, Interbay's enrollment declined and the school was closed in 1932.

Although it lived a short life, Interbay had its share of unusual happenings. Miss Kelly once heard an odd noise and rescued the janitor caught in the fan room pulley. Later there was the tragic electrocution of a workman on the roof of a portable. Built near tide flats, the southwest corner of the school grounds was a swampy area. The Mothers' Club and local area citizens made repeated requests to have this problem corrected for reasons of sanitation and safety; the problem continued without permanent solution until 1935, when the drainage was finally completed.

## Warren Avenue School, 1902-1959

Warren Avenue School was built as a 12-room school in 1902 on David Denny's Home Addition, bounded by Harrison and Republican streets, Second Avenue N., and Warren Avenue. In 1914 eight rooms were added. From its early years, Warren Avenue offered special education for the visually-impaired students of Seattle elementary schools.

The Warren Avenue school prospered, and one

*Warren Avenue school playground. Recess time, 1905. Supervising the playground was a regular part of the teacher's duties. The teacher on the left is pushing the pair of girls on the swing. Courtesy Washington State Historical Society.*

area of success was in athletics. For example, in 1939 the Warren Avenue school teams were Seattle Grade School Champions in both soccer and baseball. Student enrollments were strong and by 1959 the school's enrollment required seven portables. However, that year the school was razed to make room for the Coliseum, built for the 1962 World's Fair. Trees from the Warren Avenue School playground can still be seen bordering the Seattle Center's International Fountain.

## Coe School, 1905-present

In 1905 two temporary buildings were constructed at 2433 Sixth Avenue W. as an annex to Queen Anne School. In 1907 an eight-room, two-story building in Ionic Colonial style was erected with capacity for about 390 students. At this time the average class was 39 pupils and the school had 355 enrolled.

The school was named Frantz H. Coe Elementary School, honoring a prominent physician who served on the School Board from 1901 to 1904, and whose wife was also active in school and community affairs. By 1919 an eight-room wing was added to the building's north side and the school had eighteen teachers and 575 students. Encouraged by their teachers to participate in national events, in 1931 Coe student Grant Crouch wrote Admiral Richard Byrd a letter which was included in a volume presented to Byrd upon his return from the South Pole. Grant told Byrd, "I want to congratulate you on your kindness to dumb animals. You could easily have left those dogs

*Coe School. Drawing by Tony Cresci. Courtesy Queen Anne Historical Society.*

## The Asian Scholar's Garden

As part of the School District's overall desegregation program, Asian immigrant adjustment classes were offered at Coe School. To further the school's unique relationship with its sister school in Chongquin, China, the Asian Scholar's Garden was completed in 1991 on the north side of the school yard. A plaque in the Asian garden advises:

*If you are planning for a year, sow rice.*
*If you are planning for a decade, sow trees.*
*If you are planning for a lifetime,*
***educate people.***

*–Old Chinese Proverb*

*Photo by Isabel Egglin.*

down there and brought the airplanes back, but deep down in your heart those dogs were worth more to you than all the airplanes in the world."

In 1950 eighth grade students were moved to the Junior High School at Queen Anne High, followed in 1955 by the seventh-graders. Serving as principal from 1954 to 1972, Ernest Bartol was noted for his strong leadership and innovative programs, including the addition of a gymnasium and a learning resource center in 1972.

## Inga Ewbank

Inga Ewbank is a well-remembered and beloved Coe teacher whose Seattle teaching career began in the mid-forties. In the fall of 1959 kindergartens were eliminated because of the failure of a school levy, and Ewbank was recruited by local parents to organize and instruct in a private kindergarten in the Queen Anne area. The following year she began her kindergarten teaching career at Coe school, retiring in 1976. Up to the time of her death in 1992 at age 82, Mrs. Ewbank was an active substitute teacher as well as an outstanding volunteer in community and church projects. She left behind a legacy of love and caring.

## John Hay School, 1905-present

A shack school known as the East Queen Anne Annex of Queen Anne School was built on the block bounded by Bigelow and Fourth Avenues N. and Crockett and Newton streets in 1905, and served first and second-grade pupils. An imposing two-and-a-half-story, eight-room building, with octagonal towers framing the entrance, was completed on the site.

A unique early feature of the school was the open-air room where windows were kept open year-round. For years the principal routinely took VIP visitors to the attic to see the panoramic view. It was named John M. Hay Elementary School, in honor of President Abraham Lincoln's secretary, who later became Secretary of State under Presidents McKinley and Theodore Roosevelt. The school received an oil portrait of John Hay from his widow, which has always hung in the school.

Between 1914 and 1922 the school's burgeoning enrollment resulted in adding rooms and portables. In 1922 a one-story brick building with nine classrooms and a combination auditorium/lunchroom and two play courts was completed on Boston Street. Despite the distance separating the old and new buildings, both were used for classes. Depression-era cutbacks ended plans to demolish the original school building, which today is used by an alternative education program.

Between 1930 and 1940 the enrollment remained

*John Hay school, ca. early 1900s. Courtesy Seattle School District Archives.*

at 500 to 550 pupils. After World War II it increased to approximately 600, where it remained, despite the transfer of the seventh and eighth grades to Queen Anne Junior High School. A memory of those at John Hay in 1948 was the broadcast of Art Linkletter's "House Party" in December from the school. This was a popular nation-wide radio show, and students and faculty alike were excited and proud.

By 1977 only kindergarten through third grade were taught at John Hay, due to bussing conforming to district desegregation plans, and enrollment dropped drastically. Under Principal Louise McKinney, the Early Childhood Education Program was introduced to the Seattle school system at John Hay. This highly-individualized learning program proved to be a drawing card, and enrollment increased to nearly 500 over the next three years.

By the late 1980s, the old buildings no longer met student needs, and a new John Hay School was built on Luther Field, the old Queen Anne High School athletic field, and opened in January 1989. In September 1990 elementary school grade configurations were changed to include K-5, with the sixth grades attending the middle school. In 1990, as a way of encouraging environmental awareness and the value of recycling, the PTA decided to create a wildlife habitat on the east side of the school. The students took over the recycling, composting, and caring for the garden.

## ORTHOPEDIC SCHOOL, 1912-1953

Desiring accreditation for its teaching program at the hospital, in 1912 the staff of Children's Orthopedic Hospital (COH) requested from the Seattle School Board the assignment of a regular teacher. The hospital and detention school was given a half-time teacher. Slowly the Orthopedic staff grew to four full-time teachers. To clear any doubt as to the legality of the classes at COH, a Seattle judge decided that this facility be "construed as an annex to nearby John Hay Elementary School and to be under the supervision of that Principal."

It was a red-letter day in 1933 when President Franklin Roosevelt visited the hospital. Students from John Hay School, waving flags, greeted him as his party drove slowly down the street and up to the hospital entrance. In 1948 there were 55 patient/pupils at the hospital and its annex, a small facility on Lawton bluff. The John Hay/COH partnership ended when the hospital moved to its new north end location in 1953.

*West Queen Anne pupils learned woodworking skills from Miss Adelaide Pollock, who taught them how to build a birdhouse. Courtesy Washington State Historical Society. ca. 1905*

## NORTH QUEEN ANNE ELEMENTARY, 1913-1981

Beginning in a storefront laundry building at the southeast corner of Florentia Street and Dexter Avenue, the North Queen Anne School soon moved into a new four-room brick building that was completed at 2919 First Avenue W.

Teacher Cora Hale Gavett recalled years later:

> *There were no electric lights, no telephone, and no principal. . . Mr. E.C. Roberts, principal at Ross School, across the present Canal, shared his administrative time with us at North Queen Anne, where he would come every two weeks. The cutting down of the high bluff to the south of us to make way for the tiny school yard left a very high dirt wall, topped with the original trees of the forest. It was so dark in midwinter that there were times that I stood by the window and read to the children to save their eyes. Reading classes were lined up against the window so they could see.*

The school's Parent-Teacher Association, organized in 1916, was an active force in the school and north slope community, and was instrumental in the 1930s in closing the hazardous sandpit located near the school.

One of the beloved and well-remembered teachers is Miss Laura Deringer. A graduate of Seattle Seminary, she spent 36 of her 48 teaching years at North Queen Anne. She is recalled by former pupils from her 8th grade class in 1931 as a tiny person, wearing her hair drawn back in a tight bun, pince-nez glasses, and in complete control of the classroom—just a few taps of her pencil on the desk and the room was "at attention!" Long retired, in 1993 she was 102 years old.

The school grew steadily, requiring an eight-room addition in 1933. In 1944 the eighth grade was transferred to the new Queen Anne Eighth Grade Center.

At the beginning of World War II, the school served as community headquarters where citizens registered for ration books to obtain scarce commodities, i.e., gasoline, sugar, meat, shoes, etc. A war bond and stamp drive was held from March 1 to May 15, 1943. This "Jeep Drive" netted $4,849.60, enough to purchase five jeeps.

Marking its 50th anniversary in 1964, economic necessity forced the closure of North Queen Anne in 1981. It was leased to the Northwest Center for the Retarded for use as an Early Childhood Education Center in 1983.

### Michael Kemp-Slaughter

One of McClure's outstanding teachers was Michael Kemp-Slaughter, an avid historian. His Washington State history students researched, wrote, published and sold a 32-page booklet commemorating the 18th-century voyages of Captain George Vancouver, and funds were thus raised for a historical marker to honor this famed Northwest explorer. In 1986, Kemp-Slaughter's students organized the dedication ceremony for the installation of the marker at Phelps Park-Marshall Viewpoint on Queen Anne Boulevard. The dedication involved the entire McClure School student body, community residents, and city officials.

## MCCLURE MIDDLE SCHOOL, 1964-PRESENT

Principal Warren Arnhart welcomed the first students to the newly-constructed Worth McClure Junior High at 1915 First Avenue W. in September 1964. Most of the teachers transferred from the Queen Anne Junior Senior High School. Principal Arnhart had worked closely with the school architect, Ed Mahlum, which resulted in an extremely functional building on a sub-sized site, selected because of the adjacent Community Center and playfield, which the school shared with the Seattle Parks Department.

The school is named for Worth McClure, Seattle School District Superintendent from 1930 to 1944. A trimester plan, as contrasted with the traditional two-semester system, was put in place, and students progressed very well, with seven out of the top ten graduating seniors from Queen Anne High School being from McClure for many years.

McClure students have distinguished themselves over the years by a variety of successful projects, including putting out the *Maverick*, a school newspaper, an "International Tasting Party" and accompanying cookbook, and an award-winning jazz band.

The year 1981 was one of change for Queen Anne Hill, with the closure of the high school and two elementary schools. McClure became a middle school, changing its grade configuration to sixth through eighth. Magnolia students began attending McClure with the closing of Catherine Blaine Junior High.

McClure Middle School is proud of its multiracial student body and in 1987 the Multi-International Colors

Society (MICS) was formed by the students with Dolly Turner, Math/Computer Science head, as faculty adviser. The group's activities have grown to include year-long service and outreach activities; canned food drives for Northwest Harvest; a Math-a-thon for St. Jude's Children's Research Hospital; Christmas Magic, a children's holiday charity; "Bite of McClure", a fundraiser for UNICEF; and an annual spring Ethnic Week celebration. MICS continues to foster leadership skills, parental involvement in projects, and community responsibility.

## Schools for Special Needs

Established by Seattle Public Schools in the fall of 1991 for grades 6-8, New Options Middle School (NOMS) is a multi-cultural learning community which takes "global citizenship" as its central theme, providing an alternative program of solid academic learning. It is located in the old John Hay School at 411 Boston Street. Since 1970 the behaviorally and emotionally disturbed children served by the Seattle Children's Home have been taught at the Home in the McGraw School, an accredited elementary school.

## Queen Anne High School, 1909-1959

Queen Anne High School opened its doors at Second Avenue N. and Galer Street in September 1909 to 613 students and 33 teachers. Under 28-year-old Otto L. Luther, Principal, the teaching staff included Winona Bailey, noted international mountaineer and Latin expert; Samuel E. Fleming, history instructor and later Superintendent of Seattle Public Schools from 1945 to 1956; J. Harlan Bretz, science instructor and geologist; and Benno J. Uhl, German instructor, whose teaching style endeared him to generations of students, and who wrote the first school song.

At the school dedication, February 1910, Principal Luther declared, "Queen Anne High School exemplifies the democratization of the high school and brings vigorously to mind the thought that a high school education is now within the reach of all. The high school is the people's college."

Students flocked to Queen Anne High School, which was viewed as the newest and best in Seattle, from as far away as Port Orchard. The first decade saw Queen Anne gain wide recognition in interscholastic sports, debate and dramatics.

Queen Anne High School supported the World War I war effort with over 250 students and alumni serving in the armed forces by May 1918. Students still enrolled formed the Queen Anne "School Guard," a voluntary military organization. The war over, the first alumni reunion was held on March 26, 1920, which the *Queen Anne News* reported as marked by good music, speeches, and "a riot of fun." In 1921 the monthly school paper, the *Kuay,* become a weekly under the guidance of O.D. Stoddard.

A tradition of a gift to the school from the graduating class existed in the early years, such as the 1922 gift of a hall clock, which now hangs in the School District Archives.

In 1926, the school was greatly expanded by the addition of a new auditorium, a boys' gymnasium, a botany laboratory and greenhouse, 12 classrooms and a music room. The 1,500-seat auditorium, dedicated November 22, 1928, was the finest in the Seattle schools.

*Queen Anne High School architect's drawing, ca. 1908. Courtesy Seattle School District Archives.*

Long-time teachers who joined the faculty in the 1920s included Willard O. Baker, whose Radio Club students built the High School's first amateur radio station, and Arthur Shelton, physics and general science teacher, whose career spanned 35 years. They joined ranks which already included Mabel Furry, women's physical education teacher for 45 years, an accomplished photographer and well-known member of the Mountaineers, and Felix E. Moore, who is remembered by many as "a real character," a science teacher and boys' advisor serving 30 years.

The years of World War II saw attendance requirements relaxed. Some students interrupted their high school careers to join the armed forces or to work in war industries, and later returned to complete their secondary education. By the spring of 1945 over 2,400 Queen Anne alumni/students had joined the services, and 77 had given up their lives.

In 1955 Queen Anne High was renamed Queen Anne Junior-Senior High. Construction completed in the same year included a shop, a home economics wing, music rooms and a new lunchroom. In 1958 a new athletic field, named the Otto L. Luther Memorial Field, was developed across from the high school with the old student hangout, The Grizzly Inn, being razed in the process.

## 1960s–1981

Dramatics and music continued to be an important part of the school's curriculum. The Cantorians, under Eugene Brown's direction, won awards in Northwest music festivals, and there were few stage productions which did not draw capacity crowds to Queen Anne's auditorium. Students in Gordon Mauerman's Laboratory Writing Course began publication in 1960 of a literary magazine, *Paw Prints*, which continued into the 1970s as a showcase for student talent.

*Grizzly logo. In 1930 the student body selected the grizzly bear as the school logo, and in 1932 the school yearbook was named The Grizzly. Courtesy Queen Anne Alumni Assoc.*

### Middy Drives

A white cotton blouse with a sailor collar, known as a middy, was popular from the 1920s through the 1950s. The Queen Anne Girls' Club held a weekly Middy Drive throughout the 1930s. All girls so dressed received a tag, with the home room earning the most tags receiving lollypops for everyone.

### Student Traffic Court

In the 1950s Queen Anne High School was the only school with its own traffic court. Violators were referred by the King County Juvenile Court to the nine-judge pupil court, the judges being elected by the student body. Penalties included attending accident-prevention classes, writing themes keyed to the violations, and losing drivers' licenses up to 60 days.

### Affiliation Exchange Program

One of the most popular postwar efforts to strengthen bonds between nations was the Affiliation Exchange Program (AFEX). Queen Anne became an active participant in the 1954-55 term, with a school in Braunschweig, West Germany. The exchange grew with the years, involving students and teachers with those from many other foreign countries.

### The CCC

George S. Farmer, the principal following Otto Luther's retirement in 1951 at age 70, had a dynamic, much-respected vice principal, Walter H. Campbell. Typical of Mr. Campbell's work was the CCC—Campbell's Clean-up Committee. A 1959 graduate, Bill Tennyson, recalls that when a student was apprehended for an infraction of a rule, at that time he/she was drafted into the CCC. Reporting after school for the requisite number of days, the current CCC "members" followed the impeccably-groomed Mr. Campbell around the school grounds and adjacent neighborhood as he pointed at debris for them to collect. "We realized that we weren't being punished for our mistakes, we were being responsible for our actions."

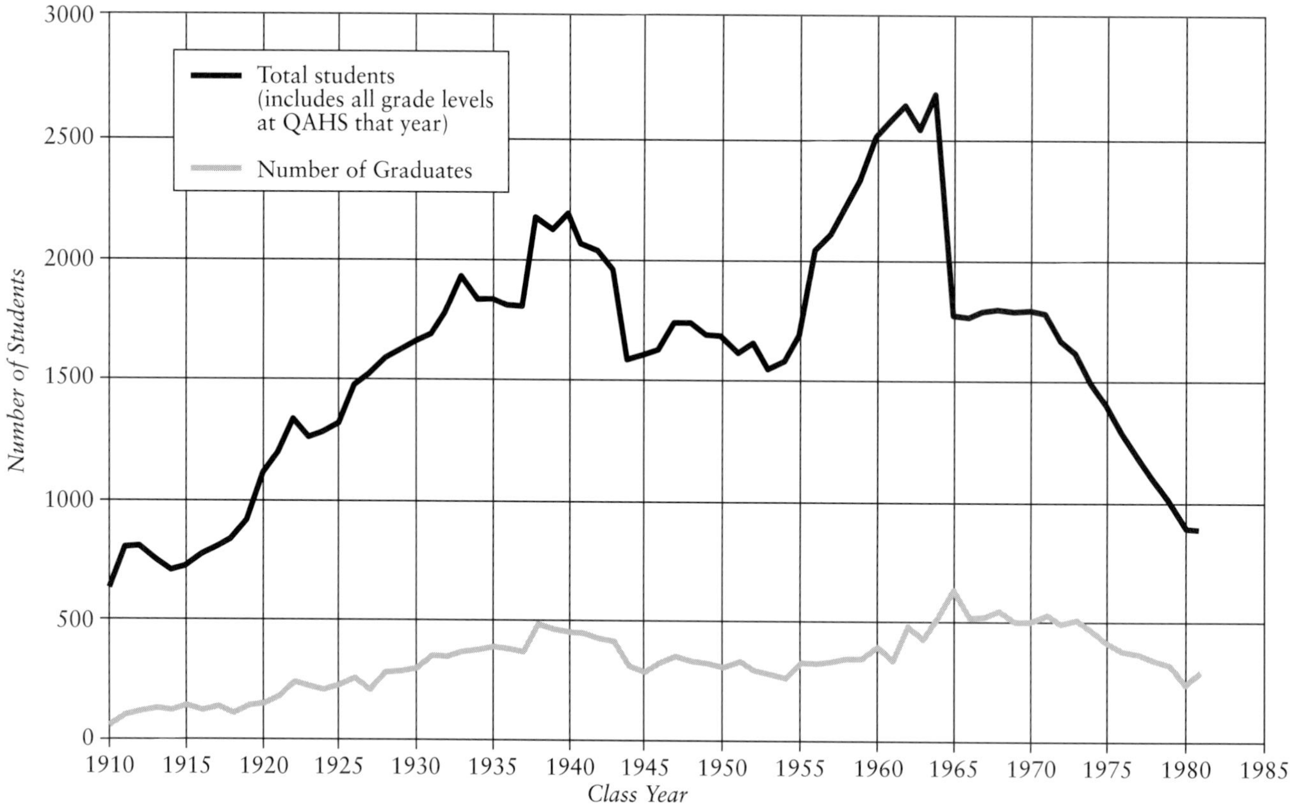


*Queen Anne High School's total enrollment and yearly graduation class size reflect the area's history. The buildup in the early decades is followed by a drop during WWII. The baby boom classes in the 60s were augmented by the 8th grade, starting in the fall of 1943, and later the 7th grade. The opening of McClure Middle School in 1964 made Queen Anne a three-year high school and the declines in the 70s ended with its closure in 1981. The total number of graduates was just under 24,000. Chart by John Hennes.*

In the 1960s Principal George Farmer and his successor William Hall had to deal with rapid social change and student unrest. With the support of the faculty, the students formed a sometimes controversial "Queen Anne Student Union" to examine current issues of concern. A new gymnasium was built across Second Avenue N. in 1961, and the well-remembered Marie Hawkins, school secretary since 1917, retired the same year. In 1964 crowding was relieved with the transfer of students to McClure Junior High School.

## Erwin Henkel

Erwin Henkel, "Henk" to his students, arrived in 1926. His six-foot four-inch physique and booming voice intimidated generations of young boys in his roles of coach, gym teacher and drill sergeant who "turned boys into men." No one ever forgot Erwin Henkel. Henk died in 1988 at age 85.

A rash of vandalism in the late 1960s, including two unsuccessful firebomb attempts on the school, prompted stronger student discipline.

In the early 1970s, after being neglected in favor of support for boy's sports, girl's athletics began to gain deserved recognition and funding. Starting in 1977, the women's volleyball team won the city title for three consecutive years.

The city-wide decline of enrollment and the deteriorating physical condition of Queen Anne High had caused consideration of the school's closure as early as 1972. As enrollments continued to drop, the decision for closure was announced in 1980, effective in June 1981.

On June 6, 1981, over 15,000 alumni and friends assembled from far and near for the "Last Hurrah," a grand farewell celebration. The day's program included a nostalgic assembly and show in the auditorium, the opportunity for a final tour of the building, and the sharing of memories with old friends. In its 72 years, slightly under 24,000 students had graduated from "Queen Anne High School on the Hilltop."

## Queen Anne High School Alumni Association

In the fall following the school's closure, a formal Queen Anne High School Alumni Association, with Maxine Amundson McMahan as its prime mover, was formed. The Alumni Association mails over 10,000 copies of its annual newsletter, the *Kuay*, edited by John Hennes for most of its life. It also holds an annual banquet, and has provided annual competitive scholarships for descendants of Queen Anne alumni, all as part of its purpose to preserve the legacy of Queen Anne High School.

# Part II
# Parochial Schools

## Sacred Heart Catholic School, 1891-1969

The first parish school in Seattle, Sacred Heart School, was opened in 1891 by Father Sigl, and was located on top of Denny Hill at what is now Sixth Avenue and Bell street. The school flourished as Seattle grew and by 1903, there were 400 pupils. The church, school and convent were relocated in 1927 to Warren Avenue and John Street due to the regrading of Denny Hill.

As the parish had fewer children of school age, Sacred Heart School began to accept children from other parishes and by 1968, of the 170 children enrolled, only 13 were Sacred Heart parish members. The school closed in 1969.

However, in 1976 a new life began as the Lifetime Learning Center opened in the school offering a wide range of classes to adults. Sharing the building since 1980 is the Little Friends Preschool. Thus students from both ends of the spectrum are still filling the school with activity and the joy of learning.

## St. Margaret of Scotland Catholic School, 1923-1971

St. Margaret of Scotland Catholic Parish opened a school in 1923 on W. Dravus Street. The school opened with 107 students taught by three sisters of St. Joseph of Peace. The children came from Smith Cove, Ross, Pleasant Valley, Magnolia, North and West Queen Anne as well as Interbay. Father Corboy, pastor for 46 years, guided the parish as the school was enlarged and modernized.

The geographical limitations of St. Margaret grew smaller and in 1971, after 47 years, the school closed. In 1977 the site of the demolished school was made into a community park, named Corboy Park in memory of Fr. Corboy's many years of service. Currently, the church, park, and rectory are used by the Seattle Catholic Polish community who are breathing new life into the St. Margaret of Scotland facilities.

*St. Anne School, 1953. A First Communion class with Fr. Thomas Quain. Courtesy Mickey Canan.*

## St. Anne Catholic School, 1923-present

St. Anne School was built at 101 W. Lee Street housing eight classrooms, three music rooms, lunchrooms, cloakrooms and offices. The school opened on September 4, 1923, and was staffed by Sisters of the Holy Names with Sister Mary Thomasina as Superior and Principal. Fr. Thomas Quain, pastor of St. Anne Parish, saw that there was no tuition charged for attending St.

### St. Anne Crab Supper

A well-known fundraiser of St. Anne Parish was the annual crab supper prepared by the Mothers' Club with its famed homemade lemon meringue pie for dessert. Years ago, the donated crabs were caught and delivered early the day of the supper. One member's vivid memory is of the time when, by noon, the waiting ladies could not be sure there would be any crab. Anxiety was high by the time it finally arrived, very late in the afternoon. "My, you never saw so many ladies working so fast as we did then!" she reports.

Anne School, in order to make a Catholic education available to all families, regardless of income. St. Anne remained tuition-free until the 1980s, when the cost of lay teachers' salaries demanded a larger income to meet expenses.

Improvements over the years include a playground (1924), tennis courts (1931) and an annex at 108 W. Lee Street with music rooms, an orchestra room, offices and kindergarten rooms (1950), and an auditorium on the west side of the school (1950). St. Anne School has been dedicated to Christian education which combines religious, social and cultural training with practical preparation for a successful life.

## Other Schools in the Community

The **Queen Anne Christian School,** located at 1716 Second Avenue N., was founded in 1979. This school is a ministry of the Queen Anne Christian Center, Assemblies of God. Serving kindergarten through twelfth grade, the school offers a program of learning with academic excellence for students of every ability. **Seattle Country Day School,** 2619 Fourth Avenue N., was founded in 1963 by parents who desired an educational alternative. The school serves grades kindergarten through eighth grade and offers a "specialized educational program dedicated to meeting the needs of intellectually gifted children with strong creative problem-solving abilities. The head of the school in 1993 was Dr. Jayasri Ghosh.

**Queen Anne School,** at 1617 First Avenue W., was founded by Kathy Napolitano in 1987 as an independent elementary school serving children ages five to twelve. The school's declared goal "is to help create confident, happy human beings by getting them off to the best possible educational start."

## Part III
## The College and Queen Anne—Seattle Pacific University

by Donald McNichols, Lit.D.

Seattle Pacific University (SPU) was founded by the Free Methodist Church as Seattle Seminary in 1891. It opened its doors to elementary students on April 4th on a five-acre plot between Third and Fifth Avenues W. and Cremona Street. The school had a single unfinished building and its campus was little more than a grazing area for the seminary cow. The next year secondary level education was added, followed by a college curriculum in 1910. Seattle Seminary was renamed Seattle Pacific College (SPC) in 1915 and was known by this name for the next 62 years.

Three men were designated by the trustees as founders: Nils B. Peterson, a resident homesteader in the Ross community who donated the original acreage from his garden plot; minister-banker John C. Norton, who chaired the committee of the Free Methodist Conference that recommended organizing a school; and Hiram Pease, who gave generously to and raised money for the seminary.

In 1891 Alexander and Adelaide Beers left their positions in a Virginia seminary to open Seattle Seminary. As the institution's first president, Alexander Beers devoted his time and energy to raising money and developing facilities, while Adelaide focused on developing curricula and teaching. The new seminary immediately attracted many students and between 1891 and 1916, three more buildings were constructed. Orrin E. Tiffany became the second president in 1916 and established the school as a college, despite the insecurities and crisis resulting from World War I in the next decade.

## The College and the Community

During these years, as the Queen Anne neighborhood grew up around Seattle Pacific, the relationship between the two communities was something like a marriage: there were times of harmony and times of acrimony. But from the perspective of more than a century, the affiliation has been warm and healthy, most often promoted by the common interests of young people.

*Alexander Hall, the first building on the Seattle Seminary campus, 1891, was named for Alexander Beers, first president. Courtesy Seattle Pacific University.*

Danna Davis, an alumna who attended Seattle Pacific from grade school through college graduation (1923-1939), recalls good times when (SPC) students and neighborhood young people played together.

> *In the '30s, students would bobsled down Third Avenue W. All the local kids got involved, from SPC and Queen Anne. It was scary but fun. The driver would lie down full length on the sled and people piled on top of him—then off we'd go down Third. There'd be lookouts at Nickerson so no one would run into streetcars or go off the bank into the canal.*

Miriam Marston Owen, alumna of SPC's grade school, high school and college, recalls that Seattle Pacific high school debaters challenged high school groups from all over the city, including nearby Queen Anne. The debates always aroused great community interest. Marston Hall is named for Miriam's father, A. J. Marston, a long-term professor.

Under Dr. C. Hoyt Watson, president from 1926-1959, the college made significant progress, including the construction of a new Student Union Building and the Royal Brougham Pavilion and Queen Anne Bowl playing field. During 1939 and 1940, President Watson secured the portion of land adjacent to Third Avenue W. known as the Peterson's sand pit. It was graded and developed with city cooperation, then deeded to the city with a 50-year lease for joint college and community use as a playfield. This idea of a dual use by SPC and the city was repeated later in developing Wallace Field adjacent to Brougham Pavilion.

President C. Dorr Demaray wanted SPC to become more of an integral part of Seattle and the Queen Anne community. Except for people working in religion, education or nursing, most Seattle residents knew little of the college. The 1962 Seattle World's Fair presented opportunities to advance Demaray's goal. The president, together with many faculty and staff members, served on fair planning committees. Later, college dormitory rooms were rented to visitors. In addition, the college worked with the Seattle Council of Churches in organizing and staffing the Christian Witness Pavilion as well as the Children's Care Center.

In 1977 the college's name was changed to Seattle Pacific University (SPU) and graduate and professional degree programs were offered. The university concept was largely the vision of Dr. David L. McKenna, whose 14 years of leadership, beginning in 1968, changed the school forever. A man of academic and theological stature, McKenna also possessed youthful vigor, skill in problem-solving, and effectiveness in the public arena.

Meanwhile, up the hill, Reverend Dick Denham watched his pews at Bethany Presbyterian fill with SPU students. "Over the years, the university blessed us with many wonderful young people." Denham remembers the mix of SPU students and his Queen Anne congregation as a happy combination. "The students took a lot of responsibility in the day-to-day running of the church and got along well with the older members. For their part, established church members accepted the newcomers well. We were all fellow seekers."

One of the most successful integrations of Seattle Pacific with the Queen Anne community has been through sports. SPU coordinates church softball, volleyball and basketball leagues, where players are drawn from churches, neighborhoods and the campus. Every

## Caroling on the Hill

A tradition that goes back to the 1920s and 1930s is annual Christmas caroling. Danna Davis remembers when groups of students would walk through Queen Anne neighborhoods singing carols. Davis recalls, "We'd use [song] booklets distributed by a local funeral parlor, then just stroll up and down the streets. Every once in a while someone would ask us in for hot chocolate."

## Outstanding SPU Professors

Paul F. Rosser, Professor of Communications, founded and directed speech competitions for Washington high school, college, and university students, and served as director of the Washington State Speech Association, 1955-70. He received a Distinguished Service Citation from the Free Methodist National Commission on High Education.

Roy Swanstrom served as Professor of History at Seattle Pacific College for 27 years, from 1949 to 1980. In 1976 he received the Outstanding Professor Award, and the Free Methodists' Higher Education Award in 1979. Professor Swanstrom's doctoral thesis chronicling the U.S. Senate of 1787-1801 has been reprinted several times by the Library of Congress. He established the Roy Swanstrom Centurion Scholarship Endowment in 1989.

spring quarter, Wallace Field, near the canal, is opened up for community Little League practice and games.

## Growth: Community Apprehensions of SPU's Master Plan

Over time, the Queen Anne welcome mat had become frayed. An SPU trustee recalls that in the early 1970s, "Some people were afraid that SPU was going to dominate the area, taking over access to the canal, and create parking problems. The community council wanted Queen Anne to stay residential."

The Master Plan was a detailed ten-year blueprint for growth which addressed the concerns of the community as well as charting the institution's path. Dr. David C. LeShana assumed leadership in 1983 and oversaw much expansion, as well as development of the Master Plan. After much negotiation, the plan, which resolved most of the community's fears, received approval from the Seattle City Council in 1991.

A happy antidote to the community's anxieties regarding the university were the SPU students themselves, who annually continue to give hundreds of volunteer hours to Queen Anne community projects. In the 1980s and 1990s students regularly volunteer with the Queen Anne Helpline and the Fremont Public Association.

The Queen Anne community has shown support and friendship to the students in many ways. Lois Roby, owner of Salladay's Pharmacy, observes,

> *We get a lot of business from SPU, and we like to support them. We take out ads in the Falcon student newspaper and we're a sponsor for the annual SPU fashion show. We get a lot of faculty members as customers, and the kids will come in asking for dorm prizes when they're having some contest. It's a two-way street and it goes well. They're very honest people.*

Since 1990, when Dr. Curtis A. Martin, lifelong faculty member, became the university's seventh president, SPU has enjoyed a stable enrollment of about 3,400. "Quality of education" is the university's priority. A $10 million library is planned for construction in the 1990s, which will be a significant asset for the university and the community. Since the 1980s SPU has welcomed retired community members to university classes as auditors, where they may broaden their education tuition-free. The generations of young people studying at the college on the north side of the hill have brought the energy and excitement of the young to a comfortable old neighborhood.

***Dr. Donald McNichols*** *is a retired Professor Emeritus of History at Seattle Pacific University and the author of Seattle Pacific University, A Growing Vision 1891-1991.*

***Marion Parker,*** *a retired librarian, attended area elementary schools and Queen Anne High (class of 1934) and the University of Washington (class of 1940.) She was a staff member at the Queen Anne Branch Library for 24 years. Two sons have attended Queen Anne schools.*

***Kim Turner*** *attended the Warren Avenue Elementary School and Queen Anne High School. A lifetime resident of Queen Anne Hill, Turner has worked for the Seattle Public Library for over thirty years in the Humanities Division.*

***Elizabeth Whitmire*** *has been a resident of Queen Anne Hill for one year and is writing a science fiction book. A graduate of Evergreen State College and the Denver Publishing Institute, she freelances in publishing work while studying graphic art.*

***Kay Yamamoto*** *is a native Seattleite and a Hill resident since 1939. An interest in Queen Anne's history began with her childrens' attendance at area schools, and grew during twenty-two years as a staff member at Queen Anne elementary schools.*

Chapter Fifteen

# Going to Church

by
Alison Nesmith

Organized religion came to Queen Anne in the pious hearts of the first settlers. A 1978 survey revealed that Queen Anne, along with Ballard, has more churches than most other Seattle districts. Indeed, the churches' determination to grow, their ability to adjust to change, and their willingness to work together has strengthened Queen Anne's sense of community. The strength of the Queen Anne Ecumenical Council in the 1990s is a testimonial to this continuing cooperative spirit.

## Houses of Worship, Centers of Community

The congregations that built the churches of Queen Anne have been energetic, optimistic and faithful. They were also willing to assume large debts. The churchgoers wanted the church to play a major role in their lives and erected not only sanctuaries of worship, but classrooms, offices, recreation rooms, libraries and meeting halls. Over the years these twentieth-century churches have been focal points of community life around the hill and supported Sunday schools, choirs, orchestras, drama troupes, and baseball and basketball teams, just to mention a few activities.

*Bethany United Presbyterian Church. Illustration by Mike Dowd. Courtesy Queen Anne Historical Society.*

During the Great Depression congregations endured extreme financial difficulties and expansion programs came to a halt. Emery Gustafson recalls that "during the Depression everyone went to church. It was a time of quiet desperation with everybody just trying to survive. And spiritual strength was all that kept them going."

The 1940s brought economic recovery, and people who worked in military and industrial efforts moved into the community. By 1960 many Queen Anne churches found their facilities inadequate to meet the needs of swelling congregations and Sunday school programs, as postwar "baby boom" children were brought to church. Some churches undertook renovations; others built brand new sanctuaries.

However, during the 1960s and 1970s church support and congregation size dwindled as a result of the decreasing number of school-age children in the area and changing attitudes towards organized religion. As commercial buildings, apartments and condominiums replaced single-family dwellings, many Queen Anne churches developed special programs for single adults and the homeless. In addition, many rented or loaned parts of their buildings to community endeavors such as day-care centers and senior citizen's programs. At the same time, the churches rededicated themselves to an ecumenism that has had a long history in the community.

## The Queen Anne Ecumenical Council

In 1920 a neighborhood Thanksgiving service was jointly sponsored by the Protestant churches of Queen Anne. This annual event quickly became the focal point of church cooperation, with the community's Catholic churches eventually joining in the effort. In 1970 this habit of working together was formalized when the churches created the Queen Anne Ecumenical Council.

Comprised of representatives from most of the neighborhood churches, the council meets monthly to share information and common spiritual concerns. High points of the year are the interfaith Thanksgiving and Easter services. The Ecumenical Council has supported many other efforts including weekly pastoral visits to retirement residences, the Queen Anne Helpline and the Bethany-Queen Anne Foodbank. When individual churches lack the resources to develop their own outreach programs, they contribute through the Ecumenical Council.

## The Women of the Church

From the earliest days, when Louisa Boren Denny donated the land for Trinity Methodist Church from her donation claim, women have played key roles in the founding and success of the community's churches. Women generally did not serve in publicly prominent roles such as pastor, deacon, or chair of the church lay leadership until late in the twentieth century. Thus, women's names have often not survived along with those of the men who served "officially" as church leaders; however, they have been the backbone supporting many churches with their work "behind the scenes."

The *Queen Anne News* reveals the year-in and year-out activities of church women's groups. The paper is filled with notices of women's rummage sales, teas, dinners, sewing bees and other fundraising activities that provided the financial support and social underpinning for literally all church efforts. At Bethany Presbyterian Church, for example, the Women's Society assumed the balance of the mortgage on the church's first building, dedicated in 1888. During the early years of Queen Anne United Presbyterian, the Women's Missionary Society furnished the pulpit and built a parsonage. In 1925 the Women's Society at Queen Anne Methodist Episcopal paid for building a kitchen in the new church hall. These are but a few examples of the kinds of church work undertaken by women. In addition, Sunday schools were frequently organized and taught by women, and many Queen Anne churches grew out of such Sunday schools.

## Churches Bring Unity and Fellowship to the Community

As the community took form churches began to appear along the south side of the hill. Among the earliest was the Congregational Church on the southeast corner of Birch (Taylor Avenue N.) and Thomas Street, established by Rev. Taylor in 1887 and active into the early twentieth century. It appears that the name Taylor Avenue derived from the old Taylor Church.

The Sanborn Fire maps, 1888-93, show the Second Presbyterian Church, now Bethany, on the southwest corner of Poplar (Third Avenue N.) and Harrison and the Church of Christ at 318 Olympic Place.

In 1890 the Second Methodist Protestant Church was built at Republican and Warren streets at a cost of

$7,000. The occasion of the electrification of the church was marked on March 23, 1891, with a celebration, the highlight being the dramatic throwing of the switch for the 30 large lights installed in the main auditorium. In 1896 the church joined the First Methodist Protestant Church with the goal of building a single strong church, rather than having each struggle along separately.

Tradition says that the German Methodist Church at 14 Howe Street was founded in the late 1880s. By 1926 it had been long abandoned by worshipers and was deemed an eyesore by the neighbors. The building boom of the late 1920s created a demand for apartments, and a developer stripped the church of its tower and converted it into the La Mance Apartments, which were "the last word in moderness." In 1993, almost 70 years later, the converted church building was still in use.

The Second Advent Church was built at Warren and Depot streets in 1890 at a cost of $850. In 1892 the church changed its name to the Central Advent Church of Seventh Day Adventists and built a finer church at 309 Poplar (Third Avenue N. and Thomas Street). By 1923 the church had moved out of the community to Boylston Avenue and Olive Way.

In 1891 the German Evangelical Church was built at Harrison and Birch streets (Taylor Avenue N.) and replaced in 1907 by a fine new church at Second Avenue N. and Valley Street which was rededicated as Evangelical Auditorium. Eventually the church closed, and the building remained boarded up until it was rehabilitated in the 1970s. A visitor pausing to run her fingers over the nearly-hidden cornerstone will be able to discern the words "First Church Evangelical Assn., 1906."

In the first three decades of the twentieth century churches literally blossomed all over the hill as the residential areas became comfortably settled neighborhoods.

Queen Anne Congregational Church, on the east side of Queen Anne Avenue between Galer and Garfield

## Churches on Queen Anne—1900 – 1929

Between 1900–1929 a number of churches came and went in the community. Little more than the name and location is known about some of these churches. Those that remain active in the community in the 1990s are discussed in this chapter.

*Bethany Presbyterian, First Ave.. N. and Roy St. (now at 1818 Queen Anne Ave. N.)
Central Advent Church (Seventh-Day Adventists), Third Ave. N. and Thomas Ave.
Chapel, 3242 Sixteenth Ave. W.
Church of Christ, 318 Olympic Place
Church of Jesus Christ of Latter Day Saints, Roy St. and First Ave. N.
*Denny Park Lutheran, Dexter Ave. N. and John St.
*City Foursquare Church, 602 Valley St.
Finnish Temperance Hall, Fifteenth W. and W. Boston
*First Free Methodist, Third Ave. W. and W. Dravus St.
First German Methodist Episcopal, 14 Howe St.
German Evangelical Church, Second Ave. N. and Valley St.
Highland Baptist Mission, 9 Garfield St.
*Interbay Covenant, 3233 Fifteenth W.
*Queen Anne Baptist, First Ave. N. and Crockett St.
*Queen Anne Christian, 1316 Third Ave. W.
Queen Anne Congregational, 1516 Queen Anne Ave.
*Queen Anne Lutheran, 2400 Eighth Ave. W
*Queen Anne United Methodist, 1606 Fifth Ave. W.
*Queen Anne United Presbyterian, 414 W. Howe St.
*Sacred Heart Church, 205 Second Ave. N.
*St. Anne Church, 1411 First Ave. W.
*St. Paul's Episcopal, 15 Roy St.
*St. Margaret of Scotland Church, 3221 Fourteenth Ave. W.
Second Methodist Protestant, Republican and Warren Streets
*Seventh Church of Christ Scientist, 2555 Eighth Ave. W.
*Seventh Day Adventist (now Queen Anne Christian Center) 1716 Second Ave. N.
Taylor Congregational, Taylor Ave. and Thomas St.
Trinity Methodist Episcopal, Mercer St. and First Ave. N.
Zion Evangelical, SW corner Harrison and Taylor

**Active in 1993*
Source: Baist Real Estate, 1905; Sanborn Fire map, 1917; Ida G. Corey, "Seattle Churches as Known Through the Seattle Newspapers." (Typewritten, 1938)

streets, was an important part of the religious community on the hill in the early years of the century. The Rev. Dr. Sydney Strong led the church between 1908 and 1921. In 1909 he held Sunday afternoon services for the entire community at Kinnear Park. The purpose was to foster community spirit by meeting together under what he called the "grandest dome ever seen." The newspapers report that often more than 1,000 people would assemble for these open-air services.

## Queen Anne United Methodist, 1606 Fifth Avenue W.

David Denny headed the board of trustees for Seattle's second Methodist congregation, which established the Battery Street Methodist Episcopal Church in 1882. In 1904 the church moved from its Belltown location to a temporary, canvas-topped structure on Queen Anne Hill. Pastor O.H. McGill preached there each Sunday, and on Monday he picked up his hammer and spent the week working on construction of the permanent building. By 1906 the new church, named Queen Anne Methodist Episcopal, was dedicated.

In 1889 Louisa Boren Denny donated a building site for the Trinity Methodist Episcopal church and parsonage. The parsonage was built at Victory (Third Avenue W.) near Olympic Place at a cost of $2,000. During 1890 the congregation met for worship at a temporary church located at the corner of Kentucky (First Avenue N.) and Thomas Street, while the new site was being built at Kentucky and Mercer. David Denny

*Wallace Seely served as church organist at Queen Anne United Methodist Church from 1931 to 1988. Photo by Isabel Egglin.*

donated lumber and W.H. Hughes donated "half a million bricks." In 1915 the church was closed and half of the congregation moved to Queen Anne Methodist Episcopal at the top of the hill.

Queen Anne Methodist Episcopal, renamed Queen Anne United Methodist after a denominational merger in 1968, became a center for youth activities and social events. In response to a growing, active membership the church added a Sunday school and community hall under the church building. It was further updated in the 1950s.

From 1974 to 1990 the church maintained Sheepshed/Lewis House, 1606 Third Avenue W., as a home for single people and families in transition. After 1990 the church expanded its mission outreach and support of the Queen Anne Ecumenical Council, Queen Anne Helpline and the Bethany-Queen Anne Foodbank.

## Bethany Presbyterian Church, 1818 Queen Anne Avenue N.

In 1885 a group of Presbyterians started a Sabbath School at Third Avenue N. and Harrison Street. Three years later, led by Pastor A.J. Canney, they completed a church nearby, "Second Presbyterian." In 1903 the church adopted the name "Bethany" and in 1906 the congregation moved to the corner of First Avenue N. and Roy Street.

In 1927 the church left this building and held services in various locations around Queen Anne while a new church was constructed at 1818 Queen Anne Avenue N. During this period and afterwards Bethany's various women's organizations worked tirelessly raising money, holding teas, musical evenings and other cultural events, and producing hand-made articles for sale. These church events also maintained a strong social network that was critical to maintaining the church community, as well as bolstering Bethany's mission.

Rev. Dick Denham, pastor from 1964 to 1989, recalls that in the early days of his pastorate, Bethany opened its doors to an "army of young people" who had set aside their material wealth to follow their vision of Christ. While these young people shocked some of the congregation with their long hair, casual dress and bare feet, Denham remembers that their "dedication and commitment... had a very positive impact on many of us." In recent years Bethany has played a key role in many important community projects including the very successful, Bethany-Queen Anne Foodbank and Queen Anne Helpline.

## QUEEN ANNE BAPTIST CHURCH 2011 FIRST AVENUE N.

A Sunday school started in 1886 evolved into the North Seattle Baptist Church by 1891. In 1925 the church opened at First Avenue N. and Crockett Street and changed its name to Queen Anne Baptist Church. In 1936 the church was further enlarged. Through the 1930s and 1940s, Queen Anne Baptist Church had an active drama troupe and its young men competed in church basketball and baseball leagues. By the 1950s, as the baby boom gained momentum, the church was ready to expand again, this time with an eye to creating space for youth activities. The new educational building, completed in 1958, enabled the church to house its own activities as well as other community endeavors.

In 1974 the church answered the needs of troubled youth with the Shelter, a home and safe place for teen runaways. A food bank, Alcoholics Anonymous and the Queen Anne Cooperative Pre-School are some of the community efforts that have benefited from using the facilities that Queen Anne Baptist Church worked so hard to establish on top of the hill.

## DENNY PARK LUTHERAN, JOHN STREET AND DEXTER AVENUE N.

In 1888 Reverend I. Tollafsen and 16 people of Scandinavian heritage created the first Norwegian Danish Evangelical Lutheran Church of Seattle. The congregation built its first home at Fourth Avenue and Pine Street. In 1904 they moved to a new location only to be forced to move again just five years later because of the first Denny Regrade project.

In 1938, the church chose a new location at Eighth Avenue N. and John Street, across from Denny Park. One of the most unique projects of the church during this time was the Lutheran Gospel Hour, a radio broadcast for people who were unable to attend services. This weekly program started in 1937 and continued for almost 40 years.

Like many of the churches described in this book, Denny Park Lutheran found itself, during the 1960s and 1970s, in a changed environment. Apartments, condominiums and commercial buildings had replaced the single-family homes that once characterized the area. In 1976 the church hired an associate pastor to reach out to young people and those who lived in multi-unit buildings. During the 1980s the church again adjusted its focus, concentrating on its ministry to the elderly in local nursing homes. Today the church also works in conjunction with Catholic Community Services to run the Denny Park Youth Shelter.

*Director Pat Sobeck, Mary Stark and Loreli Doughty prepare for a monthly clothing give away. In 1993 the Helpline also oversees the Queen Anne Food Bank. Photo by Isabel Egglin.*

### Queen Anne Helpline

The Queen Anne Helpline evolved from an informal meeting of Bethany church leaders and other concerned individuals in 1982. Rev. Denham recalls that after the initial meeting, "Queen Anne churches and many citizens of the community jumped in, and with a significant group of volunteers, this effort has continued." At first, Helpline volunteers answered the phone a few hours a week, providing Queen Anne residents with rent or utility money, clothing, transportation, referrals to shelters, and other assistance. Pat Sobeck was one of those volunteers and eventually became director of the program.

Today the Helpline is a full-time operation, with 30 volunteers who answer about 350 calls a month. One of its most innovative programs is the Bob Kussman Continuing Education Project, named in memory of one of the founders of Helpline. This program gives financial aid to single mothers who are furthering their education to cover books, daycare or other expenses. Juggling the responsibilities of school, parenthood, and in some cases part-time jobs, these women have gone into nursing, landscaping and other careers.

*The Sacred Heart Catholic Church complex includes the Lifetime Learning Center, a woman's shelter and the St. Vincent de Paul Center. These community services occupy the former convent and elementary school buildings. Photo by Isabel Egglin.*

## SACRED HEART CATHOLIC CHURCH, 205 SECOND AVENUE N.

Sacred Heart Church grew out of the energy and resourcefulness of young Father E. Demanez, who began to build a church at Sixth Avenue and Bell Street in 1889 with materials left from the Seattle Fire. Father Demanez turned the project over to the Redemptorist Fathers a few months later. By 1891 they had built the church, a convent, and a school with 107 pupils. The second Catholic church in Seattle, Sacred Heart burned in 1899 and was rebuilt by 1901.

In 1928 Sacred Heart again faced destruction, this time from the Denny Regrade project. Tearful parishioners watched as their church withstood three attempts to bring it to the ground. As one reporter wrote:

> *Bravely this gallant brick and stone edifice resisted three terrific dynamite blasts, but a fourth shot caused it to crumble and fall with colors flying—another victim to the regrade development at Denny Hill. . . .*

In 1960 the parish built a church, convent, school and rectory. Soon Sacred Heart was confronted by potential destruction when the City of Seattle attempted to appropriate the church building site for the Century 21 World's Fair in 1962. The church successfully defeated the City of Seattle in the State Supreme Court. In the end the World's Fair was a great boon for Sacred Heart as people from around the world came to visit and worship in the new sanctuary at Second Avenue N. and John Street.

The sociological changes of the late 1960s hit the parish very hard, and with only 35 families still residing in the parish, the church closed the school in 1969 and the convent in 1973. Nonetheless, Sacred Heart has remained a community center with the Lifetime Learning Center (1976) and a pre-school (1980) occupying the old school. In the 1990s the convent serves as a shelter for homeless families and single women, and as headquarters for the St. Vincent de Paul Society.

## SAINT MARGARET OF SCOTLAND CHURCH, 3221 FOURTEENTH AVENUE W.

Early in the twentieth century the Redemptorist Fathers established a mission in Interbay, which achieved parish status in 1910. Interbay's Catholics traveled "over trails, board sidewalks, and sandy roads" to celebrate their first mass as St. Margaret's parishioners on May 23, 1910. Within months of their first meeting the parishioners built a church at Fourteenth Avenue W. and W. Bertona Street, which was moved to a new site at W. Dravus Street and Fourteenth Avenue W. in 1914. The cables that stabilized the building during the move were incorporated into the interior design of the small sanctuary.

With room for only 150 people, St. Margaret's Church proudly maintains its identity as a simple place of worship. In the 1990s the little church again came under the wing of a larger parish, St. Anne. It also

*Originally dedicated in 1906 as the First Free Methodist Church, it is located at 3200 Third Avenue W. It was replaced by a new edifice in 1956. Courtesy First Free Methodist Church.*

developed a new facet to its unique identity by becoming, under the leadership of Father Joseph Calik, the home of Seattle's Polish Catholic community.

## FIRST FREE METHODIST CHURCH, 3200 THIRD AVENUE W.

Seattle pioneer Hiram Pease and Rev. John Glen built the First Free Methodist Church on Pine Street in the center of Seattle in 1880. In 1891, Free Methodists living in the Ross district organized a congregation. In 1906 they built a white frame church on the corner of Third Avenue W. and Dravus Street, across from Seattle Seminary (Seattle Pacific University.) At this time the downtown Free Methodist congregation sold its building and many members transferred to the Dravus Street Church, which then adopted the name First Free Methodist Church.

First Free Methodists were ardent temperance people who often participated in Prohibition parades in the 1910s. And though the church had to close its doors for six weeks during the influenza epidemic of 1918, grief and misfortune did not dampen the success of its revival meetings the next spring. During World War II the congregation drew close as women knit socks and mufflers, and Eleanor Eklund led the Young People's Mission Society in writing a heartfelt newsletter to servicemen abroad. Starting with a mailing list of 17, the monthly newsletter reached over 300 people by the end of the war.

In 1956 the First Free Methodists moved into a new church constructed on the same site as the original white frame building. The church's many community outreach programs have included assistance for community seniors and newly-arrived refugees. In 1970 they opened Queen Anne Day Care which serves more than 100 children. Dr. H. Mark Abbott, who was appointed senior pastor in 1982, has led the church into a new era of growth which includes increased membership and an ambitious building program.

## ST. PAUL'S EPISCOPAL CHURCH, 15 ROY STREET

St. Paul's Episcopal Church began in 1892 as an Episcopal mission of St. Mark's Church, its first members gathering for services in David Denny's old real estate office log cabin at Republican Street and Queen Anne Avenue. Under the guidance of Pastor Sidney H. Morgan, St. Paul's became one of the largest Episcopal churches in the diocese.

Under the dynamic leadership of Rev. Walter G. Horn, in 1936 St. Paul's expanded, building a hall, school rooms and two chapels. In a 1986 interview, long-time church member Mary Gustafson recalled Pastor Horn's energy:

> *He knocked on every door in the neighborhood to see if there were any children who wanted to come to Sunday school. He was a man of great personality. He was a little short man, but you'd think of him as six feet four.*

After World War II, St. Paul's began to consider relocating on top of Queen Anne Hill. However, in contrast to many other Queen Anne churches, St. Paul's elected to remain at its longtime location in lower Queen Anne, where it could focus on the problems of urban life, and, as said in the church's 75th anniversary history, "minister to all families, single persons, retired people, and transients."

Indeed, St. Paul's has remained committed to this mission. With a modern new building, completed in 1963, the sanctuary forms a dramatic five-story, A-frame structure with the organ and choir pews suspended above the main floor. During the 1980s and 1990s the church has provided spiritual guidance and other services to residents of neighborhood nursing homes and retirement centers. Congregation members have been active in feeding programs and in reaching out to people with AIDS.

## Queen Anne United Presbyterian Church, 414 W. Howe Street

In 1904 Mrs. Harold Spaulding began a Sunday school in her Queen Anne home, which outgrew the space within weeks. At this time the United Presbyterian Church bought two lots at Fifth Avenue W. and Howe Street, and a new church was completed in 1907. After this vigorous start the church continued to grow. By 1920 the Sabbath School had 301 persons enrolled and no debts, according to the *Queen Anne News*. The church's young people were involved in Christian Endeavor programs, athletic teams, and choirs.

From the beginning the church was a neighborhood institution, drawing much of its membership from the surrounding residential area. The church's 75th anniversary celebration in 1980 acknowledged its roots in Scottish Presbyterianism with bagpipe music and a theme entitled "Wee Kirk on the Hill."

## Queen Anne Christian Church, 1316 Third Avenue W.

Queen Anne Christian Church—Disciples of Christ held its first services in a building at First Avenue W. and W. Galer Street in 1906. In 1911 the congregation completed a church at Third Avenue W. and W. Lee Street. These early years were marked by the growth of social activities and children's programs.

As with many churches, Queen Anne Christian faced financial troubles during the Depression. Nonetheless, the church emerged as a focal point of social interaction and community outreach. In the late 1950s Queen Anne Christian Church completed a new sanctuary and remodeled space for Sunday school classes and other activities.

Queen Anne Christian faced the turbulent 1960s and 1970s with the Love Israel Family Commune attending services and participating in church life. Soon after, a group of church young people and Seattle Pacific University college students staged a production of *Godspell* that Pastor Laurie Rudel recalls, "changed the lives of several of the participants and crew, and touched many throughout the community."

During the 1980s and into the 1990s the church has maintained a small congregation that, Pastor Rudel notes, has offered "opportunities for spiritual growth and leadership development." Furthering its interest in interchurch harmony, the Christian Church supports the Queen Anne Ecumenical Council, Queen Anne Helpline, Childhaven and the First Avenue Service Center.

## St. Anne Catholic Church, 1411 First Avenue W.

In 1906 the Bishop of Seattle observed the rapid population growth on top of Queen Anne Hill and instructed the Redemptorist Fathers of Sacred Heart to establish a new parish there. Father Byrnes took on the task and by December 1908 the first St. Anne Catholic Church, a simple stucco building at Second Avenue W. and W. Lee Street, large enough to accommodate 400 people, was dedicated.

A rectory was built in 1913 and a new school in 1923, followed by a convent and a parish hall. The pastor during this period was Father Thomas Quain, who was "a stern and strong-willed leader. . . with Irish wit and humor who especially loved the children at St. Anne school and would often declare a holiday as a treat."

A new church, completed in 1963, involved the demolition of several houses. The church took sixteen months to build and has many beautiful details, such as handpainted murals. The parish flourished in its new home, organizing Cub Scouts, Campfire Girls, and other children's programs as well as choir work and services for the needy. By 1993 the other two Catholic parishes had closed their schools, leaving St. Anne as the only parochial school on Queen Anne.

In the 1960s St. Anne took an active role in ecumenical projects, and was a founding member when the Queen Anne Ecumenical Council was formed in 1970. St. Anne maintains its own outreach program, including work for the homeless and visits to prisoners. The church also sustains an effective St. Vincent de Paul Society which distributes funds for rent, food, clothing and emergency travel.

## Seventh Church of Christ Scientist, 2555 Eighth Avenue W.

In 1919 Christian Scientists living in the vicinity of Queen Anne Hill began to meet at Redding Hall at First Avenue W. and Roy Street, later occupied by the

*St. Anne Catholic Church broke ground for their new church at Third Avenue W. and W. Lee Street in the spring of 1960 as students and teachers from St. Anne School looked on. Courtesy Millie Hokanson.*

ACT Theatre Company. By 1928 they built, at Eighth Avenue W. and W. Halladay Street, a church and reading room where members of the public can borrow or purchase books on Christian Science and related subjects. Notable for its unique Spanish style and tile roof, the building is a designated historic landmark.

In keeping with the teachings of Christian Science, the church's community work focuses on the individual. As one of the church's leaders, Mary Davis, wrote in 1992, "spiritual giving, through church services, the activity of the reading room, and the annual presentation of at least one well-advertised lecture or talk on topics of spiritual interest and relevance to daily living is our essential outreach."

## QUEEN ANNE CHRISTIAN CENTER, 1716 SECOND AVENUE N.

One of the most recent additions to church life in Queen Anne was the establishment of Trinity Temple Full Gospel Assembly in 1957 with Nils W. Satterlund as the first pastor. In the early 1960s the church began a building program which was completed in 1969 with the help of the Northwest District Council of the Assemblies of God.

In 1965 the church changed its name to Queen Anne Assembly of God and since 1979 it has been known as the Queen Anne Christian Center. Rev. Dan Womack, who served as pastor from 1978 to 1982, helped the church establish the Queen Anne Christian School. The school, under the leadership of current Pastor Robert Johnston, serves 30 youngsters in kindergarten through twelfth grade.

## INTERBAY COVENANT, 3233 FIFTEENTH AVENUE W.

The first members of Interbay Covenant Church remember breathing soot from the temperamental coal furnace that heated the small chapel where they attended services. Built by the Presbyterian Church in 1911, the chapel had been purchased by downtown Seattle's First Covenant Church in 1941 to be used as a branch Sunday school. In 1954 the branch members formed their own self-supporting church. In 1966, a new church was built on two lots adjacent to the original property.

Children's programs have always been an essential part of Interbay Covenant's life. The small Sunday school gave way to a popular young people's recreation program, under the direction of Rev. Ralph Odham, which won a commendation from the Seattle Police Department and King County Juvenile Court.

Interbay Covenant's nursery is called "Elsa's Garden," and is dedicated to the memory of Elsa Olsen. She was one of the early members of the Interbay congregation who spent 24 years teaching the youngest members of the church. This tribute to her is an illustration of member Verna Harris's comment: "Through the years our outreach to children has been our heartbeat."

## QUEEN ANNE LUTHERAN CHURCH, 2400 EIGHTH AVENUE W.

In 1919 Pastor Jesse P. Pflueger of Queen Anne Lutheran Evangelical Church sat down to write an account of how his church began. This manuscript—which was found at a garage sale and given to Queen Anne Lutheran Pastor Reuben Sorenson in 1992—provides a lively picture of Queen Anne and one of its churches during an era of great growth.

On orders from the Ohio Synod, Pflueger arrived in Seattle in November 1916. Although he found that Seattle already had several churches—Lutheran included—he quickly pinpointed Queen Anne as an excellent place for a mission. About this time he wrote:

> *On canvassing the field, it developed that there were many unchurched people, many of whom were of Lutheran extraction, and it was learned that the Protestant churches in this section were full of former Lutherans, and that the Sunday Schools were being attended by the children of Lutheran families who held membership downtown.*

Staunch Lutheran Henry Bock, who wanted to see a Lutheran Church on the hill, offered Pflueger the use of a storeroom on Seventh Avenue W. rent free. Pflueger led the first Queen Anne Evangelical Lutheran service here on February 25, 1917. By 1921 the congregation was strong enough to build an attractive frame building at the corner of W. McGraw Street and Eighth Avenue W. The church grew and expanded over the following decades under the leadership of five different pastors. In 1959 the members dedicated a new building and, like many churches on the hill, they added a new chapel and educational unit in 1964. Since the 1970s the building has housed a thriving childcare center and pre-school, open to anyone in the community.

## City Foursquare Church, 602 Valley Street

Located in a commercial neighborhood near Aurora Avenue N., the Foursquare Gospel Church, under the guidance of Rev. Doug Heck, has an active community outreach program. Important programs at the church are a Child Development Center and the Oasis Cafe and recreation hall for young people living on the south slope of Queen Anne Hill, and transients alike. The Foursquare Gospel Church also supports the Queen Anne Ecumenical Council, Queen Anne Helpline, and the Bethany-Queen Anne Foodbank.

***Alison Nesmith*** *was born in Vancouver, B.C. and educated at Canadian universities. She lives on Queen Anne Hill with her husband Philip, a lawyer, and daughter. Nesmith Roberts Writing Service has offices in her home, where she writes on a variety of topics for many diverse clients.*

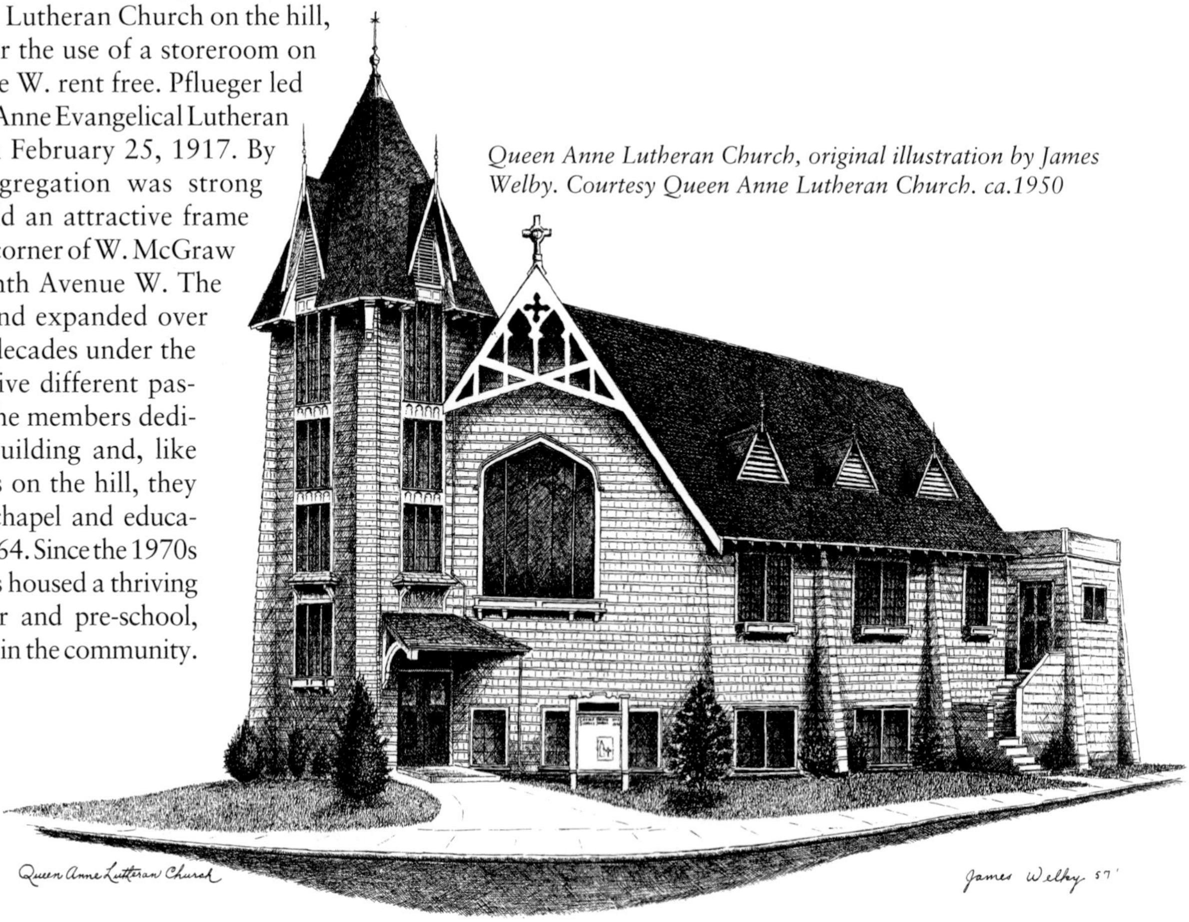


*Queen Anne Lutheran Church, original illustration by James Welby. Courtesy Queen Anne Lutheran Church. ca.1950*

Chapter Sixteen

# The Healthful Hilltop Air

by
Marina King

As an early residential suburb of Seattle, Queen Anne Hill was regarded as a healthy, "country" location, far away from the city's crowded and dirty conditions. Swept by fresh sea breezes, free of the pollution of a thousand wood and coal fires and industrial smoke, the hill was an obvious place for hospitals and convalescent homes. Many diseases in the late nineteenth century, such as tuberculosis, had no known treatment aside from long periods of complete rest. Since the 1890s Queen Anne Hill has been the location of over 25 hospitals, convalescent homes, and sanitariums. Only four of these treatment centers, among them Children's Orthopedic Hospital and the Wayside Emergency Hospital, have handled emergency or acute care.

*The Seattle Children's Home, Tenth Avenue W. and W. McGraw Street, circa 1905. The little girls' washroom, where they shared sinks and kept their personal hand towels. From the beginning, the home accepted not only orphaned children, but also children whose parents could not provide for them. Children of single fathers who labored in logging camps or made trips to Alaska, and of immigrant families who had fallen on hard times, accounted for many of the home's inhabitants. There were also orphaned children sent over from the courts who paid for their support. Courtesy Pemco Webster & Stevens Collection, Museum of History and Industry.*

In addition to health care centers, Queen Anne has been the site of numerous residential homes including orphanages and retirement centers.

## Public Health in the Nineteenth Century

From the 1860s disease and epidemics were commonplace in Seattle. Typhoid fever outbreaks were common, especially after flooding, because of the inadequate sewer system and an unprotected water supply. In 1873 over half the children in King County died of diphtheria in a few terrible months. There were deadly outbreaks of smallpox in 1876 and 1877.

At the end of the nineteenth century, medical science was beginning to embrace the germ theory of disease and to doubt the miasmic theory, which held that diseases were caused by "bad air." Seattle's doctors were very active in obtaining the latest national and international developments in medicine for the city.

During the population boom from 1880 through 1910, many well-educated physicians migrated to the city, bringing with them knowledge and training received from medical schools in the Midwest and East. The influx of physicians was fortunate, since the migrants pouring into Seattle were bringing with them the diseases that had plagued east coast cities for years.

After the 1910 census showed Seattle's death rate was the lowest of any sizable United States city, Seattle became known as the nation's healthiest city. The city had a good sanitation system as well as a progressive, efficient, health department. Much of this was the result of careful attention to health and sanitation during the rebuilding of Seattle after the Great Fire of 1889.

The worst epidemic of the twentieth century was the great flu epidemic which swept the world and Seattle in 1918. The city's death rate jumped from 9 percent to 13.7 percent that year. Drastic measures were taken, with many wearing face masks when in public. Schools were closed and all public gatherings banned.

The influenza was terrible, but did pass. Tuberculosis (TB), however, was the health horror of the twentieth century. Called the white plague, TB was the leading cause of death in the 15 to 35 age group in the first decades of this century, and elicited a sense of fear parallel to that of AIDS in the 1990s. The only known

### Early Queen Anne Hospitals and Home Care Facilities

| NAME | ADDRESS | OPERATOR | DATES | OTHER INFORMATION |
|---|---|---|---|---|
| Children's Sanitarium | 408 W. Galer St. | Bertha Keast, Matron | 1917-1928 | |
| Fairfax Home | 2604 2nd Ave. N. | Arthur G. Hughes, Superintendent | 1937-38 | Convalescent home. Hughes' earlier occupation was barber |
| Home Sanitarium, Inc. | 501 Olympic Pl. | Mabel F. Westlund, Superintendent | 1932 | |
| Industrial Home of the Boys and Girls Aid Society | 2nd N. & Republican | Emma V. Newell, Matron<br>Frank Pierce, Lawyer | 1903-04 | |
| Metropolitan Hosp. & Sanitarium | 2815 1st Ave. | | 1905-1907 | |
| The Mission Home | 614 5th Ave. W. | Rev. & Mrs. Samuel Burns, Mgrs. | 1912 | |
| Noble Emergency Hospital | 201 5th Ave. N. | Dr. Charles S. Noble | 1928-1936 | |
| Olympic View Sanitarium | 14-16 W. Harrison | Dr. G.J. Nurenberg, Specialist | 1913-14 | German specialist in chronic diseases; electrician in 1908 |
| Rauber & Baker Private Hospital for Contagious Diseases | 516 6th N. | Alice Rauber, Nurse;<br>Josephine Baker | 1910 | |
| Restview Home | 2839 14th W. | Mary E. Bettinger, Matron | 1939-40 | Convalescent home |
| St. Anne's Convent | 1305 1st W. | Sisters of the Holy Names | 1932 | |
| St. Luke's Private Hospital | 122-124 Q.A. Ave. | Ida E. Mead, Matron/Nurse | 1907-1910 | |

cure until the 1940s was convalescence, which meant complete bedrest, good food, and freedom from stress and worry for as long as a year or two. Only a few could afford such luxury, then or now. In fact, the services of a physician were not often called upon. David Denny recalled that in 24 years he and Louisa and their seven children required the services of a doctor only four times. Undoubtedly, at least once that doctor was Dr. Henry Smith, their neighbor in Smith Cove.

## Queen Anne's Pioneer Doctors—Dr. Henry A. Smith

Dr. Henry Allen Smith came to the Queen Anne area a few months after David and Louisa Denny built their cabin. Twenty-three year old Dr. Smith was Seattle's second physician, Dr. David Maynard being the first. Smith was born in Wooster, Ohio in 1830, began his medical training at Allegheny College in Meadville, Pennsylvania, and continued it in the office of Dr. Charles Roode in Cincinnati, Ohio. In 1851, having received his medical degree, he seized the opportunity to go west as the assistant physician for a covered wagon train.

*Pioneer physician Dr. Henry A. Smith built a log cabin infirmary on his donation claim in Smith Cove in 1854. There he cared for settlers and Native Americans alike who came to him via canoe. In the early years he spent most of his time clearing land and farming, like the other pioneers. Courtesy Museum of History and Industry.*

Dr. Smith staked his claim in the lowlands between Elliott Bay and Salmon Bay, which became known as Smith Cove in 1853. Dr. Smith first built a log house as an infirmary. Patients, settlers, and Native Americans were brought to him by canoe from all over Puget Sound. The infirmary was burned to the ground during the native uprising of 1856. After marrying Mary Phelan, in 1864, Dr. Smith moved to an island at the mouth of the Snohomish River he named Smith Island, where he again constructed an infirmary and looked after patients arriving by water from the surrounding five-county area. Later he served as the government physician on the Tulalip Indian Reservation.

In 1878, the Smiths moved back to Seattle with their seven children and established their home in the Cove with winters spent in Seattle until Mary died in 1880. Due to financial reverses, Smith lost much of his considerable fortune in 1893. However, he was a man of great perseverance and optimism. He continued to practice medicine at age 77 and bought 10 lots in west Queen Anne. He cleared and planted the area and constructed a house, located at 1300 W. Raye Street, in which he died in August 1915 at the age of 85. Smith Street is named for Dr. Henry Smith.

## Dr. Frederick Arthur Churchill, Horse and Buggy Doctor

Shortly after Dr. Smith returned to Seattle another physician found his way to the hill. Dr. Frederick Arthur Churchill arrived in Seattle in 1884. Born in Hillsdale, Michigan in 1856, Churchill graduated from the Chicago Homeopathic Medical College in 1882. Dr. Churchill had his office in downtown Seattle and traveled to and from his home on Queen Anne Hill by horse and buggy and later by streetcar. Churchill's office, his records and equipment were destroyed in the fire of 1889.

Dr. Churchill's wife, Martha Blanke Churchill was a highly talented pianist. Their home at 608 W. Olympic Pl. became a center of Queen Anne social life. Martha B. Churchill died in the house in 1893.

In 1895 Churchill married Emma Atkins, daughter of a "Mercer Girl," whom Asa Mercer brought out in 1863, and Henry Atkins, the first Mayor of Seattle.

In addition to his medical practice, Dr. Churchill was active in Seattle's civic affairs. He was a member of

### Lost in the Fog

Churchill did not consider himself a "country doctor," but he made many house calls, some in the middle of the night. He wrote of one such night call.

> *One night in the autumn of 1892, I was awakened about 1:30 o'clock by the ringing of my telephone and when I put the receiver to my ear, a voice said: "This is Balcom on Mercer island and my wife has taken poison. Can you come over right away?" "How shall I get there?" said I. "I will have Fred Hilt waiting for you at Leschi Park with a boat," was the answer. I agreed to go and after giving him directions for first aid, I pushed the button communicating with my man's room in the barn and when I was dressed my horse and buggy were ready for me. It was a chilly, foggy night and quite a drive from Queen Anne Hill to Lake Washington. However, I arrived at Leschi Park eventually, tied and blanketed my horse and went down to the lake shore. Sure enough, Fred was waiting with a rowboat, but the lake was covered with fog. "Have you a compass?" I asked. "No," he replied, "but we can steer by the moon." There was a full moon shining above the fog. So we set out, but after ten or 15 minutes of rowing, the fog lifted and obscured our luminary and we could not see 20 feet in any direction. Fred thought that he knew our direction, but after rowing for nearly an hour, admitted that he did not know where we were. By that time it was 3 o'clock. It was very cold and uncomfortable, but we could only float around and try to grin and bear it. Came at long last the dawn and finally we discovered we were at Laurelshadel just south of Madison Street on the same side of the lake from which we had started. So we rowed down the lake again to Leschi where I procured a small compass at the boat house and we finally arrived at our destination about 9 o'clock. I expected to find that my poor patient, over whom I had been worrying all night, had passed out by this time, but fortunately for her, the amount of poison had been so large that it had made her violently ill and she had thrown up most of it. Although she was pretty sick, she recovered ... the next day I purchased a pocket compass in order to forestall any such catastrophe in the future.*

the Board of Health from 1890 to 1893. He served on the School Board from 1893 to 1896 and on the State Medical Examining Board from 1896 through 1900. He retired in 1932, and was president of the King County Homeopathic Society shortly before his death in 1937.

## THE WAYSIDE EMERGENCY HOSPITAL

From 1899 to 1913, the Wayside Mission Hospital provided emergency care and treatment for alcoholism and drug addiction, primarily to the poor along Seattle's waterfront. Originally it was located in the *Idaho*, an old steamship moored at the foot of Jackson Street. In 1904, Dr. de Soto's lease was terminated and Mrs. Marion Babcock Baxter and Mrs. Fanny W. Cannon took over its management. In 1907 the city compelled the hospital association to move and Baxter moved the hospital to the Queen Anne location, at Second Avenue N. and Republican Street, where it became known as the New Wayside Emergency Hospital and continued to care for the sick and indigent.

The Wayside's manager, Marion Babcock Baxter, 48, was a competent manager and an outspoken feminist and prohibition worker. Arriving in Seattle in 1898, she rapidly gained notoriety as an editorial writer for the *Seattle Times*. She became President of the Wayside Mission Hospital in 1903, and the institution survived the move to Queen Anne and thrived for many years because of her skill in raising money. Upon her death in 1910, her daughter Beatrice Baxter McClure assumed management of the hospital. Like her mother, McClure was a writer on social issues as well as an accomplished musician. She lived with her husband at 115 Olympic Place until her death in 1915 of complications after surgery.

## CHILDREN'S ORTHOPEDIC HOSPITAL

In February 1907 the Women's Hospital Association, formed by Anna Herr Clise in January 1907, opened a seven-bed Children's Orthopedic Hospital Association Ward at Seattle's General Hospital. The children's ward was a small, private hospital within Seattle General. The board adopted a policy of payment according to the patient's ability to pay, with the poor having first preference. There was also an established policy that care was available regardless of race. This was the first orthopedic facility for children on the west coast and the first private hospital service in the Seattle community to have a written non-discriminatory policy.

Although the Hospital Association's aim was to care for orthopedic cases, aid was quickly extended to other types of medical problems. By 1908 the seven-bed ward had a waiting list and it was decided that a separate building was needed.

### Anna Herr Clise

Anna Herr Clise founded the Children's Orthopedic Hospital in 1907. Anna Clise lived with her husband, James W. Clise, a wealthy real estate developer, at 128 Highland Drive until 1906. The Clises had come to Seattle from Denver in 1889. In 1897 their son Willis Herr Clise died at the age of five of inflammatory rheumatism.

*Courtesy Children's Orthopedic Hospital.*

In reaction to the loss of her son to disease, Anna Clise resolved to establish a hospital in Seattle dedicated to children's needs. At that time children were placed in general wards in all the Seattle hospitals. Clise spent nine years planning her hospital for children, including visiting well-known children's hospitals on the east coast. Receiving advice from her cousin, Dr. John Musser of Philadelphia, former president of the American Medical Association, in January 1907 Clise returned to Seattle and formed the Children's Orthopedic Hospital Association, assuming the responsibilities of first President. The board was limited to 24 women and has continued to be so throughout its history. Anna Clise became blind after unsuccessful surgery for glaucoma in 1914. She remained associated with the hospital she founded, and her daughter and granddaughter served as trustees. She moved to California in retirement and died there at age 70, in 1936.

## THE FRESH AIR COTTAGE

Trustees Maude Parsons, a former student of architecture, and Bess Wilson were given the task of finding a site for a "Fresh Air Cottage." Traveling by streetcar, they explored Queen Anne Hill because it was the highest and therefore considered the healthiest location in the city. They found a vacant lot at Warren Avenue N. and Crockett Street, and a sum of $2,500 was allocated for construction of the cottage, which opened for occupancy in June 1908.

From the beginning, the Hospital Association provided a structure through which the community could support the hospital. Neighborhood guilds, made up primarily of women, met monthly to support projects designed to meet patients' needs, such as annual dues of five dollars per person which were donated to the hospital. This guild structure eventually became state- and then region-wide. The Children's Hospital Guild Association and Junior Guild Association exist today as non-profit organizations which financially support the uncompensated care the hospital provides.

## A PART OF THE COMMUNITY

The Children's Orthopedic Hospital was highly regarded on Queen Anne Hill for many reasons. As Dr. Glen S. Player, long-time Queen Anne resident and general practitioner recalls, he was so well treated for his broken arm by doctors John and Edward Le Cocq at Children's Orthopedic, that he abandoned his high school dreams of becoming an attorney and set his sights on a medical career.

The hospital provided training for generations of doctors and nurses. As a student nurse from 1937 to 1938, Beth Brook recalls that Eskimo children suffering from tuberculosis of the bones, birth defects or other illnesses, were flown in from Alaska. They would arrive at the hospital in the summertime, dressed in mukluks and parkas. The Orthopedic League members sewed little jackets for the children featuring slots for tongue depressors that kept the children from bending their arms and handling the sutured areas. Brook also recalls

*Children's Orthopedic Hospital under construction in 1911. The nurse and children are in front of the Fresh Air Cottage. Between 1954 and 1968 the hospital served as the King County Hospital clinic care facility. In 1968, the County Hospital was moved and the buildings became home to a branch of the King County Courthouse, the County's Health Department and morgue, and a branch of the Seattle District School Board. Courtesy University of Washington Special Collections.*

the metal arches the children wore under their noses, which made them "look like little ducks as they ran up and down the hall."

In 1911 a three-story, 27-bed brick hospital designed by Sommerville and Coty architects was constructed next to the Fresh Air Cottage on Crockett Street. A fourth floor was added in 1921, expanding its capacity to 78 beds. In 1928 the entire building was remodeled after a design by architect A. H. Albertson, and a new wing was added, embellished with glazed terra cotta tile and an arched entrance portico facing Warren Avenue N.

The Fresh Air Cottage became the nurses' home, then an isolation hospital, and eventually was razed. A brick nurses' home was constructed in 1923, on First Avenue N., which was occupied by the American Cancer Society in the 1980s.

In 1947 the hospital, long affiliated with the University of Washington School of Nursing, became affiliated with the university's medical school. In 1953 the Children's Orthopedic Hospital moved to Sand Point Way N.E. Eventually, all pediatric functions of the University of Washington Hospital moved to the new Children's Orthopedic Hospital buildings.

## Seattle Children's Home

The Seattle Children's Home, the city's oldest charity, was founded as an orphanage and has evolved into Washington's first comprehensive mental health center for children.

In 1884 15 women, including Sarah B. Yesler, Mary B. Leary, Babette Gatzert, and Elizabeth M. Minor, formed the Ladies' Relief Society, whose mission was to assist the poor and destitute, "regardless of creed, nationality, or color." In 1885 the society opened an orphanage in temporary quarters. David and Louisa Boren Denny donated two lots near the Denny School, at Harrison Street and Fourth Avenue N., for construction of an orphanage which was completed in August 1886.

The population boom from 1880 through 1910 found Seattle with inadequate social services and the Children's Home filled a serious need. The home required support payments from families who could afford to pay, but there was no fixed rate. By 1890 the orphanage was crowded and with relief funds from the Great Fire of 1889, the Ladies' Relief Society purchased 29 lots between Ninth and Tenth Avenue W. and Crockett and McGraw streets on Queen Anne Hill.

When the new Seattle Children's Home opened in April, 1905, it had 70 beds. Many children only stayed for a few months, thus it was not unusual for more than 100 youngsters a year to find a home there. In 1932 the old building was replaced with a new fireproof brick building.

In the 1930s, the home began shifting its emphasis away from custodial care and toward treatment. By the 1950s the focus was on mental illness in children. Building continued over the years and in 1993 there are six buildings on the campus at Tenth Avenue W. and W. McGraw Street. The Seattle Children's Home continues as a privately-run, publicly-funded organization which serves approximately 100 clients and their families yearly in a combination of residential and day treatment programs.

Helen Clark, who taught fifth- and sixth-grade classes at Coe Elementary School from 1951 through 1974, recalls that by that time the "home kids" no longer wore uniforms. Most were not orphans but children from homes where they could not be provided for. Many nationalities were represented. She recalls that the other children were "good with the home kids. Although they were well-cared for, they seemed to need love and attention."

## The Seattle Deaconess Home and Bible Training School

The Seattle Deaconess Home and Bible Training School was founded in 1906 in a private residence with two students enrolled. The purpose of the organization, founded under the auspices of the Methodist Episcopal Church, was to train deaconesses, women who were trained to give service to the community and to home and foreign missionaries. The school's 1913 pamphlet claims an enrollment of 60 over its seven-year history, with 24 graduates who served at the Deaconess Orphanage in Everett, the Spokane Deaconess Hospital, and Seattle General Hospital. The graduates acted as visiting nurses and teachers and ran the Deaconess Settlement House, now the Atlantic Street Center at 2103 S. Atlantic St.

### Citizens Object to Sharing the Healthful Hilltop Air

Queen Anne was not always accepting of health care institutions located in its midst. When Children's Orthopedic Hospital was first established there in 1908, it met with some resistance from the community. It was feared that the sight of crippled children from the hospital would upset pregnant women.

During the summer of 1909, officials of the city's newly-formed Anti-Tuberculosis League arranged to have two wagon loads of tents and supplies taken to a forty-acre site donated by Thomas W. Prosch on the north side of Queen Anne Hill. The league wanted to put up a tent colony for tuberculosis sufferers until a permanent sanitarium could be established. But the wagons were met by a brigade of women brandishing brooms and mops, who objected to the location of a large group of tuberculosis sufferers in their midst. The wagons were forced to return, and no further attempt was made to establish an encampment on Queen Anne. Fortunately, the publicity given the event resulted in many other offers of an encampment site.

Again, in 1922, when the Seattle General Hospital Association proposed construction of a new building on Queen Anne's Bigelow Avenue for TB victims, residents objected. They pointed out that over $30,000 had been spent on road improvements to build a beautiful boulevard and that a hospital would ruin the area from a residential standpoint. The hospital was not built.

*Deaconess Training School Graduates, class of 1913. The Deaconess School, under the auspices of the Methodist Episcopal Church, provided professional training for women in the social services. Courtesy University of Washington Special Collections.*

In 1910 a permanent home at 520 First Avenue N. was given to the training school by the Reverend and Mrs. G. W. Carr. Despite pleas to the public for assistance in acquiring a larger building, the school remained at that address through 1929. It closed in 1937.

## Nurses on the Hill

There were many nurses practicing in Seattle early in its history, in hospitals and as visiting nurses through the city health department. Others cared for patients in their own homes. Many of the small, private convalescent homes and hospitals located on Queen Anne Hill early in the twentieth century were operated by nurses. Several of Seattle's hospitals operated their own nursing schools. The University of Washington School of Nursing was established in 1921, long before the university medical school in 1945.

Shirley Gaston of Queen Anne graduated from the University of Washington program in 1952. During her three-month visiting nurse rotation, much of her work was teaching self-care to home-bound tuberculosis patients. She visited a child with rheumatoid arthritis every day, providing a bath and then putting the child on the dining room table to do a program of exercises.

Nurses did not normally deliver babies. That was the work of midwives. Louisa Boren Denny was probably the first midwife to live on the hill. To date no information has come to light about other midwives who practiced in the Queen Anne community, although there undoubtedly were several after 1870. *Polks Directory* reveals that Jane Josephine Rodgers was a practicing mid-wife living in Interbay in the years 1912 through 1914.

### Quarantined with Scarlet Fever

Ruth Gove Herr, who grew up on Queen Anne Hill in the 1920s and 1930s, recalls her bout with scarlet fever at the age of ten or eleven. It was three weeks before Christmas when, coming home from ice skating, she began to feel sick and went to bed. The next day she was red from head to toe and running a high fever. A Dr. Warhanik came to see her, diagnosed scarlet fever, and arranged for an ambulance to take her to Firland Sanatorium, which had isolation wards for scarlet fever and diphtheria. Her family's home was immediately fumigated and she was the only one in the family to get sick.

Martha Mae Randolph Doubt's experience with scarlet fever was slightly different. She got the disease from a child at school during the 1920s, when she was in the third grade. She was kept at home in her room, and she and her mother were not allowed to leave the house for approximately one month. Groceries were delivered to their porch. Her father had to stay in a hotel and her sisters stayed with neighbors.

## Residential Retirement Homes

The **Ida Culver Home for Retired Teachers** is Queen Anne's oldest retirement home. It was founded in 1938 by Ida Culver, a teacher at the John B. Allen School for 23 years, who was very interested in the well-being of teachers in retirement. She began her teachers' retirement service by offering her family's Queen Anne home to retired teachers in 1929. Next she formed the Seattle Education Auxiliary, a non-profit organization founded to provide housing for retired teachers.

Ida Culver Home was built with funds from Culver's estate, which she willed upon her death in 1937 to the Seattle Education Auxiliary. One of the first retirement homes for teachers in the nation, it served as a model for others. In 1950 it moved to 2315 NE 65th Street, where it continues as a retirement community. A second, larger Ida Culver residence is in operation at 12505 Greenwood Avenue N.

**Queen Anne Care Center**, 2717 Dexter Avenue N., was constructed as a retirement center by a locally incorporated business called Queen Anne Villa. It is currently a nursing facility owned and operated by the Hillhaven Corporation.

**Taylor Anne**, 1730 Taylor Avenue N., opened in 1991 in a renovated apartment building as a retirement residence with a capacity of 60 residents.

**Sunrise at Queen Anne**, 2450 Aurora Avenue N., opened in 1987 as Crestview Village, offering renters studio, one- and two-bedroom apartments with assisted living options such as two meals a day, transportation, planned activities and housekeeping services. Crestview Village was purchased by Sunrise Retirement Communities late in 1991 and the facility continues to offer similar services.

**Bayview Manor Retirement Residence,** 11 W. Aloha Street, was constructed in 1959 on the site of the home of George and Angie Kinnear. This very large, ten-story home has an extensive array of social and health services.

*Public Health nurses called on their patients to provide nursing care in the home. Beth Brook, RN, of Queen Anne, recalls her four and one-half years training at the University of Washington School of Nursing during the late 1930s. She spent two years on campus with the rest of her training being at Children's Orthopedic Hospital on Queen Anne and as a visiting nurse, through Harborview Hospital. During her visiting nurse training she resided with her parents on Queen Anne and saw patients on Queen Anne and Magnolia, using the streetcars for transportation. She visited tuberculosis patients at home to bathe them, check their vital signs and provide care information to the family. Tuberculosis patients allowed to convalesce at home were not infectious, but they needed to stay quiet. The identity of the visiting Public Health nurse and the Queen Anne homemaker are unknown. Courtesy Washington State Historical Museum.*

## Olive Kerry and Seattle Visiting Nurse Service

Olive Kerry (1891-1970) was the daughter of lumber magnate Albert S. Kerry, who lived at 421 W. Highland Drive. As a child she frequently accompanied her father to the lumber camps in Alaska and Oregon during his business ventures there. Olive Kerry devoted her life to assisting public health organizations. For many years the treasurer of the Children's Orthopedic Hospital, she also served as president and treasurer of the Ruth School for Girls. In 1929 she co-founded the Seattle Visiting Nurse Service, a non-profit organization that exists today. In 1932 the organization was described as providing bedside nursing care regardless of race, color or religion. Supported by membership fees, donations and paying patients, more than one-half of its service was done free of charge. Thirteen nurses provided 28,851 visits to 8,091 patients during 1931. The service cooperated with 20 social service agencies to provide referrals to those needing further assistance.

***Marina King** has been an architectural historian and urban planner in Cincinnati and Washington D.C. She now lives in Seattle with her husband Tom and daughter Zoe.*

Chapter Seventeen

# Business Around the Hill

by
Marina Gordon

*Van de Kamp's bakery, topped with a big windmill, opened at Mercer Street and Queen Anne Avenue in the 1920s and kept the neighborhood well-supplied with baked goods until the mid-1960s. Courtesy University of Washington Special Collections.*

*So, the streetcars are gone . . . the little neighborhood grocery stores have given way to supermarkets, and Baskin & Robbins satisfies the ice cream cravings once treated at the corner soda fountains. And Queen Anne Hill as we knew it then persists mainly in the fond memories of those of us who were there.*

Stuart Prestrud,
Long-time Queen Anne resident

Queen Anne's topography has been a major influence on the development of its business communities. Much of Queen Anne developed in the pre-automobile era and business communities sprang up along streetcar lines, which began snaking up and over the hill just after the turn of the century. These routes were determined as much by engineering skills of the day as the geography being developed.

Business growth on the hill in the first half of the twentieth century followed some general trends. A few large centers attracted shoppers from throughout the hill and the city, but it was the small, neighborhood-oriented shopping enclaves that met the residents' daily needs. Almost every neighborhood had its own grocery store, and many had a butcher shop, bakery, drug store, and beauty shop. These smaller neighborhood centers could be found at Fourth Avenue N. and Boston Street, near John Hay School; at Galer Street and Second Avenue N., the Queen Anne High School area; and at the intersection of Tenth Avenue W. and Howe Street.

Before World War I, most stores usually made deliveries of groceries by horse and wagon. Drugstores made deliveries by bicycle, and others used foot delivery. In the 1910s and 1920s, most businesses, grocery stores in particular, were smaller than they are today and often could survive by providing for only the people who lived just within a few blocks. As the popularity of the automobile (but not its reliability) rose in the 1920s, service stations sprang up and prospered.

The hardships of the Depression forced local business people to rely more on ingenuity and customers' loyalties. In 1933 *Queen Anne News* editor Clyde Dunn wrote, "Queen Anne is virtually a city in itself. . . . Just think what an outstanding business section we could build here . . . if the buying power of this vast number of people were concentrated in the community. Buying at home is the quickest way to prosperity." Business owners did not rely solely on devotion to neighborhood stores to entice people to shop locally. They came up with contests, drawings and prizes to lure customers who might otherwise shop downtown.

Although businesses had to compete against each other to survive, they also banded together for strength and formed such organizations as the Queen Anne Merchants Club, the Queeen Anne Chamber of Commerce, and the Progressive Grocer's Association. The latter was a group of eleven businesses who shared purchasing, marketing, and advertising. As the Depression came to an end, participation in these associations dwindled. The war economy helped most of Queen Anne's retail businesses, just as it did those nationwide, but rationing was difficult on some merchants.

## Primary Enclaves and Long-Term Businesses

Since the turn of the century thousands of businesses have opened and closed their doors on the hill. Many business areas can be identified but only the six primary ones are discussed here (1) Queen Anne Avenue between Galer and McGraw streets; offshoots of Queen Anne Avenue onto (2) West Galer Street and (3) Boston Street; (4) McGraw Street between Sixth and Seventh Avenues W.; (5) the Uptown area, bordered by Queen Anne Avenue, Mercer Street, and Denny Way; and (6) Nickerson Street from Queen Anne Avenue to the Ballard Bridge. Each has grown and shrunk with the vagaries of population and cultural trends that endure to this day.

This chapter chronicles the history of long-term businesses on Queen Anne Hill, both past and present, that have operated for more than 35 years in the six primary business areas identified above. Every effort was made to identify and contact all qualifying businesses, even those closed at the time of writing. However, many businesses indicated that they were not interested in participating in this effort and did not submit a history. Those histories which were submitted for Queen Anne businesses are presented here.

## Queen Anne Avenue N.— Top of the Hill

If Queen Anne is like a small town, Queen Anne Avenue is its Main Street. Since the early 1900s, the top of Queen Anne Avenue from Lee Street to McGraw has been the backbone of the business community on the top of the hill. The streetcars that were inaugurated soon after the turn of the century afforded people easy access to the hill's main business artery. Offshoots of the growth occurred on West Galer and Boston streets, coinciding with arrival of the streetcar lines. When strolling along Queen Anne Avenue in the early 1920s, one would see a fully developed, medium-sized business community with two pharmacies, three plumbing shops, Elchey's Candy and Ice Cream store, a grocery store on almost every block, a number of bakeries, a beauty shop, and the Queen Anne Theater.

In the early years of Queen Anne's growth, grocery stores on the hill were usually small, family-owned shops with the exception of **Augustine and Kyer.** This posh store on Queen Anne Avenue and Galer Street employed many of the hill's young men to deliver groceries. The half-block-long store between Galer and Garfield Streets on the west side of the block catered to "all the people who had money," claimed Fred Betts, a former delivery boy. He described his job in the following manner: "I would make about three trips a day delivering all over Queen Anne Hill. I was the swamper part of the team. A swamper stood back on the runner below the bumper, and the driver would stop near the house where the delivery was, and you'd grab ahold of the box and would run up to the house. Then you'd turn around and run back and get back on the truck and go on to the next place." Augustine & Kyer closed during the Depression.

**The Counterbalance Barber Shop** began as the Queen Anne Barber Shop in 1910, later becoming Mike's Barber Shop. In 1980 Len Hagardt bought the barber shop and renamed it Counterbalance for the old counterweight trolley system that had run past the shop for 35 years before it was replaced in 1939. Occupying the same space at 1424 Queen Anne Avenue since the building opened, the barber shop is an 80-year-old landmark business and one of the oldest barber shops in the city.

*Queen Anne Avenue and Boston Streets looking east. The Standard Drug Co. was on the northeast corner of the intersection in the location now occupied by the Standard Bakery. At the time of this photo, March 1927, the bakery was located in the middle of the block. Courtesy University of Washington Special Collections.*

The **Hilltop Tavern** opened at 2129 Queen Anne Avenue N. in 1933, the year Prohibition was lifted, and was a Queen Anne source for spirits until its 1993 closing. Above the bar hung a photo of the first Christmas the bar was open, revealing that though the neighborhood changed a great deal, the neighborhood tavern had not.

Among Queen Anne's longtime residents, two defunct movie theaters, the **Queen Anne Theater** and the **Cheerio Theater,** hold particularly strong memories. The Queen Anne Theater at Queen Anne Avenue and Boston Street was advertised as "the first neighborhood theater in the country," recalled Paul Mooney, "and this was not disputed from any quarter. It opened Christmas day, 1911, with a French hand-colored religious picture (probably Pathé). It was afterward operated by William Shaw. Opening prices were ten cents for adults; five cents for children and take off your roller skates!" The theater moved in the late 1920s, replacing the Cheerio Theater, 1529 Queen Anne Avenue.

*Cheerio Theater. Courtesy Frank B. Pomeroy.*

Dolores Graham Doyle added her recollections: "Saturday theater programs, cowboy serials, and cartoons at the two Queen Anne theaters kept many of the Magnolia kids off the street most of the day. We went in groups and had a great time for just ten cents each! Best of all was the post-show treat of double-dip ice creams for only a nickel."

## Queen Anne Avenue and Boston Street

Dr. Sam Standard owned much of the property on this corner when the hill was developing in the 1920s. One of the centers on the top of the hill, the nearby shops offered most of life's necessities, and many of its luxuries. The corner boasted popular groceries, as well as two drugstores, many doctors, and a movie theater. The *Queen Anne News* office was right down the block.

**Salladay's Drug** (formerly Standard Drug) was founded by Dr. Sam Standard at the northeast corner of Queen Anne Avenue and Boston Street. Elmer Salladay bought Standard Drug in 1956 after it had passed through a number of hands. Salladay built the present store in 1968 and sold it in 1978 to Lois Roby. Salladay has claimed that over the 20 years he owned the drugstore, his business got better and better every year, although he saw many other small pharmacies close.

*The Standard Drug Company was located on the northeast corner of Queen Anne Avenue and Boston Street from around 1908. This photograph was taken in 1910. The mustached man on the left is John Dodds, co-owner of the store. The man behind the counter in the suit is James C. Regan, druggist, and Clarence Baker is the soda jerk on the far right. Elmer Salladay bought the pharmacy in 1956. A few years later the drugstore moved across the street to its present-day location. Courtesy Salladay's Standard Pharmacy.*

Nick Muscynski, who owned and operated **Standard Bakery**, on Boston Street east of Queen Anne Avenue in the 1920s, was the shop's earliest known owner. In 1930 the new owner, a Mr. Anderson, earned a loyal following among the neighborhood children, whom coincidentally he always treated to donuts and cookies. In 1993 Standard Bakery's current owners, Mark and Dan Pavlovic, continue in that tradition, with the neighborhood's children still very much involved in bakery commerce. In addition, students of the Seattle Country Day School have brightened up the back rooms with large murals of Queen Anne.

Charles M. Brod moved the **Standard Grocery** to Boston Street near the drugstore from its location at 2132 Queen Anne Avenue N. Retiring in 1963, Brod

## "Fresher Than Morris!"

One of the most fondly remembered stores on the top of Queen Anne Hill in the twentieth century is the S&M Market and Morris Mezistrano, its proprietor. The Mezistrano family emigrated from Turkey during World War I. Morris and his brother Sam got their start selling produce in Pike Place Market, but vowed they would find surer shelter after a particularly cold winter. They moved to Queen Anne and in 1933 opened the eponymous S&M Market at 2213 Queen Anne Avenue N. They moved twice over the next 55 years, first to 5 Boston Street, then to the market's final location at the northwest corner of Boston Street and Queen Anne Avenue N.

It may, however, have been Morris' personality that drew some customers to his store. Morris did not just put out signs with prices on them; he'd add his own flourishes. A sign for flowers might say, "Fresh today! Even fresher than Morris!"

After so many decades on the hill, Morris and his store became somewhat of an institution, with the store's advertisements appearing in the *Queen Anne News* in the same space for 50 years. Very familiar with what it was like to be "hard up", Morris gave away about thirty bags of groceries every Monday during the Depression.

Competition did not bother Morris for, in his own words, "I sold cheaper than the competition." But S&M Market did eventually succumb to one large competitor: "Thriftway started staying open late, and then 24 hours, and I said it was time for me to get out." The closing of S&M Market marked the end of the era of the small grocery store. "There were about 20 grocery stores on Queen Anne that went under around this time," said Morris. Sam had died in 1967, and Morris worked on alone until the store closed in 1989. The S&M Market was best known and appreciated for its fresh produce, which Morris and Sam personally selected for the Queen Anne community's pleasure for half a century. *Courtesy University of Washington Hamilton Collection.*

had been in the grocery business on Queen Anne for 50 years. Paul Mooney characterized Brod as "the very last in the city of the 'old telephone-order, deliver, 30-day-billing corner grocers' and quite a man." Morris Mezistrano was one recipient of his kindness. When he opened his own grocery, the S&M Market, at the corner of Boston Street and Queen Anne Avenue, he asked Brod for $50 to help get his business started. Said Mezistrano, "He lent me the money and wouldn't let me pay him back. He said that this was my wedding present."

## West Galer Street

Location has meant everything for businesses along W. Galer Street. At the northern end of the old Counterbalance, business spilled in two directions, down Queen Anne Avenue N. and down W. Galer. Businesses flourished along W. Galer to Fourth Avenue W. because of the streetcar line that ran from Sixth Avenue W. to Queen Anne Avenue N.

In 1925, a local could have had a suit pressed at the Queen Anne Pressery, shopped for groceries at Cook, Gregory & Company, gotten a haircut at Mr. Carter's (after which, according to his ad, "*She* will think more of you and you will look better"), and picked up repaired shoes at Austin Banks ("Mender of Bad Soles; Surgeon to Old Shoes").

M.J. Nelsen and his sister Elizabeth opened **Nelsen's Quality Grocery** on the south side of W. Galer Street and Fourth Avenue W. in 1919. In the 1930s and 1940s M.J.'s sons, Fred and Don, joined the family business, which was moved across Fourth Avenue W. Fred Nelsen retired in the 1980s and Don has continued to operate the store. Nelsen's Quality Grocery has the distinction of being the oldest continuous family business on Queen Anne Hill.

*The Seventh Avenue W. and McGraw Street business district developed in the 1920s and 1930s when it was a thriving commercial center for those living on the north side of the hill. In the 1980s and 1990s the district is experiencing a revival of activity as small businesses move into the storefronts. Courtesy University of Washington Special Collections.*

## High School Hangouts

There were many hangouts for Queen Anne High students on W. Galer. Among the most fondly remembered was **Al's Hamburgers,** located on W. Galer and Queen Anne Avenue N. First opened in 1926, by the 1950s Alexander Gordon had moved his business to 1517 Queen Anne Avenue N. Paul Mooney described Gordon as "a man of great resistance, contending with those generations of high school characters, and a friend and confidante to all of them." Others are more apt to remember the 15-cent hamburgers.

**The Grizzly Inn**, across the street from Queen Anne High, was a home away from home for many students. Dee Simmons Hepworth recalled that in the early 1940s, "The Grizzly Inn was north of the school and became our headquarters. George Lammereaux owned the Inn and was good to the students. He employed them, sheltered them from the attendance office 'spies,' and allowed the bricks in the fireplace at the west end of The Inn to be painted with our names." Such an honor was not free. Another Queen Anne student remembers paying 50 cents to have her name painted on the bricks over the fireplace.

## West McGraw Street and Five Corners

By the 1920s the enclave along West McGraw Street between Sixth and Seventh Avenues W. was a thriving district. Mary M. Bauders remembers, "We had our own little business district between Sixth and Seventh W. on West McGraw—a drug store, shoe repair, dry cleaners, gift store, bakery, service station, grocery stores, a dime store, barber shop, and at one time a florist, and hardware store." The grocers were guaranteed almost daily visits from the local homemakers.

Joseph Kildall opened **Kildall's** in 1938 at 820 W. Halladay Street as a real estate business. He later moved to 610 W. McGraw Street and expanded the services to provide insurance, safety deposit boxes and money orders. His son Tom now runs the business. Mary M. Bauders vividly remembered that "the sight of the large steel door at the back of the establishment was very awesome to the eyes of a child."

Rex Miller opened the **Laurel Beauty Salon** in the 1930s at 1529 Queen Anne Avenue near Galer Street. By 1960 Miller had moved three times and was settled at 623 W. McGraw Street, where the beauty shop has survived four changes of ownership. Since 1987 Litsa Polychronopoulos has operated the salon as Litsa's West McGraw Street Salon.

At the corner of W. McGraw Street and Seventh Avenue W. for more than 40 years, **Maughan's Pharmacy** was originally part of the Jamison chain of drug stores. Maughan sold the store to Bernie Hoover, who changed its name to Queen Anne Pharmacy and moved it to the corner of W. McGraw Street and Sixth Avenue W. Chuck Paulson is the current owner.

The ovens in the **McGraw Street Bakery** have been in almost continuous use since 1924, the date that is stamped on them. The original founders of the bakery are unknown, but in 1930 the bakery was operated first by Chris Anderson and then by Frank and Virginia Mock, who changed its name to Banks and Mock Bakers. Mary Bauders remembers, during the years of World War II, "We would stand in line for bread during the rationing period, because of the scarcity of ingredients such as eggs, flour, shortening and especially sugar. The bakery had lots of goodies after the rationing ended." In the 1950s the Mocks sold the bakery to Chuck Sylvester and his wife who renamed it Sylvester's Queen Anne Bakery. Jessica Reisman currently operates the old landmark as the McGraw Street Bakery.

Chuck Gerrish and Bob Garrison opened **Quality Fruit and Vegetables** on Sixth Avenue W. near West McGraw Street in 1932 with an investment of $500 between them. Gerrish recalls that opening a business in the middle of the Depression did not yield much profit and that grocers could not charge much for food. In 1940 they moved to 600 W. McGraw, replacing Ben Franklin Grocery and Meats. The new store was three times larger than the previous one and the new partner was Ing Taigen.

**A & J Meats** opened at the corner of Sixth Avenue West and W. McGraw Street in 1951 inside Quality Market and was named for its owners, Al Ploe and Jerry Friar. Rick Friar, the current owner and son of its co-founder, recalls that the clientele grew so large over the first 20 years that A & J's original location was no longer adequate. In 1970, they moved to their current location at McGraw Street and Queen Anne Avenue.

**Reliable French Cleaners** opened in 1920 on the north side of W. McGraw Street. Early ownership records are lost. However, a Mr. Clark acquired it in the early 1940s and moved the establishment into a bigger building across the street. After two changes of ownership Charles and Anne Hoen, former employees of the shop, bought the business in November 1952. The cleaners had become more than just a business to the Hoens; it had sentimental significance. In 1946 Charles and Anne became engaged and were married in the shop. After Charles' death in 1973 Anne ran the business alone until 1991, when she sold it.

Down the block, at the five-way intersection of W. McGraw Street, W. McGraw Place, and Third Avenue W., sits the tiny Five Corners enclave, which developed as a convenient midpoint between the larger business areas at Queen Anne and Sixth avenues. **Five Corners Hardware** has been an anchor store here since 1940, when "Uncle Sam Jr." Jensen began business with $500 in insurance money he had collected in compensation for losing a finger. Sam Sr. joined the business in 1944 and, after World War II, two sons joined the family business. In 1961 Jim Forkey bought the store and his daughter Jean has operated it since 1987.

## Nickerson Street

Since the 1910s Nickerson Street has been lined with light industry. Scattered along Nickerson east of the Ballard Bridge have been businesses in boat moorage, construction and repair, milling and wood products, and others.

**Northwest Millwork** began producing cabinets, doors and other wood products in 1958, under the direction of Frank Stipek, whose son Ronald is a co-owner today. The commercial demand for their products has not diminished since the booming 1950s, when the University of Washington, hotels, resorts, banks and schools made up the bulk of their clients. Since the early 1990s many of Northwest Millwork's products have been exported to Pacific Rim customers. **Nordquist & Engstrom,** which has been in business for one hundred years, began at the corner of Third Avenue W. and

*The William O. McKay Co., located at Westlake Avenue and Mercer Street, would send out its service car to help troubled motorists. Courtesy University of Washington, Hamilton Collection.*

Nickerson Street, which is now the site of Seattle Pacific University's Royal Brougham Pavilion. The business is now a part of Northwest Millwork.

## On the East Side of the Hill

After owning a number of garages along Fifth Avenue, weathering the Depression, and having to close up shop during World War II, Frank Pantley opened **Frank Pantley Auto Rebuild** at 113 Dexter Avenue North in 1946. He remained in this building until 1968, when Virg Fuhrman, who bought the shop from Pantley in 1957, relocated the business to 225 Roy Street, where it closed in early 1993.

In 1955, when **Dag's** first began serving hamburgers on Aurora Avenue N., hamburgers were 19 cents; fries, 11 cents; and shakes, 14 cents. Brothers Boe and Edmund Messett founded Dag's, with the Dag Beefy Boy logo, on the grounds of the Sunset Monument Company, which the Messetts owned. Named in honor of their father, Boe Messett recalls that their philosophy of a quality product with fast, friendly service delivered from a neat and clean kitchen won immediate support from Queen Anne residents and all of Seattle, as well as set an industry standard. Dag's closed in 1993.

## Lower Queen Anne

The south slope of Queen Anne in the twentieth century has become known as the Uptown district and is something of a satellite to downtown Seattle. In the late 1880s, following residential migration from the center of Seattle to the hill, businesses that served the home quickly sprouted along lower Queen Anne Avenue N., First Avenue N. and Mercer Street. *Polk's Directory* reveals that by the 1910s grocery shops, butchers, a restaurant, a dry cleaners and a dye works were operating in the area.

There is consensus among longtime Queen Anne residents that Uptown has been a transitory neighborhood in the twentieth century, one to which these people often did not have close ties. Those who were raised in the Uptown district are likely to recall a great deal of class-consciousness: rich people lived on top of hill, workers lower down. Those who grew up on the top of the hill tend to disagree. They acknowledge social stratification but do not feel that this created problems. The young people had opportunities to play and interact with each other without worrying about their parents' positions, geographic or otherwise.

July 1 has been a lucky day for the Smith's. Preston and Frances Smith opened the **Five-Point Cafe** on Cedar Street on July 1, 1929 and **The Mecca Cafe** at 526 Queen Anne Avenue North on July 1, 1930. Their son Dick Smith took over on July 1, 1974. The end of prohibition saw

*Aasten's Grocery, 300 Queen Anne Avenue, was a typical family-run corner grocery store—with a difference. The Aastens sold very fresh produce all season long from their own store garden. The large garden was behind the store and next to their home. Molly Aasten, who worked in the store as did everyone in the family, recalls that the milk came from Kristofferson's Dairy, Turner & Pease provided the eggs and butter, potatoes and onions came from Dahlgren's on the waterfront, and most of the canned goods came from Schwabacher Bros. Courtesy Molly Aasten.*

The Mecca boom, with sales as high as 75 kegs of beer a day. In 1991 Preston Smith, then 86 years old, recalled the depression era struggles and World War II shortages and noted, "I didn't have sense enough to quit."

**Green's Tavern** is probably best remembered for having occupied a well-known Queen Anne landmark, the historic Denny Real Estate log cabin on Republican Street and Queen Anne Avenue. Green's had opened in the same building as the Uptown Theater in 1927 before later moving to the log cabin.

In 1920 the **Marqueen Garage,** then known as the Kuay Garage, opened, claiming to be "the largest single garage in the city." For more than 50 years, the garage and its "doctors of motors" serviced cars from its Queen Anne Avenue location between Roy and Mercer streets, in the building of the Seattle Engineering School which operated the garage. The building is now the Marqueen Apartments. The school was begun to retrain blacksmiths to work at the Ford assembly plant at the south end of Lake Union. Hugh Hustwayte and Fred Myers bought the garage in 1950, took in partner Kurt Arnold and changed the name to Marqueen. Upon retirement of his partners, in 1977 Arnold became the sole owner, and in 1979, moved the garage to the top of the hill.

Edwin and Josephine Anderson opened the **Olympic Grocery** on Queen Anne Avenue south of Mercer Street in 1928, where it shared a building with Busy's Meat Market. At that time a Seattle city ordinance forbade selling meats and groceries in the same establishment. Thus, if a grocery store customer wanted meat, the Andersons would call the order over the half-wall that divided the two shops and Busy would toss the wrapped meat over. There were many other grocers in the area, so the Andersons kept the store open from noon to midnight, seven days a week, whereas most of their competitors closed at five or six o'clock. Olympic Grocery moved twice, to Mercer Street between First Avenue N. and Queen Anne Avenue in 1937, and then to 118 W. Mercer Street. The Andersons closed the store in 1965, when they leased the space to Brownie's Tavern.

Lou Bunich opened **Scissor's Palace Barber & Style Shop** at 10 W. Mercer Street in 1945 and it has remained there to this day, though the business has been renamed Bert & Lou's Barber and is co-owned with Tony Romero.

**Rudd Paint**, at 1630 15th Avenue W., on the west side of lower Queen Anne began life in 1912. It was bought out by Donald M. Cummings in 1942 and subsequently operated by Alan M. Park in the mid-50s. As the Rudd Co., Inc. it continues today with Alan M. Park, Jr. as president.

Along Elliott Avenue **Blackstock Lumber** made its appearance at 545 Elliott Avenue W. in 1930. It had been located at 2325 Western Avenue between Battery and Bell streets since 1912 when Carl Blackstock purchased the old Lee Lumber & Mfg. Company. A major fire in September, 1941, required extensive rebuilding. In December 1988 they moved to their current location at 1039 Elliott Avenue W. The old lumber yard, empty and no longer Blackstock's, was swept by fire in September, 1989, claiming the life of a Seattle firefighter. Carl's sons, Ray and Carl, operated the store for many years. Since 1988 it has been owned by Ray's two sons, Jim and Scott Blackstock.

The **Queen Anne Stationery & Office Supply**, 524 First Avenue N., was originally a portrait studio owned by Frank and Josie Pomeroy. In 1950 the Pomeroys opened the first formal office supply store on Queen Anne, eventually expanding to include a Hallmark card and gift store. Harry and Irene Tenneson purchased the store in 1976 in partnership with Chris and Jane Bihary. It is now owned by the Biharys and Keith and Sally Brooks.

## Queen Anne's Business Districts Change, 1950-1990

Marion Parker, who grew up on Queen Anne, left the community in 1944 and returned in 1958 to find that drug stores had consolidated and more large grocery stores had been built. In addition, several small grocery stores had consolidated or closed and the movie theater had become a popular bowling alley. Queen Anne Avenue N., although a strong business magnet since the inauguration of streetcars, was fully coming into its own in the 1950s when centralization was the order of the day.

The **Safeway** store was first opened at the corner of Blaine Street and Queen Anne Avenue N. and then moved to First Avenue N. and Mercer Street in the 1950s. In 1961, the supermarket moved back to the top of the hill, to its present location on Queen Anne Avenue N. between Boston and Crockett streets. A second Safeway at First Avenue W. and Mercer Street opened in 1952.

The Zorich brothers, Joe, Marty and Sam, opened their 12,000-square-foot **Thriftway** in 1960, but the next year it was dwarfed by the new Safeway nearby, which had more than twice the square footage. Dick Rhodes bought the store in 1974, and maintained a commitment to the basics: a clean store, pleasant em-

*Besides the retail lumber business, Blackstock's interest pioneered one of the first co-op ventures for building materials in the Northwest. Called Lumber Supply, the co-op was originally created as a means of increasing the buying power of its members. Some of the early participants in the co-op were the Brace, Alki and Compton lumber companies. Later Lumber Supply was sold and Carl Blackstock continued in business with his family. Courtesy Blackstock Lumber Co.*

ployees, and lots of service. In order for Thriftway to compete with its larger neighbor, Rhodes remodeled and expanded the store in 1981. He kept a close ear to the customers, feeling that the store would compete best if it responded to changes in the community.

Don Nelsen, owner of Nelsen's Grocery, thought the World War II and post-War years were the most prosperous for West Galer businesses. During the 1940s he remembers numerous small groceries, a pharmacy, two gas stations and a garage on the street. Then, Nelsen says, business declined in the 1960s. He offered two reasons: "Everything started centralizing on Queen Anne Avenue North. West Queen Anne and Queen Anne High School closing hurt us more than anything; there are hardly any kids around here anymore."

Down in the Ross district the loss of the small business community came early. By the early 1930s most of the small businesses clustered around Nickerson Street and Third Avenue W. had closed, never to reopen. Most businesses that continue to line Nickerson are light industries geared towards the construction trade—same as in the earlier days. Since the 1980s professional office buildings have been built along the Ship Canal from the Fremont Bridge to Cremona Street.

The Uptown area had been a busy district for almost a century and, until the World's Fair, was composed of "mom and pop" stores and small businesses catering to residents in the immediate area. To make way for the Fair, many homes and a school were torn down. In the years since, apartment buildings have increased and the area has become high-density, with many restaurants, theaters, shops and parking lots. Although many long-time residents dislike the crowds and crime that come with growth, as a business district it is thriving.

*Marina Gordon is an editor, freelance writer, and newcomer to Queen Anne. She often amazes friends and relatives with her ability to recite the location and history of almost any business on the Hill.*

Chapter Eighteen

# Apartments and Development on the Hill

by
Kim Myran and Scott Jennings

## Part I
## Architecture and Development on the Hill, 1890-1940

by Kim Myran

After the Great Fire of 1889, when Seattle began rebuilding, American architecture was in the second phase of the Eclectic Movement. The first, beginning about 1860, was related to the Gothic Revival, which led to an interest in a Romanesque Revival and to the Arts and Crafts movement in Britain. The second phase, which lasted until about 1930, was more aca-

*The Chelsea Family Hotel, 620 W. Olympic Place, is typical of the late Eclectic Movement. The Chelsea is a mix of English, Renaissance and Italian villa styles. The English element appears in the U-shaped plan, with the two flanking wings of the building establishing a symmetry that is repeated throughout the building in the bay windows, leaded glass transoms and other features. The Italian influence is evident in the tiled arches that lead one from the entrance to the courtyard. This photo, taken at the building's completion, shows the arbor for the rooftop. Courtesy Pemco Webster and Stevens Collection, Museum of History and Industry.*

*The Denny Mansion, at the corner of Queen Anne Avenue and Republican Street, after remodeling into a multi-family residence. ca. 1930s. Courtesy University of Washington Special Collections.*

demic, influenced by the L'Ecole des Beaux Arts in Paris. It sought inspiration from great past architectural periods, such as the Italian and French Renaissance, ancient Greek and Roman, and late Gothic. These architectural styles are much in evidence in the early apartments on Queen Anne Hill.

World expositions at this time were instrumental in introducing the general public to new technological advances in science, industry, engineering, and architecture. The 1892 Chicago Columbian Exposition did much to heighten awareness of architectural styles. The 1909 Alaska Yukon Pacific (AYP) Exposition had an impact on the Northwest, especially Seattle, that was as powerful as the Columbian Exposition nationally. A population educated by the AYP demanded buildings according to the current styles.

Located at the corner of Queen Anne Avenue and W. Highland Drive, the **Gable House**, One W. Highland Drive, was built in 1901 by Bebb and Mandel for Harry Whitney Treat. Inspired by the English Arts and Crafts Movement, the Gable House has a brick base, while tawny bricks and stucco appear in the gable area half-timber detailing. Through the beveled glass windows is a grand view of Elliott Bay and the city skyline. The house was originally constructed with 18-inch I-beams in anticipation of a third story.

Between 1922 and 1970 the house was used alternately as an apartment building and a private residence. In 1975, Gary Gaffner, a lifelong Queen Anne resident and developer with a strong interest in history, purchased the fine old house. Under Gaffner's sensitive supervision the Gable House has been tastefully converted to apartments that respect the original design of the building.

## Eclectic Architectural Expressions

Vintage architecture on Queen Anne Hill is largely an expression of the second phase of the Eclectic Movement in building design that characterized American architecture from the 1890s to 1930s. Perhaps the most magnificent surviving example of a multiple residence on the hill is the De La Mar.

*Historical records show that multifamily residences were being built on Queen Anne in the 1880s. Called tenements, these were often two- or three-family homes which are referred to as duplexes and triplexes in current times. These triplexes stood at 411 and 417 Ninth Avenue N. Courtesy University of Washington Special Collections.*

*The De La Mar entrance courtyard is entered through a wrought-iron gate, flanked by a pair of brick posts capped with terra cotta. In the courtyard there is a pond also trimmed in terra cotta and adorned with a statue of a maiden on a lamppost designed by Julian Everett. Entering the building, one is greeted by a mosaic tile coat of arms on the floor emblazoned with "De La Mar" and the sentiment "I think better by the sea" in Latin. Photo by Isabel Egglin.*

The **De La Mar**, 115 W. Olympic Place, was built in 1908 by George Kinnear as a grand guest house for his friends visiting the AYP Exhibition. The building is an example of the neoclassical style favored by the Beaux Arts Movement in the 1890s. Its foundation and ground floor are made of simulated rusticated stone in terra cotta. The terra cotta ornamentation makes a handsome contrast to the yellow-colored brick that faces the building.

Twentieth century restoration work has returned the handsome interior to its original appearance. The "marble" columns and the wainscoting in the entry were made using a lost technique, a cast material covered with a faux marble veneer of crushed colored particles that has the look and feel of marble. Planned on a grand and elegant scale, the lobby entrance is graced by statuary, stained glass windows, a pair of grand staircases, and richly carved mahogany. Today the De La Mar has 39 apartments with high ceilings and much original woodwork. Earlier restoration work was improved upon by Mel Kaufmann and a local group of investors in the early 1970s, and in 1978 the De La Mar was designated a Seattle City Landmark.

The **Chelsea Family Hotel** was built in 1907 through the collaboration of Charles R. Collins, engineer, and Harlan Thomas, architect. Built to initially serve AYP Exposition visitors in 1909, the goal was to create an elegant building with spaces that would remind the guests of home, or a place one would want to call home. It would offer the refined visitor a quiet retreat from the hubbub of the city and a grand view of the Olympic Mountains, Mount Rainier, and Puget Sound. The Kinnear-line streetcar stopped across the street and it was only a ten-minute ride to downtown Seattle, where a connecting car went north to the AYP site, on the University of Washington campus. For the first ten years, the hotel was the scene of many social occasions, including dinners, weddings, and Halloween parties. In 1913 a Montessori school was started at the hotel.

The Chelsea project had a major impact on Collins' and Thomas' lives and work. For a number of years Charles Collins lived with his family at the Chelsea. Thomas went on from the Chelsea, his first major project, to design the Sorrento Hotel, the Corner Market Building in the Pike Place Market, the Seattle Chamber of Commerce Building, the Rosita Villa Apartments, and the Amalfi apartment building. He built his family home at 804 W. Lee Street and eventually became a highly influential figure in Northwest architectural design, serving as the Director of the University of Washington School of Architecture from 1928 to 1940 and a partner in the architectural firm of Thomas, Grainger and Thomas.

Around 1917 the elegant hotel was sold to an investment company, which converted it into apartments and enclosed part of the lobby and lower dining room. It was not well maintained and by the 1960s it had badly deteriorated.

However, the Victorian Revival sparked renewed appreciation of turn-of-the-century buildings and in 1977 Dr. Steven Yarnall rehabilitated the building and restored it to its original appearance in every detail, including the leaded-glass windows. In 1978, largely through the efforts of architectural historian Miriam Sutermeister and the Queen Anne Historical Society, the exterior of the Chelsea, including the loggia, was officially designated a Seattle Historic Landmark. On October 3, 1991, the building was damaged by a major fire. However, restoration work was completed immediately.

*Kinnear Apartments, 905 Olympic Way W., 1909, Architect W.P. White. Illustration by Jim Stevenson. Courtesy Queen Anne Historical Society.*

The **Amalfi**, named for the Amalfi Coast of Italy, 1306 Queen Anne Avenue N., was designed by Harlan Thomas. Built in 1915, the Amalfi is less refined than the Chelsea and the exterior of the building is eclectic in a less formal, rustic, Italian style. Overall the building has a bulky, massive look, with heavy, graceless balconies on the front. The original balconies were cantilevered and support beams span the entire depth of the building.

The Amalfi was designed for residents with an active social life and includes a ballroom in the basement. But few balls were ever held there and eventually the space was converted to an apartment during the post World War I housing shortage. In 1950, the Amalfi was converted to a cooperative. In 1992 the building received a facelift.

The **Victoria Apartments**, 120 W. Highland Drive, were designed by John Graham Sr. in the Tudor style of English Gothic, which is reflected in the details of the portals and the window moldings. A center courtyard provides the surrounding 44 apartments with good natural light while assuring tenants' privacy. The exterior is composed of red brick with terra cotta trim around the entrances, windows, and cornice, with cast-stone lintels and sills. The interior is rich in detail and color. At the entrance vestibules and elevator halls there are marble floors with matching marble wainscot. The Victoria Apartments were renovated in the 1970s.

## The Arts and Crafts Movement

After World War I the Northwest experienced tremendous growth. Several architectural styles were predominant in the apartments that were constructed as a part of the building boom. The influence of the Arts and Crafts Movement continued and is seen in the popular English brick, half-timber style. The typical apartment building designed by Fred Anhalt, a local builder, is characterized by this style and by close attention to landscaping around the buildings. In addition, bungalow and courtyard apartments became popular and were a step closer to the feeling of having one's own place—even if it just meant a back stoop.

The apartments at **1320 Queen Anne Avenue N.** are a fine example of the Arts and Crafts Style as interpreted by Fred Anhalt. They were originally built in 1927 as family apartments and meant to be homes. Anhalt designed a series of entrances shared by several apartments. Built in the English Tudor style, with steeply-pitched roofs, random brick colors, stucco and a half-timber look, the apartments are nestled into the nearby steep hill.

## The Mediterranean Style

Paralleling the Arts and Crafts Style was the Mediterranean Style, which was viewed as very romantic and found expression in the bungalow and courtyard designs of the late 1920s. Typical features include stucco exterior, flat roofs, arched windows and doorways, and narrow casement windows, often with leaded glass.

**Seville Court,** at the corner of Aloha Street and First Avenue N., is an Anhalt Mediterranean courtyard complex. The detailing on these apartments is similar to that of a courtyard complex at the corner of Boston Street and

Bigelow Avenue N. Both of these buildings have stucco walls, tiled roofs, leaded glass windows and an applied, detailed scrolled arch embellishment. The leaded glass on the Boston building has a slightly different pattern than the typical leaded glass of this period.

The **Villa Costella,** 348 W. Olympic Place, was built in 1928 on the site of John Kinnear's grand house. Thought to have been built by John Beardsley and Fred Anhalt, the Mediterranean theme is carried out in the interior of the building, which retains much of its original character. The floors of rich red Spanish tile alternate with wood and those made of a combination of tile and polished slate. The walls are thick plaster with timber-beamed ceilings. Each unit has an electric faux fireplace just deep enough for one metal log textured to simulate bark. Building manager Val Reel affirms that after 60 years, most of the electrical logs still function and even give off enough heat to make the room cozy. From the living rooms, French doors open onto spacious decks, from which tenants enjoy a sweeping view of downtown Seattle. A deep overhang provides outdoor seating sheltered from the rain.

*The Sea View, 579 W. Roy Street, is the grandest example of Art Deco on Queen Anne. The building has a yellow brick exterior which is topped by a very wide detailed band that imparts a heavy feeling to the structure. In the courtyard is found a whimsical spouting pony fountain. The entry doors, made of honey-colored stained wood, appear to be polished brass in the sunlight. Photo by Isabel Egglin.*

## THE ART DECO MOVEMENT

In 1925 a design and ornamentation concept was introduced to the general public at the Exposition Internationale des Arts Decoratifs et Industriels Modernes, held in Paris. The style was meant to complement the machine age and one of the principal characteristics was its emphasis on the future. It was one of the first popular styles in the United States to break with the revival traditions represented by the Beaux Arts period. Soon Art Deco themes and forms were used in literally every aspect of art and design from household appliances to building design.

*The Victoria Apartments, 120 W. Highland Dr. Illustration by Jim Stevenson. Courtesy Queen Anne Historical Society.*

The application of Art Deco elements to architectural design added variety and emphasis to facades, as well as breaking down the building mass to a friendlier scale. Classic details on buildings were replaced by Egyptian, Assyrian, Celtic, Persian, Mayan, Incan and Native American geometry,

## Selected 20th Century Multi-Family Residences on Queen Anne Hill

*(by construction dates if known)*

| BUILDING NAME | ADDRESS | CONSTRUCTED | SPECIAL FEATURES |
|---|---|---|---|
| W. Queen Anne School | 1401 5th W. | 1894-1916; conv. 1984 | 49-unit, Romanesque-style former school. Red brick, stone trim, arched windows. Nat'l. & Seattle historical landmark.; condo. |
| Court Apartments | 1701-03 2nd N. | 1899 | English Tudor, attractive arched garage doors. |
| Duplex | 1324 4th W. | 1903, ren. 1951 | Now a condominium. |
| De La Mar Apartments | 115 W. Olympic Pl. | 1906-9; ren. 1908 | 39 units, originally George Kinnear's hotel. Florentine villa copy. Views, pond, courtyard, terracotta, stonework, statuary, stained glass, etc. |
| Chelsea Apartments | 620 W. Olympic Pl. | 1907; ren. 1917, 1978, 1992 | 55 units, originally Harlan Thomas hotel. Mixed English, Renaissance, Italian villa styles, courtyard, fountain, roof garden. Nat'l. & Seattle historical site. |
| Etruria Apartments | 69 Etruria | 1909 | Square box, beveled siding, double-hung windows. |
| Kinnear Apartments | 905 Olympic Wy. W. | 1909 | W.P. White architect. |
| White Apartments | 1946 11th W. | 1909 | Seven units with Puget Sound view, horizontal siding, plain. |
| Q A Apts.(High School) | 201 Galer | 1909; ren. '29, '55, '85 | 139-unit classical style former high school. Concrete/masonry, terracotta detailing. Nat'l. & Seattle historical landmark converted to apts. in 1985. |
| 600 West Howe | 600 W. Howe | 1910 | Six townhouses; long covered porches, interesting stairs, cottage windows. |
| Grocery Store Apts. | 1800 8th W. | 1912; ren. 1933 | Originally grocery store, then dance studio, then apartments. |
| Highland Court | 1216 1st W. | 1914 | First U.S. apartment building with a lanai. |
| Courtyard Apts. | 1701 Taylor N. | 1914 | Curving stairway. |
| Amalfi Apartments | 1306 Queen Anne N. | 1915 | Architect/builder Harlan Thomas, same as Chelsea. Spanish style, balconies. |
| Victoria Apartments | 120 W. Highland Dr. | 1921 | 55 units, Tudor Gothic style, brick/terracotta, courtyard, largest apt. lawn on QA. Views, rich detail inside & out. Recent addition controversy. |
| Valley St. Apartments | 201 & 211 Valley St. | 1926, ren. 1957 | Built by Gust Holmberg, similar to 200 Aloha. |
| 1320 Queen Anne N. | 1320 Queen Anne N. | 1927 | Fred Anhalt-built English Tudor style, brick/stucco/1/2 timber, leaded glass, family apartments nestled into wilderness-like hill in rear. |
| Lee Courtyard Apts. | 205 Lee St. | 1927 | Brick/stucco U-shape, courtyard, in single-family neighborhood. |
| Marcanna Apartments | 102 Galer St. | 1927 | Six units built by Albert Geiser & R.P. Hemmingsen. Originally the Ella. |
| Chateau Apartments | Howe & Taylor Sts. | 1928 | Brick/stucco, pitched roofs, individual entrances. |
| Elise Apartments | 1627 10th W. | 1928 | Eight unit brick, arched mahogany doors, coved ceilings, original tile. |
| Triplet Apartments | 1902/06/12 5th N. | 1928 | Amherst, Aladdin, Sargent Apts. Different roof & window details. |
| Villa Costella | 348 W. Olympic Pl. | 1928 | Kinnear land, Anhalt built, Mediterranean style & details, view decks, tile. |
| 405 Prospect | 405 Prospect | 1929 | 5 stories on one side; 3 stories on the other. Original Denny land and small adjoining house. |
| Alexander Hamilton | 1127 Olympic Wy. W. | 1929 | 22 units, views, unusual leaded glass entry doors, tiles. |
| La Charme | 600 W. Roy, 3rd W. | 1929 | 39 units, originally a hotel, leaded glass entry windows. |
| Anhalt Mediterranean | 1108 9th Ave. W. | 1930 | Fred Anhalt-built bungalows; stucco, tile, leaded glass, ornamentation. |
| Lola Apartments | 326 W. Mercer | 1930 | Appears exact mirror of La Charme. |
| Iris Apartments | 415 W. Roy | 1931, ren. 1990s | Brick, Art Deco trim and ornamentation. |
| Sea View Apartments | 519 W. Roy | 1932 | Art Deco style. |
| 200 Aloha | 200 Aloha St. | 1945; ren. 1957 | Built by Gust Holmberg, courtyard feel, balconies, "unusual" character. |
| Aloha Terrace Apts. | 212 Aloha St. | 1947 | 19 units, Stuart & Durham architects, courtyard, two 3-story brick bldgs. |
| Queen Vista Apts. | 1321 Queen Anne N. | 1949; ren. 1983,89 | 85 units, Stuart & Durham architects, International Style |
| Queensborough Apts. | 101 W. Olympic Pl. | Constructed 1950 | 146-unit reinforced concrete apt./hotel. Bomb shelter. Built by Stringfellow. |
| Skyline House | 600 W. Olympic Pl. | 1956 | 85-unit award-winning Durham & Co. Int'l. Style. T-shape, balconies |
| Bayview Manor | 11 W. Aloha St. | 1961 | Retirement home on Kinnear mansion site. Graham & Co. Modern style. |
| Aloha House | 100 Aloha St. | 1962 | 48 units on Dillis Ward mansion site. 3-story ext. mosaic of Space Needle |
| 2101 Nob Hill | 2101 Nob Hill | 1978 | Six-unit modern condominium designed and built by owners. |
| Cascade Terrace | 602 Galer | 1987 | 144 units in NE Queen Anne Greenbelt. |
| Wharfside Pointe Apts. | 3811 14th W. | 1987 | 130 units, apts. & retail, rec. facilities. Project had permit & site difficulties. |
| Windwatch Condos. | 2400 Aurora N. | 1987 | 20 Roger Newall designed townhouses, terraced, sound screened. |
| Highland Parc | 105 Highland Dr. | 1992 | Six-unit condo, brick, iron balconies, designed to blend with older bldgs. |
| Le Parc Condominiums | 1231 5th N. | 1992 | 13 units terraced into slope overlooking downtown & Lake Union. |
| Cornerstone Q.A. | 500 Aloha | 1993 | 35-unit mixed use project on former pickle factory site |
| Nautica Condos | 1425 Dexter N. | 1993 | 56-unit mixed use project, terraced, roof decks. |

*On Fourth Avenue W. between W. Roy and W. Mercer streets are four buildings of Art Deco style, the Marianne, Charmaine, Naomi, and Franconia. The horizontal and vertical banding found on these neighboring brick apartment buildings adds interest and breaks down the structural mass to smaller, more digestible building parts. In this way, a comfortable balance to the overall mass of the building is achieved. The Charmaine displays a Celtic theme, and the Naomi an Egyptian fan design. The Marianne (top) features a repeated botanical motif and a pair of rising suns above the door. The entrance of the Franconia (bottom) is located in the corner of the building and creates a unique alcove with a repeated triangle motif that draws one in. The decorative ironwork on the doors and windows and in the leaded glass conveys a Spanish ambiance. Photos by Isabel Egglin.*

incised in stone, wood and bronze. The wide use of Egyptian motifs reflected excitement resulting from the discovery of King Tut's tomb. With their bold horizontal banding, these buildings are impossible to ignore. Ornamentation was focused at the base and top of the buildings. The movement reached its height at the time of Seattle's construction boom of 1928 to 1931. As a result, the city has the best preserved collection of Art Deco buildings north of San Francisco.

## Part II
## Architecture and Development—1940 to 1993

by Scott Jennings

Looking down on Queen Anne Hill late in 1940, one could easily have seen various buildings devoted to specific uses, such as hospitals, hotels, clubs and apartments. At this time there were very few buildings over 40 feet high except on the south and north slopes, where some reached 60 feet. Uniformity of yard size in the residential districts would also have been obvious. These and other characteristics of the community's buildings were shaped by a series of city zoning regulations determining allowed uses, lot coverage and building height.

### The Zoning Codes

Queen Anne was typically zoned for R-2 use along most of the lower level sloped areas and arterial streets such as Queen Anne Avenue, West Galer and Boston streets and Aurora Avenue. Seattle's zoning codes of the late 1940s explicitly stated that R-2 zoning designation allowed apartment houses, boarding houses, hotels, clubs and fraternal societies, memorial buildings, uses permitted in the less restrictive R-1 zone, and in some cases hospitals. Most of the hill was also governed by a 40-foot height restriction, although some parts of the north and south slope had 65-foot limits and the Uptown area, from Harrison to Roy streets, had an 80-foot limit. This kind of zoning is reflected in the large number of typically small, brick, two- or three-story apartment buildings scattered over the hill. These patterns continued with a few exceptions until a new zoning code went into effect in 1955.

*Looking north from Fifth Avenue W. and Mercer, apartment buildings rise like terraces up Queen Anne Hill. Photo by Isabel Egglin.*

In 1955 the existing Seattle zoning code was totally revamped, with new designations assigned to the zones. No longer was the language of the code succinct. Building heights were now limited by both an area's classification and by the location of the building on its site. The effect of the new regulations was that high-rises became legal in some areas formerly restricted by lower height regulations. The code also required off-street parking for tenants, which in effect reduced the number of rental units that could be built on a parcel of land.

## Architectural Styles at Mid-Century

Architecture in the United States in the late 1940s and early 1950s was undergoing a transformation. Since the early 1920s, progressive American architecture was under the influence of the International Style. Originating in Germany at the Bauhaus School, under the leadership of Walter Gropius, the International Style was devoid of the ornament and decoration that had characterized architectural design for centuries. Concrete, steel and glass were the most commonly used materials. Structural expression, glass banding and a strong horizontal emphasis were trademarks.

Many found the International Style somewhat harsh and a radical change from the well-established norms of architectural design. Eventually, this harshness was softened by the influence of elements of Functionalism and Rationalism. In addition, regional and personal variations were expressed through color, lively surfaces and textures.

The architectural firm of Stuart and Durham designed two apartment buildings on the hill, the **Queen Vista Apartments**, 1321 Queen Anne Avenue, completed in 1949, and the 19-unit **Aloha Terrace**, 212 Aloha Street. Built in 1947 as two three-story buildings clustered around a stepped courtyard, the Aloha Terrace design reflects the preference of this period for simply massed, non-adorned brick buildings. The originally rented apartments were converted to a cooperative in 1957. The Queen Vista has 85 apartments and, reflecting contemporary regulations, has 53 underground parking spaces.

**Skyline House,** 600 W. Olympic Place, won an American Institute of Architects award in 1956 for its designers, Durham, Anderson, and Freed. Built by E. S. Lovell, the original design incorporated 85 luxury units in an eight-story T-shape featuring multicolored balconies that offered residents a spectacular view of Puget Sound and the Olympic Range. The entry is defined with two massive columns which support the cantilevered apartments above, and the sound of gurgling fountains welcomed the residents as they entered the glass lined lobby when the building was new. By the 1990s the building had been painted a drab mustard color and the fountains were filled with cedar chips, but the building continues to be an important Seattle example of an innovative period of architectural history.

### The Queensborough, a Home for Visiting Artists

In 1950, Virgil Stringfellow, an active developer, in the 1930s and 1940s, built his largest project in Seattle, the 146-unit **Queensborough** at 101 W. Olympic Place. Designed by architects Granger, Thomas and Baar, the Queensborough has simple lines devoid of ornamentation. During the 1962 Seattle World's Fair, Stringfellow rented some apartments on a daily basis to fair visitors. In the following decades, Stringfellow made the Queensborough's hotel rooms available to the numerous performers and celebrities who visit Seattle to perform at the many theaters and concert halls on Queen Anne.

By the late 1950s, Queen Anne Hill, with its good public transportation service and fine views, was often chosen as an ideal place for retirement. **Bayview Manor**, 11 W. Aloha Street, is designed to take advantage of the stunning location on Queen Anne Hill's south slope. The main residential portion of the ten-story building forms a concave, south-facing curve. In designing the very large structure, John Graham and Co. used simple massing, long horizontal forms, a variety of texture and the original use of primary colors to highlight the balconies.

Built on the site of George and Angie Kinnear's mansion, reminders of the Kinnear era are a carved mantel near the library and some stained glass windows outside the chapel. Out on the grounds the trees planted by Angie Kinnear continue to shade the site. The Italianate fountain topped by cherubs is all that remains of the extensive south-facing gardens that once surrounded the gracious home.

## The Tumultuous Seventies

The 1970s were a time of struggle for Queen Anne between commercial interests and those wishing to preserve the neighborhoods. Battles were fought, laws were changed, and a few came out winners. Memories still linger for those who were deeply involved.

The 1950s zoning code, which permitted high density residential housing in selected inner city neighborhoods, started the problem. While the concept was very reasonable in light of Seattle's population growth, the residents of Queen Anne's south slope opposed this trend and the ordinance prompted many citizens to request down-zoning of their neighborhoods. When the Dillis B. Ward mansion was destroyed and the Continental Apartment Building at 100 Ward Street went up in what was considered a "single family neighborhood," people became alarmed and angry, but nothing happened.

However, diligent citizens were watching and in the late 1960s a multitude of citizen groups formed, determined to preserve the neighborhood and the view corridors. These groups included Concerned West Slope Residents, the North Queen Anne Preservation Association, the Galer Street Community Action Committee, the Steering Committee of West Slope Residents, and the North Queen Anne Association. In 1968 The Queen Anne Community Development Council, an informal community government organization, drew up recommendations for preserving the residential character of the community's neighborhoods which were not approved by Seattle City Hall.

In the early 1970s the United South Slope Residents (USSR), formed a dynamic citizens' group that successfully reversed the commercialization of the south slope residential neighborhoods. Headed by architect Art Skolnick, the ad hoc group was well-organized, well-connected and, equally important, well-funded when the need arose. A petition was circulated and 4,800 signatures were gathered demanding that all high-rise property on the south slope be down-zoned to low-rise. The stage was set for the battle to begin.

The developers were busy obtaining permits for projects before any zoning changes were approved. Polygon Realty Corporation was one which had a permit denied. Alfred Petty, City Building Permit Superintendent, concluded that "established zoning on Queen Anne does not appear to be in the best interest of the local community." Polygon promptly filed two lawsuits: the first one contested the superintendent's decision, the second contested the city's decision to down-zone some of Queen Anne Hill.

USSR joined in the court case, financing lawyers' fees with grass roots fund raising efforts, including tours of the community's elegant old houses. The citizens were victorious, for the courts sided with the city and upheld the denial of Polygon's permit. The decision, based on environmental concerns, was a major one, since it clarified that all future projects would have to be evaluated on environmental grounds as well as zoning laws to obtain permits. USSR has remained a viable citizens' organization since its inception as it continues its watchdog role, periodically reviewing controversial projects.

## New Lives for Old Schools

During the 1960s and 1970s Queen Anne's demographics changed and the number of school age-children dropped drastically. West Queen Anne School was slated for closure and possible demolition. However, the neighborhood quickly rallied and was successful in achieving protection for the old school through placement on the National Register of Historic Places in 1975, and designation as a Seattle City Landmark in 1977. The school closed in 1981.

The building was converted to a 49-unit condominium building that retained the historic character of the school. The playfields were converted into landscaped gardens with parking hidden beneath. Through creative lease agreements with the school district, Historic Seattle was able to ensure that West Queen Anne School will be preserved for many years to come.

Following this precedent a similar program was followed at the closure of Queen Anne High School in 1981. Conversion of the school to the apartment building The **Queen Anne** is the hill's finest example of adaptive reuse of a historic building. Designed in 1909 by James Stephen, the Beaux Arts Movement design took its inspiration from the late English Renaissance palace style. It is constructed of concrete, unreinforced masonry, and heavy timber, and features elaborate terra cotta detailing at the cornice and entries.

As with the West Queen Anne School conversion into condominiums, the Seattle Preservation and Development Authority and the Seattle School District cooperated to preserve the historic building while transforming it into a 139-unit luxury apartment building. Following the design of the Bumgardner Architects, the 1929 auditorium and gymnasium wings were demolished and the exterior terra cotta detailing was restored. The old Queen Anne High School was placed on the Washington State and National Register of Historic Places in 1985, became an Official City of Seattle Landmark in 1984, and welcomed new residents. Queen Anne High School, living a new life, continues to stand proudly at 201 Galer Street.

In 1974 the old Queen Anne Community Church building, several old neighboring houses, and Hansen's Sunbeam Bakery were redeveloped into a restaurant-shop complex named the Hansen Baking Company. The buildings were connected with covered walks, and a central court, complete with fountains, benches and landscaping, provided a reprise from the outside world. The complex was not a successful venture and the Hill and Roats Co., acquired the property in 1988. After a bitter battle between the developers and the preservationists, the old church and baking building were demolished in 1993 as plans progressed for its re-development.

## Housing for Low-Income Citizens

The Seattle Housing Authority (SHA) was created in 1939 to provide low income housing and related services for the people of Seattle, including the elderly, handicapped, and disabled citizens. Although noble in its cause, the authority's projects are not typically welcomed by neighbors on the hill. Of the 10,000 Department of Housing and Urban Development (HUD) housing units in Seattle, in 1992 there were 363 units in six Queen Anne locations:

**Center West,** 533 Third Avenue W., 1969, 92 units, designed by Price and Assoc.; **Olympic West,** 110 W. Olympic Place, 1971, 76 units, designed by Sullam Smith and Assoc.; **Queen Anne Heights,** 1212 Queen Anne Avenue N., 1971, 53 units, designed by John Y. Sato and Associates; **Carroll Terrace,** 600 Fifth Avenue W., 1985, 26 units; **West Town View,** 1407 Second Avenue W., 1978, 59 units, designed by Dudly and Ekness; and **Michaelson Manor,** 320 W. Roy Street, 1985, 57 units, designed by Architects Virgil and Bradbury.

*In 1974 Richard Hoyt, Jr., grandson of the original baker Jim Hansen, developed the old bakery building and adjacent structures into a commercial complex called the Hansen Baking Company. The complex was heralded as "urban renewal—the restoration of classic old buildings." It was demolished in May 1993. Courtesy Bob Frazier.*

## Scarce Land

By the late twentieth century, land available for building large apart-

## The Chandelier Returns

Deloris Kaczor's dream was to have a home with a chandelier just like the one that hung in the dining room of a bungalow on Highland Drive. In 1965, George and Deloris Kaczor built a modern $850,000 retirement home on the site of the bungalow and carefully installed that chandelier. After George passed away, Deloris solicited her son Michael to help plan the next home on the site. They decided to build a condominium tower with six units. The property was zoned for high rise construction, and after meeting with the local community groups and the City of Seattle, the project was permitted to continue. In 1988, the Hobbs Architecture Group was given the task of designing a building with the most modern amenities, but made to look as old as its neighbors. Consequently, the six-story building Highland Parc, with one unit per floor, was detailed with field laid brick and iron balconies on a form that is modulated as in earlier times. When Deloris Kaczor moved into her new home at Highland Parc, the chandelier that hung in the early bungalow was placed in her kitchen.

ment and condominium complexes was scarce on Queen Anne Hill and developers turned to building on the more difficult sites around the hill.

The **Wharfside Pointe Apartments,** 3811 Fourteenth Avenue W., is an example of the problems that can accompany development on marginal building sites. As excavation started in 1987 the history of the site began to unfold. Pre-construction soils testing had failed to reveal extensive charcoal dump sites. Also, a former fuel depot from the early 1900s had left behind leaking tanks with contaminated soil to be cleaned. A soils engineer was required on the site full-time to analyze soil as the project proceeded. In addition to these problems, there were difficulties with new zoning regulations which required that the building be of a mixed-use type. New city regulations also required community participation in the planning of the project. After considerable discussion several thousand square feet of retail space was built into the ground floor of this 130-unit apartment building.

At times zoning code changes made with the intention of creating a more pleasant environment for the community resulted in a proliferation of poorly-designed structures built with the sole intent of crowding the maximum development allowable on the parcel of land, thus increasing developers' profit margin. Occasionally, good projects are built by competent architects and developers such as **Le Parc Condominiums,** designed by Roger Newell and developed by James Paul Jones in 1992. The four-story, 13-unit project, located at 1231 Fifth Avenue N. overlooking Lake Union, proves that it is possible to design within the constraints of the current zoning codes and create a pleasant environment for both the users and the community.

## From Pickles to "Mixed Use"

The **Cornerstone** condominiums epitomize what multifamily construction will be like in the years to come. In 1993 vacant land to build new projects is nonexistent. Zoning laws are firm and any future multifamily structures will have to be built on sites occupied by single-family homes located in multifamily zones, on industrial sites no longer able to expand, or on sites occupied by dilapidated apartment structures.

Fortune Development's Cornerstone project, on Aloha Street and Fifth Avenue N., is built on the former site of the Green Garden Food Co., a pickle factory that had outgrown its facilities. The mixed use project, designed by Lagerquist and Morris, has 35 condominium units with 52,000 square feet of commercial or retail space on the ground floor.

***Scott Jennings** is a Florida-raised transplanted architect living on Queen Anne Hill with his wife Kim, also an architect, and son John. His hobbies include renovating historical structures and boating in local waters.*

***Kim Myran** is an architect. Originally from Hawley, Montana, she joined the Army after school and was educated at the University of Idaho. She lives in Seattle, is a captain in the Army Reserve, and resides in a historic apartment building on Queen Anne.*

Chapter Nineteen

# Community Life—Organizations and Newspapers

by
Betty Renkor and Todd Davidson

Many factors contribute to the transformation of a group of people living in close proximity into a community. Local newspapers and organizations based on common cares and interests are central to its development. Queen Anne has both enjoyed and benefited from its local newspapers and organizations—strong threads which continue to hold the fabric of its community together.

Contemporary community organizations were invited to participate in this history by submitting written accounts of their own individual histories. Those who did so are chronicled in this chapter; additional community organizations may be found elsewhere in the book. Some of the individual histories were incomplete or did not contain current information. This does not mean the organization has disbanded. As much history as was made available is included here.

*First known as Redding Hall, this red brick building has seen many uses, including periods as a ballroom, dance studio, union hall, badminton club and newspaper office. Since 1965 it has been the home of A Contemporary Theatre (ACT). Photo by Isabel Egglin.*

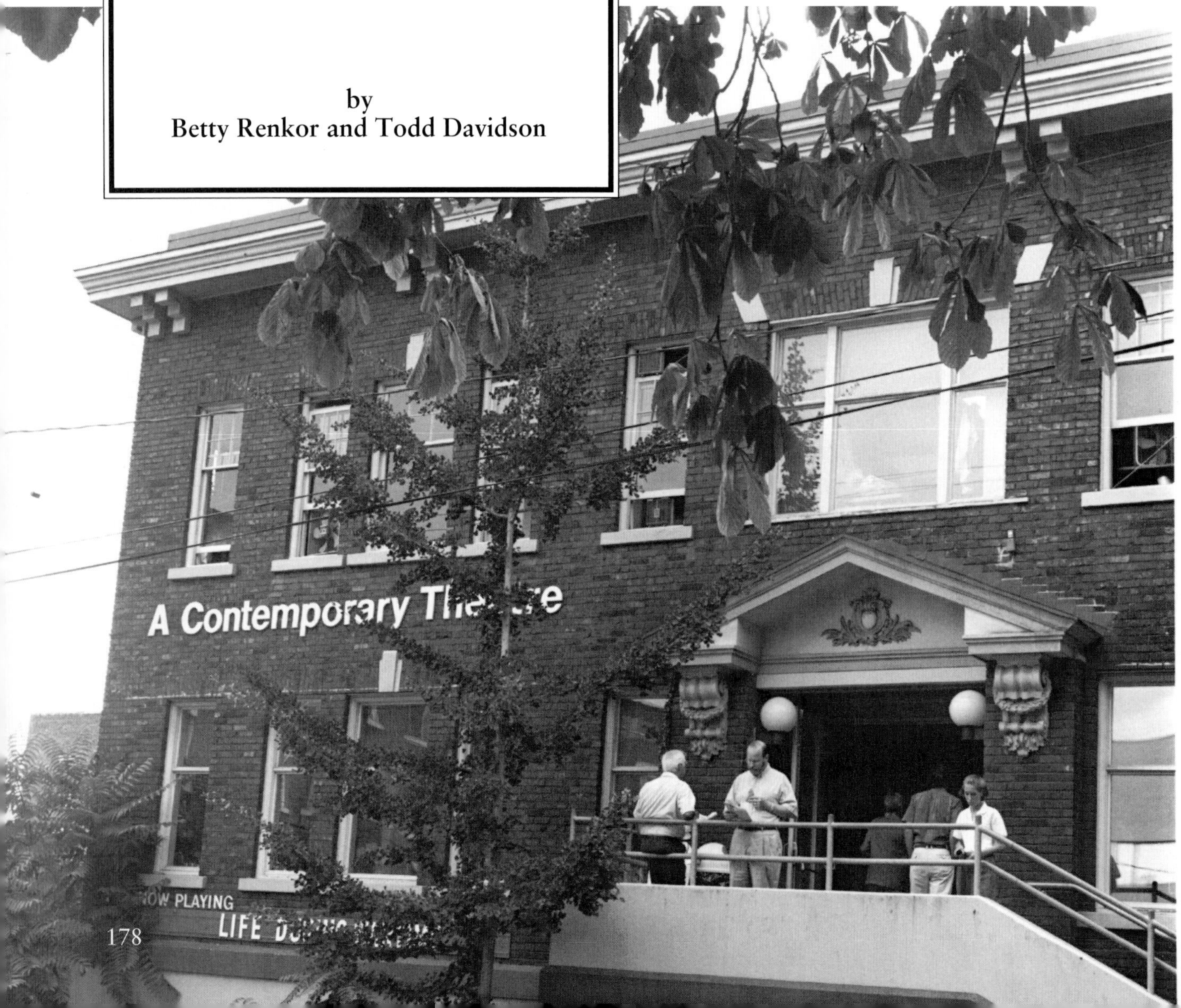

# PART I
# ORGANIZATIONS BUILD THE COMMUNITY

by Betty Renkor

## CIVIC ORGANIZATIONS

In 1968 the **Queen Anne Community Council** formed to oppose proposed zoning changes which would allow multiple family residences in single-family zoned areas on Queen Anne Hill. The council serves as a forum for community members to voice their concerns. It is independent, non-profit and non-partisan. Board members are elected by the community at an annual public meeting. Throughout the years, the Queen Anne Community Council has worked to develop a strong relationship with Seattle City Hall in order to keep abreast of and respond to development proposals, to lobby for community improvements, and to guide land-use planning on Queen Anne.

**Girl Scout** troops were in full swing in the Queen Anne area when the Seattle Girl Scout Council was organized in 1927 and have continued to be active in the area, with most troops meeting in homes. Queen Anne troops have joined with those in Magnolia and other north Seattle neighborhoods for district and neighborhood events. Girl Scouts sell cookies in local stores during annual fundraisers and attend camps with troop earnings. Scout activities range from outdoor pursuits to traditional crafts to local volunteering. Highlights of Girl Scouting on Queen Anne include the International Friendship Get-Together for all Queen Anne Girl Scouts held in 1970. This event was hosted by the Queen Anne Cadettes. **Brownie** and **Junior Girl Scout** community volunteerism in 1992 and 1993 included stenciling storm drains on Queen Anne, warning about water pollution.

*Girl Scout Brownie Troop Number 46, 1955. L. to r., back row; Sara Hughes, Anne Crippen, Sandra Kleinlein, Louise Hoeschen, Sheryl Simpson; front row, Terry Samuelson, Barbara Brewer, Valerie McBride and Jeri Samuelson. Courtesy Jeri Jones.*

**Campfire Girls**, including a Queen Anne group, were first organized in Seattle in 1919. By the late 1930s there were seventeen Camp Fire units for younger girls, later called Bluebirds. The Queen Anne community was considered one of the most active Camp Fire districts in the city during the 1930s. Campfire activities continue on the hill in 1993.

**Boy Scouts** have been active on Queen Anne since 1916, providing leadership training and recreational fellowship. The hill's first Eagle Scout, George McCauley, Jr., was a member of Troop 72, which still exists today. Troop 65, chartered 1920, came under the dynamic leadership of Scoutmaster Clark Schurman in 1921. Meeting at the library for the next 25 years, the more than 300 Scouts set standards never since equalled. Although disbanded in 1946, members still hold reunions. Troop 70, chartered 1921, moved from West Queen Anne School in 1923 to the Queen Anne Methodist Church, its sponsor, where it continues to meet. Cub Scout Packs, organized in 1930, support troop programs.

The **Black and White Boys Club** was based on a shared interest in football in the 1920s. Love of the game drew boys, ages sixteen to eighteen to the Queen Anne Congregational Church on Sunday mornings. Tracy Strong was the general secretary for the Seattle Young Men's Christian Association, a high school football referee, and the son of the church's pastor. He would review the previous day's football game with the boys and teach them a Bible lesson. About a dozen boys from the Sunday class formed the Black and White Club, which met at the Strong home on the east side of Queen Anne Hill from 1920 to 1922. Through the club's many athletic activities, Strong emphasized the four-way development of a boy to manhood: mental, physical, spiritual and social growth. Close friendships were formed among the members which have lasted a lifetime for Carl Carlson, Pat Gallagher, Wilmar Wallace, Hal Moran, Julian Beck and Wendel Jefferies, who still met regularly in the 1980s.

The **Young Men's Christian Association (YMCA)** was organized locally in 1919 by a group of Queen Anne men who felt a need for organized activities for boys on the hill. The men raised money, hired Charles G. Norman as secretary, and established the Y headquarters in the Leibly building at Queen Anne Avenue and Boston Street. Until the YMCA was funded by the Community Fund, the annual Y budget of $4,000 to $6,000 was met by community donations.

In the first years, the Y coordinated the efforts of existing agencies that sponsored activities for boys. In March 1920, a recreation center was opened at headquarters for boys sixteen and over, complete with pool and billiard tables, checkers, ping-pong and a reading corner. Two years later, the center was open to boys of all ages.

The Y clubs were church-based until about 1930, when they were reorganized as school groups, with clubs for the Friendly Indians, boys aged nine to twelve, being the most popular. In 1935, the Y moved to 1615 Queen Anne Avenue, a more central location. Two years later, the Y opened a new clubhouse at 1520 Queen Anne Avenue, formerly the old Queen Anne Congregational Church building. The **Girl Reserves** were sponsored by the Young Women's Christian Association.

**Don Sprinkle's football teams** on Queen Anne Hill were without school affiliation but achieved great success. Sprinkle was a varsity fullback for the Queen Anne High School Grizzlies in the 1930s and later King County Sheriff. The Queen Anne Boys Club football team, sponsored by the Queen Anne Commercial Club and Queen Anne Post of the American Legion, was coached by Sprinkle and won many championships.

## SERVICE ORGANIZATIONS

The **Hilltop Unit of Ryther Child League** was formed in 1956 by a group of Queen Anne women, most of whom had children at Coe Elementary School and who desired to devote time and energy to a charity. After reviewing many organizations they chose the Ryther Child League, which supports treating emotionally disturbed and chemically dependent children. The League was founded in 1947 to provide financial and emotional support to Ryther Child Center.

The **Queen Anne-Magnolia Lions Club**, founded in 1945, has organized a variety of service projects for local communities in maintaining its focus on befriending and helping blind people. The club's Blind Peoples' Fishing Derby is unique in King County and the first in the nation.

The Lions Club also honors two outstanding students from McClure Middle School for "Service Above Self." Over the years, club members have raised funds for service projects through pancake breakfasts, rummage sales and other events. Many prominent citizens have been members. For twenty years, the club members met at the old Crawford's restaurant on Seattle's waterfront. At this writing, it meets at the Executive Inn near the Space Needle.

**Children's Orthopedic Guild** was founded in 1907 to support Children's Orthopedic Hospital. The Queen Anne Guild was the first formed and is the oldest of the 450 guilds. The specific work of its volunteers has changed over the past eighty-six years. In recent times members work not only in the Children's Hospital but in the five fund-raising shops. Della Bovard, born in 1899, is its oldest living member.

The **School Program Involving the Community Elderly** program, or **SPICE**, was formed for older people who wanted to be actively involved in the community. The Queen Anne SPICE meets each weekday for lunch and activities at the Queen Anne Community Center. SPICE seniors have a warm, sup-

*The Queen Anne-Magnolia Lions Club Banquet was held at the Federal Old Line Life building on Queen Anne Avenue N. The attendees include Roland Adams, president of Arthur A. Wright and Sons; Ed Perry, past president of Perry's Moving and Storage Co.; Senator Victor Zednick; Don Moyle, grocer and real estate broker; Oral (Buz) Wittauer, Wittauer's Appliances; Dr. J.H. Wadeson; and Gene Belcourt, Queen Anne Hardware. Courtesy Tom Kildall. ca. 1940*

*Gertrude Sawyer Canan of Queen Anne, was "Miss Brunette" in a 1918 World War I community war relief drive. Courtesy* Queen Anne News.

portive relationship with the McClure Middle School students, whose building they share. They work one-on-one with the students, helping with school studies and offering friendship.

## Social Clubs

The **Queen Anne Garden Club** was founded in 1939 by members of Coe School P.T.A. who loved the feel of rich garden soil and the joy of harvesting flowers and vegetables. Gardeners from Magnolia as well as Queen Anne belong to the club.

The garden club is a working group with members following a flower show format, including judging and awarding ribbons at each meeting. Club members have an excellent reputation in gardening circles and bring home blue ribbons from Washington State Federation of Garden Club events for flower arrangements and horticulture specimens. Members also tour gardens and flower shows, take classes and support the community service activities. The club contributed a London Plane tree for the Bertona Street park at Seattle Pacific University.

The **Seattlean Club** was formed in 1925 by ten young women committed to promoting literary, cultural, and philanthropic interests. In the early days the club met in members' homes, where they read papers on topics of interest and shared refreshments. During the Depression club members sewed and knitted for unwed mothers and gathered baskets of food for families. The club has also paid the tuition for a nursing student, bought a wheelchair for an invalid, supported a Chinese orphan and sent money for famine relief to Bangladesh. Membership has always been by invitation only. However the club has not been exclusive and welcomes those who share its interests.

**Sigma Rho** was formed in 1937 by four young women who desired to become acquainted with other young homemakers. They called themselves "The Better Halves." Early informal monthly gatherings evolved into a more formal organization focusing on programs with broad cultural interest, including providing scholarships for Seattle Pacific University students.

The **Queen Anne Moose Lodge** was an active community men's club for many years with its lodge located at Third Avenue N. and Mercer St. from 1962 to 1977. In 1978 the building was sold and the lodge moved to North 152nd Street and Aurora Avenue North.

**Queen Anne Chapter No. 209, Order of the Eastern Star** has had a history of dedication and service to the community since it was organized on November 1, 1924. Early service projects included endowing a room at the Masonic Home in Zenith, Washington, forming a Red Cross unit in 1941, and selling war bonds in 1942. In 1952, the chapter supplied clothing for refugees in Germany. The chapter has also supported Grand Chapter service projects including cancer research, scholarship funds and the Eastern Star Nursing Home. Social events have included card parties, picnics and luncheons.

The **Queen Anne Rainbow Assembly** for girls was founded in 1927 by the Eastern Star Chapter No. 209.

Both the Eastern Star and Rainbow groups have a close working relationship with the Queen Anne Job's Daughters and Queen Anne DeMolay and have helped with service projects sponsored by the Grand Assembly. Masonic organizations located in the community in the past include Mecca Chapter No. 220, Order of the Eastern Star, and Queen Anne Court No. 23, Order of Amaranth. The **Shriners'** Nile Temple building at Seattle Center was purchased by the city of Seattle in 1979 as part of a Center improvement project.

*The Wisteria Dance Club of Queen Anne enjoys a dance at Redding Hall, April 19, 1913. This historic hall, located at Roy Street and First Avenue W., was later renamed Queen Anne Hall. The strong interest in "oriental" culture that predominated at the turn of the century is reflected in the hall decorations that include Chinese lanterns and placards with Chinese script. Courtesy Lloyd Repman.*

The **Queen Anne Masonic Lodge** evolved in 1920 from regular neighborly discussions held in the evenings by a group of men who gathered at Lambert Peterson's Queen Anne Florists greenhouse at Seventh Avenue W. and W. Raye Street. It was formally established in July 1921 as the Queen Anne Lodge despite opposition from the regional office, where some deemed it inappropriate to name a Masonic Lodge after not only a woman, but, more significantly, a Catholic queen. Nevertheless, the name Queen Anne was adopted.

The telephone building, 1608 Fourth Avenue W., has been the home of the Queen Anne Lodge since 1925. Through the years, the Masonic Lodge has supported numerous community activities.

## ARTS ORGANIZATIONS

In the late twentieth century lower Queen Anne has become a center for arts and culture in Seattle. Queen Anne residents are fortunate that many regional arts organizations offer a plethora of music, theater and dance within walking distance. These major arts groups currently include the Seattle Symphony Orchestra, the Pacific Northwest Ballet, the Intiman Theatre Company, A Contemporary Theatre (ACT), the Seattle Opera, the Seattle Repertory Theatre, the Seattle Children's Theatre, and the Group Theatre.

The **Intiman Theatre Company** was founded in 1972 and occupies a 424-seat playhouse at Seattle Center. The mainstage season, which emphasizes the classics, runs from May through December.

A Contemporary Theatre, or **ACT**, was founded in 1965 by Gregory A. Falls and is among the oldest contemporary theaters in Seattle. Located in historic Redding Hall at 100 West Roy Street, ACT presents a six-play mainstage season and an annual school touring production. ACT focuses on bringing new plays to northwest audiences and has a reputation for consistent excellence.

The **Seattle Opera Association**, formed in 1964, is the largest performing arts organization in the Pacific Northwest. With five to six productions a season the association has earned an international reputation for presenting opera that is both musically accomplished and theatrically compelling under the direction of Speight Jenkins. The Seattle Opera has gained much international acclaim for its productions of Wagner's complete *Ring* cycle.

# Part II
# Newspapers Serve the Community

## The Frontier's Vigorous Press

by Betty Renkor

Frontier newspapers were important to the exploration and settlement of the Puget Sound area. Since 1853, more than 2,200 newspapers have been published in the territory and state of Washington. The first paper was *The Columbian*, later called the *Washington Pioneer*, which began in Olympia in 1852. Frontier newspapers were published weekly and provided readers with national news, particularly on such events as the Civil War, in addition to local news and advertising.

After 1870, nearly every town over 1,000 people in Washington Territory was served by two weeklies, often representing opposing political philosophies. In some cities a third paper with a religious affiliation was published.

Government printing contracts were a major source of income, thus political connections were helpful in founding and publishing a newspaper. Newspapers also received revenue by publishing land and timber claim notices that were required by law. Town merchants, recognizing the value of newspaper advertising, sometimes provided free office and printshop space to editors and owners as a means of stabilizing a sometimes risky enterprise.

Seattle's first newspaper, *The Gazette*, was founded in 1863. The next year, the *Weekly Intelligencer* began publication. In the following decades, a number of papers were started, flourished, and died or merged with other papers. A few months after Washington achieved statehood in 1889 there were four daily newspapers published in Seattle: the *Post-Intelligencer, The Times, The Evening Press* and *The Journal.*

## Queen Anne's First Newspapers

As Seattle grew into a city of distinctive neighborhoods in the 1890s, local newspapers were founded to chronicle local news and promote that community's character. The papers served merchants' needs to tout their wares and citizens' needs to know about their neighborhood, schools, churches and club activities. The community newspapers often took on the role of community activist, advocating change and sponsoring activities. The *North Seattle Advocate*, published from 1888 to 1890, was the earliest known Queen Anne newspaper. Unfortunately, no copies of this paper are known to exist, hence the exact character of the paper is unknown. After *Advocate* folded, twenty-five years passed before Queen Anne's next local paper, the *Queen Anne American*, appeared.

## The *Queen Anne American*

In 1915 James W. Bryan, a former Washington State Senator and United States Congressman living on Queen Anne, founded the *Queen Anne American.* In his first editorial in the November 19, 1915 edition, Bryan announced his sincere hope to "make this a real adjunct to the activities of the community" and sought "the aid and advice of all." He assured his readers that he saw the role of the *Queen Anne American* as providing news about church activities, school events and athletics, and helping teachers and parents communicate.

Only four issues of the paper have been found, and those gave good coverage to society and club notes, meeting announcements, and general news about the Queen Anne community, as well as select Seattle activities and national news. The editor encouraged residents to trade with local merchants. The last known issue of the *Queen Anne American* is dated January 21, 1916, less than a year after the paper had begun.

## The *Queen Anne News*

by Todd Davidson

Beginning January 2, 1920, the Queen Anne community gained another voice, the *Queen Anne News.* This newspaper was founded by Mrs. Katherine L. Hamilton, her daughter Juanita, a teacher, and her son Rupert, a journalism student at the University of Washington. Rupert, then twenty, became the editor. The newspaper office was located in the newly-opened YMCA Center in Leibly Hall at Queen Anne Avenue N. and Boston Street, in space donated by YMCA secretary Charles G. Norman, who recognized the need for a local newspaper to publicize the Y and other community activities.

Additional assistance came from Rupert Hamilton's university professors and the head of the University of Washington Printing Department, who helped arrange the printing of the *Queen Anne News* at the *University*

*Herald* print shop. Katherine and Juanita Hamilton financed the founding of the community newspaper with great personal sacrifice.

> *This is the opening number of the Queen Anne News. From now on, it will appear every Friday afternoon. Carriers will bring it to your doorstep and place it where you will get it. The present plan of the Queen Anne News is to distribute without charge, the ads paying all expenses. . . . The Queen Anne News is your paper. If you have something to say about conditions on Queen Ann Hill, send it to the paper and your influence for good will make itself felt through our clums [sic]. We will welcome all criticisms and suggestions.*

Initially Rupert wrote the newspaper copy. However, this proved too much for him alone, and soon Juanita began writing as the news release editor. In the first weeks her duties expanded to include advertising copy editor, bookkeeper and office manager. Rupert eventually found that rather than writing copy he preferred spending his time walking around the community with Arthur Bailey, the paper's advertising salesman, selling advertisement space and picking up news items. At the end of 1920 the little paper had a circulation of 3,500.

In 1921 F. Clyde Dunn, a college classmate of Rupert Hamilton, bought the *Queen Anne News* and was editor for the next eighteen years. Dunn's news coverage centered on local and state politics as well as on the community's schools, especially Queen Anne High School. Community improvement projects, such as street paving, sidewalks, sewers, parks and trolley lines, were also the frequent focus of the news. The inside pages were devoted largely to social notices.

Local representative in the state legislature, Victor Zednick, wrote a regularly-featured column. Brief reports also appeared on city government doings and special events at the University of Washington.

Retaining ownership, Dunn turned the editorship over to Curtis Barnard in December 1939. By 1941 Barnard joined the armed forces, leaving the paper under Charles A. Gerold's editorship, who bought the paper in 1943. In the burst of prosperity that followed the war, the *Queen Anne News* expanded to eight pages. Local and downtown Seattle stores regularly ran one-half and full-page advertisements. The focus of the news was primarily on local activities and concerns.

In August 1953, John S. Murray bought the paper for $12,000. The circulation of the paper at that time was 9,600. In the thirty-seven years Murray owned the *Queen Anne News*, the paper underwent numerous changes as Murray expanded his operation from that of a single newspaper publisher to one of the largest printing companies in the region.

During his publishing years John Murray lived on Queen Anne and was very active in community affairs, serving as the president of the Queen Anne Community Club, and other local organizations. He was also a state representative from 1967 to 1970 and a state senator from 1971 to 1978, and wrote a popular column on news from Olympia.

Mickey Canan joined the staff in 1953 and was a key employee for over 30 years. With her long-term business management skills, and the excellent editorial work by Maribeth Bunker Morris, Florence Ekstrand, Patricia Paquette and others, the paper flourished. By 1980 the paper was twenty pages and the circulation was 13,500.

In early 1960 the *Queen Anne News* launched a Magnolia edition as a response to outside competition. Since the 1980s the *Queen Anne News* and the *Magnolia Journal* have been published out of the same office using "switch pages" devoted solely to Magnolia or Queen Anne topics, with most of the news and advertising appearing the same in both. In 1975, a new community paper, *Queen Anne Today*, appeared briefly on the hill.

In 1990 the *Queen Anne News* was sold to the Pacific Media Group Corporation. The new owners assured the Queen Anne community that they wanted "our newspapers to be the very best source of information in the communities they serve." While the *News* has undergone some content and style changes since 1990, its mission continues to be to inform the Queen Anne community of local news and provide a place for advertising.

***Betty Renkor*** *is a Queen Anne resident, avid hiker and cross-country skiier. A former newspaper reporter, she continues to write on a freelance basis and currently works as a planner for King County.*

***Todd Davidson*** *was editor of the Queen Anne News 1990-93.*

## The Queen Anne Historical Society

*The Kinnear House; the Queen Anne Historical Society's logo. Illustration by Jim Stevenson.*

The Queen Anne Historical Society was founded in 1971 by the History Committee of the Queen Anne Community Council under the leadership of Louise Locke. The organization incorporated as non-profit and adopted the Kinnear Mansion as the society's logo. For over two decades the society has worked in many areas to advance its mission of preservation of the community's historic heritage. The society maintains a community history archive and holds bimonthly meetings which feature programs emphasizing community and Washington history.

**Highlights of the Queen Anne Historical Society Achievements with the Names of Leaders**

| | |
|---|---|
| 1992-93 | Sponsored Queen Anne Community History Book Project — Bob Frazier |
| 1990 | *C. H. Black House & Gardens, 615 W. Lee St. |
| 1989 | Published reprint of *Homes & Gardens of the Pacific Coast, Seattle, 1913* — Michael, Ethel & James Kemp-Slaughter |
| 1987 | Sponsored first annual Christmas lighting contest focusing on historic Queen Anne Blvd. |
| 1986 | Dedication of Captain Vancouver plaque at Betty Bowen Viewpoint and celebration – Michael Kemp-Slaughter |
| 1986 | Co-sponsored the restored Ballard Mansion grand opening, September 1-2, 1986 — Michael Kemp-Slaughter |
| 1986 | *Bethany Presbyterian Church, 1818 Queen Anne Ave. N. |
| 1985 | *Queen Anne High School, 215 Galer St. |
| 1984 | *Stuart/Balcom House, 619 W. Comstock St. |
| 1984 | *Bowen/Huston Bungalow, 715 W. Prospect St. |
| 1983 | Society Newsletter founded; "Great Queen Anners" list of historic community leaders compiled for the state "Great Washingtonians" project — Kathryn Seymour |
| 1983 | *Handschy/Kistler House, 2433 9th Ave. W. |
| 1981 | Queen Anne Oral History Project — Ron Palmer |
| 1981 | *North Queen Anne Bridge, over Wolf Creek Canyon |
| 1980 | *Brace/Moriarty House, 170 Prospect St. |
| 1980 | Cleaned pioneer graves and mapped Mt. Pleasant Cemetery, 1980 — Ray Bronson |
| 1980 | *Parsons/Gerrard House, 618 W. Highland Dr. |
| 1980 | Parsons Memorial Garden, immediately west of 618 W. Highland Dr. |
| 1980 | *McFee/Klockzien House, 524 W. Highland Dr. |
| 1979 | *Ballard/Howe House, 22 W. Highland Dr. |
| 1979 | *Fourteenth Ave. W. Group, 2000–2016 Fourteenth Ave. W. |
| 1978 | *Chelsea Apartment Building, 620 W. Olympic Pl. |
| 1978 | *Cotterill House, 2501 Westview Dr. W. |
| 1978 | *De La Mar Apartment Building, 115 W. Olympic Pl. |
| 1977-81 | Queen Anne heritage calendar produced; 1977, Jan Clow; 1979, Pauline Hanover; 1980, 1981, Ray Bronson. |
| 1977 | *West Queen Anne Elementary School, 515 W. Galer St. |
| 1976 | *Wilcox Wall, west side 8th Ave. W. to 8th Pl. W. |
| 1976 | Assisted with historical research in production of historical U.S. Bicentennial edition of the *Queen Anne News*, 1976 —Jon Bartlett, Susan Christenson, Alice Ellis |
| 1976 | Historic walking tour and tour brochure produced — Howard Lovering, Alice Ellis |

**Designated official City of Seattle Landmark*

Chapter Twenty

# Staying on Queen Anne Forever

by
Del Loder

The settlers who reached the shores of Puget Sound were a hardy lot, and funerals and cemeteries were not in their immediate plans. Burial sites were needed, nonetheless, and established near the heart of the settlement. The settlers' first burying ground adjoined the Methodist Episcopal Church, "the White Church," at the southeast corner of Second Avenue and Columbia Street. It was dedicated in May 1855. Some twenty persons were buried at another cemetery, on Denny Hill near Second Avenue and Stewart Street, the present location of the Moore Theater.

As town improvements encroached on these locations, there was clearly a need for a burial site safely away from future city expansion. It was found near the southeast foot of Queen Anne Hill in 1864 when David and Louisa Boren Denny gave five acres of their donation claim, located on the northeast corner of Dexter Avenue and Depot Street (Denny Way), for a cemetery.

*Mount Pleasant Cemetery is one of Seattle's oldest graveyards. Illustration by Dan Tuttle. Courtesy Queen Anne Historical Society.*

*Nils B. Peterson family. Back row, from left to right: Joseph, Sarah, Nelly, Henry, Lily, Mattie. Front row, left to right: Mabel, Nils, Charles, Karen Mary. Mount Pleasant Cemetery is located on the Peterson homestead on the north slopes of Queen Anne Hill. Courtesy Seattle Pacific University.*

Already a Native American burial ground, the site was far out of town and only reached by a narrow wagon road. The Seattle Common Council established the Seattle Cemetery on the Denny land along with a potter's field on January 3, 1873. By 1878, one hundred twenty-four graves occupied the new cemetery.

By 1883, the Seattle Cemetery contained more than 200 graves and was no longer "way out in the wilderness." The following year, the Dennys drew up a new deed rededicating most of the cemetery property for use as a public park, with the gravesites to be removed at city expense. Oliver C. Shorey, a local undertaker, was paid $3,000 for "the exhuming, removal and re-interment of 221 bodies from Seattle Cemetery to [other local] cemeteries selected by the friends, relatives, or persons interested in the deceased. The removal and replacement of all monuments, stonework and fencing. . . [and] the construction of 221 cedar boxes for the encasing of the coffins before re-burial."

The majority of the graves were transferred to the new City Cemetery on Capitol Hill, from which they later were moved to make way for Volunteer Park. Thirty-three bodies were re-interred at the Masonic Cemetery (Lakeview) immediately to the north of the city's Capitol Hill site, and 29 Chinese went to the new Chong Wa Cemetery adjoining that of the Masons'. Twenty-eight Catholic graves were moved to the newly consecrated Catholic cemetery, and the remaining seven went to the cemetery on the north side of Queen Anne Hill, soon to be known as Mount Pleasant.

The Seattle Cemetery Commission recommended repairing the fencing around the old cemetery site to protect the shrubbery left on the grounds against damage by stock that might be running at large. Later that year, the Seattle Common Council approved renaming the property Denny Park.

## Mount Pleasant Cemetery

Mount Pleasant Cemetery commands an outstanding view on the north side of Queen Anne Hill at 700 W. Raye Street. A walk through the cemetery is a pleasant experience at any time of the year. It is filled with large, mature maple and chestnut trees as well as beautiful yews, cedars and other evergreens. The grounds are well-maintained by the current owner, William Edwards, and his groundskeepers. The northeastern slope affords a panoramic view stretching from Ballard past the George Washington Memorial Bridge, the University District and the Cascade Mountains. A study of the grave markers takes one back to the pioneers and leaders of early-day Seattle, as well as illustrating the ethnic and religious diversity of the city.

The property occupies 40 acres of the original 80 acres homesteaded by Nils B. Peterson in 1878. In 1879, the Independent Order of Odd Fellows purchased ten acres nearby for a cemetery. The boundaries were not clear and in error interment began on Peterson's land. When he discovered this, Peterson filed protests both in Olympia and Washington, D.C. State officials sug-

### Funeral Costs at Mount Pleasant—1888

| | |
|---|---|
| Date: | December 6, 1888 |
| Deceased: | Lander Lambert |
| Cause: | Consumption |
| Age: | 19 years - American |

| | |
|---|---|
| 1 coffin | $ 25.00 |
| Hearse | 10.00 |
| Attendants | 2.50 |
| Box & delivery | 4.50 |
| Hauling from concrete house | 1.00 |
| Single grave | 4.00 |
| Dig grave* | 3.50 |
| Emit fluid & keeping | 2.00 |
| Shave, wash & dress | 10.00 |
| Total | $ 62.50 |

* *Families had the option to dig the grave themselves to save costs.*

*Source: 1888 invoice from the Mount Pleasant ledger*

gested he move his claim over to adjacent vacant land and Peterson asked his church, the Free Methodist Church, for advice. The pastor wrote Peterson urging him to accept the settlement suggested by Olympia, and added that Mr.Peterson would do well to join the Odd Fellows to enhance his popularity.

On June 28, 1879, Peterson officially transferred ten acres to the Odd Fellows for use as a cemetery forever. The price was $100. In 1882, he sold ten more acres to the Free Methodist Church for a cemetery. Eventually, this property was purchased by the S.O. Cross family, and by 1895 it had been sold to the James W. Clise family with the name Mount Pleasant firmly attached. In a letter dated December 17, 1906, H.R. Clise stated to Queen Anne resident Clarence B. Bagley that a sixteen-foot lot in the main portion of the Mount Pleasant Cemetery would sell for $400. In 1903 the same lot would have sold for $200.

Several record books were destroyed in an office fire at the cemetery in the 1890s, making facts on early ownership, gravesite locations and inventories somewhat sketchy. However, it is known that in the nineteenth century the cemetery company allocated sections to various social, religious and ethnic groups. The following cemeteries are a part of Mount Pleasant: The Independent Order of Odd Fellows (established in 1879); Congregation Chaveth Sholem Cemetery, Seattle's first Jewish cemetery (1890); Seattle Hebrew Benevolent Association Cemetery (1895); Temple de Hirsch (Sinai) Cemetery (1911); Chong Wa Society Chinese Cemetery, establishment date unknown.

A Muslim section was established in 1979 and burials are arranged with the permission of the mosque. Strict burial customs are observed and it will be immediately noticed that all Muslim graves are oriented in the same direction so the faithful will be facing Mecca. The Hills of Eternity are operated as a separate facility by the Temple De Hirsch. All the other ethnic and religious sections are operated under Mount Pleasant.

## Mount Pleasant and Air Defense During World War II

In early 1942, the United States Army commandeered several sites in King County for anti-aircraft installations, including a site at Mount Pleasant Cemetery that was chosen for its height above Puget Sound. The site was located in the northwest corner in Section Five, the only open area in the cemetery. The army fenced it off and installed tents and an anti-aircraft gun. There were also listening devices to detect approaching aircraft. The command consisted of about two dozen soldiers who manned the station 24 hours a day. They were headquartered out of the main command post at Woodland Park, where their meals were prepared and delivered to the site. As army life in tents was not a pleasant experience in the cold, rainy Seattle weather, the tents were later replaced by wooden Quonset huts.

*Gravestone of Clarence Bagley. Photo by Isabel Egglin.*

### A Chinese Funeral Procession

The Chong Wa section evokes images of the traditional Chinese processions described by Sophia Frye Bass, who grew up in Seattle in the 1870s and 1880s and witnessed many Chinese funeral processions. In *Pig-Tail Days in Old Seattle* (1937), she describes such a procession, many of which ended at the Chong Wa Benevolent Society Cemetery at Mount Pleasant.

> *Every good "China boy" on his way to Celestial Heaven had to be protected from the devil. So a friend sat with the driver of the hearse-with its nodding plumes-and scattered bits of perforated white paper in the breeze. The devil would be so busy picking up the papers that he could not follow the procession. Besides, there were street corners to turn on the way to the cemetery, and the devil cannot turn a corner. So, between the corners and the bits of paper, he would become hopelessly lost, and the spirit of the departed could go serenely on.*
>
> *The procession was always led by a brass band, and if the "China boy" was in good standing, there would be a long line of hacks filled with his cousins and friends—and a wagon containing roast pig, many chickens and much rice to be placed about his grave.*

Today, walking through the cemetery one finds markers for a number of notable people from Queen Anne's history: Jacob Galer, former Governor John H. McGraw, Asa Mercer, David and Catherine Blaine, Daniel and Susannah Bagley, Clarence Bagley, B.F. Day, James and Anna Clise, Frederick and Mary Emma Churchill, John and Mary Ross, and George Cotterill. Finally, attention is drawn to a low granite headstone with the word "FATHER" in large letters. Drawing near, the full inscription is plainly visible: Nils B. Peterson 1846 – 1918. Here on his own ground Nils rests on the "... lone couch of his everlasting sleep."

By 1957, the cemetery was in a state of disrepair. Some tombstones were toppled and broken and lawn and shrubs were overgrown. It was at this time that the Neil Edwards family bought the property and began clearing the grounds and improving the site.

## A New Service: The Washington Cremation Association

Arthur A. Wright came to Seattle in 1888 and after the turn of the century saw potential for a new service industry. In 1904 Wright formed the Washington Cremation Association, to be located on the southeast corner of Mount Pleasant Cemetery. Wright supervised the building of a crematory, which, according to the *Seattle Post-Intelligencer,* would be the ninth west of the Mississippi River and the first in the state.

The crematory was designed with an incineration room, small chapel, retiring room and organ room. In the basement of the crematory was a crypt containing 800 niches where the urns were kept.

During the construction, thousands of people visited the crematory and Columbarium, which cost $35,000 to build. As most people were accustomed to traditional burial, the crematorium was not immediately popular. However, by 1916 the numbers averaged 80 a month.

The main mortuary building was leveled in 1930. It was replaced by an authentic reproduction of a sixteenth-century Italian monastery chapel. Seating approximately 400 persons, the chapel was equipped with a custom-built imported 680-pipe church organ. Arthur A. Wright died before the completion of the new chapel and his son Charles G. Wright became the new president. The company concluded that it would be in its best interests to enter the undertaking business, and in March 1931 it became a full-service mortuary. By mid-1920, the company had changed its name to Arthur A. Wright and Son, Mortuary and Columbarium.

In May of 1940, the Wright Mortuary formally dedicated and opened a new, larger columbarium, adjoining and behind the chapel-mortuary. Planned by Arthur A. Wright, designed by Seattle architect Henry Bittman and erected under the direction of Charles Wright, the building occupies a commanding site. Here, in niches formed of solid bronze castings and backed by steel partitions, is space for more than seven thousand cinerary urns.

At the opening Charles Wright said, "One of my early recollections was my father's dislike for the feeling of dread attached to the passing of loved ones. He resolved then to build an enduring memorial building—and this new columbarium expresses tangibly the plans he laid."

Charles died later that year and the business was then taken over by Merlin E. Frease, Roland E. Adams and Ralph T. Carpenter. Adelaide Wright served as

*Arthur B. Wright and Son Funeral Home and Columbarium was built in the 1930 and expanded in 1940. Courtesy Butterworth's Arthur A. Wright.*

family representative to the company. The company is now owned and managed by the Butterworth family.

## BLEITZ FUNERAL HOME

The founder of Queen Anne's other funeral home, Jacob J. Bleitz, was born August 5, 1867, in Sandwich, Illinois and graduated from the Chicago College of Embalming in 1900. He came to Seattle in 1904 and soon established a funeral home in the Green Lake area. He moved from this site in 1919 to the foot of Queen Anne Hill on Florentia Street, where the company remains today.

The building is a full-service facility constructed in an eclectic Gothic style. The Moeller organ in the chapel is a twin to the one in Bethany Presbyterian Church, as

*Bleitz Funeral Home on Florentia Street is a landmark near the Fremont Bridge. Photo by Isabel Egglin.*

they were purchased at the same time. Jacob died in 1939 and the management went to his two sons, James C. and Lawrence L. The Bleitz Funeral Home was among the first to recognize that people needed alternatives to current funeral home practices and entered into an agreement with the non-profit People's Memorial Association, currently the oldest and largest memorial society in the continental United States. In 1989, a 5,000-square-foot extension was added to the west side of the building, still retaining the architectural integrity of the original structure. The funeral home is now owned by Uniservice.

## FULL SERVICE FOR QUEEN ANNE

Queen Anne is certainly a city within a city, with full service from womb to tomb. For this last stage of life, earlier residents of the area had more than funeral homes and cemeteries. By 1917, they also had the services of the Washington Casket Company at 400 W. Mercer Street and, later, the Pacific Casket Company at 508 Third Avenue W., one of the largest manufacturers on the Pacific Coast. In addition, the Norwalk Vault Company, a concrete burial vault factory, was located at 121 Queen Anne Avenue. Custom tombstones were available from the Art Marble Company at 731 Westlake Avenue or Sunset Monument Company on Aurora Avenue at Valley Street. By 1950, the fashion for elaborate tombstones and monuments ebbed and the Messett Brothers, owners of Sunset, disposed of their inventory and transformed the property into the forerunner of a successful chain of hamburger stands.

*Sic Transit Gloria Mundi*

***Del Loder*** *is a graduate of Queen Anne High, a veteran Boy Scout leader and member of the Boy Scout National Council, where he serves as vice chairman of the Order of the Arrow.*

# References

## Chapter 1 — The Geology of Queen Anne Hill

### Published


Hall, J.B., and K.L Othberg. *Thickness of unconsolidated sediments, Puget lowland, Washington.* Washington Division of Geology and Earth Resources Geologic Map GM-12. Olympia: Washington Division of Geology and Earth Resources, 1974.

Yount, J.C., G.R. Dembroff, and G.M. Barats. *Map showing depth to bedrock in the Seattle 30' x 60' quadrangle, Washington.* U.S. Geological Survey Miscellaneous Geologic Investigations Map MF-1692. Denver: U.S. Geological Survey, 1985.

Booth, D.B. "Timing and Process of Deglaciation Along the Southern Margin of the Cordilleran Ice Sheet." *North America and Adjacent Ocean During the Last Glaciation, Geology of North America, Vol. K-3*, ed. W.F. Ruddiman and H.E. Wright, Jr. Boulder: Geological Society of America, 1987.

Waldron, H.H., B.A. Liesch, D.R. Mullineaux, and D.R. Crandell. *Preliminary geologic map of Seattle and vicinity, Washington.* U.S. Geological Survey Miscellaneous Geologic Investigations Map I-354. Denver: U.S. Geological Survey, 1962.

Mullineaux, D.R., H.H. Waldron, and M. Rubin. *Stratigraphy and chronology of late interglacial and early Vashon glacial time in the Seattle area, Washington.* U.S. Geological Survey Bulletin 1194-O. Denver: U.S. Geological Survey, 1965.

Booth, D.B., and B. Goldstein. "Patterns and processes of landscape development by the Puget lobe ice sheet." *The Regional Geology of the State of Washington.* Olympia: Washington Division of Geology and Earth Resources, 1992 (to be published).

Galster, R.W., and W.T. Laprade. " Geology of Seattle, Washington, United States of America." *Bulletin of the Association of Engineering Geologists* 28, no. 3 (August 1991): 235-302.

Lamb, J. *The Seattle Municipal Water Plant.* Seattle: Moulton Printing Co., 1914.

McWilliams, M. *Seattle Water Department History, 1854 - 1954.* Seattle: City of Seattle Water Department, 1955.

Tubbs, D.W. *Landslides in Seattle.* Washington Division of Geology and Earth Resources Information Circular 52. Olympia: Washington Division of Geology and Earth Resources, 1974.

Morse, R.W. "Regrading Years in Seattle." In *Engineering Geology in Washington.* chaired by R.W. Galster. Olympia: Washington Division of Geology and Earth Resources, 1989.

Chrzastowski, M.J. *Historical Changes to Lake Washington and Route of the Lake Washington Ship Canal, King County, Washington.* U.S. Geological Survey Water Resources Investigations WRI 81-1182. Denver: U.S. Geological Survey, 1983.

Galster, R.W. "Geologic Aspects of Navigation Canals of Western Washington." In *Engineering Geology in Washington.* Chaired by R.W. Galster. Olympia: Washington Division of Geology and Earth Resources, 1989.


### Unpublished


Bagley, Clarence B. "Scrapbooks" : "Forty Years' Span, "Vol: 6, 11, University of Washington, Allen Library Special, Collections.


## Chapter 2 — Off the Beaten Track: Native Americans and the Queen Anne District

### Published


American Indian Policy Review Commission. *Final Report, May 17, 1977.* Washington, DC: US Government Printing Office, 1977.

Andrisevic, Kathy. "Queen Anne Still Reigns," *The Seattle Times Pacific Section*, October 5, 1986.

Ballard, Arthur C. *Some Tales of the Southern Puget Sound Salish.* Seattle: University of Washington Publications in Anthropology, Vol. 2, No. 3, 1927.

Bagley, Clarence E. *History of King County Washington, Vol. 1.* Seattle: SJ Clarke Publishing Co. 1929.

Bagley, Clarence E. *Indian Myths of the Northwest.* Seattle: Lowman and Hanford Co., 1930.

Buerge, David. "Seattle Before Seattle," *The Weekly,* December 1980.

Buchanan, C.M. "Rights of the Puget Sound Indians to Game and Fish," *Washington Historical Quarterly,* 6 (1915).

Cohen, Fay. *Treaties on Trial.* Seattle: University of Washington Press, 1984.

Collins, June M. "Influence of White Contact on the Indians of Northern Puget Sound." In *Coast Salish and Western Washington Indians*, Vol. 2. New York: Garland Publishing, 1974.

Denny, Arthur A. *Pioneer Days on Puget Sound.* Seattle: C.B. Bagley, Printer, 1888.

Denny, Emily Inez. *Blazing the Way: True Stories, Songs and Sketches of Puget Sound and other Pioneers.* Seattle: Rainier Printing Co., Inc., 1909.

Duwamish Tribal Cultural Center and Museum. *Duwamish Tribe Conceptual Operations Plan*, 1991.

Ekrom, J.A. *Remembered Drums: A History of the Puget Sound Indian War.* Walla Walla, WA: Pioneer Press Books, 1989.

Gunther, Erna. *Northwest Coast Indian Art.* Exhibition information, Seattle World's Fair, April 21 - October 21, 1962.

Haeberlin, Hermann and Erna Gunther. "Mythology of Puget Sound," *Journal of American Folklore,* Vol. 37 (1924); 371 - 438.

University of Washington Publications in Anthropology, Vol. 4, No. 1. *The Indians of Puget Sound.* Seattle: University of Washington Press, 1930.

Hilbert, Vi. *Haboo: Native American Stories from Puget Sound.* Seattle: University of Washington Press, 1985.

Meeker, Ezra. *Pioneer Reminiscences of Puget Sound: The Tragedy of Leschi.* Seattle: Lowman and Hanford Stationary and Printing Co., 1905.

Seattle, City of. "Population changes in the City of Seattle: 1960-1965." *Current Planning Research Bulletin*, February 1, 1966. City of Seattle: City Planning Commission.

Seattle, City of. "Population Changes in the City of Seattle: 1960-70." *Current Planning Research Bulletin No. 32*, June, 1971. Prepared by City of Seattle, Research Section, Goals and Program Division Department of Community Development.

Seattle, City of. "Population Changes in Seattle, 1980-1990." *Current Planning Research Bulletin Number 51*, April 1, 1991. City of Seattle, Office for Long-Range Planning.

Thompson, Nile Robert. "The Original Residents of Shilshole Bay," *Passport to Ballard*, ed. Kay F. Reinartz. Seattle: *Ballard News Tribune,* 1988.

Tollefson, Kenneth. "The Snoqualmie: A Puget Sound Chiefdom," *Ethnology,* 28 (1987); 121-136.

Tollefson, Kenneth. "Political Organization of the Duwamish," *Ethnology,* 28 (1989); 135-149.

Tollefson, Kenneth. "The Political Survival of Landless Puget Sound Indians," *American Indian Quarterly,* 16 (1992); 213-235.

*United States v. Washington.* 459 F. Supp. (1987).

*Washington v. Washington State Commercial Passenger Fishing Vessels Association.* 443 U.S. 658, 1979.

Washington State Department of Public Assistance. "Washington Indians Progress." *The 39er,* October 1959.

Waterman, Thomas Talbot. "The Geographical Names Used by the Indians of the Pacific Coast." *Geographical Review.* vol 12, pt. 2 (April 1922); 175-194.

Waterman, Thomas Talbot. "Notes on the Ethnology of the Indians of Puget Sound." *Indian Notes and Monographs,* Miscellaneous Series No. 59. New York: Museum of the American Indian, Heye Foundation, 1973.

### Unpublished

Buerge, David. *Significant Native American Sites in King County.* 1992. Typewritten.

Hansen, Karen Tranberg. "American Indians and Work in Seattle: Associations, Ethnicity, and Class." Seattle: Department of Anthropology, University of Washington, 1979. Typewritten..

Sherwood, Don. "Indian Playfields and Recreation." Handwritten. Government Research Assistance Library Collection, Seattle Public Library, 1975.

Sherwood, Don. "Indian Sites that Became Seattle Parks." Handwritten. "Description and History of Seattle Parks Department. Government Research Assistance Collection, Seattle Public Library, 1975.

Tollefson, Kenneth. "In Search of Recognition." Paper presented to the Annual Meeting of the Pioneers Association of Seattle, June 27, 1987.

Washington Pioneer Project. *Told by the Pioneers: Tales of Frontier Life As Told By Those Who Remember The Days of the Territory and Early Statehood of Washington.* Vol. III. *Washington Pioneer Project: Work Projects Administration Project No. 5841.* Olympia, WA: 1938.

## CHAPTERS 3 – 11

by Kay Reinartz

### Published: Books

*A Volume of Memoirs and Genealogy of Representative Citizens of the City of Seattle and County of King, Washington.* New York: The Lewis Publishing, 1903.

Andrews, Mildred. *Seattle Women: A Legacy of Community Development, A Pictorial History 1851-1920.* Seattle: YWCA of Seattle/King County.

Baist Real Estate Atlas. "Surveys of Seattle." Philadelphia: G. Wm. Baist, 1905.

Bagley, Clarence B. *History of Seattle,King County.* 3 vols. Chicago: S. Clarke Pub., 1916, 1929.

Bass, Sophie Frye. *Pig-tail Days in Old Seattle.* Portland, OR: Metropolitan, 1937.

Bass, Mrs. Sophie Frye. *When Seattle was a Village.* Seattle: Lowman & Hanford, 1947.

Buerge, David M. and Junius Rochester. *Roots and Branches.* Seattle, WA: Seattle Council of Churches, 1988

Denny, Arthur. *Pioneering on Puget Sound.* Fairfield, WA: Galleon Press, 1965.

Denny, Emily Inez. *Blazing the Way.* Seattle: Rainier Printing Co., 1909.

Dickey, Maud Ward. "Memoir," in *Told by the Pioneeers: Tales of Frontier Life As Told By Those Who Remember The Days of the Territory and Early Statehood of Washington.* Vol. III. *Washington Pioneer Project: Work Projects Administration Project No. 5841.* Olympia, WA: WPA, 1938.

Dickey, William A. and Dillis B. Ward. Family documents. "Highlights of the Dillis B. Ward Collection," prepared by Shorey Book Store, Seattle: Typewritten.

Doyle, Dolores Graham. *Three Hundred Years in America with the Mercers.* Baltimore: Gateway Press Inc., 1991.

Ficken, Robert E. and Charles P. LeWarne. *Washington, A Centennial History.* Seattle: University of Washington Press, 1988.

Grant, Frederick James, ed. *History of Seattle, Washington.* New York: American Publishing & Engraving Co., 1891.

Hanford, C.H. *Seattle and Environs,* 3 vols. Chicago & Seattle: Pioneer Historical Publishing Co., 1924.

Lamb, John. *Seattle Municipal Water Plant.* Seattle: Moulton Printing Co., 1914.

Meeker, Ezra. "Pioneer Reminiscences of Puget Sound." Seattle: 1905; rpt. 1980.

Nelson, Kay, "Keeping Healthy on Salmon Bay." In *Passport to Ballard* by Kay Reinartz. Seattle: Ballard News-Tribune, 1988.

Newell, Gordon. *Westward to Alki, the Story of David Denny and Louisa Boren.* Seattle: Superior Publishing Co., 1977.

Phelps, Myra L. *Public Works of Seattle Narative History of Engineering Department 1875-1975.* Seattle, WA.: Seattle Engineering Dept., Kingsport Press, 1978.

Polk, R.L. Seattle City Directories, 1890-1920.

Reinartz, Kay F. *Passport to Ballard.* Seattle: Ballard News-Tribune, 1988.

Reinartz, Kay F. *Tukwila, Community at the Crossroads.* Seattle: City of Tukwila, 1991.

Reynolds, Chang. *Pioneer Circuses of the West.* Los Angeles: Westernlore Press, 1966.

Sanborn Fire Map of Seattle. Seattle: Sanborn Map & Publishing Co., 1905,1917.

*Seattle Leaders.* Edited by Edward Desmond. Pioneer Printing Co., 1923.

Thompson, Nile R., "The Original Residents of Shilshole Bay," *Passport to Ballard* by Kay F. Reinartz, ed. Seattle: Ballard News-Tribune, 1988.

Watt, Roberta Frye. *Four Wagons West.* Portland, OR: Binfords & Mort, Publishers, 1931.


### Published: Periodicals


*Duwamish Valley News:* "Mercer's Daughters," "Mrs. Susanah Graham is Honored by Pioneer Daughters," Apr. 9, 1936.

*Queen Anne News:* "Church News," Feb. 6, 1920; "Elsie Ferguson Recalls How Queen Anne Got Name," Sep. 13, 1967; "Cotterill House Approved for Landmark Designation," June 1, 1977.

*Seattle Mail and Herald:* "The Independent Telephone Company of Seattle," Dec. 19, 1903; "Independent Telephone Company," Dec. 17, 1904.

*Seattle Post-Intelligencer:* "Real Estate Transactions," 1884-93; "The Damages Assessed," June 17, 1888; A.S. Mercer, "The Gilman of His Day," Sep. 6, 1888; "Rapidly Improving," Sep. 15, 1888; "The Record of Houses Erected in Seattle During 1888," Dec. 30, 1888; C.P. Stone, "Desirable Building Lots in Lake Union Addition," Jan. 15, 1889; "Wanted," July 2, 1889; "A Water Famine," Nov. 4, 1889; "Queen Anne Town will have to Use Spring Water Two Weeks," Nov. 5, 1889; "For Better Streets, Commissioner Alexander's Work Begins to Tell" Nov. 8, 1889; "North Seattle Water Supply." "Cost of New Streets," Jan. 30, 1890; "A Worthy Enterprise." Apr. 18, 1890; "Pioneer Dwelling Making Room for a Brick Block," June 14, 1890; "Hanging the Fire Bells," July 6, 1890; "An Uncounted City," Jul. 13, 1890; "Fire Department Notes," July 18, 1890; "Last Session of the Year for the Common Council," July 25, 1890; "The Fire Department," Aug. 15, 1890; "Their Silver Wedding," Dec. 26, 1890; "Driven for the Community" Jan. 21, 1891; "Paying for Sewerage," Mar. 8, 1891; "Fire on Queen Anne," July 14, 1891; "Work for the Council," July 19, 1891; "Anxious for a Park," Sep. 20, 1891; "The Sarah B. Yesler," Sep. 20, 1892; "No Fire Protection," Aug. 29, 1893; "Fire in the Early Morning," Nov. 24, 1891; "The City Council Reports, Protection from Fire in the Residential Districts." Sep. 2, 1893; "A Good Woman's Life," "Diana Gilmore Tobin Smithers, Obituary." Aug. 3, 1894; "Mrs. Thomas Mercer Dead." Nov. 13, 1897; "William H. Shoudy Dead," Obituary. Sep. 20, 1901; "Housekeeping in Seattle Fifty Years Ago," Jan. 22, 1905; "Erasmus Smithers Dies in Renton," Nov. 22, 1905; Abbie Denny-Lindsley, "A Pioneer Child's Life in Seattle," July 22, 1906; Leigh D. Bruckart, "When Santa Claus Comes to Seattle," Dec. 20, 1908; "High and Humble Unite to Mourn John H. McGraw," June 25, 1910; "Prosch's Tribute to Alki Pioneers," Nov. 19, 1911; "Aged Mrs. Bagley, Pioneer, is Dead," "Pioneer Woman Dies," "Jos. Dickerson, War Veteran and Pioneer, is dead," Oct. 12, 1913; Edmond S. Meany, "Living Pioneers of Washington, Isaac Bigelow," Jan. 19, 1916; "Seattle in 1860: A Husky Village with City Hopes," Nov. 27, 1919; C.T. Conover, "Panic of 1893 Ended Boom Era Here; Banks Kept Open," "New Era Follows the Panic of 1893," Apr. 17, 1938; "Gold Rush Booms Realty Here," Apr. 24, 1938; Susannah Mercer Graham, "Eyewitness Story of Seattle, 1853 to 1938"; "The Success of Charlie Plummer," *Northwest Section,* Apr. 27, 1980.

*Seattle Star:* Dr. Henry A. Smith, "Early Reminiscences," Nov. 5, 1887.

*Seattle Times:* "Ships in Port Reference Tables," May 23, 1900, June 16, 1900; "Mrs. Alice M. Bagley Summoned by Death," May 10, 1926; "Mrs. Susan Mercer Graham," Aug. 2, 1932; "Youthful Naval Officer did not like 'Seattlepol'," November 8, 1934; "Mrs. Graham, 93, Recalls Attack by Indians in 1856," Sep. 30, 1936; "G.F. Cotterill, Father of City Water Plan, Here 53 Years," Jan. 2, 1938; "New Era Follows the Panic of 1893," Apr. 17, 1938; "No War - Just Happiness for Mercer's Daughter," Sep. 30, 1941; "Mrs. Graham, One of Mercer Family, Dies." June 25, 1942; "Mercers, Early Pioneers." "Susie Mercer Graham," *Rotogravure,* Oct. 31, 1943; "Bagley Home to be Replaced," "Notes on the Bagley Mansion," Jan. 16, 1944; Margaret Pitcairn Strachan, "Early-Day Mansions, No. 24—George Kinnear," Feb. 11, 1945; Margaret Pitcairn Strachan, "Early-Day Mansions, No. 25—John Kinnear," *Magazine Section,* Feb. 17, 1945; Margaret Pitcairn Strachan, "Early-Day Mansions, No. 46—Dillis B. Ward," *Magazine Section,* July 15, 1945; Margaret Pitcairn Strachan, "Early-Day Mansions, No. 23, William H. Shoudy, " *Magazine Section,* Feb. 4, 1945; Lucille McDonald, "Origin of Seattle Street Names," June 14, 1953; Lucille McDonald, "Ranks of Old-Time Seattle Mansions Rapidly Thinning." *Magazine Section,* Dec. 21, 1958; "Just Cogitating: G.F. Cotterill Was Leader in Temperance Movement," June 19, 1960; Helen N.Freece, "Seattle's 'Horse and Buggy' Doctor," June 21, 1964.

*The Olympian,* "Food and Supplies, 1857 Prices," Oct. 3, 1857.

*Weekly Intelligencer,* "Ira Utter Taken into Custody," Nov. 28, 1870, Jan. 9, 1871; "The Seattle of '61," Sep. 15, 1988.

Ward, Dillis B. "From Salem, Oregon, to Seattle in 1859." *Pacific Northwest Quarterly* (Jan. 1906):100-106.

### Unpublished

Bagley, Clarence B. "Scrapbook": Vol. 1, pp. 668, 673, 676, 677, 678, 680, 678-79, 702, 670, 683, 687-88; Vol. 2, pp. 38, 569, 668, 693, 788-790, 840-41; "First Flower Garden Planted in Seattle," Vol 5; "Forty Years' Span," "Thomas Mercer Dead," Vol 6, p. 11; "Pioneer of King County Dies," Vol. 8; Dr. Henry Smith, "Early Reminiscences, Coming North in 1852" Vol. 11, 10; "Early Reminiscences, Governor Isaac Stevens" Vol. 11, 18,; Susannah Mercer Graham, "Eyewitness Story of Seattle, 1853 to 1938" Vol. 80, pp. 15-16; Margaret Pitcairn Strachan, "Early-Day Mansions, No. 30 Clarence Bagley," Vol. 84, pp. 25-26; "Early-Day Mansions, No. 31 Rezin W. Pontius," Vol. 84, 28; University of Washington, Allen Library, Special Collections.

Cameron, Frank B. "Bicycling in Seattle, 1879-1904." 1982. Typewritten.

Correspondence File, Election Records, Petition File, 1869-1940. City of Seattle Archives, Seattle Municipal Building.

Correspondence Files, 1890-1940. City of Seattle Parks Department. Seattle Municipal Building.

Corey, Ida G. "Seattle Churches as Known Through the Seattle Newspapers." 1938. Typewritten. Seattle Public Library.

Denny, E. Inez. "By the Dreaming Shores," Handwritten. No date. University of Washington, Allen Library, Special Collections.

Dickey, Maud Ward. Letter to Mrs. Edmund Bowden, Seattle, Washington, June 9, 1933. University of Washington, William Dickey File, Allen Library Manuscript Collection and Archives.

"Extracts from the diary of Dillis B. Ward ...1865-1878," Typewritten. University of Washington, Allen Library, Special Collections.

Federal Decennial Census of Seattle, 1900, 1910, 1920. National Archives and Records Administration, Seattle, WA.

Hamilton, Laura. "Queen Anne Fire Stations." 1975. Typewritten. Queen Anne Historical Society Files.

"John McGraw, Second Governor, Queen Anne Resident," prepared by the Queen Anne Historical Society, Typewritten. No date.

King County Real Estate Records and Plat Records. King County Administration Building.

King County Census, 1860. National Archives and Records Administration, Seattle, WA.

Kinnear, C.A. "Arrival of the George Kinnear Family on Puget Sound, and Early Recollections by C.A. Kinnear, One of the Children." Typewritten. University of Washington, Allen Library, Special Collections.

Local Improvement District (LID) Records, Street Improvement Files. City of Seattle Archives, Seattle Municipal Building.

Meany, Edmond S. "Living Pioneers of Washington. Mr. and Mrs. Dillis B. Ward", University of Washington, Allen Library, Special Collections.

Nordstrom, Carl J. "Queen Anne Water Towers." 1993. Typewritten.

*Olmsted Report,* published in the Park Commisioner's Report, City of Seattle, 1909. City of Seattle Parks Department. Seattle Municipal Building.

Park Commissioner's Report, City of Seattle, 1909. City of Seattle Archives, Seattle Municipal Building.

Prosch, Thomas. "A Chronological History of Seattle from 1850 to 1901." Typewritten. University of Washington, Allen Library, Special Collections.

Prosch, Thomas. "Scrapbook," University of Washington, Allen Library, Special Collections.

Queen Anne Community Study. Seattle Public Library, Public Service Division. 1978.

"Seattle Street Names Old and New, 1896." Printed by the City of Seattle. City of Seattle Engineers Office. Seattle Municipal Building.

Schneider, Lt. Richard. "Queen Anne Fire Department History." 1992. Typewritten.

Sherwood, Donald. "History of Seattle's Parks." Handwritten. City of Seattle Archives, Seattle Municipal Building.

Spaulding, Florence, letter, 1919. Provided by Carl Nordstrom.

Water Department Records. City of Seattle Water Department, Seattle Municipal Building.

## CHAPTER 12 — DEPRESSION AND WAR— THE 1930S - 1940S

### Published

Lawren, William. *The General and the Bomb.* New York: Dodd, Mead & Co., 1988.

*Queen Anne News,* various numbers 1930-1950.

Watson, Emmett. *Digressions of a Native Son.* Seattle: Pacific Institute, 1982.

### Unpublished

Palmer, Ronald. "Hard Times on the Hill: Queen Anne in the 1930s." 1981. Typewritten.

Palmer, Ronald. "Queen Anne Enters the War: Local History, International Context." 1989. Typewritten.

## CHAPTER 13 — IN OUR TIME— 1950 - 1993

### Published

*Celebrating 100 Years of Husky Football.* New York: Professional Sports Publications and the University of Washington Athletic Dept., 1990.

Duncan, Don. *Meet Me at the Center.* Seattle: Seattle Center Foundation, 1992.

Duncan, Don. *Washington, The First One Hundred Years.* Seattle: The Seattle Times Company, 1989.

Frare, Aleua L. *Magnolia—Yesterday and Today.* Seattle: Magnolia Community Club, 1975.

*Greenbelts.* Planning Commission Report, City of Seattle, May 13, 1959.

*The History of Seattle Center.* Seattle Center, City of Seattle, 1991.

Jasny, Barbara R. AIDS 1993: Unanswered Questions. *Science* 260:1219, May 28, 1993.

*The KUAY.* Queen Anne Alumni Association annual newsletter, Seattle, WA, 1982-1992.

*Queen Anne News.* Oct. 5, 1939; Mar. 3, 1949; Feb. 11, 1970; Nov. 8, 1972; Aug. 31, 1976; Sept. 2, 1976; Aug. 9, 1978; Dec. 20, 1978; Nov. 5, 1986; May 30, 1990; April 1, 1992; May 27, 1992; Nov. 4, 1992.

*Queen Anne Today.* April 14, 1976.

*Residents' Guide to Queen Anne and Magnolia.* Seattle: *Queen Anne/Magnolia News,* 1990.

Ridge, Don. *Take a Lap—Seattle Ramblers Football Club.* Seattle, 1989.

*Seattle Post-Intelligencer.* May 8, 1946; Oct. 10, 1953; Apr. 19, 1957; May 11, 1974; Apr. 20, 1975; Mar. 16, 1976; May 14, 1978; May 22, 23, 1983; June 17, 1985; Dec. 9, 1985; Mar. 6, 1986; Mar. 9, 1989.

*Seattle Sun.* Dec. 3, 17, 1975.

*Seattle Times.* Mar. 20, 1957; Feb. 5, 1958; Jan. 25, 1972; Apr. 11, 1973; Jan. 3, 1974; Apr. 25, 1976; July 18, 1976; May 10, 1977; Jan. 14, 1979; Jan. 23, 1982; June 18, 1983; Dec. 6, 1984; Feb. 4, 1986; Nov. 13, 1987; Aug. 11, 1988; Sept. 4, 1990; Mar. 10, 1991; June 24, 1992; Aug. 11, 1992; Dec. 23, 1992; May 23, 1993; June 28, 1993.

*The Weekly.* Dec. 7, 1982; June 18, 1986.

### Unpublished

Ballard air pollution. Correspondence of Seattle Dept. of Buildings with Seattle City Council, Oct. - Dec., 1963.

Bishop, Robert O., Sr. "Little Cabin Lost and Other Tales of the Uptown Area." 1992. Typewritten.

Codling, Donald. "Reminiscences — 1948 to Present." 1993. Typewritten.

Edwards, Mrs. Harlan H. Correspondence regarding West Queen Anne playfield with Seattle City Council, and various community members, 1968.

Intlekofer, Charles F. "Burlington Northern and the History of Interbay." 1993. Typewritten.

*Oral Sources - TV Towers*: Bud Alger. Chief engineer, KTZZ-TV; Ken Hermanson. Former KING Broadcasting employee; Del Loder, Former KING Broadcasting employee; Don Wilkinson, Vice-president and Director of Engineering, KOMO Radio and TV.

*Oral Sources - Community History*: Hilda and Jim Blaikie; Chris Crosby; Gary Gaffner; Emery Gustafson; Anne Hoen; Millie Hokanson; Jack and Louise Locke; Carl J. Nordstrom; JoAnn Storey; Lee Zobrist.

Parker, Marion. "Queen Anne Branch Library." 1993. Typewritten.

"Parsons Garden." Correspondence of Seattle Park Department with George Parsons and Anne Parsons Frame, 1956-1959. Seattle City Archives, Seattle Municipal Building.

Queen Anne Community Club. "Guide to the Queen Anne Community Council." 1974. Pamphlet.

"Queen Anne Field house Dedication Program." Seattle Park Board, April 28, 1950.

"Queen Anne Swimming Pool." Memorandum, Dept. of Community Development, City of Seattle, March 4, 1970.

"Report on Queen Anne Club Building." Seattle Parks Dept. memo, Apr. 27, 1936.

"Report of the Queen Anne Parks and Recreation Committee." Report of survey of Queen Anne park needs. Queen Anne Community Council, 1970.

Schneider, Lt. Richard. *History of Fire Department on Queen Anne*. 1992. Typewritten.

Sherwood, Donald. "Notes and descriptions of Seattle Parks." Sherwood File, Seattle City Archives, Municipal Building, Seattle, WA.

"35 Years of Broadcasting." KING Broadcasting, Seattle, WA, 1983.

## CHAPTER 14 — A CENTURY OF SCHOOLS ON THE HILL

### Part I — Public and Private Schools

#### Published

"A History of Children's Orthopedic Hospital." Queen Anne Historical Society. Typewritten.

"A Lesson in Recycling: Schools Integrate Sludge Compost into Projects." *Monitor*. May 1991.

Erigero, Patricia C. *Seattle Public Schools: Historic Building Survey Summary Report*. Seattle: Historic Seattle Preservation and Development Authority, 1989.

John Hay *Bugle*. April 28, 1939.

"McClure Middle School and McClure PTSA." McClure *Maverick*, April 1986.

Queen Anne Christian School. *The Queen Anne Christian School*. Seattle, WA: Queen Anne Christian School. Pamphlet.

Queen Anne High School. *Grizzly*. Various years 1933-1980.

Queen Anne School. Pamphlet.

"Queen Anne Students Rap School Bombings." Queen Anne High School *Kuay*, February 20, 1970.

*Queen Anne News*, April 3, 1920; June 16, 1922; May 14, 1926; January 28, 1927; Novcember 30, 1928; October 31, 1930; April 14, 1965; September 1, 1971; May 20, 1981; March 28, 1984; May 6, 1988; June 1, 1988; May 29, 1991

Seattle Country Day School. Pamphlet.

Seattle Public Schools, Dept. of District Relations. Sara Levant, ed. Seattle School Histories, 1869-1974.

Seattle Public Schools. Seattle School Histories. 1951.

Seattle Public Schools. "An Exciting New Choice for Public Middle School in Seattle." Pamphlet, 1991.

Seattle School Board. *Record*, various numbers, 1904 - 1958.

*Seattle Times*, February 5, 1910; April 7, 1956; August 28, 1988; November 18, 1991; March 5, 1990

#### Unpublished

Arhhart, Warren. Address at Silver Anniversary Celebration, Worth McClure Middle School, November 7, 1992.

"Fifty-Five Years at West Queen Anne," 1945. Handwritten.

Hennes, John. "Queen Anne High School Alumni Association," 1993. Typewritten.

"History of F. H. Coe School," 1948. Handwritten.

"History of John Hay School," 1948. Handwritten.

North Queen Anne Parent-Teacher Association, *Scrapbook*. 1945.

Skolnik, Arthur M., ed. "Facing the Consequences; What Will Happen to Our Community if West Queen Anne School is Closed? A Citizens' Report." Special Project Committee, Queen Anne Community Council. August 13, 1974.

Tennyson, Bill. Letter to John Hennes, 1992.

### Part II — Seattle Pacific University

#### Published

Beers, Adlaide Lione. *The Romance of a Consecrated Life: A Biography of Alexander Beers*. Chicago: Free Methodist Publishing House, 1922.

McNichols, Donald. *Seattle Pacific University, A Growing Vision 1891-1991*. Seattle: Seattle Pacific University, 1989.

*Seattle Post-Intelligencer,* various dates 1889-1988.

*Seattle Times*, various dates 1896-1988.

Shay, Emma Freeland. *Mariet Hardy Freeland: A Faithful Wilness*, 2nd edition. Chicago: Free Methodist Publishing House, 1914.

Walls, Alice E. ; Ruth L.; Rose; Mary Loretta. *Eighty Years: Historical Sketch of the Woman's Missionary Society of the Free Methodist Church*. Winona Lake, Indiana: Light and Life Press, 1975.

### Unpublished

Crawford, Rachel B. "Hiram and Merci Pease, the Forgotten," 1975. Typewritten.

Demaray, C. Dorr. "Yes, We Can!" Seattle Pacific University Centennial History, 1891-1991." 1981. Typewritten.

Hedges, Richard G. "A Historic Study of Seattle Seminary and Seattle Pacific College, 1891-1925." Master's thesis, University of Washington, 1962.

Schoenhals, Lawrence R. "Higher Education in the Free Methodist Church in the United States." Unpublished Ph.D. dissertation, University of Washington, 1935.

Seattle Pacific University Board of Trustees Minutes, June 24, 1891-January 22, 1907; April 21, 1908-June 6, 1913; March 14, 1914-1988.

Watson, C. Hoyt. "Life Stream: The Story of the First Seventy-five Years of Seattle Pacific College, 1891-1966. 1968. Typewritten.

## CHAPTER 15 — GOING TO CHURCH

### Published

Buerge, David M. and Junius Rochester. *Root and Branches*. Seattle: Seattle Council of Churches, 1988.

Morgan, Murray. *Skid Road, An Informal Portrait of Seattle*. New York: Viking Press, 1952.

Newell, Gordon. *Westward to Alki, the Story of David Denny and Louisa Boren*. Seattle: Superior Publishing Co., 1977.

"Queen Anne Community Study." Public Services Division, Seattle Public Library, 1978.

*Queen Anne News*, Various dates. 1920-1930.

*Queen Anne News*, Fiftieth Anniversary Issue, February 11, 1970.

### Unpublished

Corey, Eda Grace. *Seattle Churches as Known Through the Seattle Newspapers*. 1938. Seattle Public Library. Typewritten.

"Dedication of Saint Anne Church May 19, 1963." Booklet.

Denny Park Lutheran Church, 1888-1988. Centennial booklet.

Pflueger, Rev. Jesse P. and Rev. E. C. Knorr. Queen Anne Luthern Church. Typewritten.

"Queen Anne Lutheran Church 1917-1967." Anniversary booklet.

"Redemptorist Fathers and Brothers Centennial 1891-1991." Sacred Heart Catholic Church booklet.

"Sacred Heart Church - A Brief History 1889-1989." Centennial booklet.

"Saint Paul's Episcopal Church, 75th Anniversary." Booklet.

"Seattle First Free Methodist Church of Seattle Washington, 1880-1980." Centennial booklet.

"Seventy-fifth Anniversary, 1905-1980." Queen Anne United Presbyterian Church booklet.

## CHAPTER 16 — THE HEALTHFUL HILLTOP AIR

### Published

American Medical Association. *American Medical Directory, Register of Legally Qualified Physicians of the U. S. and Canada*. Chicago: American Medical Association Press. Various years, 1880-1990.

Andrews, Mildred. *Seattle Women: A Legacy of Community Development, A Pictorial History 1851-1920*. Seattle: YWCA of Seattle/King County.

Anti-Tuberculosis League of King County. *Sketches of Anti-Tuberculosis League Activities in Seattle and King County 1937-1938*. Seattle: Anti-Tuberculosis League of King County, Seattle, WA, 1938.

Bagley, Clarence B. *History of King County, Washington*. 4 Vols. Chicago: S. J. Clarke Publishing Co., 1929.

Bagley, Clarence B. *History of Seattle*. 3 Vols. Chicago: S. J.Clarke Publishing Co., 1916.

Chase, Cora G. *Unto the Least, A Biographic Sketch of Mother Ryther*. Facsimile reproduction. Seattle: The Shorey Book Store, 1972.

Deaconess Training School. "What You Do When You Help the Deaconess Training School." Pamphlet. Seattle: The SeattleDeaconess Training School, 1913.

Frare, Aleua L. *Magnolia Yesterday and Today*. Seattle: Magnolia Community Club, 1975.

Hamley, Frederick G. *Firland: A Story of Firland Sanatorium*. Work of Compiling, Edited and printed by Occupational Therapy Department of Sanatorium, 1935/1936.

King County Medical Society. *King County Medical Society 1888-1988: 100 Years*. Seattle: King County Medical Society, 1988.

Ladies Relief Society of the City of Seattle. "1927 Year Book of the Seattle Children's Home." Maintained by the Ladies Relief Society of the City of Seattle, 1884, 1927.

*Queen Anne News*, May 26, 1922; July 20, 1923; August 12, 1948; July 23, 1953; March 29, 1956; September 18, 1968.

Reinartz, Kay F. *Tukwila, Community at the Crossroads*. Tukwila, WA: City of Tukwila, 1991.

Rockafellar, Nancy, and James W. Haviland, M.D., Eds. *Saddlebags to Scanners: First 100 Years of Medicine in Washington State*. Seattle: Washington State Medical Association, 1989.

*Seattle Post-Intelligencer*, August 30, 1908.

*Seattle Times*, June 25, 1931; January 10, 1932; March 21, 1933; January, 1937; November 16, 1942; January 18, 1953; December 28, 1954; December 15, 1957; January 14, 1959; November 8, 1959; December 13, 1959; April 30, 1961; August 22, 1961; June 21, 1964; September 23, 1965; November 11, 1966; January 11, 1967; March 6, 1983; February 11, 1993.

Schwabacher, Emilie B. *A Place for the Children, A Personal History of Children's Orthopedic Hospital and Medical Center*, revised, ed. Heidi Rabel. Seattle: Children's Orthopedic Hospital and Medical Center, 1982.

*Seattle City Directory*. Seattle: R. L. Polk and Company. Various Years., 1880-1940.

Smith, Clarence A., M.D. "Seattle Hospitals." *Northwest Medicine*, 17 (July 1918), 199-208.

Swick, Dr. Edward Lyndon. *The Science of Personal Magnetism and the Art of Its Application for the Treatment of Disease, Including Treatise on Massage and the Diet*. Seattle: Pigott Printing Concern, Inc., 1923.

Whorton, James C. "Drugless Healing in the 1920's: The Therapeutic Cult of Sanipractic." *Pharmacy in History*. 28, no. 1 (1986) 14.

### Unpublished

Charles Bodemer Papers. Acc. 3379-88-17. University of Washington Libraries, Boxes 11, 12 and 13.

Department of Community Development. Landmarks Preservation Board. "Old Children's Orthopedic Hospital." Seattle Historic Building Data Sheet, December 10, 1975.

Douglas, Thomas E., M.D. Letter to Dr. Kay F. Reinartz, October 26, 1992.

"Final report on the Seattle Area Chest X-Ray Program, September 9,1948 through January 15, 1949." Compiled by the Program Director, General Chairman and Executive Committee. Sponsored by the King County Medical Society, the Anti-Tuberculosis League of King County, Seattle and King County Department of Public Health in cooperation with Firland Sanatorium, State Department of Health and the U.S. Public Health Service. Seattle.

Fitch, Bonnie. Letter to Dr. Kay F. Reinartz, October 24, 1992.

Rockafellar, Nancy Moore. "Public Health in Progressive Seattle 1876-1919." Masters Thesis, University of Washington, School of Medicine, 1973.

## Chapter 17 — Business around the Hill

### Published

*The Falcon*, November 12, 1982.

*Queen Anne News*, May 31, 1929; September 26, 1930; November 14, 1930; February 7, 1952; September 25, 1952; October 25, 1956; August 3, 1961; December 27, 1961; January 3, 1963; February 11, 1970; October 28, 1981.

## Chapter 18 — Apartments and Development on the Hill

### Published

Brambilla, Roberto and Gianni Longo. *Learning From Seattle*. New York: Institute for Environmental action, 1979.

Chambers, S. Allen, Nancy B. Schwartz, John C. Poppeliers. *What Style is it?* Washington, D.C: The Preservation Press, 1983.

Hatje, Gerd. *Encyclopedia of Modern Architecture*. New York: Harry N. Abrams, Inc., 1954.

"Hearing Due for Polygon Corp.'s Full-block Queen Anne Project," *Seattle Daily Journal of Commerce*, November 20, 1978.

Heyer, Paul. *Architects on Architecture*. New York: Walker and Co., 1978.

*High Rise Apartments—A Report to the Seattle City Planning Commission*. Seattle: Clark, Coleman & Repeiks Inc., July 17, 1964.

Kreisman, Lawrence. *Art Deco Seattle*. Seattle: Allied Arts, 1979.

Kreisman, Lawrence. *West Queen Anne School: Renaissance of a Landmark*. Seattle: Seattle School District, 1978.

Palmes, J.C. *Sir Banister Fletcher's A History of Architecture*, 18th ed. New York: Charles Scribner's Sons, 1975.

*Queen Anne - An Inventory of Building and Urban Design Resources*. Seattle: Historic Seattle Preservation and Development Authority, 1975.

*Queen Anne News*. May 19, 1976; October 11, 1978; May 20, 1981; December 2, 1992

Seattle Housing Authority. *Seattle Housing Authority Annual Report 1989/1990*. Seattle: Privately printed, 1990.

*Seattle Post-Intelligencer*. May 11, 1974; January 28, 1979; May 23, 1983;

*Seattle Sun*. September, 1976; October 27, 1976; April 28, 1977; July 13, 1977; August 24, 1977; August 9, 1978

*Seattle Times*. March 28, 1968; July 21, 1968; May 29, 1969; November 30, 1969; July 26, 1970; November 10, 1979

*Seattle Weekly*. October 8, 1986; February 21, 1990.

Steinbrueck, Victor. *A Guide to Seattle Architecture 1850-1953*. New York: Reinhold, 1953.

*The Weekly*. July 28 and August 3, 1976.

Woodbridge, Sally B. and Roger Montgomery. *A Guide to Architecture in Washington*. Seattle: University of Washington Press, 1980.

Zoning Ordinance. Seattle, WA. 1923, 1947, 1955.

### Unpublished

Historic Seattle Preservation & Development Authority. "Queen Anne High School." Seattle, WA.

## CHAPTER 19 — COMMUNITY LIFE—ORGANIZATIONS AND NEWSPAPERS

### Published

*North Side News*, November 30, 1911.

*Notable Men of Washington*. Tacoma, WA: The Perkins Press, 1912.

*Queen Anne American*, November 19; December 5, 19, 1915; January 21, 1916.

*Queen Anne News*, various numbers, 1921-1992.

*Seattle Times*, May 21, 1954; August 27, 1956; August 3, 1958; March 29, 1978; December 22, 1988.

### Unpublished

Nickerson, Harold H. "The Social Organization, Queen Anne Hill." 1938. (Typewritten)

Mitchell, Marlene. "Washington Newspapers: Territorial and State," unpublished thesis, University of Washington, 1964.

Palmer, Gayle L., ed. *Washington State Union List of Newspapers on Microfilm*. Olympia, WA: Washington State Library, 1991.

## CHAPTER 20 — STAYING ON QUEEN ANNE FOREVER

### Published

Bagley, Clarence. *History of Seattle, King County*. 3 vols. Chicago: S. Clarke Pub. Co., 1916, 1929.

Bagley, Clarence B. "Scrapbooks," Vol 2.

Bass, Sophie Frye. *When Seattle was a Village*. Seattle: Lowman and Hanford. 1947.

*Choirs Directory*, Seattle, WA, 1878.

Mah, Byron. "History Haunts Mount Pleasant." *Queen Anne News*, December 2, 1981.

Newell, Gordon. *Westward to Alki*. Seattle: Superior Publishing. 1977.

Seattle, City of. City Cemetery Ledger, City of Seattle Archives.

Seattle, City of. Ordinance Nos. 36, 571, City Archives.

Seattle, City of. Denny Park records, Parks Department file, City of Seattle Archives.

*Seattle Post-Intelligencer*, March 5, 1905; September 24, 1905; November 5, 1911; April 16, 1919; May 31, 1983.

*Seattle Times*, May 25, 1914; May 3, 1940; April 28, 1990.

Watt, Roberta Frye. *Four Wagons West, The Story of Seattle*. Portland, OR: Binfords & Mort., 1931.

### Unpublished

Driggers, Mary Ellen. "The History of Mt. Pleasant Cemetery." 1974. Typewritten.

# Appendix A: Distinguished Queen Anne Citizens

A diverse group of Queen Anne citizens met as a committee in the summer of 1992 to start the process for this list of citizens. A form was developed that was to be used in nominating those who had distinguished themselves in local, state or national arenas over the years. This form and a covering letter explaining its purpose were mailed to members of over fifty community organizations, inviting members to submit nominations. From those submitted, the committee then chose the persons included here. In addition, many more distinguished Queen Anne citizens are mentioned throughout the book. The focus of this list is the twentieth century.

## Arts and Entertainment

**Christopher P. Bollen**—Pen and ink and watercolor artist of the Northwest scene. Published book *I Don't Know Much About Art, but I Know What I Like!*

**Howard Costigan**—Radio news commentator. Active in the Washington Commonwealth Federation during the 1930s.

**John Danz**—Founder and president of Sterling Theater chain and noted philanthropist.

**Edmund J. Donohoe**—Editor of the *Washington Teamster*, noted for its controversial column, "Tilting the Windmill."

**Florence Ekstrand**—Editor of *Queen Anne News* for fifteen years and writer of Scandinavian books. Under her editorship the *News* became a much stronger voice.

**Winifred R. Emmanuel**—Organist who played at theaters and radio stations around the Northwest.

**Emery O. Gustafson**—Community leader, journalist, pharmacist. Member of Queen Anne Alumni Assoc. and Queen Anne Historical Assoc. Columnist ("The Passing Scene") for the *Queen Anne News.*

**Alicia Hokanson**—Award-winning poet, teacher and writer.

**Randolph H. Hokanson**—Concert pianist who toured internationally before and after World War II and Professor of Music at the University of Washington for 35 years. Performed locally with the Seattle Symphony and many other orchestras.

**Elizabeth Huddle**—Actress and artistic director of Seattle's Intiman Theatre.

**Milton Katims**—Virtuoso violinist and conductor of the Seattle Symphony for many years. Recently returned as a guest and received a standing ovation.

**Bill Knight**—Sports editor of the *Seattle Post-Intelligencer.*

**Mildred Lopeman**—Creator of porcelain figures.

**Jean H. Lunzer**—Newspaper columnist and editor of the *Seattle Times*, woman's page.

**Erika Hokanson Michels**—Actress in films and in radio and television commercials.

**Kevin Nicolby**—Locally renowned gardener and botanical illustrator whose works are in the J. Paul Getty Museum in Texas.

**Jean Gray Ohnstad**—Singer, model and actress. Sang in various musical productions and for public events.

**Ruth Prins**—Creator and star of longtime children's television show "Wunda Wunda."

**John M. Spargur**—First-rank violinist and orchestra conductor for the Seattle Philharmonic.

**Emily Lindsay Squier**—Dramatist and songwriter for first graduating class at Queen Anne High School. Noted Southwest writer.

**Anna Louise Strong**—Seattle School Board member, mountaineer, and emigre to Soviet Union and China.

## Leaders in Business

**Frank E. Best**—Inventor of the Best Lock, president of Best Lock Co., and author of technical books.

**Charles C. Cawsey**—Pioneer contractor who built first building after the Great Seattle Fire, also Carnegie Library and Lowman Building.

**William A. Clark**—Realtor in Seattle and Alaska, founder of Ewing and Clark Realty.

**Michael Dederer**—Member of Queen Anne Community Club and founder of Seattle Fur Exchange.

**Elsie Fauble**—Owner of Queen Anne Variety Store, a longtime local establishment on Queen Anne Avenue, and lover of children.

**C. Arthur and Wedell O. Foss**—Co-presidents of Foss Tug and Marine oil transportation.

**Jack Garrison**—Owner of Consolidated Freightways, the world's largest trucking company.

**Paul C. Harper**—Investment banker and director of Title Insurance Company. President of Seattle School Board.

**Gary Kildall**—Inventer of CP/M, the first operating system for mini-computers and forerunner of the DOS system.

**Joseph Kildall**—Founder of Kildall Nautical School and Kildall Realty.

**Charles H. Lilly**—Founder of Charles H. Lilly Co., the internationally-known grain and flower seed business.

**William O. McKay**—Established Seattle's first car dealership. Civic leader.

**Walter B. Nettleton**—President of West Coast Lumberman's Association and founder of Nettleton Lumber Co.

**Reginald H. Parsons**—Banker. President of Parson's Investment Company and Seattle Trust and Saving. Noted for his community service; Boy Scout camp Parsons named in his honor.

**"Alki" Al Salisbury**—Publisher of 500 locally-authored books of Northwest history.

**Leroy Stradley**—Founder of *Weekly Index,* a shipping newspaper serving the Pacific Northwest. Founder of Cama Beach, Camano Island's first salt water resort, in 1934.

**John F. Strom**—Owner of Interbay Pharmacy, Washington State Representative, Travel Service.

**James B. Warrack**—Construction engineer on schools, hospitals and hotels in Alaska.

**George V. Whittle CPA.**— Owner of George V. Whittle and Co., CPAs, since 1919.

## COMMUNITY

**Frank S. Bayley**—Member of Seattle School Board and president of the YMCA.

**Della Bovard**—Active member of Queen Anne Orthopedic Guild for 46 years.

**Ada E. Breen**—Facilitator in the purchase of Children's Orthopedic Hospital to form King Co. Hospital No. 2.

**Bill Clemmens**—Volunteer at the Queen Anne Bethany Food Bank for 7 years; Director for 3 years.

**Mrs. Robert N. Cowan**—President of Queen Anne High School PTA in the 1940s. Oversaw distribution of games made by Seattle school children to military service personnel.

**Marie Dalton**—"Perpetual" U.G.N. volunteer; church and community worker.

**Robert W. Frazier**—Past president of the Queen Anne Historical Society and longtime volunteer at the Seattle Public Library.

**Les and Laura Hamilton**—Researchers of Queen Anne Hill's history and collectors of numerous photographs, now preserved as the Hamilton Collection, Allen Library, University of Washington.

**Orville and Beverly Johnson and sons Paul and Billie Pearson**—Noted as helpful neighbors who provide many complimentary services.

**Helena M. Johnson**—A mainstay of North Queen Anne PTA holding many offices, including President. Served 25 years in Girl Scouts.

**Kathryn Katica**—Active volunteer, including the Red Cross.

**Robert Kildall**—Chairman of the Seattle Park Board, President of the Magnolia Community Club and founder of the "Friends of Discovery Park" who involved Queen Anne in the project.

**Arthur W. Lampkin**—Assisted in organizing the Bethany Food Bank and Queen Anne Helpline, serving on the Board.

**Sol G. Levy**—Owner of the Commission Co., a whole grocer supplier. Internationally—recognized worker in the Boy Scouts. Initiated the Cub Scout Packs in this area.

**David M. Marriott Jr.**—Recipient of the Queen Anne Chamber of Commerce Scholarship and producer of a historical video on Queen Anne churches.

**Mary C. Mascarella**—Coordinator of selection process for Queen Anne Chamber of Commerce scholarship recipients.

**William and Louise McCutchin**—Named "oldest sweethearts" in contest in 1938, their 71st year of marriage.

**Harmon E. Meecham**—Civil War veteran and community worker.

**Mrs. George T. Myers**—Children's Orthopedic Hospital in the 1920s.

**Patricia S. Nordlund**—Volunteer with Queen Anne Helpline and active in the Women's Auxiliary of Swedish Club.

**Florence S. Nordstrom**—Member of many military and civic organizations around the time of World War II, and an active member of Queen Anne Historical Society.

**Marion L. Parker**—Staff member of the Queen Anne Branch Public Library for 24 years. Community and church volunteer.

**Pat Sobeck**—One of the founders and currently the director of the Queen Anne Helpline. A strong community leader caring for the needy of all ages.

**Thelma S. Waring**—President of West Queen Anne PTA, originated the now-nationwide "Halloween Make-up for Safety Campaign."

## Government and Law

**George Benson**—Pharmacist, Seattle City Councilman, and advocate for improved transportation and the revival of the Waterfront Trolley.

**Hugh DeLacy**—United States Congressman and, in 1936, the youngest member of Seattle City Council.

**William Dwyer**—Lawyer, United States District judge, and civil libertarian.

**Russell V. Hokanson**—Attorney active in Queen Anne politics and zoning policies.

**Stephen Hull**—State Representative and financier.

**C. Montgomery Johnson**—Political activist and campaign manager for many Republican candidates in Washington and Alaska.

**Warren G. Magnuson**—One of Washington's outstanding public servants, serving 37 years in the U.S. Senate.

**Donald A. McDonald**—Attorney, Washington State Representative and Superior Court Judge.

**Paige Miller**—Port Commissioner. Involved in Pier 91 zoning and land-use requirements.

**Ray Moore**—Washington State Senator, advocate for schools and affordable housing, and volunteer with Queen Anne Helpline.

**Charles P. Moriarty, Jr.**—Lawyer and Washington State Representative and Senator.

**Charles P. Moriarty, Sr.**—Assistant U.S. Attorney and Superior Court Judge.

**Albert E. Pierce**—Civil engineer and superintendent of Seattle Municipal Street Railway.

**Joel Pritchard**—Washington State Representative and Senator, U.S. congressman, and Washington State Lt. Governor.

**William B. Severyns**—State and county sheriff, criminal investigator, and Seattle's youngest police chief.

**Evangeline Starr**—King County Prosecuting Attorney, Divorce Proctor, Justice of the Peace, and King County District Court Judge.

**Daniel B. Trefethen**—Oldest practicing attorney in Washington at the time of his death at age 93.

**Victor Zednick**—Lt. Governor and State Representative and Senator.

## Military Service

**Robert Galer**—Congressional Medal of Honor, World War II.

**James Harvey**—World War II veteran honored at Fort Lawton's Reserve Center.

**Robert J. Leisy**—Congressional Medal of Honor, Vietnam. The Reserve Center at Fort Lawton named for him.

**Capt. Philip H. Luther**—Merchant Marine officer, licensed Master Mariner for any ship or ocean.

**Capt. Roger W. Luther**—Naval officer and commander of first U.S. Navy ship to visit the Soviet Union following World War II.

**Major General William F. Marquat**—Served in World War I and II. Received Distinguished Service and Silver Star for gallantry. Did postwar work in Japan.

## Science and Medicine

**Harry E. Allen**—Physician and surgeon, Medical Corps in Philippine Campaign 1900-1902. Chief of surgical staff during World War I.

**Michael Copass**—Neurologist, Deputy Director of Medic One and Professor at University of Washington School of Medicine.

**Frank P. Maxon**—Physician and surgeon for Seattle Fire Department and staff surgeon at several Seattle hospitals.

**G. L. Tanzer**—Analytical chemist, developed Seattle's first pure milk campaign after discovering impurities in raw milk. Established the first City Laboratory.

# Appendix B: Business District Maps from 1915–1935

Hundreds of businesses, small and large, have existed on Queen Anne since its beginning. Chapter 17 tells some of this story. A few major business intersections are mapped out in this appendix, showing the ebb and flow of our local history as businesses started, moved, disappeared, and in a few cases, endured.

The data are from the classified section of the Polk Seattle City Directories for 1915, 1920, 1925, 1930 and 1935. The business names known to our residents were not always listed in the directory. For instance, Alec Gordon's restaurant at 13 W. Galer is our long-time Al's Hamburgers. Businesses that came and went between the five-year intervals are not shown. The listings also do not show private homes and apartments and the maps are simple schematics drawn just to show locations.

## Queen Anne and Boston Business District

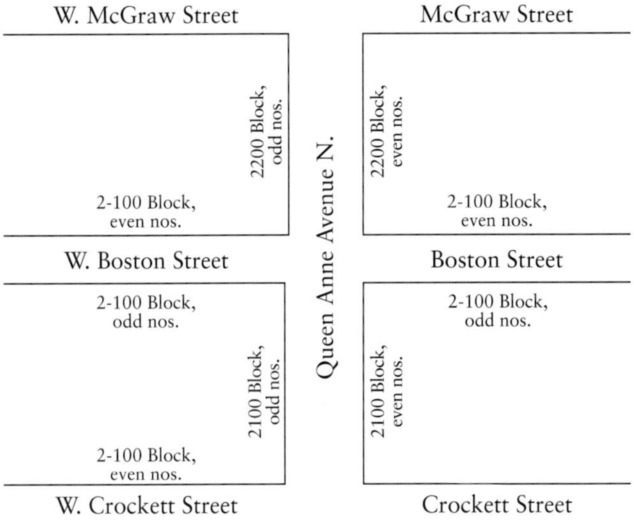


## Sixth W. and McGraw Business District

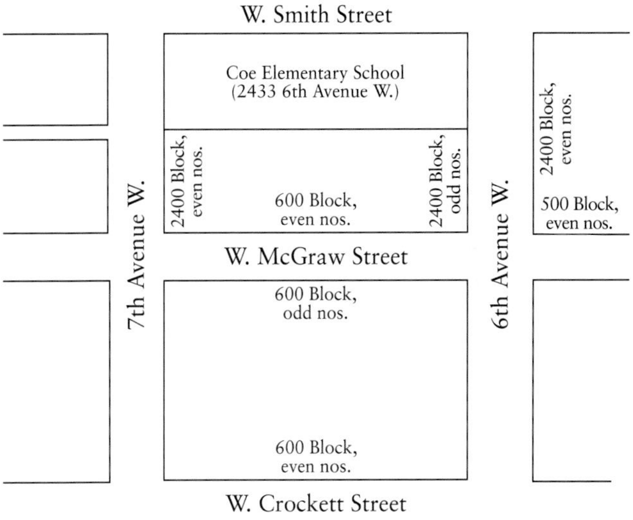


## Queen Anne and Galer Business District

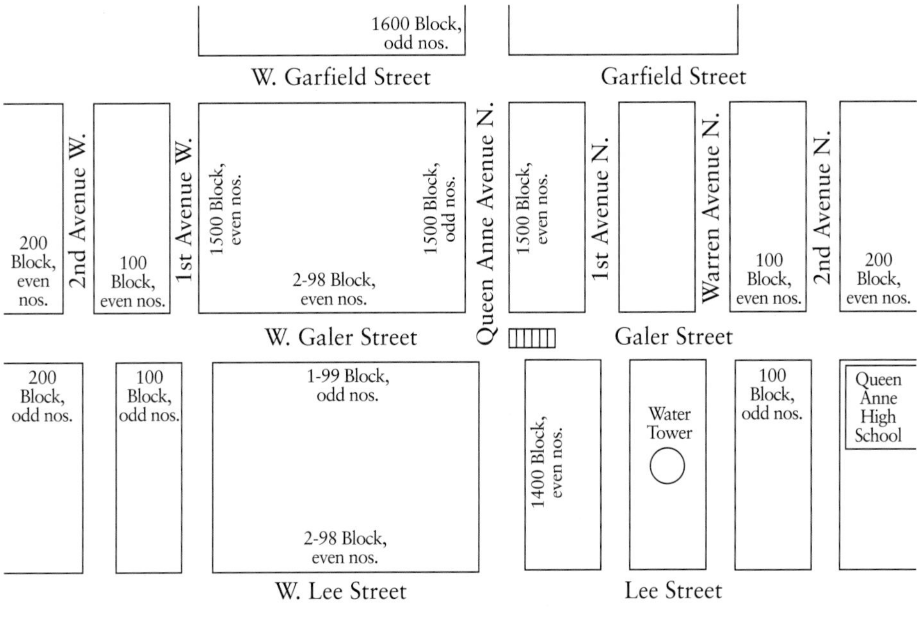


Maps not to scale.

## QUEEN ANNE AND GALER BUSINESS DISTRICT, 1915-1935

| Address | Businesses ca. 1915-1920 | Businesses ca. 1925-1930 | Businesses ca. 1935 |
|---|---|---|---|
| 1420 Q.A. | | | Galer Court Service Auto Garage |
| 1421 Q.A. | | | Hill Davis & Co./Keystone Real Estate |
| 1424 Q.A. | | | Katherine Cook Library |
| 1426 Q.A. | | | Grace Martin Beauty Shop |
| 1427 Q.A. | | Ferguson & Peabody Notions | |
| 1428 Q.A. | | Keystone Realty | |
| 1429 Q.A. | | Parker & Marin, Radiant Beauty Shoppe | |
| 1500 Q.A. | Galer St. Pharmacy | Galer St. Pharmacy | Galer St. Pharmacy |
| 1501 Q.A. | G. Estey Drugs, T. Nicholas Grocery | L.A. Kiehl Grocery, H. Fisher Restaurant | Wade Walker Beer Parlor |
| 1502 Q.A. | | W.E. Nicholas Grocery | |
| 1503 Q.A. | | John Ericksen Meat Market | H. Bingham Meats/Q.A. Central Grocery |
| 1504 Q.A. | | Top O' the Hill Baking Co. | |
| 1505 Q.A. | S. Blummer Bakery, R. Paschal Bakery | Paul Bischof Bakery, Q.A. Radio Store | |
| 1507 Q.A. | Augustine & Kyers Grocery | Augustine & Kyers Grocery | Augustine & Kyer Grocery |
| 1508 Q.A. | | Cheerio Garage | Wm. Randish/D. Peha Grocery/Produce |
| 1509 Q.A. | 1/2 Chas. B. Williams Barber | 1/2 W. Allen Barber, J. R. Havlik Realty | Havlik Realty |
| 1511 Q.A. | R. Culver Realty, A. McGee Furniture | Van Runyan Hardware | |
| 1519 Q.A. | | | Les McDowell Barber |
| 1521 Q.A. | | | Pandora Beauty Salon |
| 1523 Q.A. | | Highland Garage | |
| 1525 Q.A. | | Jos. Sheehan Barber | |
| 1527 Q.A. | | | Cheerio Bookshelf Library |
| 1529 Q.A. | | Cheerio Movie Theater | Queen Anne Movie Theater |
| 1531 Q.A. | | Cheerio Candy Kitchen/1/2 Dainty Lunch | Chet Larson Restaurant |
| 1607 Q.A. | | A.D. McPherson Grocery, Wee Best Groc. | Chas. Pelham Grocery |
| 1609 Q.A. | | E.S. Alexander Barber | Walter Hemmingsen Barber |
| 1611 Q.A. | Anna Wheeler Confectioner | Galer Dye Works | |
| 1613 Q.A. | | Queen Anne Furniture House | |
| 1615 Q.A. | John A. Lucas Dyers & Cleaners | Galer Dye Works & Cleaners | |
| 1617 Q.A. | R. Dunn Groc., 1/2 Thuleen Shoe Repair | M.A. Yarrow Grocery | |
| 1619 Q.A. | | | Frank Ching Laundry |
| 1631 Q.A. | | | Galer Dye Works Cleaners |
| 182 Galer | John M Stephens Confectioners | | |
| 183 Galer | | A.B. Stubbs Restaurant | Arthur Stubbs Restaurant |
| 193 Galer | | Pings Restaurant | |
| 214 Galer | | Louie's Place Restaurant, Grizzly Inn | Grizzly Inn Restaurant |
| 3 W. Galer | | Tom Niclos Grocery | Thomas Nicholos Grocery |
| 5 W. Galer | | Angus Cowan Barber | Queen Anne Barber Shop |
| 6 W. Galer | | | Thos Jeske Shoe Repair |
| 7 W. Galer | | A. Mochinski Dyers/Cleaners,QA Pressery | Anthony Mochinski Cleaners |
| 8 W. Galer | Thos. Stempel Shoe Repair | | |
| 9 W. Galer | | Nelson Shoe Repair, Jeskey Shoe Repair | |
| 11 W. Galer | | E.E. Hortman Bakery, QA Barber Shop | Fred McKenzie Restaurant |
| 12 W. Galer | Mrs. M.G. Rittenhouse Shoemaker | Cheerio Tailor Shoppe | |
| 13 W. Galer | Wm A. Lynch Dyers & Cleaners | Kugener Shoe Rep./1/2 McAlpin, Salter Barber | Alec Gordon Restaurant |
| 14 W. Galer | Henry Mullins Shoe Repair | | |
| 15 W. Galer | Brod & Baker Grocery/Banks Cobbler | 1/2 -W. Allen Barber | |
| 23 W. Galer | | | Mary White Beauty Shop |
| 117 W. Galer | | Martin Iverson Grocery | |
| 125 W. Galer | | Central Pharmacy | Central Pharmacy |
| 126 W. Galer | Gideon & Oleson Garage | Queen Anne Garage | Queen Anne Garage |
| 215 W. Galer | | Garfield Auto Garage | Garfield Garage |
| 224 W. Galer | | L.H. Webster Grocery, R. Taylor Grocery | Peter Comera Grocery |
| 225 W. Galer | | W. Galer Tailor | |
| 233 W. Galer | | Mrs. J.E. Long Confectioners | |

## Queen Anne and Boston Business District, 1915-1935

| Address | Businesses ca. 1915-1920 | Businesses ca. 1925-1930 | Businesses ca. 1935 |
|---|---|---|---|
| 2101 Queen Anne | | | Tarbet Grocery |
| 2117 Queen Anne | | Peterson Tailor, QA Coat & Dress Shop | |
| 2119 Queen Anne | | Sheridan's Restaurant | Knapp Bakery |
| 2123 Queen Anne | | Duguid Grocery | Fritz Grocery |
| 2125 Queen Anne | Herber Tailors | | Morris Mezistrano & Gerrish Grocery |
| 2127 Queen Anne | | | Van de Kamp's Bakery |
| 2129 Queen Anne | Muller & Driscoll Hardware | | Hilltop Tavern |
| 2131 Queen Anne | | Muller Hardware | QA Hardware |
| 2132 Queen Anne | Lauderdale Grocers | Duguid & MacAuley Grocery | Wills Real Estate |
| 2134 Queen Anne | Standard Drug | Standard Drug | QA Drug |
| 2135 Queen Anne | Leo Kline Shoe Repair | | |
| 2201 Queen Anne | QA Theater | | Piggly Wiggly |
| 2203 Queen Anne | Martinez Realty | Piggly Wiggly | |
| 2204 Queen Anne | | QA News | |
| 2205 Queen Anne | Weil Confectionery | QA Candy Shop | |
| 2207 Queen Anne | Eckert Barber | Hook Cleaner | Garfield Cleaners & Dyers |
| 2209 Queen Anne | | Martinez Realty | Martinez Realty |
| 2211 Queen Anne | Arbogast Real Estate | | |
| 2212 Queen Anne | | Standard Grocery, Joos Real Estate | Standard Grocery |
| 2213 Queen Anne | | Gust QA Dry Good | |
| 2231 Queen Anne | | Ward Gas Station | Ward Gas Station |
| 4 Boston | Stelzner Meat Market | | Guthmuller Meat Market |
| 6 Boston | Roth Shoe Repair | Boston Shoe Repair | Henning Shoe Repair |
| 7 Boston | | | Mezistrano Produce |
| 8 Boston | Lawrence Bakery | Standard Bakery | Standard Bakery & Lunch |
| 10 Boston | | Wheatman & Wittauer Radio | |
| 10 1/2 Boston | | Beardsley Watch Repair Kiddies' Shop | |
| 11 Boston | | Standard Barber Shop, Standard Shoe Repair | |
| 11 1/2 Boston | | | Helder's Shoe Repair |
| 12 Boston | | Lewis Dye Works | |
| 13 Boston | | Merkley's Meat Market | Burton's Restaurant |
| 14 Boston | Culver Real Estate | | |
| 15 Boston | | QA Cafe | Bazzetta & Costello Grocery |
| 16 Boston | | | Lewis Cleaners |
| 3 W. Boston | | | Willson's Gas Station |
| 6 W. Boston | | | Ojala's Beauty Shop |
| 8 W. Boston | | | Storr's Barber Shop |
| 10 W. Boston | | | QA News |

## SIXTH WEST AND MCGRAW BUSINESS DISTRICT, 1915-1935

| Address | Businesses ca. 1915-1920 | Businesses ca. 1925-1930 | Businesses ca. 1935 |
|---|---|---|---|
| 514 W. McGraw | Patterson/Bailey Grocery | Mayflower Grocery | Bailey's Grocery |
| 600 W. McGraw | | Groceteria<br>Annex Meat market | Benjamin Franklin Grocery<br>Hoffmeister Meat |
| 601 W. McGraw | | | Gas Station |
| 602 W. McGraw | | Kenyon's Dry Goods | Coffman's Dry Goods |
| 603 W. McGraw | | Q.A. Super Service Gas | |
| 610 W. McGraw | | | Gardner's Cleaners |
| 612 W. McGraw | | | Helberg's Restaurant |
| 612½ W. McGraw | | | Cisney's Barber Shop |
| 615 W. McGraw | | Anderson's Bakery | Anderson's Bakery |
| 617 W. McGraw | | | Weese's Barber Shop |
| 618 W. McGraw | | Reliable French Cleaners | Richardson's Beauty Shop |
| 619 W. McGraw | | Lowman's Meats | Lowman's Meats |
| 620 W. McGraw | Maxon Barber Shop | Danielson Barber Shop | DePuydt Meats |
| 621 W. McGraw | | Piggly Wiggly | Piggly Wiggly |
| 623 W. McGraw | | | Gibson Shoe Repair |
| 624 W. McGraw | | | Harvey's Grocery |
| 625 W. McGraw | | Baker Drug (1930) | |
| 633 W. McGraw | | Gibson Shoe Repair (1930) | |
| 600 W. Crockett | De Bruler/McKay Grocery | Tarbet Grocery | Dainty Lunch |
| 602 W. Crockett | | | Mazon's Beauty Shop |
| 604 W. Crockett | Geddis Meat market | | |
| 606 W. Crockett | | DeBruler Grocery | |
| 608 W. Crockett | | Smith Restaurant | |
| 610 W. Crockett | | K. Sasaki Shoe Repair<br>OK Shoe Repair (1930) | Tonkecheff Shoe Repair |
| 2433 6th W. | Coe Elementary School | Coe Elementary School | Coe Elementary School |
| 2442 6th W. | Gerling Coal Co. | | |
| 2400 7th W. | Baker Drug | Baker Drug | |
| 2404 7th W. | Van Winkler Grocery | | |
| 2406 7th W. | | Asmuth Meat Market | |
| 2408 7th W. | Barrett & Roach Grocery | Laurel Grocery | |
| 2412 7th W. | | Gibson Shoe Repair | |
| 2433 7th W. | | Baker's Restaurant | Bothwell & Keay's Candy Shop |
| 2435 | | Bowden Grocery<br>Wild Rose Grocery (1930) | |

# Appendix C: Street Name Changes

Names of Queen Anne's streets and avenues have unique stories of their own. As each area was platted the developers would make up their own street names. Early Queen Anne street names, including many still in use, reflected such personal visions as: a) Family ties (Thomas Street for David Denny's second son, Thomas); b) Political beliefs (Temperance Street became Queen Anne Avenue south of Galer, north of Galer it was Villard Avenue; Republican Street was named for Denny's political party); c) Land developers' promotional names (Etruria, Florentia); and d) Hoped for civic development (Depot Street, now Denny Way, for a hoped for railroad terminal).

The lack of a systematic naming policy, duplications of names by land developers throughout the city, and resulting confusion for postal, fire and police departments led, in 1895, to a widespread renaming of Seattle's streets. Listed here are the Queen Anne area old and new street names. The list, from city and newspaper records, does not contain every such name change nor any changes made in recent decades. It does, however, show the imagination of our ancestors who built this community on the hill.

| ORIGINAL NAME | PRESENT NAME |
|---|---|
| Allee St. | Ward/Kinnear Pl./Olympic Pl./ Aloha |
| Anna St. | 5th Ave. W. |
| Arthur St. | Barrett St. |
| Ash St. | Nob Hill N. |
| Baltimore St. | Armour St. |
| Banner St. | 1st Ave. W. |
| Benjamin St. | Lee St. |
| Birch St. | Taylor Ave. N. |
| Blaine St. | Hayes/Garfield Sts. |
| Bluff St. | Olympic Pl. |
| Bowman St. | 5th Ave. N. |
| Box St. | 4th Ave. N. |
| Bradley St. | Highland Ave. (west side) |
| Clay St. | Crockett St. |
| Cleveland St. | Armour St. |
| Cove St. | 12th Ave. W. |
| Crawford St. (Mt. Pleasant Cemetery) | 4th Ave. W. |
| Decatur St. | Denny Way |
| Denny St. | Barrett St. |
| Depot St. | Denny Way |
| Dexter St. | Dexter Ave. |

| ORIGINAL NAME | PRESENT NAME |
|---|---|
| Diomeda St. | Galer St. |
| Division St. | Howe St. |
| Elliott St. | 7th Ave./Kinnear Pl. |
| Farm St. | Aurora Ave./7th Ave. N. |
| Farragut St. | Highland Ave. (east side) |
| Filbert St. | Valley St. |
| Front St. | Elliott Ave. |
| Garfield St. | Ray St.* |
| Gayler St. | Galer St. |
| George Ave. | 3rd Ave. N. |
| Gould Ave. | 1st Ave. W. |
| Grand Blvd. | Dravus St. |
| Grant St. | Bay/9th Ave. W. |
| Hawthorne St. | Denny Way |
| High St. | Aloha/Kinnear Pl./Olympic Pl. |
| Jacobs Ave. | Warren Ave. |
| Jackson St. | Emerson St. |
| James St. | Blaine St. |
| Jesse St. | Howe St. |
| Kearney St. | 2nd Ave. N. |
| Kentucky St. | 1st Ave. N. |
| Lake Union Blvd | Westlake Ave. |
| Lakeview Ave. | 4th Avenue N. |
| Law St./Law's Ave. | 11th Ave. W. |
| Lawrence St. | 10th Ave. N. |
| Leary Ave./St. | 9th Ave. W. |
| Massachusetts St. | Lee St. |
| Light St. | 2nd Ave. W. |
| Lombard St. | 6th Ave. N. |
| Lynn St. | McGraw St. |
| Madison St. | Aurora Ave. |
| Manitoba Ave. | Newell St. |
| Marion (Marietta) | 4th Ave. W. |
| Montgomery St. | 2nd Ave. N./3rd Ave. N. |
| Oak St. | 3rd Ave. N. |
| Olympia Ave. | Olympic Pl. |
| Orange Ave. | 2nd Ave. N. |
| Orion St. | 9th Ave. N. |
| Park St. | 8th Ave. N. |
| Payne St. | Lee St. |
| Pennsylvania Ave. | Lee St. |
| Poplar St. | 2nd Ave. N./3rd Ave. N. |
| Powell St. | Prospect St. |
| Prohibition Ave. | Fairview Ave. |
| Quilcene St. | Howe St. |
| Quimper St. | Garfield St. |

| ORIGINAL NAME | PRESENT NAME |
|---|---|
| Ridgely Ave. | 10th Ave. W. |
| Rollin St. | Westlake Ave. |
| Roy St. | Thomas St./Roy St. |
| Scott St. | Armour St. |
| Scurry St. | 5th Ave. W. |
| Seattle St. | Ray St.* |
| Smith St./Smith's Ave. | 10th Ave. W. |
| Smithers Ave. | Taylor Ave. |
| Stacy Ave./St. | 8th Ave. W. |
| Swim St. | Comstock St. |
| Temperance St. | Queen Anne Ave. south of Galer |
| Thomas Ave./St. | Roy St. |
| Vanderbuilt Ave. | 1st Ave. N. |
| Victory St. | 3rd Ave. W. |
| View St. | Highland Ave. |
| Villard Ave. | Queen Anne Ave. |
| Villard St. | Ward St. |
| Vine St. | 8th Ave. N. |
| Warren St. | Warren Ave. |
| Wheeling Ave. | Blaine St. |
| White St. | 6th Avenue West |
| Wiley Ave. | 10th Ave. W. |
| William St. | 14th Ave. W. |
| Willow St. | 5th Ave. N. |
| Woodland Ave. | 4th Ave. N. |
| 1st Street | Aurora Ave. |
| 3rd Ave. E. | 15th Ave. W. |
| 3rd Street | Blaine St. |
| 4th Ave. E. | 14th Ave. W. |
| 4th St. | Howe St. |
| 5th Ave E. | 13th Ave. W. |
| 5th St. | Crockett St. |
| 6th Ave. E. | 12th Ave. W. |
| 6th St. | Boston St. |
| 7th Ave. E. | 11th Ave. W. |
| 7th St. | Ray St.* |
| 7th St. | McGraw St. |
| 8th St. | Smith St. |
| 9th St. | Ray St.* |

**Ray became Raye because of post office confusion with Roy*

# The Trolley Club

Quorum Real Estate

Best Plumbing

Nadine Belcher

Phil and Mickey Canan Howard

Butterworth's Arthur A. Wright

Robert W. Frazier

Queen Anne Thriftway

Roger & Susan Belanich

L. Dankers Real Estate Group /
Apple Property Management

Fay Johnson

John S. Murray

Read Products, Inc.

Seattle Mortgage Company

The Queen Anne Historical Society is extremely grateful to the above contributors for their donations of $500 to the Queen Anne History Book Project.

*Kinnear Park Trolley—early 1900*
*Courtesy Queen Anne Historical Society*

# The Counterbalance Club

Marqueen Garage
Hobb's Hilltop Automotive
Frederick V. Betts
A & J Meats & Seafoods
Nancy's Sewing Basket
Key Bank
Metcalf Real Estate

Jas. J. Backer Co.
Russell V. Hokanson
Queen Anne Pharmacy, Inc.
Queen Anne Avenue Books
Mecca Cafe
Video Isle
Sorry Charlie's Restaurant

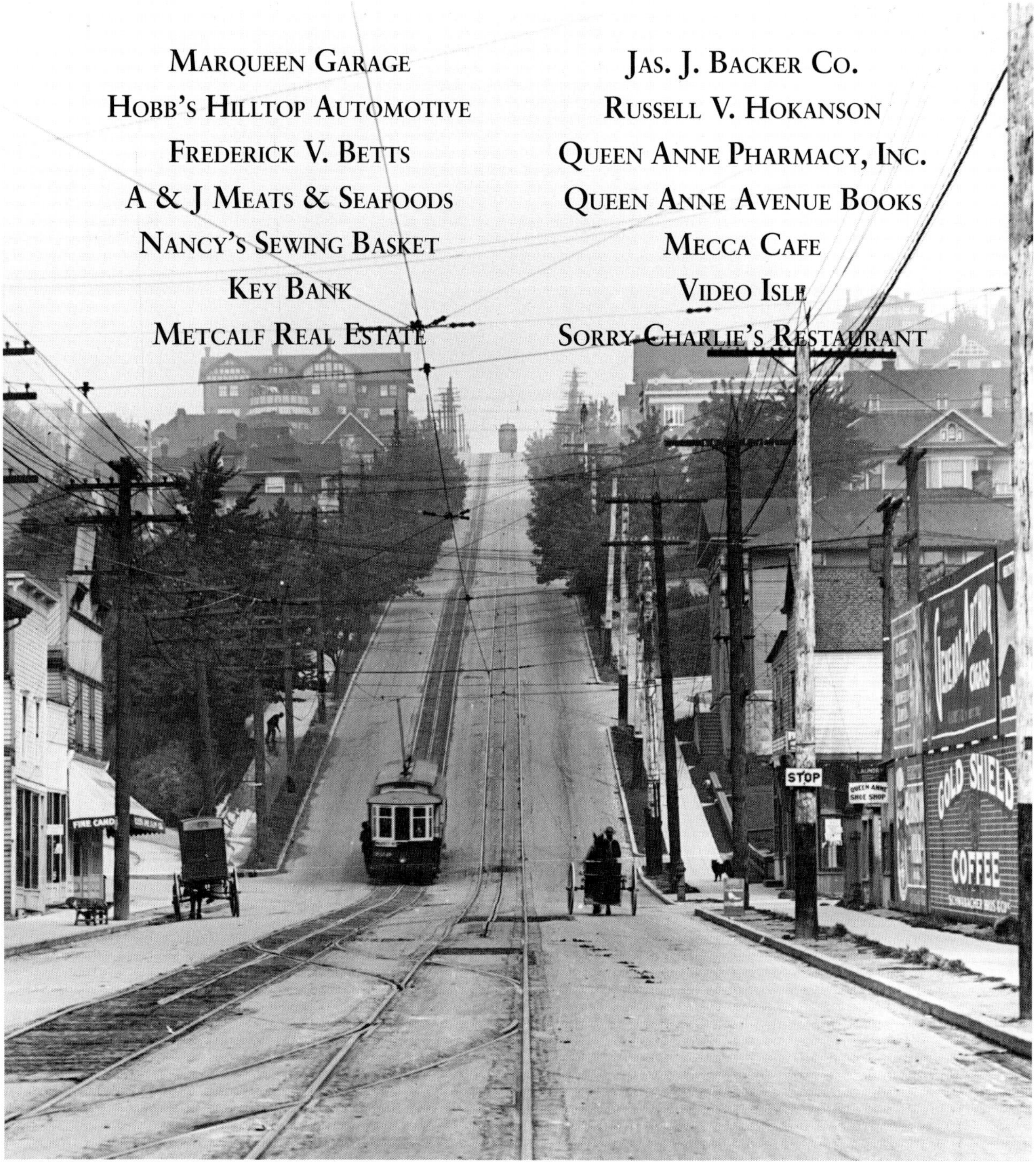


*Early photo of Queen Anne Avenue North. "The Counterbalance"—1910. Courtesy Museum of History and Industry.*

A hearty thank you to the above donors
who contributed $250 to the
Queen Anne History Book project.

# Queen Anne Boosters

**DAVE PRINDLE'S BOSTONIAN BARBER SHOP**
11 Boston St. 286-1477
Mon - Fri 10 - 7, Sat 10 - 3

**SUNRISE AT QUEEN ANNE**
A retirement community—
Independent living with support services
2450 Aurora Ave. N. 282-5777

**PROVIDENCE MEDICAL CARE CENTER**
Queen Anne—Family practice in your neighborhood
2211 Queen Anne Ave. N. 283-1842

**NANCY'S SEWING BASKET**
One stop sewing center
2221 Queen Anne Ave. N.
282-9112

**O'HARA'S PET CENTRE**
"Pets & their supplies"
4 Boston St. 285-6503

**QUEEN ANNE MANOR**
Retirement community offering assisted/catered living
100 Crockett St. 282-5001

**READ PRODUCTS, INC.**
A family owned business since 1945
3615 15th Ave. W. 283-2510

**SENATOR JOHN S. MURRAY**
Murray Publishing Co.
1963 - 1990

**DR. MICHAL FRIEDRICH, D.D.S.**
Family Dentistry
14 Boston St. 284-2136

**PISTON SERVICE OF WESTLAKE**
Your complete auto parts store
1420 Queen Anne Ave. N.
282-9900

**US BANK**
530 Dexter Ave. N.
Seattle 98109 344-2383

**DEXTER DELI**
The Brannon Family
30 years of service to Queen Anne
1201 Dexter Ave. N.
284-5508

**HOUSE OF PAINTINGS**
Red Skelton Collection
619 Queen Anne Ave. N.
282-8727

**TOM LIVENGOOD DESIGN**
An architectural and interior design firm specializing in the renovation of Queen Anne's older homes.
6 1/2 Boston St., Suite #8
282-9795

**UNIVERSITY SAVINGS BANK**
First in customer service
1600 Queen Anne Ave. N.
282-8787

**KIWANIS CLUB OF DOWNTOWN SUNRISERS**
"We build through community service!"
100 Wall St. (206) 932-7698

**QUORUM REAL ESTATE**
On the "Hill"
Quorum is Queen Anne
320 W. Galer 281-8000

**WILLIAM A. BAIN, ASSOC.**
Serving Queen Anne & The Greater Seattle Area since 1972
1200 Westlake Ave. N. #406
283-5200

**BEST PLUMBING**
Proudly serving Queen Anne since 1968

**BAYVIEW MANOR**
Gracious living in a garden setting
11 W. Aloha 284-7330

**SHERWOOD FOREST**
"Queen Anne's Full Service Florist for 20 years."
2215 Queen Anne Ave. N.
284-1077

**RAFAEL CARRABBA VIOLINS, INC.**
Member of the American Federation of Violin and Bow Makers
405 W. Galer (206) 283-5566

**RHINESTONE ROSIE**
Vintage and Costume Jewelry
Repair & Sales
606 W. Crockett 283-4605

**RELIABLE CLEANERS**
on Queen Anne since 1920
619 W. McGraw
282-0272

**A & J MEATS & SEAFOODS**
A family owned business since 1951
Queen Anne Ave. & McGraw St.
284-3885

**STANDARD BAKERY**
"A Queen Anne Tradition Since 1930"
No. 2 Boston St. 283-6359

**SAFEWAY PHARMACY**
Expect The Best
2100 Q.A. Ave. N. 284-4226

**FIVE CORNERS HARDWARE CO.**
Family Owned Since 1940
305 W. McGraw 282-5000

**BIRKELAND & ASSOCIATES**
Real estate management since 1972
1321 Queen Anne Ave. N., suite B
285-1835

**RON METCALF**
Certified Residential Broker
Since 1973. Experience
Makes A Difference
When It Comes to Good Advice.
Quorum Real Estate 281-8000

**JAMES KEMP-SLAUGHTER, ASA**
P.O. Box 19704 Queen Anne Sta.
Seattle, WA 98109 285-5711
Antiques and Fine Art
Appraised Since 1977

**NATHANIEL BELO**
323 W. Raye St, Seattle
Quorum Real Estate - Buy & Sell
With a Queen Anne Native
281-8000 282-3336

**QUEEN ANNE PHARMACY, INC.**
Chuck & Karen Paulsen
601 W. McGraw 282-2888

**KILDALL AGENCY**
Since 1938
610 W. McGraw (206) 282-1230

**APPLE PROPERTY MGT.**
L. Dankers Real Estate
Management & Real Estate Service
of Quality & Professionalism
285-2352 / 285-2333

**FLAIR FOR HAIR**
A Friendly & Caring Atmosphere
1901 Queen Anne Ave. N.
282-5318

**SI-RO'S**
We groom all breeds since 1968
1422 Queen Anne Ave. N.
283-4996

**LOU'S LIVE JUICES**
Fresh squeezed juices made
just for you!
1523 Queen Anne Ave. N.
283-4208

**THE QUEEN ANNE COFFEE HOUSE**
A place to meet friends or curl up
with a good book. Come in and
hang out.
1625 Queen Anne Ave. N.
281-1931

**BODY WORKS MASSAGE**
"Body Works"
... if yours doesn't, I can help.
Professional healing specializing
in injury treatment.
Lori Bielinski, LMP
2 Nickerson St. Suite 103 284-7811

**CREATIONS IN GOLD**
Custom Jewelry Design
9 Mercer St. 283-3614

**DON-DIANE FUN TOURS**
One day & longer escorted tours
& cruises. Our 20th year.
508 2nd Ave. W. 282-3508

**PHOTOMASTER**
Fast quality film processing
1519 Queen Anne Ave. 282-2040

**UPTOWN SALON**
Full service hair care for men
& women
515 Queen Anne Ave. N. 282-9333

**STARBUCKS COFFEE COMPANY**
Glad to be part of Queen Anne
2201 Queen Anne Ave. N 285-3711

**WILD SALMON MARKET**
Premium Fresh Seafood
Fishermen's Terminal 282-2407

**RUDD COMPANY, INC.**
Since 1912
1630 15th W. 284-5657

**BENLA WATER HEATERS**
Since 1944
3008 16th Ave. W. 283-7676

**TEACUP**
Mary Noe, 20-year QA resident
Specializing in tea, tea pots,
& tea related items.
2207 Queen Anne Ave. N.
283-5931

**TSUBOTA INDUSTRIAL SUPPLY CO., INC.**
A family owned business since 1934
1837 15th Avenue W.
282-1844

**BARTELL DRUGS**
Locally owned & operated
since 1890.
23 Mercer Street 284-1353

**CITY CATS**
Seattle's favorite cat collectible store.
1509 Queen Anne Avenue N.

**"LIKE A GOOD NEIGHBOR"**
Chuck Dagg - State Farm Ins.
3206 16th Ave. W. 285-3003

**THE MOUNTAINEERS**
A great place for lunch or a meeting.
300 Third Ave. W. 281-7775

**VIDEO ISLE**
Your friendly neighborhood video
store.
2213 Queen Anne Ave. N.
285-9511

**QUEEN ANNE CHAMBER OF COMMERCE**
Serving Queen Anne from top
to bottom.

**GUADALAJARA HACIENDA**
"Fine Mexican Dining"
1531 Queen Anne Ave. N.
283-0788

**QUEEN ANNE ANIMAL CLINIC**
Quality health care for your pets
since 1971
1800 Queen Anne Ave. N.
284-2148

**OLYMPIC PIZZA**
The Best Pizza In Town
1500 Queen Anne Ave. N.
285-5550

**MUSEUM QUALITY DISCOUNT FRAMING**
Your affordable custom framer
on Queen Anne
1905 Queen Anne Ave. N.
285-9656

**13 BOSTON HAIR DESIGN**
Quality Hair & Skin Care
13 Boston St.
282-3377

**FIRST FREE METHODIST CHURCH**
Celebrating 112 years of history
3200 3rd Ave. W. 281-2240

**THE STEWART SALON**
16 years of quality service with quality staff - come and feel good!
1501 Queen Anne Ave. N.
285-6301

**BEECH TREE MANOR BED & BREAKFAST**
"A Queen Anne Tradition"
1405 Queen Anne Ave. N.
281-7037

**SINGER GALLERIES**
Antiques & Appraisals since 1981
1621 Queen Anne Ave. N.
285-0394

**ERNEST JONSON & CO., P.S.**
Certified Public Accountants
216 Queen Anne Ave. N.
285-2100

**RON'S COBBLER SHOPPE**
Full service shoe repair
2131 Queen Anne Ave. N. 283-1031

**SOFT COVERINGS**
Home Fabric Specialist
323 W. Galer St. 286-7638

**RAZZ M'TAZZ**
Seattle's finest consignment boutique
623 Queen Anne Ave. N. 281-7900

**HOME BUILDERS CENTER**
For all your building needs
1110 W. Nickerson 283-6060

**S & M MARKET 1933 - 1988**
Morris Mezistrano, one of the best known persons on the Hill.
Queen Anne Ave. & Boston

**COUNTERBALANCE BARBER SHOP**
Precision haircuts since 1910.
Len Hagardt
1424 Queen Anne Ave. N. 284-3162

**QUEEN ANNE CAFE**
A good place to eat
2121 Queen Anne Ave. N.
286-1421

**STARR CHIROPRACTIC CENTER**
Chiropractic for your health.
Deborah Starr-Neal
8 W. Mercer 281-7827

**THOMAS G. ROBERTS, DDS**
We offer optimum dental care in a comfortable, relaxed environment.
100 W. Harrison, N. Tower,
Suite 150 284-4412

**NORTHWEST MILLWORK**
Manufacturer of custom millwork, doors & cabinetry.
360 W. Nickerson 284-6440

**REED WRIGHT HEATING CO.**
Service since 1938
2212 Queen Anne Ave. N.
283-1234

**QUEEN ANNE MAIL & DISPATCH**
"The Best Little Shipper in Seattle"
1509 Queen Anne Ave. N.
286-1024

**UNITED SOUTH SLOPE RESIDENTS**
Proud to be part of Queen Anne's history
510 W. Prospect 282-7493

**BLACKSTOCK LUMBER CO.**
Quality millwork & lumber since 1912.
1039 Elliott Ave. W. 284-1313

**WERNER'S CRASH SHOP**
Same location since 1974
710 Taylor N. 285-0780

**TOP CUSTOM CLEANERS**
Quality Cleaning on Top of the Hill
1617 Queen Anne Ave. N.
284-1433

**QUEEN ANNE 7 - 11**
Twenty four hour convenience
1607 Queen Anne Ave. N.
284-8166

**DR. ZEENY TEJA**
Smile with style - orthodontics for all ages
1805 Queen Anne Ave. N.
285-7755

**SEAFIRST BANK**
Expect Excellence
100 W. Mercer St.
358-1909

**SORRY CHARLIE'S RESTAURANT**
Home style dinners - piano bar
529 Queen Anne Ave. N. 283-3245

**THE HERBFARM**
Enjoy everything herbal from our farm in Fall City
1629 Queen Anne Ave. N.
284-5667

**THE HOMING INSTINCT**
Essential tools for homemaking
1622 Queen Anne Ave. N.
281-9260

**MECCA CAFE**
Oldest family owned cafe & lounge in Seattle - since 1929
Dick & Darlene Smith
526 Queen Anne Ave. N. 285-9728

**ALPHAGRAPHICS**
Printshops of the future.
402 Cedar Street 448-9100

**WESTSIDE STORIES BOOKSTORE**
Used, rare, out of print, book searches
12 Boston 285-2665

**QUEEN ANNE BP SERVICE**
Serving your automotive needs since 1973
1929 Queen Anne Ave. N.
282-0462

**KEY BANK**
America's neighborhood bank
434 Queen Anne Ave. N.
447-5733

**F.T. CROWE BUILDING**
329 2nd Avenue W.

# Queen Anne Cobblestone Family Album

Queen Anne Ecumenical
Parish, Formed 1920
Chartered 1969

In memory of Nicholas
Belanich who came to
Queen Anne in 1897

Les Bleiler - QA '53
Grateful for supportive
parents, many friends

Fond memories at Interbay,
Coe, Q.A. High 1919 - 1928
Wm. H. Holm

In memory of
Florence Spaulding Nordstrom
Queen Anne Class - 1915

Van R. Peirson
School Tennis Champion
1926

Chuck & Mary McGrew
Ole & Russ Carlson
1835 7th Ave. W.

In memory of
Betty Bowen

Eddie A. Bolton Family
Queen Anne residents
1900 - 1915

Jeanne Kohl, State Rep
36th District
January 13, 1992

Donna Moriarty Family
Queen Anne classes
'52, '76, '77, '78, '81

Sarah Ellison &
Douglas Fischer,
Marion 1988 - Mark 1991

Pauline Runnels
Sue, Dave, George,
Eileen, Chris & Paul

The Queen Anne Helpline
People helping people
Since 1982

A light on top of the hill
Q.A. Baptist Church
2011 1st N. 282-7744

Honoring grandparents
Martin & Cassandra Marston
(arrived in) 1898 in Queen Anne

With happy memories of
Richard Dwyer
Q.A. resident 1972 - 1991

Krijn, Judy & Saskia
de Jonge
Residents since 1984

In memory of Oscar
and Mary Welden
From their son

Six Stones say "Hurrah"
Jim - Eline - Claire -
Sig - Hank - Dorothy

Part of the spirit of Queen Anne
since 1906
St. Anne's Catholic Church
1411 1st Ave. W.

John & Margaret Hennes
May Queen Anne
live long and prosper!

Anne / Charles Hoen
Reliable Cleaners
619 W. McGraw
11/17/52–4/13/91

The Bartlett Family
Fred - Ida - Erla - Beth
416 Halladay

Judith Rogers Dearden
St. Anne's, Queen Anne 1954
Mensan, two children

Don, We Miss
You a lot!
Love, Mona & Dave

Graduate John Hay
Queen Anne High School
(Jan. 1954)
Mildred Excell Olson

The Loacker Family
Walde, Arlyne, Lynn and John

Carrol (Sutton) Read
"Aloha" to the 1954
Queen Anne graduates!

Anne Anderson Questad
Kuay '44
Teacher of Piano

Hugh DeLacy, Statesman
Remembered with love by
daughter, Margaret DeLacy

Wilcox Family
John Hay Grade
Queen Anne High
Before 1892-1931

Wm. & Etta Ardery
Lycurgus & Malinda Ardery
1890's - 1920's

Family of
Judge Charles P. Moriarty
1932

Begg Family
West Queen Anne Grade
Queen Anne High 1911

In memory of
Chief John Brittain
Seattle Fire Dept.

Richard Stark
QAH class of
1963

Wyeth Barclay
Born July 7, 1983
1107 7th West, Seattle

Jean Beegle Yardy ('42)
Panama, Sports, Teacher, SPC
Wes, Cynthia, Gordon

Dick & Jan Manning Family
Bruce, Brian, Patty,
Ann & Mike

Dee (Simmons) Hepworth
QA - '43
Living in Spokane since 1954

Arthur Whitehill Family
Arthur, Henrietta, Jane, Allan
& Richard – 35 years

The Metcalf Family
Ron & Sheila, Liz & Emily
Since 1973

In memory of
Rachel Okerlund (Ernst)
Class of 1919

Bruce Johnson, Paige Miller
and Marta, Winslow and
Russell Johnson

In memory of
Michael Kemp-Slaughter
Past President of the
Queen Anne Historical Society

Queen Anne pioneers
Mort & Cassandra Marston
leave 77 descendants

Helen Sommers, Representative
First elected by Q.A. in
November, 1972

Reg, Arloa, Sidney
and Kim Turner,
Q.A. residents 1940+
(QA -'59) (QA -'61)

In memoriam
Josie Gore Healy and
Frank J. Healy

Bethel & Jim Savino
Married Aug. 8, 1942

Kuay Forever
Kelley Canan Wood '77;
MikeCanan '64;
Tim Canan '66

Also attended
Queen Anne High School
Gertrude Sawyer Canan '17;
Donald J. Canan '40

Howard Jensen '39
"Broken Promises,
Shattered Dreams"
Ellen Schille '40

Aegea Barclay
Born July 29, 1985
700 W. Lee, Seattle

The Belo Family
Gasat & Perla
Nathan & Ariele

What endures is
what matters
AAF & GRH

The Willson Family 1975-Present
Bettina & Richard
Stuart, Duncan & Vanessa

James Etue Family
Residents Queen Anne 40 yrs.
Attended St. Anne's

In memory of Graham & Grace
Betts who moved to 700 W.
Kinnear Pl. in 1906

The Anderson Family
QA High School - Corinne '29
Gary '58, Grover '61, Connie '63

"The Yenter Famiy"
Bill - Sharon
Ben - Jason

The Bush Family
Bill, Janet, Anne & Jane
Since 1974

Dolores Graham Doyle
Queen Anne High
Class of '46

Steve Ordal Family
Proud owners on
Nob Hill since 1976

The Lewis Family
David, Susie, Andrew
and Torrey

Tom Walsh - Elaine Winters
David Winters Walsh
1415 7th West

N.D. Johnson, Contractor
503 - 504 Pioneer Bldg.
1900 - 1911

Maternal Grandparents
Charles & Florence Morse
1909 - 1944

In memory of
John B. Mullally Family
Helen Jean Mullally

J. Dean Henderson, Jr.
Family residents
1951 - 1987

Bonnevie Family
Robert, Karen, Karl
on "the Hill" since 1970

Storey Family
B.J., Jo Ann, Jon, Paul,
Pamela & Melissa - 1950

Anderson - Hall
Four Generations
1928 - present

Love to all my grandparents
near 8th & Halladay
Curtis Sandy

Will Clan - Q.A. Alums
Ed 1942, Hal 1944,
Doug 1974

The Oien Family
Willard, Ione, Marilynne, Ardyth,
Lorene, Keith & Ronald
since 1941

Betty Jorgensen
Remembered with love by
daughter, Margaret DeLacy

Bill & Peggy Laney
Jane '48 - Bill '50
Sallie '52

The Sobeck Family
Don, Pat, Susan,
Steven & Garry

Tallant
Millard "Tal" James
DeAnn Miller Markham
Joy Amanda 1984

Paul Birkeland & Family
Affiliated with
Queen Anne since 1948

Anne Marie Stark
QAH class of
1966

We love Queen Anne
1962 - 1991
Dick & Vivian Hedrich

O God our help in ages past
Queen Anne Lutheran Church
Since 1918

Thomas Lister Samuelson Family
Lister, Alice, Terry, Jeri, Tom, Fred, Trig & Beth
on 10th West 1912 - 1989

The Joe Daniels Family
Queen Anne residents
1941 - 1991

A proud "class of 1949"
Queen Anne Graduate
Bob Houbregs

Miriam T. Askren
She loved children
1892-1988

Berg Family Graduates
Norman '42; Kimberly '59;
Knute '62;Karin '67; Janice '68;
Jean M. Wood '44

1st Lt. Maylon D. Price
Korea
Queen Anne 1940

Denny Carmichael '43
Donna Clark '50
Retired on Orcas Island

Carl Ramberg & Karen Richeson
are proud to be
Grizzlies

The Williams Family
Since 1942
John, Astrid, Joan, Western

Greetings from Oregon
Molly Sylvester Saul
Class of 1937

In remembrance of
Earl & Helen Condie
Claire Condie Bigbie

The Van Valey Family
Roger & Ann
Carla, Ruth, Roger, John

Q.A.'s First Orchestra Violinists
Lotta Wilson - 1914
Icia Wilson - 1915

Roy Kinnear Family
Since 1885

Carol McHenry Strom '43
my love forever!
Jack Strom '41

The Etue Family
In memory of Dad
1952 - Present

In memory of Martin Budinich
who came to
Queen Anne in 1900

The Ketcham Family
Queen Anne Residents
1924 - 1938

Hagman-Ryan Family
Queen Anne residents
1956 - present

Last owner D.B. Ward mansion
Paul F. Rosser, Sr. Family

Florence Ekstrand, Editor
Queen Anne News
1966 - 1980

In memory of James and
Ali-Lou Frazier

The Walls Family
Burt, Ralene, Preston,
Annie and Goldie

3rd and 4th Q.A. generations
Chuck, Linda, Eric,
Mark Dagg

We love Queen Anne too
Leyrer Family
Mavis, Bill & Libby

The Marks Family
Sandy, Chuck & Diane

Grace & Elmer Weaver 1922 - 37
Union Oil Co. & Q.A. Baptist
Church, Betty Weaver '35,
Margie Weaver '37
& Carolyn Weaver '38

In memory of Gladys Brittain,
mother ofJune (1942) and
Dorothy (1939)

Luft Clan - QA Alums
Patrick Spencer - 1956
Carol Jean - 1967

The Alhadeff Family
Joseph, Doreen,
Loren & Mitchell

Griffins Wallaces Densmores
1904 1946 1973
111 Tower Place

"The Wee Kirk on the Hill"
Queen Anne Presbyterian Church
414 W. Howe 283-6644

In memory of Bill &
Dorothy Burrow
Since 1973

Hokanson Family
Russ & Millie
Connie, Erika, Alicia, Sarah,
Russ Jr., Johanna

Gene M. Uttinger
Queen Anne resident
since 1982

Jackie Cedarholm since 1937
in memory of mother
Glen Morgan Cedarholm

Leanne Olson and Jim Bailey
1524 Seventh Avenue West

The Hanover Family
since 1946
In memory of Pauline
Hanover

1939 - 1993
Queen Anne Garden Club
salutes "The Book"

Seeking Light - Sharing Love
Queen Anne United
Methodist Church
Since 1892

Best wishes to the Queen Anne
Community
From Dr. Zeeny Teja

Eda M. Goodwin Circle,
Seattle Milk Fund, helping our
community since 1952

Shdo's have called Q.A. home
for four generations - what
memories!

To Jennifer, Tom & Dymphna
with love, Ma

Wally Barrow &
Josie Browne Barrow - QA '48

Elmer & Marguerite Salladay
Suzanne - Drake - Peter - Paul
Queen Anne 1943 - ??

In loving memory of
John & Rhoda Campbell
Q.A. residents 1941 - 91

Steve and Inez Selak Family
South Slope residents since 1932

Queen Anne Manor
A residential retirement
community
100 Crockett St 282-5001

Westenberg Family
Roy, Sylvia, Christine, Grant

From the Kildalls
Bob, Ruth, Katie (Bucy),
Maria & Kristian

Willia Sutherland
Q.A. supporter 1947 - 1990

Kelly & Toner
with love from
Mike, Andrea, Connor & Sean

In loving memory of my wife,
Emmilla Dagg.
Ralph Dagg

Frank Pracna '31 & Mary Jane
Tvete '35 married - 1937

Boy Scout Troop 70:
Oldest on Queen Anne Hill

Lewis Arthur Wallon
Mary Gove Wallon
to Queen Anne, 1908

Sacred Heart Catholic Church
since 1889

Interbay Evangelical
Covenant Church
Serving Q.A. - Magnolia since '42
3233 15th W.

Q.A. Hill since 1920
Roberta House Gadberry,
Q.A. Alum '37

Our Home Since 1988
Bernard, Carole, Celeste,
Benjamin Jalbert-Jones

Arthur, Dean & Loretta
Morgan –
Queen Anne residents.

Mr. & Mrs. M. Brace
Humor, Life & Love
Married Sept. 24, 1977

In memory of
Mary E. Gustafson
Emory O. Gustafson KUAY 1936

You're the tops, Queen Anne!
Patricia Paquette

Miles Family
Don, Pamela, Katherine,
Lesley & Nicole
Residents since 1976

In memory of Betty Galbraith
Beloved longtime resident

In memory
Margaret Hamlin House
Burt House, Q.A. since 1920

I remember St. Anne's
& riding the Counterbalance
1928 - 1937
Gene Schroers

Jerry, Sharee & Kristen Olson
Kody & Eileen Lyons
Since 1973

Boy Scout Troop 65:
The Grand masterwork of
Clark E. Schurman

Boy Scout Troop 72:
Serving Queen Anne Boys
since June, 1919.

In memory of Betty Heeter
Queen Anne Resident
1904-1987

T.J.A.K. & M.A.K.
In love on
Queen Anne Hill

We love Queen Anne
Harry & June Delaloye
Tropics Motel 1958 - 1976

The Brickell Family
Ruby, T.L., Christine & Tim
Since the 40's

The Killions:
Judy, Gerry, Laura, Mike, Gail
1945–?

# INDEX


A & J Meats, 163
A & P Grocery, 114
A Contemporary Theatre (ACT), 147, 182
Aasten, Molly, 164
Aasten's Grocery, 164
Abbott, Dr. H. Mark, 145
Abbott, Martin, 11
*Across the Plains in 1853*, 19, 20
ACT. *see* A Contemporary Theatre
Adams, Roland E., 180, 189
*Addie* (barge), 55
*Advocate* (newspaper), 183
Affiliation Exchange Progam (AFEX), 133
Agnew, Henry Clay, 122
air defense during WWII, 188
air raid precautions, 113
Aladdin apartments. *see* Triplet apartments
Alaska Yukon Pacific Exposition, 94, 168
Albertson, A.H., 154
Alexander Hall, 137
Alexander Hamilton apartments, 172
Allen, Brian. *see* Israel, Logic
Allen (John B.) School, 156
Aloha House, 172
Aloha Street apartments, 172
Aloha Street Substation, 93
Aloha Terrace apartments, 172, 174
Al's Hamburger Shop, 110, 162
Amalfi apartments, 169, 170, 172
American Cancer Society, 114, 154
American Indian Movement, 11
American Indian Policy Review Commission, 11
American Indian Women's Service League, 10
American Legion. Queen Anne Post, 180
Amherst apartments. *see* Triplet apartments
Anderson, B. Roy, 114
Anderson, Chris, 163
Anderson, Edwin, 165
Anderson, Josephine, 165
Anderson, Mr.(of Standard Bakery), 161
Anderson, Ralph, 123
Anhalt, Fred, 170, 171, 172
Anhalt Mediterranean apartments, 172
Animal Control Center, 93
Ankeny, Rudolf, 10
Ankeny House, 10
Anti-Tuberculosis League, 155
Apex Dairy, 90
architectural styles, 10, 62, 82, 84, 105, 123-124, 128, 167-177, 190
Arnhart, Warren, 131
Arnold, Kurt, 165
Art Marble Company, 190
arts organizations, 182
Asian Scholar's Garden, 129
Aspasia Club, 100
Assemblies of God. Northwest District Council, 147
Astor, John Jacob, 13
Atkins, Emma. *see* Smith, Emma Atkins
Atkins, Henry, 151
Atlantic Street Center, 155
Auditorium Field. *see* Civic Field
Augustine and Kyer (store), 159
Aurora Bridge, 107
Avon Club, 69

Bagley, Alice Mercer, 15, 18, 22, 27, 39, 40, 45, 48, 49, 70, 71, 127
Bagley, Clarence, 56, 60
  on growth of area, 35, 59
  and herbal medicine, 19
  early settler, 15, 16, 18
  education and marriage, 39, 40
  home, 62, 83
  Mt. Pleasant Cemetery, 188, 189
  supports women's suffrage, 70
Bagley, Daniel, 18, 19, 37, 39, 43, 62, 189
Bagley, Susannah Whipple, 18, 189
Bagley Wright Theater, 116, 121
Bailey, Arthur, 184
Bailey, James, 109
Bailey, Winona, 132
Baily, Almira, 96
Baker, Clarence, 161
Baker, Josephine, 150
Baker, Willard O., 133
Ballard/Howe House, 185
Ballard Mansion, 185
Banks, Austin, 162
Banks and Mock Bakers. *see* McGraw Street Bakery
Barnard, Curtis, 112, 184
Barnum amd Bailey circus, 103
Bartell's, 114
Bartlett, Jon, 185
Bartol, Ernest, 129
Bass, Sophia Frye, 189
Battery Street Methodist Episcopal Church. *see* Queen Anne Methodist Episcopal Church
Battle of Seattle (1856), 31, 95
Bauders, Mary M., 162-163
Baxter, Marion Babcock, 152
Bayview Manor Retirement Residence, 118, 157, 172, 175
Beardsley, John, 171
Beattie, John, 98
Bebb & Mandel (builders), 168
Beck, Julian, 179
Beeler Plan for transportation, 112
Beers, Adelaide, 136
Beers, Alexander, 136, 137
Belanich family, 124
Belcourt, Gene, 180
Bell, Sarah, 60
Bell, William, 22, 23, 60
Ben Franklin Grocery and Meats, 163
Bert & Lou's Barber shop, 165
Bethany-Queen Anne Foodbank, 140, 142, 148
Bethany United Presbyterian Church, 137, 139, 140, 142, 148, 185, 190
Bethel party, 18, 19, 40
"Better Halves, The", 181
Better Homes in America Committee, 100
Bettinger, Mary E., 150
Betts, Fred, 97, 159
"Bhy" Kracke Park, 116, 117
bicycles, 83
Bigelow, Isaac N., 66, 71
Bigelow's First, Second additions, 66, 74
Bihary, Chris, 165
Bihary, Jane, 165
birds, 54
Bishop, Bob, 99
Bite of McClure, 132
Bite of Seattle, 121
Bittman, Henry, 189
Black, Emilia, 96
Black and White Boys Club, 179

Black (C.H.) House & Gardens, 185
Blackstock, Carl, 165, 166
Blackstock, Carl, Jr., 165
Blackstock, Jim, 165
Blackstock, Ray, 165
Blackstock, Scott, 165
Blackstock Lumber Co., 116, 165
Blaine, Catherine, 189
Blaine, David, 189
Blaine (Catherine) Junior High School, 131
Blaine's (Catherine) home school, 127
Blanke, Martha. *see* Churchill, Martha Blanke
Bleitz, Jacob J., 190
Bleitz, James C., 190
Bleitz, Lawrence L., 190
Bleitz Funeral Home, 190
Blethen, Alden, 105
Blewett, Carrie, 64
Blewett, Edward, 64
Blind Peoples' Fishing Derby, 180
Bluebirds (Campfire Girls), 179
Bock, Henry, 148
Boeing Company, 114, 116, 121
Boeing Field, 1, 13
Bolcom Canal Lumber Co., 76
Boren, Billie, 45, 49, 50
Boren, Carson, 28, 29, 50
Boren, Gertrude, 41
Boren, Louisa. see Denny, Louisa Boren
Boren (Louisa) Park, 56
Bovard, Della, 180
Bowen, Betty, 118
Bowen, Leola, 111
Bowen (Betty) Viewpoint, 95, 185
Bowen/Huston Bungalow, 185
Bowman, C.E., 78
Bowman, Mr., 43
Bowman fire, 79
Boxley, David, 11
Boy Scout troops No.65,70,72, 179
Brace/Moriarty House, 185
Brazean, Elizabeth Wallon, 101
Bretz, J. Harlan, 9, 132
Brewer, Barbara, 179
Brod, Charles M., 161-162
Bronson, Ray, 185
Brook, Beth, 153, 157
Brooks, Keith, 165
Brooks, Sally, 165
Brown, Eugene, 133
Brownie's Tavern, 165
Brownies (troop), 179
Bryan, Edgar, 79
Bryan, James W., 183
Bumbershoot, 121
Bumgardner Architects, 176
Bunich, Lou, 165
Burke, Judge Thomas, 70
Burns, Mrs. Samuel, 150
Burns, Rev. Samuel, 150
business areas, growth of, 159-166
business occupations, 87-88
Busy's Meat Market, 165
Butterworth, Cal, 111
Butterworth family, 190
Byles, Sarah. *see* Ward, Sarah Isabel Byles
Byrd, Admiral Richard, 128
Byrnes, Fr., 146

cable car, 73
cable powerhouse, 67
Calik, Fr. Joseph, 145
Camp Orkila, 110
Campbell, Walter H., 133
Campbell's Clean-up Committee, 133
Campfire Girls, 179
Canal Mill, 76
Canan, Gertrude Sawyer, 181
Canan, Mickey, 184
Canney, Pastor A.J., 142
Cantorians, 133
Carlson, C. G., 75
Carlson, Carl, 179
Carlson, Eddie, 120
Carnegie Corporation, 105
caroling, 137
Carpenter, Ralph T., 189
Carr, Edmund M., 22, 25, 26, 28, 29, 30, 31, 71
Carr, Olivia Holgate, 31
Carr,Mrs.G. W., 156
Carr,Rev.G. W,, 156
Carroll Terrace, 176
Carter, Mr. (barber), 162
Cascade Terrace, 172
CATE. *see* Citizens Against Tower Expansion
Catholic cemetery, 187
Catholic Community Services, 143
Cedar River water supply system, 84
celebrations
  Christmas, 40, 41, 48, 139
  Fourth of July, 40
  Thanksgiving, 34
cemeteries, 37, 186, 189
Center West, 176
Central Advent Church. Seventh Day Adventists, 141
Central Lumber, 76
Central School, 57
Century 21 Exposition, 116, 120, 137, 144
Century Club, 100
*Changing Form* (sculpture), 118
Chapel, 141
Charley (horse), 26, 27, 40
Charmaine (building), 173
Chase, Doris Totten, 118
Chateau apartments, 172
Cheerio Theater. see Queen Anne Theater
Chelsea apartment, 172, 185
Chelsea Family Hotel, 167, 169
Cherberg, Johnny, 110, 116
Childhaven, 146
children
  banking, 126
  library and reading, 50, 105
  play, 49-50, 101, 102
  work, 48-49
Children's Care Center, 137
Children's Home, 66
Children's Hospital Guild Association, 153
Children's Orthopedic Guild, 180
Children's Orthopedic Hospital, 109, 130, 152-153, 155, 157, 180
Children's Orthopedic Hospital Association Ward, 153
children's programs, 146, 179
Children's Sanitorium, 150
"China Boys". *see* Chinese
China Gardens, 71
Chinese, 54-55, 70-71
Chittenden Locks, 7
cholera, 15, 18, 19, 82
Chong Wa Benevolent Society Cemetery, 187, 188, 189
Chongquin, China sister school, 129
Christenson, Susan, 185

Christian Witness Pavilion, 137
Christman, Lana Anderson, 124
Christmas Magic, 132
Church of Christ, 140, 141
Church of Jesus Christ of Latter Day Saints, 141
Church of the Armageddon, 116, 121
churches, 139-148
Churchill, Dr. Frederick Arthur, 63, 69, 151, 152, 189
Churchill, Martha Blanke, 69, 151, 189
Churchill, Mary Emma, 189
circus, 103
Citizens Against Tower Expansion (CATE), 123
City Cemetery, 187
City Foursquare Chuch, 141
Civic Auditorium, 56, 119
Civic Center, 119, 120
civic cooperation, charitable, 109
Civic Field, 119
Civic Ice Arena, 119
civic oganizations, 179-180
civil defense measures, 111
Clark, Helen, 154
Clark, Mr. (cleaner), 163
Clise, Anna Herr, 152-153, 189
Clise, James W., 153, 188, 189
Clise, John, 89
Clise, William Herr, 153
Clise family,, 63
Clow, Jan, 185
Coast Artillery Anti-Aircraft Battalion, 118
Cocknane, Agnes, 102
Coe Elementary School, 110, 116, 126, 128-129, 154, 180, 181
Cohen, Lou, 114
Coliseum, 121
Collins, Charles R., 169
Collins, Diana Borst, 13
Collins, Lucinda, 13
Collins, Luther, 13
Collins, Stephen, 13
*Columbia Rediviva* (ship), 13
Columbian Exposition, Chicago, 168
*Columbian* (newspaper), 183
Columbus Day storm, 116
Columbia Center, 123
Community Chest, 114
Community Fund drives, 109
community organizations, 100-101
Concerned West Slope Residents, 175
Congregation Chaveth Sholem Cemetery, 188
Congregational Church, 110
Consolidated Fuel Co., 100
"Contact, The," 4
Continental apartment building, 175
Cook, Gregory & Company (grocers), 162
Cooke, Alistair, 120
Corboy, Fr., 135
Corboy Park, 135
Corner Market building, 169
Cornerstone condominiums, 177
Cornerstone Queen Anne apartments, 172
Cotterill, Cora R. Gormley, 84
Cotterill, George, 77, 83, 84, 189
Cotterill House, 185
Council for Defense, 106
Council for Patriotic Services, 106
counterbalance, 85, 88, 97, 113, 124, 162
Counterbalance Barber Shop, 160
counterbalance hill, 118
Court apartments, 172
Courtyard apartments, 172
Cowan, Mrs. Robert, 111
Craig, Anne, 87
Craig, Charles, 87
Crawford's Restaurant, 180
Crestview Village, 156
Criddle, Fredrick J., 86
Criddle, Fredrick P., 86, 101
Criddle, William J., 86
Crippen, Anne, 179
Crockett, S.D., 71
Cross, S.O., 188
Crouch, Grant, 128
Cub Scout Packs, 179
Culver, Ida, 156
Culver Home for Retired Teachers, 156
Cummings, Donald M., 165
cyclone, 38

Dagg, Linda, 123
Dag's, 164
Dahl, Perry, 114
Dahlgren's, 164
Dailey, Sally, 115
Davidson, Fredrick J., 98
Davidson, Howard, 98
Davidson, Jane Skinner, 98
Davidson, Todd, 184
Davis, Danna, 137
Davis, Mary, 147
Day, B.F., 75, 189
Day, F.G., 103
Day, Frances R., 103
Daybreak Star Indian Cultural Center, 10, 11
De La Mar apartments, 95, 168, 172, 185
Deaconess Home and Bible Training School, 155-156
Deaconess Orphanage, Everett, 155
Deaconess Settlement House. see Atlantic Street Center
*Decatur* (ship), 95, 118
Decatur Terrace, 63, 82
Delius, Ted, 101, 103
Delma (hired girl), 96
DeLong, Eleanor, 101
Demanez, Fr. E., 144
Demaray, C. Dorr, 137
Demerts, Dr. William, 11
demographics, 87-88
DeMolay, 182
Denham, Rev. Dick, 137, 142, 143
Denny, A.A., 43
Denny, Abigail Lenora
*see* Denny-Lindsley, Abigail Lenora
Denny, Anna Louisa, 45, 51
Denny, Arthur, 16, 22, 23, 67
Denny, Carrie V. Palmer, 70
Denny, Catherine, 16
Denny, David Thomas
  and Chinese, 71
  and church, 142
  business concerns, 58, 59, 60, 63, 68, 70, 79, 82
  civic concerns, 35, 36, 62, 77, 81
  death, 82
  donations of land, 154, 186
  family life, 45, 48, 50, 55, 151
  homes, 9, 27, 32, 34, 82
  marriage, 23, 24
  native uprising,1856, 30, 31
  pets, 47
  temperance movement, 41, 77
  travel and early settler, 13, 15, 16, 17, 18, 19, 22, 23

Denny, David Thomas, Jr. (Davie), 45, 48
Denny, Emily Inez
and forest fire, 39
and Fourth of July, 40
and Native Americans, 29, 46
childhood, 23, 45, 48, 49, 50
education, 57
illustration by, 24, 36
Licton Spring, 4182
reminiscences of, 16, 21, 27, 34, 36, 37, 38, 44, 53-54
social issues, 70, 71
temperance movement, 41
Denny & Hoyt Addition, 63, 64
Denny, Inez. *see* Denny, Emily Inez
Denny, John, 16, 48, 58, 63, 70
Denny, John B., 63, 68, 71, 81
Denny, Kate, 35
Denny, Loretta, 71
Denny, Louisa Boren
and cyclone, 2338
and Native Americans, 30, 54
and Chinese, 71
Christmas menu, 41
death, 82
garden, 56
health care, 151, 156
homes, 9, 27, 32, 33, 34, 82
land donations, 140, 142, 154, 186
marriage, 23, 24
social concerns, 70, 71
travel and settler, 13, 15, 16, 17
Denny, Madge Decatur, 23, 30, 40, 45, 46, 48, 51
Denny, Mary Boren, 23
Denny, Tom, 27
Denny, Victor Winfield Scott, 45, 48
Denny-Boren party, 16, 45
Denny Cemetery, 65
Denny Clay Co., 67
Denny-Lindsley, Abigail Lenora, 40, 45, 48, 51, 52
Denny mansion, 61, 168
Denny Park, 66, 187
Denny Park Lutheran Church, 141, 143
Denny Park Youth Shelter, 143
Denny Real Estate log cabin, 165
Denny Regrade, 4-5
Denny School, 126
Denny's Additions, 59, 63, 74, 127
depression era, 107, 159
Deringer, Lura, 131
Design Standards Advisory Board, 120
deSoto, Dr., 152
Devin, William, 114
Dickerson,Capt. Joseph, 59
Dingwall, Ewen, 120
diptheria, 150
Discovery Park, 2, 11
*Documented History of the Origin of Washington Geographic Names*, 62
Dodds, John, 161
Donation Land Grant Acts (1850 and 1851), 13-14, 15
Doubt, Martha Mae Randolph, 156
Doughty, Loreli, 143
Doyle, Dolores Graham, 160
*Dr. Allen's Temptation*, 100
Dudley & Ekness (architects), 176
Dukelow's Grocery, 99
Dunn, F. Clyde, 109, 184
Duplex apartments, 172
Durham, Anderson & Freed (architects), 174
Durham & Co., 172
Duwamish River Valley, 13
Duwamish tribe, 8, 11

Eagle Scout, 179
Early Childhood Education Program, 130
earthquake, 36, 116
East Queen Anne Improvement Club, 104
East Queen Anne Playground, 104
East Queen Anne trolley, 106
Eben, Judge, 90
economic initiatives, 108
Eden Additions, 59
Eden Hill, 27, 28, 31, 36, 39, 53
Edwards, Neil, 189
Edwards, William, 187
Eklund, Eleanor, 145
Ekstrand, Florence, 106, 184
Elchey's Candy and Ice Cream store, 159
electric lights, 83
Electrical Workers Building, 114
Elise apartments, 172
*Eliza Anderson* (riverboat), 50
Ella apartments. *see* Marcanna apartments
Ellis, Alice, 185
"Elsa's Garden," 147
Engine Company No. 8, 94
Epstein, Jesse, 112
Erdman, Paul. *see* Israel, Love
Ernst, Sam, 98
ethnic population, 54-55, 86-88, 90, 127
Ethnic Week, 132
Etruria apartments, 172
Evangelical Auditorium, 141
*Evening Press* (newspaper), 183
Everett, Julian, 169
Evergreen Park, 92, 103
Ewbank, Inga, 129
explorers of Northwest, 13

Fairfax Home, 150
Falls, Gregory A., 182
Famine Emergency Drive for Europe and China, 114
Far West Emigration Expedition, 24
Farmer, George S., 133, 134
Federal Old Line Insurance Co., 114
Federal Old Line Life Building, 180
Federal Way Historical Society, 60
Ferry, Elisha P., 69
Field Artillery Armory, 111
Fifth Avenue W. Fire Station, 93, 94
Finnish Temperance Hall, 141
fire (1889), 81
Fire Alarm Office, 94
fire protection, 78, 93-94, 119
Firland Sanitorium, 156
First Avenue Service Center, 146
First Church Evangelical Association, 141
First Covenant Church, 147
First Free Methodist Church, 141, 145
First German Methodist Episcopal, 141
First Methodist Protestant Church, 141
Fisherman's Terminal, 26
Fitzgerald Fountain, 121
Five Corners Hardware, 163
Five-Point Cafe, 164
Flatow, Isador, 87
Flatow Laundry Co., 87
Fleming, Samuel E., 132

flowers, 56
Folklife Festival, 121
Follow Through, 127
food and supply prices (1857), 32
Food Circus, 120
forest fires, 39
Forkey, Jean, 163
Forkey, Jim, 163
Fort Decatur, 30, 31
Fort Lawton. *see* Discovery Park
Fortnightly Club, 100
Fortune Development, 177
Forty-first Infantry Division, 111
Forward Thrust bond issue, 116, 117
Fourmile Rock, 8
Foursquare Gospel Church, 141, 148
Fourteenth Avenue W. group, 185
Fourth Avenue N. Station (fire), 94
Franconia (building), 173
Frank (horse), 94
Frank Pantley Auto Rebuild, 164
Franklin Playground, 95
Franklin School, 116
Fraser River gold rush, 34
Frazier, Bob, 185
Frease, Merlin E., 189
Free Methodist Church, 136, 188
Fremont, Gen. John C., 16
Fremont Cut, 6
Fremont Mill, 64
Fremont Public Association, 138
fresh air cottage, 153
"fresh produce car," 99
Friar, Jerry, 163
Friar, Rick, 163
Friendly Indians (boys club), 180
Frink, J.M., 89
Front Street Cable Railway Power House and Car Barn, 68, 97
Frost, Osmine, 22, 28, 42, 43
Frye, George, 40, 48
Fuhrman, Virg, 164
funeral costs, 188
Furry, Mabel, 133

Gable House, 168
Gaffner, Gary, 168
Galer, Bob, 114
Galer, Jacob, 189
Galer Hill, 61, 62
Galer Street Community Action Committee, 175
Gallagher, Pat, 179
Gallup, Stanley, 114
game animals, 41-42
gardens, 56
Garfield Place, 101
Garrison, Bob, 163
Gaston, Shirley, 156
Gatzert, Babette, 154
Gavett, Cora Hale, 131
Gaylor, Jacob, 61-62
Gayway Amusement Area, 120
*Gazette* (newspaper), 183
Geise Associates, 124
Geiser, Albert, 172
General Construction, 3
General Hospital (Seattle), 153
geology of Queen Anne area, 1-6
George Washington Memorial Bridge. *see* Aurora Bridge
German Evangelical Church, 141
German Methodist Church, 141
Gerold, Charles A., 184
Gerrish, Charles, 108, 114, 163
Ghosh, Dr. Jayasri, 136
Girl Reserves (YWCA), 180
Girl Scouts, 179
Glen, Rev. John, 145
Goff, Bruce, 123
gold rush, 34
Golden West Dairy, 90
golf course, 116
Good Templars Lodge No. 6, 77
Goodwill Industries, 109
Gordon, Alexander, 162
Gordon, Marina, 166
Gorham-Seagrave 800 pumper truck, 94
Gormley, Cora R.. *see* Cotterill, Cora R. Gormley
Gould, Harry, 90
Gould Lumber, 76
Graham & Co., 172
Graham, David, 37, 59
Graham, Eliza Anne Mercer, 15, 18, 19, 22, 27, 36, 37, 45, 71, 127
Graham, George, 37
Graham, John, 120
Graham, John Sr., 170
Graham, Susannah Mercer, 5937
Graham, Walter, 36, 37, 62, 71, 79
Graham, William, 37, 79
Grand Army of the Republic. Washington and Alaska Division, 59
Gray, Robert, 13
Greater Defense Chest, 111
Green Garden Food Co., 177
Green Lake addition, 74
Greenbelt Ordinance, 118
Green's Tavern, 165
Griffin, Leah, 113
Griffith, Lyman H., 64, 69
Griffith Co., 64, 83
Griffith Water System, 4, 79
Grizzly Inn, 162
Grocery Store apartments, 172
grocery stores, 99, 161, 165
Group Theatre, 182
Growth Management Act (Washington), 6, 116
Gustafson, Emery, 140
Gustafson, Mary, 145

Hagardt, Len, 160
Hall, Osborn, 22, 23, 28
Hall, William, 134
Hamilton, Juanita, 183, 184
Hamilton, Katherine L., 183, 184
Hamilton, Rupert, 183, 184
Hammond, William, 41
Handschy/Kistler House, 185
Hanford, Cornelius, 25, 31, 40, 71
Hanover, Pauline, 185
Hansen, Jim, 176
Hansen Baking Company, 116, 176
Harbor View Park, 117
Harborview Hospital, 157
Harris, Verna, 147
Hawkins, Marie, 134
Head Start, 127
Headquarters Hall, 41
Heck, Rev. Douglas, 148
Hemmingsen, R.P., 172
Henkel, Erwin, 134
Hennes, John, 124, 135
Hepworth, Dee Simmons, 162
Herd Laws, 75, 90
Herr, Ruth Grove, 104, 156
*H.F. Alexander*(ship), 102
High School Memorial Stadium, 120
Highland Baptist Mission, 141
Highland Court, 172
Highland Parc apartments, 172, 177

Hill & Roats Co., 176
Hillhaven Corporation, 156
Hills of Eternity (cemetery), 188
Hilltop Tavern, 160
Hilt, Fred, 152
Hobbs Architecture Group, 177
Hoen, Anne, 163
Hoen, Charles, 163
Hoeschen, Louise, 179
Hoglund, Alfred, 88
Hokanson, Barbara, 112
Hokanson, Bina, 112
Hokanson, Dorothy, 112
Hokanson, Erik, 112
Hokanson, Patricia, 112
Hokanson, Randolph, 112
Holgate, Olivia. *see* Carr, Olivia Holgate
Hollinger, Brandt, 124
Holloway chemical wagon, 93
Holmberg, Gust, 172
Holmes, Frances L., 105
home care facilities, 150
Home Guard, 106
Home Sanitarium Inc., 150
homemaking, 98
Homestead Act, 13-14
Hoover, Bernie, 163
"Hooverville," 107
Horn, Walter G., 145
Horton, Dexter, 18, 19, 33, 49
Horton, Eliza Shoudy Horton, 18
Horton, Rebecca, 18
Hose Company No. 24, 94
hospitals, 150, 152-55
Howe Field. *see* West Queen Anne Playfield
Hoyt, Judge John P., 63
Hoyt, Richard Jr., 176
Hudson's Bay Company, 13
Hughes, Arthur G., 150
Hughes, Sara, 179
Hunter, Bill, 102, 103, 104
Hunter, Helen, 104
Hunter, Phil, 104
Hunter, Will, 104
Hunter, William C., 94
hurricane, 60
Hustwayte, Hugh, 165

ice skating, 37-38
immigrants, 71, 86
improvement clubs, 91-92
Independent Order of Good Templars, Seattle Lodge No. 6, 41
Independent Order of Odd Fellows, 187, 188
Independent Telephone Co., 83
Indian Athletic Association, 11
Indian war (1856), 29
Industrial Home of the Boys and Girls Aid Society, 150
influenza epidemic, 150
Interbay Covenant Church, 141, 147
Interbay dump and landfill, 116
Interbay School, 127
International Fountain, 120, 121
Interurban Station, 90
Intiman Theatre Company, 121, 182
Iris apartments, 172
Israel, Logic, 121, 122
Israel, Love, 116, 121, 122. *see also* Love family
Israel, Serious, 122

Jack (dog), 47
Japanese-Americans, 113, 114
Jeep Drive, 131
Jeffries, Wendel, 179
Jenner, Charles H., 92
Jenner, J. Kirkham, 92, 99, 102
Jensen, Sam Sr., 163
Jensen, "Uncle Sam" Jr., 163
Jim (crow), 46
Job's Daughters, 182
John Graham & Co., 175
John Hay School, 126, 129-130
John Hay school, 132
Johnson, Anne Howell, 99
Johnson, Hugh, 108
Johnson, Ronald, 11
Johnson Mill, 68
Johnston, Pastor Robert, 147
Jones, James Paul, 177
*Journal* (newspaper)
Junior Guild Association, 153

Kaczor, Deloris, 177
Kaczor, George, 177
Kaczor, Michael, 177
Kail, Seymour, 111
Kaldal, Jim, 111, 114
Kaufmann, Mel, 169
Keast, Bertha, 150
Kelley, Maynard, 114
Kelly, L. Maxine, 127
Kemp-Slaughter, Ethel, 185
Kemp-Slaughter, James, 185
Kemp-Slaughter, Michael, 131, 185
Kerry, Albert S., 157
Kerry, Albert S., Sr., 95
Kerry, Olive, 157
Kerry Park, 95, 116, 118
Ketcham, Hank, 110, 116
KEVR (radio station), 122
Kilbourne,Dr. E.C., 64
Kilbourne's, Dr. Green Lake Addition, 74
Kildall, Joseph, 163
King, Marina, 157
King County Commissioners, 29
King County Courthouse, 154
King County Health Department, 154
King County Homeopathic Society, 151
King County Hospital, 154
KING (television station), 122
King Tut exhibit, 116, 121
Kingdome, 121
Kinnear, Angie Simmons, 8, 60, 70, 72, 95, 157, 175
Kinnear, Becky, 69
Kinnear, Charles, 8, 60
Kinnear, George, 8, 60, 62, 69, 70, 71, 72, 78, 90, 95, 112, 114, 157, 169, 172, 175
Kinnear, George, Jr., 8, 60
Kinnear, John Ritchey, 69, 70, 71, 171
Kinnear, Rebecca Means, 69, 70
Kinnear, Roy, 68, 97
Kinnear Addition, 74
Kinnear apartments, 170, 172
Kinnear family, 63
Kinnear Mansion, 118, 185
Kinnear Park, 68, 72, 77, 83, 95, 97, 101, 142
Kinnear streetcar line, 97
Kinnear Water System, 4, 79
Kinnear's Addition, 60
KIRO (television station), 122
Kleinlein, Sandra, 179
Knutsen, George, 89, 102
Knutsen, Knute, 90
Knutsen, Sigrid Rongve, 90
Knutsen, William, 90

Knutsen Dairy, 90
KOMO (television station), 122
Kracke, Werner H. "Bhy," 117
Kristofferson's Dairy, 164
KRSC (television station), 122
*Kuay* (alumni newsletter), 132
Kuay Garage. *see* Marqueen Garage
Kussman (Bob) Continuing Education Project, 143

La Charme apartments, 172
Ladder Company No. 6, 94
Ladies Musical Club, 69
Ladies' Relief Society, 154
LaFontaine, Frank, 11
Lagerquist & Morris, 177
Lake Union, 5, 31, 34, 35, 37
Lake Union Mill, 68
Lake Union Road, 64-65
Lake Union sewage tunnel, 81, 82
Lake Union Women's Christian Temperance Union, 77
Lake Washington, 5, 31, 68
Lake Washington Ship Canal, 2, 5, 6, 58, 76
Lakeview cemetery, 37
LaMance apartments, 141
Lambert, Lander, 188
Lammereaux, George, 162
land grants
Donation Land Grant Acts, 1850 and 1851, 13-14
Homestead Act, 13-14
Oregon Territory Donation Land Act, 15
Preemption Land Act, 13-14
"proving up", 14
Timber Culture Act, 13-14
Land Use Review Committee, 122
Landes, Bertha, 100
Landmark cedar, 10
landmarks, historic, 75, 84, 126, 169, 172, 176
landslides, 3, 4, 6, 118
Langlie, Arthur, 109
Laprade, Bill, 6
Laurel Beauty Salon. *see* Litsa's West McGraw Street Salon
Law, James, 58
Law's Second Addition, 58
Le Parc condominiums, 172, 177
Leary, John, 70
Leary, Mary B., 154
LeCocq, Edward, 153
LeCocq, John, 153
Lee Courtyard apartments, 172
Lee Lumber & Mfg. Company, 165
Lee Street Fire Station, 79, 94
Leibly Hall, 180, 183
LeShana, David C., 138
Lewis and Clark Expedition, 13
libraries, 40, 105-106, 118-119
Licton Springs, 82
Liebow, Edward, 11
Lifetime Learning Center, 135, 144
lights, electric, 83
Lindsley, Abigail Lenora Denny-. *see* Denny-Lindsley, Abigail Lenora
Lindsley, Edward, 60
Linkletter, Art, 130
Linkletter, Doris, 114
Linkletter, Doris McClure, 89, 114
Litsa's West McGraw Street Salon, 163
Little Friends Preschool, 135
Local Improvement District (LID), 92
Locke, Louise, 185
Loder, Del, 190
Loeb Mill, 76
Logic Israel. *see* Israel, Logic
Lola apartments, 172
Longmire party, 15
Lookout tree, 10
Love family, 121, 122, 146
Love Israel. *see* Israel, Love
Lovejoy, George, 108, 112
Lovell, E.S., 174
Low, John, 17, 18
low-cost housing, 112, 176
Loyal League, 71
Lumber Supply Co-op, 166
Luther, Otto L., 114, 132
Luther Field, 116, 130
Luther Memorial Field, 133
Lutheran Gospel Hour, 143
Lyon, R.H., 103

Macdonald, Jeannette, 104
Machmeier, Teresa, 113
Maggs Water System, 4, 79
Magnolia Branch Library, 118
*Magnolia Journal* (newspaper), 184
Magnolia School, 127
Mahlum, Ed, 131
Maple, Jacob, 13
Maple, Samuel, 13
Marcanna apartments, 172
March of Dimes, 114
Marianne (building), 173
Marion, Marion Baker, 101
Marqueen apartments, 165
Marqueen Garage, 165
Marshall, George, 118
Marshall, Margaret, 118
Marshall Viewpoint, 95, 116, 118
Marston, A.J.(Archie), 76, 137
Marston, Charlie, 76
Marston, Clarence, 76
Marston, Martin, 76
Marston Hall, 137
Martin, Dr. Charles A., 138
Mary Thomasina, Sr., 135
Masonic Cemetery (Lakeview), 187
Masonic Home, 181
Masonic organizations, 182
Master Builders Association, 112
Matsushita, Kazuyuki, 121
Mauerman, Gordon, 133
Maughan's Pharmacy, 163
*Maverick* (school newspaper), 131
Mayfair Land Company, 91
Mayfair Park, 116, 117
Maynard, Dr. David "Doc," 23, 24, 28, 151
McBride, Valerie, 179
McCallum, Linda Humphrey, 124
McCauley, George, Jr., 179
McClintock, John, Jr., 114
McClure, Beatrice Baxter, 152
McClure School, 116, 131, 134, 180, 181
McCombs, James, 79
McDonald, Agnes, 102
McDonald, Mayme, 102
McDougall,Rev. A.C., 41
McFee, Donald, 114
McFee/Klockzien House, 185
McGill, Henry M., 34
McGill, O.H., 142
McGraw, John H., 71, 89, 189
McGraw School, 132
McGraw Street Bakery, 163
McGraw Street Bridge, 3
McKenna, Dr. David L., 137
McKenzie, Dean Vernon, 111
McKinney, Louise, 130

McLane, Margaret, 102
McMahan, Maxine Amundson, 135
McMillan, Rev. David, 32
McMillan, Mary Jane. *see* Ross, Mary Jane McMillan
McNatt, Francis, 22, 28, 29
McNichols, Dr. Donald, 138
Mead, Ida E., 150
Meany, Edmond, 62, 69, 70, 71
Meany, Lizzie Ward, 70
Mecca Cafe, 164
medical care, 151-157
Melby, Carrie, 96
Memorial Shrine, 120
Memorial Stadium, 121
Mengadoht's Meat Market, 99
mental health center for children, 154
Mercer, Alice
*see* Bagley, Alice Mercer
Mercer, Asa Shinn, 37, 151, 189
Mercer, Eliza. *see* Graham, Eliza Anne Mercer
Mercer, Hester Loretta Ward, 15, 19, 20, 36, 37, 63, 70, 71
Mercer, John B., 45
Mercer, Mary Jane. *see* Parsons, Mary Jane Mercer
Mercer, Nancy Brigham, 18, 19, 26
Mercer, Susannah, 15, 18, 22, 27, 30, 35, 45, 46, 48, 49, 127
Mercer, Thomas
  and Native Americans, 30, 31
  civic activities, 62, 81
  early settler, 15, 22
  herbal medicine, 55
  home and family, 26, 27, 32, 45, 50
  land business, 59, 63
  marriage, 36
  naming lakes, 31
  public office, 30
  supports suffrage, 70
  wagon train party, 18, 19
Mercer Island named, 31
Mercer School, 103, 126, 127
Mercer Street named, 62
Mercer's Additions, 63, 74
Merchant's Club, 110
Messett, Boe, 164
Messett, Edmund, 164
Messett Brothers, 190
Methodist Episcopal Church, 31, 34, 155, 186
Methodist Protestant Church, 19, 40
Metropolitan Hospital and Sanitarium, 150
Mezistrano, Morris, 161
Mezistrano, Sam, 161
Michaelson Manor, 176
Mickey Mouse Club, 111
mid-wives, 156
"middy drive", 133
Mike's Barber Shop. *see* Queen Anne Barber Shop
Milham, Samuel, 79
Military Road, 33, 108
Miller, John Franklin, 95
Miller, Rex, 163
Millikin, Earl, 112, 114
Minor, Elizabeth M., 154
Minute Men, 106
Miskey, C.F., 108
Mission Home, 150
Miyauchi, Yoshi, 113
Mock, Frank, 163
Mock, Virginia, 163
Moeller organ, 190
Montessori school, 169
Mooney, Paul, 108, 160, 162
Moore, Felix E., 133
Moore Theater, 186
Moran, Hal, 179
Morgan, Pastor Sidney H., 145
Moriarty, Judge Charles, 109, 114
Moriarty, Mrs. Charles, 109
Morris, Jack, 114
Morris, Maribeth Bunker, 184
Mount Pleasant Cemetery, 58, 64, 75, 91, 113, 118, 121, 186-188, 187, 189
Moyle, Don, 180
Multi-International Colors Society (MICS), 131-132
Municipal League, 112
Municipal Street Railway Maintenance Shop, 93
Murray, John S., 184
Muscynski, Nick, 161
Muslim cemetery, 188
Musser, Dr. John, 153
Myers, Fred, 165
Myrtle Edwards Park, 117
Nagle, John H., 22, 25, 28, 29, 36, 41
Naomi (building), 173
Napolitano, Kathy, 136
Naramore, Bain, Brady and Johanson, 120
National Guard, 114
National Recovery Act (NRA), 108
Native American cemetery, 187
Native Americans, 7, 8, 9, 30, 45-46
Nautica condominiums, 172
Neighborhood Resource Center, 118-119
Nelsen, Don, 162, 166
Nelsen, Elizabeth, 162
Nelsen, Fred, 162
Nelsen, M.J., 162
Nelsen's Quality Grocery, 127, 162, 166
Nelson, Don, 114
Nesmith, Alison, 148
"New Frontier," 123
New Options Middle school, 132
"New System 44 wet wash," 98
New Wayside Emergency Hospital. *see* Wayside Emergency Hospital
Newell, Emma V., 150
Newell, Roger, 177
newspapers, 183-184
Nickerson, Harold, 110
Nickerson Street business area, 163-164
Nile Temple building, 182
Nob Hill Addition, 74
Nob Hill apartments, 172
Noble, Dr. Charles S., 150
Noble Emergency Hospital, 150
Nordquist & Engstrom, 163
Nordstrom, Carl, 93
Norman, Charles G., 179, 183
North Queen Anne Association, 175
North Queen Anne Bridge, 185
North Queen Anne Elementary school, 126, 131
North Queen Anne High School, 116
North Queen Anne-Nickerson Community Club, 109
North Queen Anne Preservation Association, 175
North Seattle, 58, 61, 62, 63

*North Seattle Advocate* (newspaper), 183
North Seattle Baptist Church. *see* Queen Anne Baptist Church
north slope gravel pit, 104
Northern Pacific & Great Northern (water) system, 79
Northwest Center for the Retarded, 131
Northwest Football League, 112
Northwest Millwork, 163
Norton, John C., 136
Norwalk Vault Company, 190
Norwegian Danish Evangelical Lutheran Church of Seattle. *see* Denny Park Lutheran Church
Nurenberg, Dr. G.J., 150

Oak Park Cemetery, 82. *see also* Washelli Cemetery
Observatory Park, 93
occupations and wages, 73, 74, 87
Odham, Rev. Ralph, 147
Old Chemical Wagon No. 3, 93
Olmsted Plan, 89, 117
Olsen, Elsa, 147
Olympic Grocery, 165
Olympic View Sanitarium, 150
Olympic West, 176
Open Door Inn, 122
Opera House. *see* Seattle Opera House
Order of Amaranth. Queen Anne Court No. 23, 182
Order of Good Templars. *see* Independent Order of Good Templars
Order of the Eastern Star. Mecca Chapter No. 220, 182
Order of the Eastern Star. Queen Anne Chapter No. 209, 181, 182
Oregon Territorial Law, Section 4, 15
Oregon Territory Donation Land Act, 15
Oregon Territory Surveyor General's report, 15
Oregon trail, 15, 17
Orptic Club, 100
Orthopedic school. Children's Orthopedic Hospital, 130
Osborne, James, 119
Osgood, F.H., 62, 124

Owen, Miriam Marston, 98, 137

Pacific Casket Company, 190
Pacific Electrical Co., 83
Pacific Media Group Corporation, 184
Pacific Northwest Ballet, 182
Pacific Science Center, 120
Palmer, A.L., 71
Palmer, Carrie V.. *see* Denny, Carrie V. Palmer
Palmer, Ronald, 114, 185
Pantley, Frank, 164
Paquette, Patricia, 184
Parcel, Peggy, 114
Paris, Ben, 108
Park, Alan M., 165
Park, Alan M., Jr., 165
"Park of State", 72
Parker, Marion, 111, 138, 165
parks, 95, 116-118
Parsons, Henry G., 36
Parsons, Mary Jane Mercer, 15, 18, 22, 27, 36, 45, 127
Parsons, Maude, 153
Parsons, Reginald, 109, 114
Parsons/Gerrard House, 185
Parsons Memorial Gardens, 116, 118, 122
Paulson, W. Chuck, 163
Pavlovic, Dan, 161
Pavlovic, Mark, 161
*Paw Prints* (school magazine), 133
Payne, Howard, 112
Pearl Harbor, 113
Pease, Hiram, 136, 145
Penfield, Lima, 57
Pennoyer, Douglas, 11
People's Memorial Association, 190
Perry, Ed, 180
Perry's Moving and Storage Co., 180
Peterson, Charles, 187
Peterson, Henry, 187
Peterson, Joseph, 187
Peterson, Karen Mary, 187
Peterson, Lambert, 182
Peterson, Lily, 187
Peterson, Mabel, 187
Peterson, Mattie, 187
Peterson, Nelly, 187
Peterson, Nils B., 64, 103, 104, 136, 187-188, 189

Peterson, Sarah, 187
Peterson family, 43
Peterson Water System, 4, 79
Peterson's sand pit, 137
pets, 46-48
Petty, Alfred, 175
Pflueger, Jesse P., 147-148
Phelan, Mary, 151
Phelps, Thomas Stowall, 95, 118
Phelps Park, 95, 131
philanthropic cooperation, 109
Phoenix Lumber & Fuel, 76
physicians, 151-152
Pierce, Frank, 150
Pierce, Henry K., 22, 23, 24, 25, 28
Pifer House, 123
*Pig-Tail Days in Old Seattle*, 189
Pike Place Market, 99
Player, Glen S., 153
playgrounds, 114
Ploe, Al, 163
Plummer, Charles, 25, 48
Plummer, Ellender Smith, 15, 22, 24, 25, 28
Plummer's Mercantile, 34, 41
Point Elliott Treaty, 11
political activism, 108
*Polk's Seattle City Directory*, 1890, 73
Pollard, Lancaster, 85
Polley, Dean, 1254
Pollock, Adelaide, 126, 130
pollution of lakes, 68, 80-81
Polychronopoulos, Litsa, 163
Polygon Realty Corporation, 175
Pomeroy, Allan, 114
Pomeroy, Frank, 165
Pomeroy, Josie, 165
Pontius, Ann M., 71
Population statistics, 15, 35
Port of Seattle Grain Terminal, 116
*Post-Intelligencer* (newspaper), 20, 60, 66, 68, 74, 78, 82, 183, 189
Post Office Building, 114
potlatch, 9
Potlatch Meadows, 9, 121
potter's field, 187
Powell, Isabell, 86
Powwow tree, 9, 10
"Prairie Houses," 123
Preemption Land Act, 13-14
press. *see* newspapers
Prestrud, Stuart, 86, 102, 158

Price & Associates, 176
Proctor, Dr. Oscar, 109
prohibition era, 77, 108
prohibition political party, 41, 77
property, cost of, 74-75
Prosch, Thomas W., 73, 155
Prospect St. apartments, 172
public health, 150-151
public health nurses, 157
Public School Administrative and Service Center, 114
public transportation, 97, 112
public utilities, 92-93
Puget Sound Traction Light and Power Station, 93

Quain, Fr. Thomas, 135, 146
Quality Fruit and Vegetables, 163
Quality Market, 163
*Queen Anne American* (newspaper), 183
Queen Anne apartments (High School), 172
Queen Anne Assembly of God Church. *see* Queen Anne Christian Center
Queen Anne Avenue N. business area, 159
Queen Anne Baptist Church, 141, 143
Queen Anne Barber Shop. see Counterbalance Barber Shop
Queen Anne Blvd., 89
Queen Anne Bowl, 64, 110, 137
Queen Anne Boys Club, 180
Queen Anne Cadettes, 179
Queen Anne Care Center, 156
Queen Anne Chamber of Commerce, 112
Queen Anne Christian Center, 136, 147
Queen Anne Christian Church, 141, 146
Queen Anne Christian School, 136, 147
Queen Anne Commercial Club, 115, 180
Queen Anne Community Center, 180
Queen Anne Community Church, 176
Queen Anne Community Clubhouse, 91, 101, 109, 111, 116, 122, 184
Queen Anne Community Council, 110, 122, 123, 179, 185
Queen Anne Community Development Council, 175
Queen Anne Congregational Church, 141, 179, 180
Queen Anne Council of Clubs (QACC), 109
Queen Anne Day Care, 145
"Queen Anne Days," 110
Queen Anne Demolay, 182
Queen Anne district and Native Americans, 7-11
Queen Anne Ecumenical Council, 139-140, 142, 146, 148
Queen Anne Eighth Grade Center, 131
Queen Anne Field House, 114, 116, 117
Queen Anne Florists, 182
Queen Anne Garden Club, 181
Queen Anne Girls' Club, 133
Queen Anne Hall, 182
Queen Anne Hardware, 180
Queen Anne Heights, 176
Queen Anne Helpline, 116, 138, 140, 142, 143, 146, 148
Queen Anne High School, 102, 110, 112, 113, 116, 122, 129, 130, 131, 132-135, 136, 176, 184, 185
Queen Anne Hill district annexation, 61
Queen Anne Hill geologic profile, 2
Queen Anne Historical Society, 60, 169, 185
Queen Anne Improvement Club, 90, 93
Queen Anne Job's Daughters, 182
Queen Anne Knickers Club, 100
Queen Anne Library, 105-06, 116, 119
Queen Anne Lutheran Church, 141, 147-148
Queen Anne-Magnolia Lions Club, 180
Queen Anne Masonic Lodge, 182
Queen Anne Men's Club, 100, 110
Queen Anne Methodist Church, 179
Queen Anne Methodist Episcopal Church, 140, 142
Queen Anne Moose Lodge, 181
*Queen Anne News*, 106, 108, 109, 112, 113, 132, 140, 146, 160, 161, 183-184
Queen Anne Nomadic Circle, 100
Queen Anne North apartments, 172
Queen Anne Park, 89, 91, 108
Queen Anne Pharmacy, 163
Queen Anne Pool, 1, 2
Queen Anne Post Office, 92
Queen Anne Pressery, 162
Queen Anne Rainbow Assembly, 181-182
Queen Anne Recreation Center, 117
Queen Anne Sand and Gravel, 110
Queen Anne Sand Co., 104
Queen Anne School, 126, 136. *see also* West Queen Anne School
Queen Anne School Guard, 132
Queen Anne Second Addition, 62
Queen Anne Stationery & Office Supply, 165
Queen Anne Student Union, 134
Queen Anne Study Club, 100
Queen Anne style (architecture), 82
Queen Anne Swimming Pool, 117
Queen Anne Theater, 111, 159, 160
*Queen Anne Today* (newspaper), 184
Queen Anne Town, 61, 62, 70, 73-84
Queen Anne United Methodist Church, 141, 142
Queen Anne United Presbyterian Church, 140, 141, 146
Queen Anne Villa, 156
Queen City Bicycling Club, 84
Queen City Bowl, 114
Queen City Good Roads Club, 84
Queen Vista apartments, 172
Queensborough apartments, 172, 174
quilting, 54

radio stations, 114
Raffs house, 123
railroad, 62
railway, public street, 82
Rainbow groups, 182
Rauber, Alice, 150
Rauber & Baker Private Hospital for Contagious Diseases, 150
Real Estate Board, 112
real estate market, 89

recreation, 101, 102, 104-105, 131, 160
Red Cross, 109
Redding Hall, 146, 178, 182
Redemptorist Fathers, 144, 146
Reel, Val, 171
Regan, James C., 161
Reichert, Robert, 123
Reisman, Jessica, 163
Reliable French Cleaners, 163
Renkor, Betty, 184
"restoration fever," 124
Restview Home, 150
retirement homes, 156-157
Rhodes, Dick, 165-166
Rhyther Child League. Hilltop Unit, 180
Rich, Silas, 108
Ringling Brothers and Barnum and Bailey, 103
Ritchy, John, 69
roads, 35-36
Roberts, E.C., 131
Robinson's Hardware, 76
Roby, Lois, 138, 160
Rodgers, David, 103
Rodgers, Jane Josephine, 156
Rodgers Park, 92, 103
Roe, Michael, 11
Romero, Tony, 165
Roode, Dr. Charles, 151
Roosevelt, Franklin D., 130
Rosita Villa apartments, 169
Ross, David, 71
Ross, John, 15, 22, 25, 26, 28, 29, 30, 31, 32, 36, 42, 43, 57, 58, 64, 70, 189
Ross, Mary Jane McMillan, 15, 32, 57, 58, 70, 189
Ross District, 65
Ross district, 64, 92, 166
Ross Marche Mercantile, 64, 75, 102
Ross Post Office, 64
Ross School, 57, 64, 131
Ross Station, 64
Rossellini, Victor, 127
Rosser, Paul F., 138
Rover (dog), 96
Roy Swanstrom Centurion Scholarship Endowment, 138
Royal Brougham Pavilion, 137, 164
Rudd Co. Inc., 165
Rudel, Laurie, 146
Ruth School for Girls, 157

S & M Market, 116, 161
Sacred Heart Catholic Church, 141, 144
Sacred Heart Catholic School, 135
Safeway, 165-166
Salish culture, 8
Salladay, Elmer, 160
Salladay's Standard Pharmacy, 138, 160, 161
Salmon Bay Fishermen's Terminal, 93
Salmon Bay School, 127
Samuelson, Jeri, 179
Samuelson, Terry, 179
sand pit, 104
Sandvigan, Alex, 96
Sandvigan, Buster, 96
Sandvigan, Emma, 96
Sandvigan, Gilbert, 96
Sandvigan family, 96
Sargent apartments. *see* Triplet apartments
Sato (John Y.) & Associates, 176
Satterlund, Nils W., 147
scarlet fever, 156
Schneider, Lt. Richard, 124
School Program Involving the Community Elderly (SPICE), 180-181
schools, 57, 125-138
Schurman, Clark, 179
Schwabacher Bros., 164
Scissor's Palace Barber & Style Shop. *see* Bert & Lou's Barber
sea travel, 15
Sea View apartments, 171, 172
Seafair Indian Days, 10
Seafair Parade, Queen Anne's entry, 115
*Seattle and Environs*, 71
Seattle Brass Band, 40
Seattle Catholic Polish community, 135
Seattle Cemetery, 187
Seattle Center, 9, 10, 116, 119, 121
Seattle Chamber of Commerce, 112, 169
Seattle Children's Home, 109, 132, 149, 154
Seattle Children's Theatre, 182
Seattle Coal and Transportation Company, 55, 60
Seattle Common Council, 187
Seattle Council of Churches, 137
Seattle Country Day School, 136, 161
Seattle Education Auxiliary, 156
Seattle Electric Light Co., 83
Seattle Engineering Department, 4, 6
Seattle Engineering School, 165
Seattle General Hospital, 155
Seattle Grade School Champions, 128
Seattle Hebrew Benevolent Association Cemetery, 188
Seattle Housing Authority (SHA), 176
Seattle Indian Center, 10
Seattle Lake Shore and Eastern Railroad, 70
Seattle Library Board, 105
*Seattle Mail and Herald* (newspaper), 100
Seattle Municipal Water System, 79, 80
Seattle Opera, 27, 36, 71, 120, 182
Seattle Pacific College, 102, 110, 138. *see also* Seattle Seminary
Seattle Pacific University, 10-11, 26, 136-138, 164, 181
*Seattle Post-Intelligencer. see Post-Intelligencer*
Seattle Preservation and Development Authority, 176
Seattle Repertory Theatre, 121, 182
Seattle School District, 116, 119, 176
Seattle Seminary, 131, 137. *see also* Seattle Pacific College
*Seattle Star* (newspaper), 42
Seattle Steam Laundry, 68
Seattle Symphony Orchestra, 121, 182
*Seattle Times*, 105, 152
*Seattle Times* (newspaper), 102
Seattle Visiting Nurse Service, 157
Seattle World's Fair. *see* Century 21 Exposition
Seattlean Club, 181
Second Advent Church, 141. *see also* Central Advent Church. Seventh Day Adventists

Second Methodist Congregation, 142
Second Methodist Protestant Church, 140-141
Second Presbyterian Church. *see* Bethany United Presbyterian Church
Seely, Wallace, 142
Semple, Eugene, 70
Sensitive Areas Ordinance (Seattle), 6
service organizations, 180
Seventh Church of Christ Scientist, 141, 146-147
Seville Court, 170
sewage pollution, 81
sewer system, 79, 80-83
Seymour, Kathryn, 185
shantytown, 107
Sheepshed/Lewis House, 142
Shelton, Arthur, 133
Shilshole tribe, 8
Shimizu, Hideki, 121
shopping, grocery, 99
Shorey, Oliver C., 187
Shoudy, John, 41
Shoudy, William, 18, 70
Sigl, Father, 135
Sigma Rho, 181
Simmons, Angie. *see* Kinnear, Angie Simmons
Simpson, Sheryl, 179
Sisters of the Holy Name, 135, 150
Skokomish Indian Reservation School, 58
Skolnick, Art, 175
Skyline House, 172, 174
Slaughter, Michael Kemp-. *see* Kemp-Slaughter, Michael
smallpox, 150
Smith, Dr. Henry
  and Native Americans, 31
  and neighbors, 28, 43, 60
  civic activities, 30, 35
  first settler, 15, 22, 23
  home and family, 24, 34, 41, 45
  land business, 63
  lost in the woods, 25
  medical practice, and portrait, 151
  natural disasters, 36, 39
  *Reminiscences*, 36
  women's suffrage, 70
Smith, Abigail Teaff, 15, 22, 24, 25, 28, 31
Smith, Dick, 164
Smith, Ellender
*see* Plummer, Ellender Smith
Smith, Emma Atkins, 151
Smith, Frances, 164
Smith, Mary Phelan, 41, 45, 151
Smith, Preston, 164
Smith, Robert, 114
Smithers, Diana Gilmore Tobin, 31
Smithers, Erasmus M., 22, 28, 30, 31
Snohomish tribe, 46
Snoqualmie Hall. *see* Headquarters Hall
Snoqualmie tribe, 8
Sobeck, Pat, 143
social clubs, 181
Somervell and Thomas, 105
Sommerville and Coty, 154
Sorenson, Reuben, 148
Sorrento Hotel, 169
Soundview Terrace, 116
Space Needle, 94, 119, 120
Sparkman, Harold, 114
Spaulding, Florence, 93
Spaulding, Mrs. Harold, 146
Spaulding, Richard, 119
special education at Warren Avenue School, 127
SPICE. *see* School Program Involving the Community Elderly
Spike (horse), 94
sports, 110, 116, 121, 137, 180
springs, 3
Sprinkle, Don, 114, 180
St. Anne Catholic Church, 146
St. Anne Catholic School, 135-136
St. Anne Church, 141
St. Anne Crab Supper, 136
St. Anne Parish Mothers' Club, 136
St. Anne School, 78
St. Anne's Convent, 150
St. John's Lodge of Free and Accepted Masons, 41
St. Jude's Children's Research Hospital, 132
St. Luke's Private Hospital, 150
St. Margaret of Scotland Catholic School, 135
St. Margaret of Scotland Church, 141, 144-145
St. Margaret Parochial School, 127
St. Mark's Church. Episcopal Mission. *see* St. Paul's Episcopal Church
St. Paul's Episcopal Church, 141, 145-146
St. Vincent de Paul Society, 109, 144, 146
Standard, Dr. Sam, 160
Standard Bakery, 160, 161
Standard Drug Co., 160
Standard Grocery, 161-162
Stanley, David, 22, 28, 30, 42, 43
Stark, Mary, 143
Steen, Lee, 108
Steinbrueck, Victor, 120
Stephen, James, 176
Stephens, Isaac, 25
Stetson and Post Lumber Co., 87
Stevenson, Jim, 89
Stewart, A.B., 62
Stickeen (tribe), 46
Stipek, Frank, 163
Stipek, Ronald, 163
Stoddard, O.D., 132
street maintenance, 67
street railway, 82
streetcars, 85, 97
Strickler, William, 22, 28, 29, 30
Stringfellow, Virgil, 174
Stringfellow (builder), 172
Strong, Sydney, 142
Strong, Tracy, 179
Stuart and Durham, 172, 174
Stuart/Balcom House, 185
student traffic court, 133
Sullam Smith & Associates, 176
Sunrise Retirement Communities, 156
Sunset Monument Company, 164, 190
Sunset Telephone Co., 83
Suquamish tribe, 8
Sutermeister, Miriam, 169
Swanstrom, Roy, 138
Sweetbrier Bride, 23
Sylvester, Chuck, 163
Sylvester's Queen Anne Bakery. *see* McGraw Street Bakery

Taigen, Ing, 163
Taylor, Gene, 123

Taylor, Rev.(Congregational Church), 140
Taylor Anne, 156
Taylor Congregational Church, 140-141
Taylor house, 123-124
telegraph line, 35
Telephone Exchange Building, 83
telephone service, 83
television age, 114
television towers, 122-123
temperance movement, 41, 77
Temple deHirsch (Sinai) Cemetery, 188
tenements, 168
Tenneson, Harry, 165
Tenneson, Irene, 165
tennis, 95, 104
Tennyson, Bill, 133
Territorial University, 32, 37, 39, 47, 48, 57, 127
Terry, Lee, 18
Terry family, 51
Thiry, Paul, 120
Thomas, Grainger & Thomas, 169
Thomas, Harlan, 169, 170, 172
Thompson, Reginald H., 5, 83
Thornton, Jesse Quinn, 12
Thriftway, 161, 165-166
Tib (horse), 26, 27, 40
Tiffany, Orrin E., 136
Tillman, Helen. *see* Zednick, Helen Tillman
Timber Culture Act, 13-14
*Times* (newspaper), 183
Tobin, Diana Gilmore. *see* Smithers, Diana Gilmore Tobin
Tollafsen, Rev. I., 143
Tollefson, Kenneth, 11
Town Meeting Club, 100
Townsend Club, 100
Towser (dog), 47
traffic problems, 121
transportation, public, 82, 85, 88, 92, 97-98
Treat, Harry Whitney, 168
Trinity Methodist Church, 140
Trinity Methodist Episcopal, 142
Trinity Temple Full Gospel Assembly. *see* Queen Anne Christian Center
Triplet apartments, 172
trolleys, 97
tuberculosis, 150
Tulalip Indian Reservation, 151
Turner, Dolly, 132
Turner, Kim, 138
Turner & Pease, 164
typhoid fever, 150

Uhl, Benno J., 132
Union Electric Co., 83
Union Water Company, 80, 81
Union Water System, 4, 79
Uniservice, 190
United Indians of All Tribes Foundation, 10, 11
United Sales Company, 114
United South Slope Residents (USSR), 175
United States Science Pavilion, 120
University of Washington, 100, 110
University of Washington Printing Department, 183
University of Washington School of Nursing, 156, 157
Uptown district, 164, 166
Uptown Theater, 100, 165
Urban Village, 116
U.S. Dept. of Housing and Urban Development, 176
Utter, Francis, 43
Utter, George, 43
Utter, Ira Wilcox, 22, 23, 28, 30, 42, 43, 58

Valley Street apartments, 172
Van Asselt, Henry, 13
Van de Kamp's bakery, 158
Vanni, Edo, 110, 114
Victoria apartments, 170, 171, 172
Villa Costella, 172
Virgil & Bradbury, 176
*Visit from Our Tillicum*, 36
Vista apartments, 174
Vitamilk (dairy), 90
Volunteer Park, 110, 187
voting rights for women, 70

Wadeson, Dr. J.H., 180
Walker, Gordon, 123
Wallace, Wilmar, 179
Wallace Field, 137, 138
Wallon, Lewis Arthur, Jr., 101
Wallon, Mary Gove, 101
Wang, Laura, 118
War Dance, 10
Ward, Agnes, 69
Ward, Clarence, 69
Ward, Dillis
  and Hester Ward, 37
  as teacher, 57, 58
  business affairs, 64, 69, 70
  civic activities, 71, 77, 78, 90
  early days in Northwest, 15, 16, 19, 20, 36
  home and family, 69
  pioneer party, 12
  women's suffrage, 70
Ward, Eliza "Lizzie," 69
Ward, Hester. *see* Mercer, Hester Ward
Ward, Jesse, 20, 37
Ward, Kate, 69
Ward, Mabel, 58, 69
Ward, Maud, 69
Ward, Sarah Isabel Byles, 15, 58, 69, 70, 71
Ward family, 63
Ward party, 19, 20
Ward Street Pumping Station, 93
Warhanik, Dr., 156
Warren Avenue Elementary School, 103, 120, 126, 127-128
Warren Avenue Fire Station, 94
Washelli Cemetery, 82, 110
Washington Casket Company, 190
Washington Cremation Association, 189
*Washington Pioneer* (newspaper), 183
Washington Sand and Gravel, 110
Washington State Armory, 119
Washington State Coliseum, 120
Watch (dog), 42, 47, 48
water rates, 80
water rationing, 116
water service, municipal, 79
water supply systems, 4, 79, 92
water tower, 93
Waterman, Thomas Talbot, 10
Watson, Dr. C. Hoyt, 137
Watson, Helen, 105
Watt, Roberta Frye, 16, 54
Wayside Emergency Hospital, 149, 152
weather, 36-38, 59, 60, 101
Wedgewood Building, 114
*Weekly Intelligencer*, 183

*Weekly Intelligencer* (newspaper), 43
West Galer Street business, 162
West Howe apartments, 172
West McGraw Street business area, 162
West Point, 7, 9
West Queen Anne Playfield, 109, 116, 117
West Queen Anne School, 91, 100, 116, 125, 126, 127, 172, 175, 179, 185
West Seattle, Lake Union and Park Transit Co., 70
West Slope Residents. Steering Committee, 175
West Town View, 176
Western Mill, 68
Westlund, Mabel F., 150
Wet Wash Laundry, 98
Wetmore, John, 42
Wharfside Pointe apartments, 172, 177
Wheeler family, 63
White, W.P., 172
White apartments, 172
Whitmire, Elizabeth, 138
Wilcox family, 53
Wilcox Wall, 89, 185
Wiley, W.W., 113
Wilke, Charles, 75
Williams, Benezette, 81
Williams, Donna Everett, 102
Williams, Lane, 124
Wilson, Bess, 153
Windwatch condominiums, 172
Wineberry, Jesse, 116
Wisteria Dance Club, 182
Wittauer, Oral (Buz), 180
Wolf, Mervin, 124
Wolf Creek ravine, 91
Wolgemuth, Alice DeLong, 101
Womack, Rev. Dan, 147
women
  and church, 140
  homemaking, 98
  hotel, 74
  voting rights, 70
Women's Christian Temperance Union, 105, 106
Women's Hospital Association, 152
Women's Single Tax Club, 100
Woodland Park, 63, 109, 188
Works Progress Administration (WPA), 106, 108, 109
World War II, 111-114
World's Fair. *see* Century 21 Exposition
Wright, Adelaide, 189
Wright, Arthur A., 189
Wright, Charles G., 189
Wright & Son, Mortuary and Columbarium, 180, 189, 190

Yamamoto, Kay, 138
Yamasaki, Minoru, 120
Yarnall, Dr. Steven, 169
Yesler, Henry L., 24, 40, 43
Yesler, Sarah B., 40, 154
Yesler Terrace, 112
Yesler Women's Hotel, 74
Yesler's Hall, 40
Yesler's Mill, 25, 29, 68
Yesler's mill, 27, 33, 34, 35
Yesler's wharf, 26, 34, 50
Young Men's Christian Association, 110, 122, 179-180, 183
Young People's Mission Society, 145
Young Women's Christian Association, 180
Younger, Erin, 11
Youth Service Project, 111

Zednick, Helen Tillman, 100
Zednick, Victor, 100, 108, 114, 180, 184
zoning codes, 173-174, 177
Zorich, Joe, 165
Zorich, Marty, 165
Zorich, Sam, 165

# No relief from Japan's new toilets

## *Some find high-tech controls confusing*

BY MARY JORDAN AND KEVIN SULLIVAN
*The Washington Post*

TOKYO – An American diplomat was at a dinner party in a Japanese home when he excused himself to go to the bathroom. He did his business, stood up, and realized he didn't have a clue about how to flush the toilet.

The diplomat speaks Japanese, but he still was baffled by the colorful array of buttons on the complicated keypad. So he just started pushing.

He hit the noisemaker button that makes a flushing sound to mask any noise you might be making in the john. He hit the button that starts the blow-dryer for your bottom.

Then he hit the bidet button and watched helplessly as a little plastic toothbrush-shaped arm appeared from the back of the bowl and began shooting a stream of warm water across the room and onto the mirror.

And that's how one of America's promising young Foreign Service officers ended up frantically wiping down a Japanese bathroom with a wad of toilet paper.

Just as many foreigners finally mastered the traditional Japanese "squatter" with no seat, they are being confused anew by the latest generation of Japanese toilets: super-high-tech sit-down models with a control panel that looks like the cockpit of an airplane.

Already selling well are toilets that clean themselves, have coatings that resist germs and spray pulsating water to massage your backside.

The toilets look like the standard American model, except for the control pad.

The bottom-washer function, combined with the bottom blow-dryer, is designed to do away with the need for toilet tissue. Other buttons automatically open and close the lid. Some toilets even have a hand-held remote control.

Manufacturing company Toto sells about $400 million worth of high-tech Washlet toilets a year and now wants a piece of the U.S. market.

The U.S. Toto – a $600 seat, lid and control panel that attaches to a regular American toilet bowl – features a heated seat, the bottom washer and a deodorizing fan.

Many foreigners say that once you get used to these toilets, it's hard to do without them.

Tom Quinn, a Californian who does play-by-play analysis of sumo matches on Japanese television, isn't one of them.

He said he wishes he had a plain old American toilet.

"I don't want rocket controls on my toilet," he said.

# CONTINUED FR

# *Savvy decisions earn praise*

**NUDELMAN**

CONTINUED FROM PAGE 1

ing the Woodland Park Zoo, the Pacific Science Center and the Greater Seattle Chamber of Commerce list Nudelman as a friend and financial supporter.

But instead of savoring his accomplishments, Nudelman suddenly finds himself on the defensive.

The Ph.D. and master's degrees listed on his résumé come from an unaccredited California college characterized by some as a diploma mill.

For years, Group Health press releases have said Nudelman earned three bachelor-of-science degrees from the University of Washington, but last week university officials said he received only two.

To his supporters, the focus on Nudelman's educational background is a painful distraction from his years of good service.

Others say Nudelman is not who he appears to be, and neither is Group Health.

The 50-year-old cooperative has strayed from its ideological roots under Nudelman's term, his critics say, and the Kaiser deal further dampened its democratic spirit.

Nudelman maintains that he is ashamed of nothing and is more prepared than ever to shape Group Health's future.

"I believe in what I have done, and ... I'm doing," he said in an interview Friday. "It was not my intention ... in the spotlight. It is my ...n to change the health-care ...n this country."

intent... system ...

**Class p...**

Nudelma... Portland, th... housewares ... pilot's licen... was 16 be... the UW. At th... came...

**...resident for two years**

...n was born and raised in ...e second son of a ...man. He earned a ... he

ly," reads the caption underneath a photograph of a grinning Nudelman in the UW's 1956 yearbook.

"Phil had a nice sense of humor and didn't take himself too seriously," said Charles Mertel, a classmate who is now a King County Superior Court judge. "I didn't sense that he was inappropriately ambitious. He brought a lot to the table that made him a good leader."

But the 1957 class president left the UW without a diploma. Nudelman joined the Air Force reserves several credits short of a degree, a move he blames on his out-of-school distractions.

"I was overzealous in my extracurricular activities, so I had to finish a credit or two," toward a bachelor's degree.

However, a spokesman for the UW said Nudelman was not close to finishing the degree. Last week, Nudelman revised his résumé. Instead of saying he earned a B.S. in microbiology in 1957, it now reads: "Major work completed – degree not awarded."

After a stint in the Air Force and a job as a commercial airline pilot, Nudelman joined a national drug company as a salesman. He worked as a pharmacist in Bellevue and went back to the UW to earn a bachelor-of-science degree in zoology in 1963 and another bachelor-of-science degree in pharmacy three years later.

In 1973, he was asked to serve as a consultant to Group Health's pharmacy division. After two months, he was hired full time.

**No Ph.D., no promotions**

Nudelman rose swiftly through the ranks at Group Health and conceived several innovations that are still i... intr...

an advanced degree. And he was not speaking as a concerned mentor.

"They were not friendly conversations," Nudelman said. "But it stuck with me."

Nudelman resigned from Group Health, but returned a few months later after Shaver had left. In 1982 he was named senior vice president and chief operating officer.

By that time, he had received a master's degree and a Ph.D. from Pacific Western University, a California-based school that has no classrooms or examinations and awards degrees based partially on what the student has already learned.

Given the nature of the health-care industry, it's no surprise Nudelman heeded Shaver's advice. Many members of Group Health's leadership are doctors with the "M.D." behind their names, and the health-care profession places enormous prestige on academic performance.

On Oct. 8, 1990, after serving five different presidents, Nudelman was named to Group Health's top post. The press release announcing his promotion said Nudelman was a graduate of the UW in pharmacy, zoology and microbiology.

"One of the reasons Phil stood out in our decision to hire him was his values were consistent with our higher expectation of ourselves," said Aubrey Davis, longtime board member and past president of Group Health. "He has understood the problems of balancing our culture and the marketplace."

**'Circling the wagons'**

Last month, Group Health members voted by a wide margin to form an alliance with Kaiser health plan of Oakland, Calif., the nation's largest health maintenan...